Designing SPEED in the Racehorse

by Ken McLean

"Discovery consists of seeing what everybody has seen,
and thinking what nobody has thought."
- Albert von Szent-Gyorgy

Darshaan winning the Prix de l'Arc de Triomphe Gr-1 from Sadler's Wells and Rainbow Quest.

Cover design & layout by Bosetti Production Art & Design

Library of Congress Cataloging-in-Publication Data

McLean, Ken.

Designing speed in the racehorse / by Ken McLean.

p. cm.

Includes bibliographical references and index.

ISBN-13: 978-0-929346-80-9 (hardcover)

1. Thoroughbred horse--Pedigrees. 2. Race horses--Breeding. 3. Race horses--Genetics. 4. Race horses--Speed. I. Title.

SF293.T5M45 2006

636.1'22--dc22

2005037697

Published by

The Russell Meerdink Company, Ltd.

1555 South Park Avenue, Neenah, Wisconsin 54956

USA

(920) 725-0955

www.horseinfo.com

Printed in Colombia by Imprelibros S.A.

SECRETARIAT - one of greatest racehorses in the world, bred on the Nasrullah / Princequillo cross.

TWO FAMOUS TRIPLE CROWN WINNERS

SEATTLE SLEW with Karen and Mickey Taylor at Three Chimneys Farm, Kentucky.

"Lucy and I would like to win the Kentucky Derby one day."
- William T. Young, five years before
Grindstone made the dream come true.

The author has a chat with STORM CAT at Overbrook Farm, Kentucky.

Other Thoroughbred breeding books written by the author

Quest For A Classic Winner

Tesio - Master of Matings

Genetic Heritage

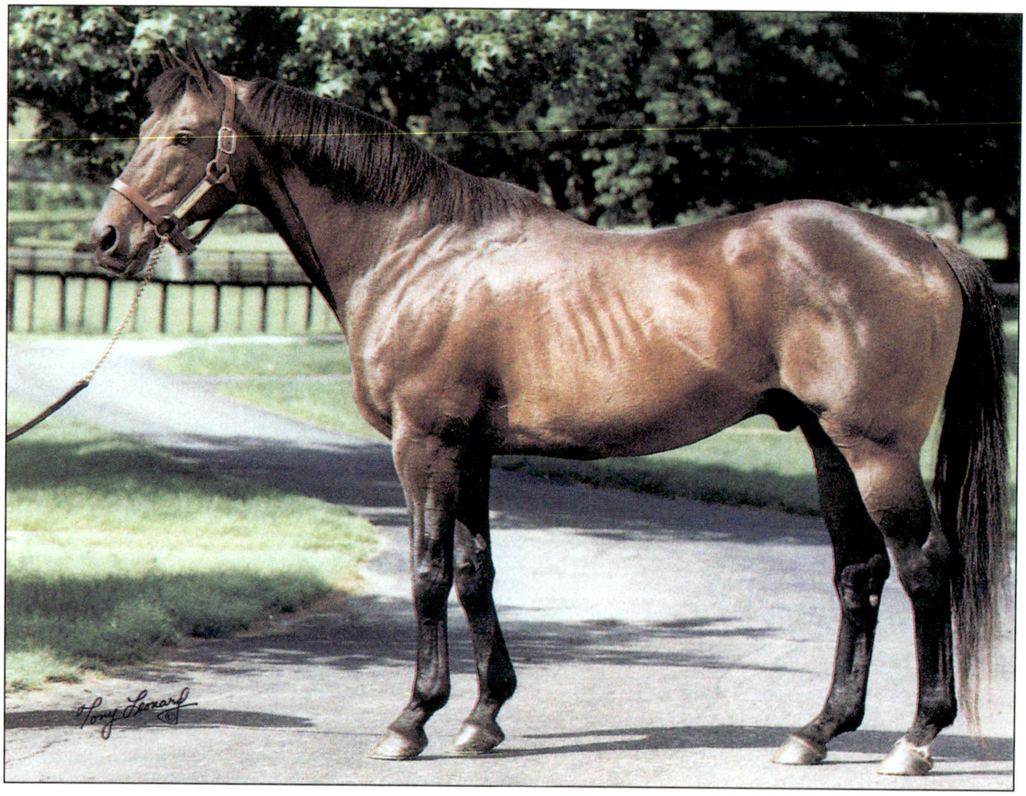

MR. PROSPECTOR (Raise A Native - Gold Digger by Nashua), leading sire and broodmare sire in North America.

CONTENTS

My father's new book, *Designing Speed in the Racehorse*, is a wonderful resource for the serious breeder of racehorses. It contains more than 50 years of pedigree research and performance results compiled for the reader. Since we seem to be always in a hurry to get results, this reference book, written for the analytically-minded person, should provide the reader with a gift of information.

Nothing would please my father more than to know breeders might use some of the information to plan matings that will produce future stakes winners.

The breed needs to be sustained with greatness and strength and everything depends upon the selection process. Thoroughbred breeding is a passion. I grew up on horse farms, including William T. Young's beautiful Overbrook Farm, Lexington, Kentucky, so it would seem strange to me not to have a passion for horses. I used to ride around Overbrook on my black mare and watch the weanlings develop into yearlings. I saw many newborn foals that were bred on specific bloodlines. I would visit the yearling and broodmare sales with Dad where he would teach me about conformation and type.

We were fortunate to attend the races with Mr. Young when he had a horse running at Keeneland. It was a real eye opener for me – a different world – an exciting world that is everchanging. Each day there is always something to learn.

We went to Newmarket, England, and saw horses train on the downs. I remember staying with Sir Philip Payne-Gallwey at the B.B.A's house near the saleyards. He would sing in the shower. In the early mornings we would be woken from sleep by the sounds of hoofbeats.

Sir Philip often stayed with us in Lexington. He taught my father many things about horse breeding.

My husband, Jamie, and I breed horses of a different kind – versatile Australian Stock Horses. At the moment we stand three well-bred stockhorse stallions at our farm and enjoy breeding working horses. I now realize how much I learned from Dad who in turn learned so much from experienced horsemen, men like old Mr. Gentry who managed Darby Dan Farm many years ago.

I trust you will enjoy reading this book – there is a considerable amount of detail to digest. Great ancestors responsible for improving speed are well documented with their pedigrees. I am very proud of my father.

Tanya Shaw,
Jaytee Stud, Tamworth,
N.S.W., Australia.

NATIVE DANCER (Polynesian - Geisha by Discovery) after winning the Belmont Stakes.

NORTHERN DANCER (Nearctic - Natalma by Native Dancer)
shown with Ben Miller at Windfields Farm, Maryland.

Carla and I have had the pleasure of meeting many interesting people in the Thoroughbred breeding industry. We have visited some of the world's leading Thoroughbred stud farms and along our fascinating journey, made many friends.

Breeding the racehorse is a real challenge. One needs dedication, patience, a stout heart, time for research and above all, admiration for one of nature's most beautiful species. Successful racehorse breeders need to be observant and skillful in the selection process, seeking answers as to why genetic inheritance behaves the way it does. The more knowledge we acquire, the more we realize how much is yet to be learned. On a weekly basis, an incredible amount of information needs to be absorbed.

We have enjoyed personal contact with leading Thoroughbred breeders throughout the world and have listened intently to their stories of heartbreak and success. Many years ago, Sir Philip Payne-Gallwey shared knowledge with three lads – Tim Richardson, manager of the Niarchos family's Haras de Fresnay-Le-Buffard, France, his brother Chris Richardson, manager of Mr. and Mrs. Thompson's Cheveley Park Stud, England, and myself. How Philip put up with the three of us I'll never know, but we are exceedingly grateful for his friendship, guidance and expertise.

Twenty years ago I was hired to work in Kentucky for a wise and wonderful man, William T. Young, owner of Overbrook Farm. It was he who introduced us to many successful owner-breeders in North America and Europe. Our objectives were to develop and expand the farm and select foundation mares, as it was Mr. Young's goal to be more involved in what he called a legitimate business. In 1986, he sent his homebred colt Storm Cat to trainer Johnathan Sheppard and contemplated a much larger racing stable. These were very happy days and we want to thank everyone at Overbrook as well as the farm's advisor, Dr. Robert Copelan. Mr. Young selected D. Wayne Lukas to train his horses – one of the hardest working guys in the business.

We made special friends in Kentucky, among them Mary and Monty Hinton, David and Betsy Hager, Peter and Gina Kirwan, John and Susannah Prather, Ben and Harriet Giles, Bill and Barbara Green, Rich Decker, Bruce and Nancy Jensen and Bob McCann. The talented Ben Giles was mainly responsible for implementing William T. Young's visionary ideas. Today, Overbrook Farm is a truly beautiful Thoroughbred nursery and home of North America's leading sire, Storm Cat.

It's impossible to mention everyone who enlightened and enriched our lives, but a big thank you in North America goes to Josephine Abercrombie and her manager Clifford Barry (Pin Oak Stud), Robert and Blythe Clay (Three Chimneys Farm), Henry White, Arthur B. Hancock III and his wife Staci (Stone Farm), Joanne Nor (Norfields), Len and Lois Green, Robert B. Berger, Antony Beck (Gainesway Farm), Duncan Taylor and his brothers (Taylor Made Farms), John Phillips (Darby Dan Farm), Pope McLean and sons (Crestwood Farm), Allen Kershaw (Gainsborough Farm), Robert Courtney, Richard Bonnycastle, Bobby Spalding, Phyllis Allen, Dottie Ingordo, Ernie Paragallo and Steve Cauthen.

In Australia we especially wish to thank Les and Peggy Bridge, Dr. Percy Sykes, Norman and Anne Carlyon, and in New Zealand Jack Glengarry who travels the world promoting pedigree research.

In Europe, we are grateful to Chris and Annie Richardson, Tim and Mimi Richardson, Michael Goodbody, Stephen Gill, Robert and Amelie Ehrnrooth, Pat Downes (Gilltown Stud) and the team at Gainsborough, Ballysheehan and Woodpark Studs, namely Paddy Bowles, John Brady, Kate Ryan, Brian Malony, Jenny Bailey and Sarah Norris.

SEASIDE ATTRACTION (Seattle Slew - Kamar) wins the Kentucky Oaks Gr-1 for William T. Young's Overbrook Farm. She produced Champion 2YO filly Golden Attraction, Red Carnival, Cape Canaveral and Cape Town.

STORM CAT (Storm Bird - Terlingua by Secretariat), the leading sire in North America and seven times leading juvenile sire.

To our publishers, The Russell Meerdink Company Ltd., thank you so much for your creative ideas and assistance. To my lovely wife Carla, thanks "Toots" for everything; and to my wonderful daughters Kiersten and Tanya, thanks guys for helping me out – I love you both, heaps.

Also, I must thank two extremely gifted scientists in Dublin who made me think harder and longer – Professor Paddy Cunningham and Dr. Richard K. Porter whom we had the pleasure of meeting at Trinity College (Genetics & Biochemistry Departments). Paddy introduced us to one of my heroes, Dr. James Watson, who shared the Nobel Prize in 1962 with Dr. Francis Crick for the discovery of the molecular structure of DNA (the double helix).

Finally, I dedicate this book to my two grandsons, Mitch Harrison and Jackson James. God bless them.

Ken McLean
146 Carthage Street,
Tamworth. NSW 2340
Australia.

April, 2005.

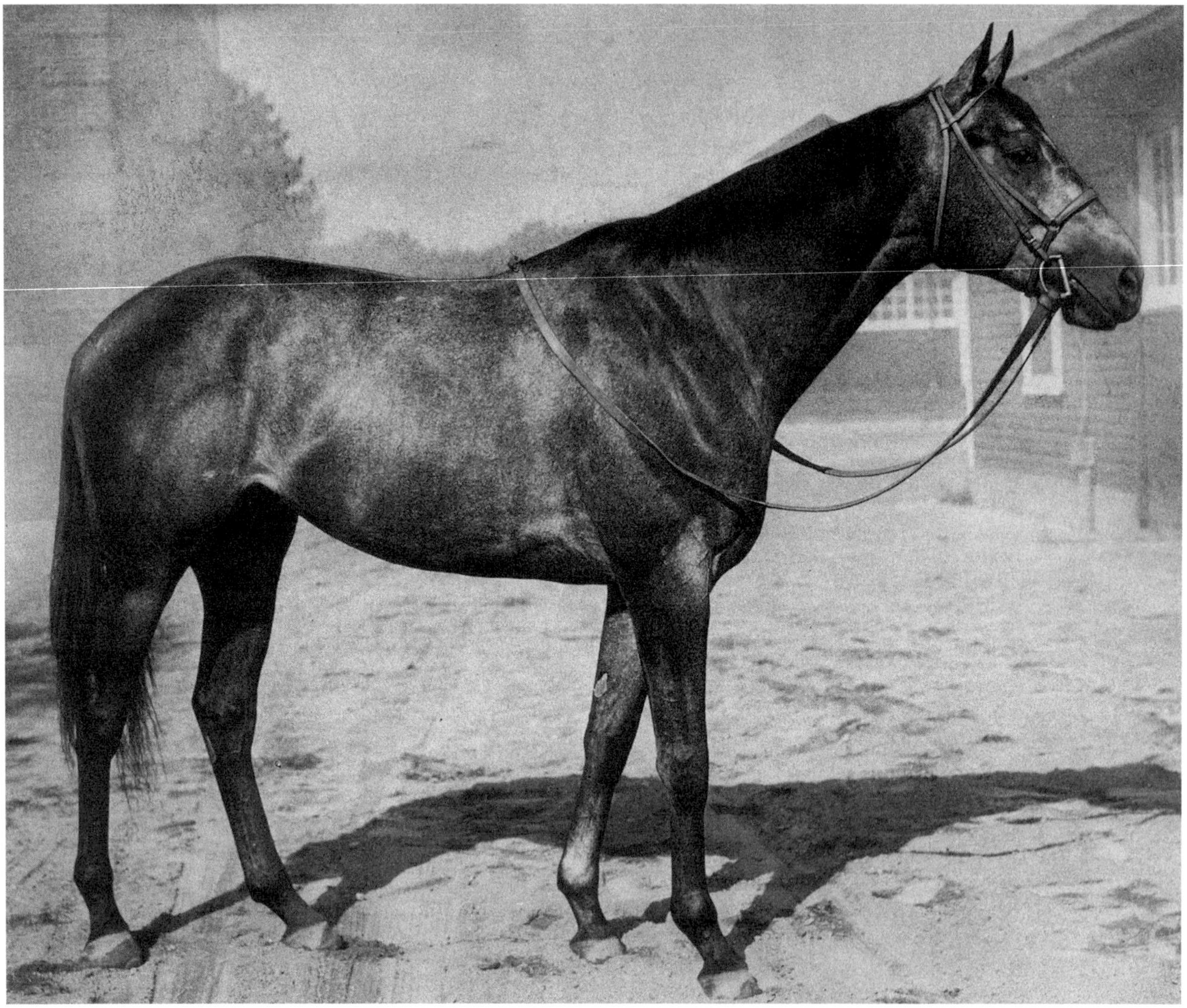

America's Horse of the Year NATIVE DANCER is a phenomenal sire of speed. His sire, champion sprinter Polynesian, is inbred to brother and sister Sainfoin and Sierra four times. Native Dancer was foaled on March 27, 1950.

"The whole debate on numbers and over-production seems to me to hinge on one important fact. No one forces a mare owner to use a specific stallion."
- Darryl Sherer (Pacemaker magazine)

The word "Thoroughbred" inaptly describes the racehorse. Strictly speaking it is a "hybrid" breed, inheriting its genotype (genetic make-up) from ancestors developed in the Middle East of mainly Arabian descent. Because of their unique genetic mix, stallions and mares rarely breed true-to-type. Instead, they provide horse breeders with many surprising results owing to "genetic probability factors" – i.e., genetic variation. The Thoroughbred as a breed was established in England.

Perhaps the most recent, significant change in the racehorse industry began without fanfare in the early 1990's when the management of Irish-based Coolmore Stud implemented a new strategy. John Magnier and partners decided to increase the number of mares booked to Coolmore-based stallions.

It was no small increase by any stretch of the imagination; rather, it was an increase that would buck tradition, shake up the way other commercial stud farms conducted their business and alter substantially the way one would forecast annual income from stallion fees.

At the time I thought Coolmore's main objective was simply to outbid the competition and secure fashionable Group or Graded stakes winners to add to their stallion portfolio. The concept was simple – in any one year, the more mares a stallion covered, the more income could be earned. This new strategy would help enable the Irish farm to outbid rivals for potential stallions. In hindsight, Coolmore's objective was to own outright and seek control of commercial stallions and be able to shuttle certain stallions to farms based in the Southern Hemisphere. Magnier saw syndication as being too restrictive.

One should recall 20 years ago many commercial sires were syndicated in North America, Europe, Japan, New Zealand and Australia. Nearly all stallion syndicate agreements legally prevented large books of mares. However, by the early 1990's this was not the scenario at either Coolmore Stud in Ireland or Ashford Stud in Kentucky where unsyndicated horses filled the stallion barns. No legal hindrance would affect their particular style of flexible management. The Irish team wanted full control of their stallions and if possible, income from Northern and Southern hemispheres.

The success of influential shuttle stallion Danehill (Danzig-Razyana by His Majesty), initially owned jointly by Coolmore Stud in Ireland and Arrowfield Stud in Australia, changed everything. Danehill proved to be a very fertile horse, capable of covering large books of mares. Eventually Coolmore gained sole ownership and the bay stallion's solid performance in the breeding shed in both hemispheres convinced John Magnier and partners to amend their objectives. Coolmore Stud had invested many millions of dollars to acquire the remaining half ownership of Danehill, therefore it had to be anticipated Magnier and partners would want a decent return on their financial outlay. Hence, Danehill kept shuttling without respite.

Although Danehill's service fee increased, so too did the number of mares he covered in both hemispheres. Coincidentally, by the mid-1990's in Japan, a dominant black stallion named Sunday Silence (Halo-Wishing Well by Understanding) caused a sensation. Almost overnight, Sunday Silence topped Japan's Sires' List and what followed was enormous demand for his services. Pressure from clients forced the management of Shadai Farm to open up the stallion's book. Japanese breeders owning quality mares tried desperately to acquire nominations to Sunday Silence whose fee was raised. The stallion's book was increased to accommodate strong demand and fortunately for the Yoshida family, Sunday Silence proved to be an extremely fertile horse, handling his amorous task well. He seemed to be an ideal replacement for Japan's leading sire Northern Taste.

Subsequent yearling crops by Sunday Silence (offered at public auction) experienced a dramatic increase in average sale price, this despite a faltering Japanese economy. Sunday Silence's success as a sire of Group winners was consistent. He was revered by Japanese racehorse owners and trainers and quickly gained international respect. The stallion quite simply amazed everyone including his co-breeder Arthur B. Hancock III (Stone Farm, Kentucky) who always believed in the stallion's potential.

These two influential stallions, Danehill and Sunday Silence, had managed to succeed in covering large books of mares without affecting progeny results on the racetrack. Both possessed high fertility and remained healthy. Were they exceptional stallions? Yes. Will each make a lasting impression on the breed? Highly probable because both were superior individuals and transmitted desirable racing genes to a vast majority of their progeny. There is no reason to doubt their descendants will make a memorable impression on the breed, long-term. However, these stallions are unique examples. Let's be realistic. Of all young stallions standing at stud, only about one in 10 actually succeeds. Rarely are we able to mention in the same breath sires as successful as Danehill and Sunday Silence.

Influential sires earn the right to cover reasonably large books of mares. Once a successful sire's genetic dominance is established he merits special consideration; but what of young unproven stallions who cover excessive books – some in excess of 130 mares in any given breeding season?

Breeders must consider the risks involved. If young stallions happen to fail as sires of winners and stakes winners, they are quickly banished to far off lands because commercial breeders act without hesitation concerning disappointing sires. However, consider the widespread damage associated with unsuccessful sires. Produce records of well-bred mares are so easily spoiled. A mare's value diminishes with regular use of inferior sires.

Yet, there are commercial breeders who gamble religiously on the selection of first-season sires. Risk takers put their trust in first-season sires hoping the popular trend will continue from anxious yearling buyers and eager "pinhookers." However, should an era of over-production suddenly hit a soft market, the ballgame will change.

Coolmore Stud never shuttled their star performer Sadler's Wells.

Sadler's Wells is an exceedingly valuable stallion. He quickly achieved fame as a sire of turf runners throughout Europe and his son El Prado is one of the most successful sires in North America, where his progeny excel on dirt and turf.

Sadler's Wells may be ranked with the most influential sires ever to stand at stud in Europe. His progeny seem to show their best form on yielding tracks.

Sadler's Wells (Northern Dancer-Fairy Bridge) will be added to an illustrious list of influential sires that shaped the breed.

Leading owner-breeder Edward P. Taylor stood Northern Dancer at his Windfields Farm, Canada. This Champion 3YO colt in North America won the Kentucky Derby in record time and his stud career was carefully supervised. The stallion syndicate agreement restricted the number of mares Northern Dancer could cover in one season. Later, when Northern Dancer was transferred from Canada to Windfields Farm, Maryland, the agreement was never changed.

Furthermore, only a limited number of Northern Dancer yearlings came on the market. The little bay stallion's share price and service fee skyrocketed. At time of writing, the record price ever paid for a yearling remains at a hefty $13.1 million for the colt by Northern Dancer out of Seattle Slew's dam, My Charmer. At Keeneland, Robert Sangster commissioned bloodstock agent Joss Collins (B.B.A.) to buy the colt who was named Seattle Dancer.

Multi-million dollar yearlings sired by Northern Dancer were sold at Keeneland and everyone wanted to own one. Eddy Taylor's stallion covered some of the most outstanding stakes producers and stakes winners residing in North America and during 1985, I seem to recall a Northern Dancer season (nomination) fetched $1 million. Within a short space of time, Northern Dancer's sons proved themselves as sires of Group winners – sons like Lyphard, Nijinsky II, Danzig, Storm Bird, Nureyev, Fairy King and Sadler's Wells. Demand for Northern Dancer's yearling colts saw unprecedented spirited bidding duels between the big spenders from Europe and Japan – bidding duels that captured headlines in the general press. We were all captivated at the time. Windfield's strategy was working out beautifully.

Imagine – all this was achieved from a very limited number of mares covered by Northern Dancer each year.

Tony Morris, a long-standing member of the Thoroughbred Breeders' Association in England, whom I deeply respect, wrote the following paragraphs in the January 2005 issue of *Pacemaker* magazine:

> "But in the sixties we had an ordered industry, with genuine syndication of stallions whose books rarely exceeded 45. Eyebrows were raised when the odd horse covered more than 50. Breeders took shares in horses and knew their value, and when they bought a nomination they had a fair idea of the level of risk. Like as not, when they came to sell their yearling by an acknowledged commercial sire, there would be no more than 20 or 30 of his crop on offer in the whole season."
>
> "Of course, by the nineties things were beginning to go haywire, but there were still few Flat stallions with books larger than 60, and those with 80-plus were confined to a small number of studs in Ireland. In 1994 the foal crop in these islands numbered under 12,000, the lowest for six years. The final tally for 2004 is likely to be in excess of 17,000, and there is a larger one to foal shortly, the results of a breeding season in which no fewer than 44 Flat-only stallions covered three-figure books – Cape Cross heading the list with 188, with Hawk Wing, in his first season, on 172."
>
> "Ireland no longer holds a monopoly of excess in this regard. There is wanton exploitation of breeders, too, in England, and very few stallion studs apply quality controls or set limits on the activity of a horse who is capable of taking a huge book."

Obviously from these comments Tony Morris believes there is reluctance for the British industry to address what he thinks might be a serious problem.

If one considers a shuttle stallion might cover in excess of 100 mares in the Northern Hemisphere and perhaps another 100 mares or so in the Southern Hemisphere, is this milking a young horse's sperm bank? To be blunt, I am amazed at the large number of mares covered by some of the unproven first-season sires in Europe and North America.

In Kentucky, for example, I was surprised to learn about the large book of mares covered by first-season sire Grand Slam (Gone West-Bright Candles by El Gran Senor). The number came as a shock.

At the time of signing breeding contracts, few breeders would have guessed Grand Slam would be represented by 127 named foals on the ground in his first crop, and a year later would have a huge number of yearlings entered for public auction. (In retrospect, one wonders how the numbers affected the stallion's first-crop average yearling sale price.) In 2002, Grand Slam covered 215 mares from which 151 foals resulted, while in 2003 he covered 197 mares resulting in 149 foals.

Commercial stallion operators in North America and Australia are jumping on the bandwagon. To show by example let's take excerpts from page 5946 of *The Blood-Horse* magazine, October 30, 2004 issue, listing North American stallions bred to 100 or more mares in 2004.

There were 140 stallions making this list. Here are 17 sires with the largest books, i.e. those covering in excess of 150 mares:

Mares covered in 2004

Hold That Tiger	199
Fusaichi Pegasus	193
Grand Slam	191
Van Nistelrooy	186
Tale of the Cat	185
Doneraile Court	184
Stormy Atlantic	183
Buddha	182
Johannesburg	175
Chief Seattle	166
Mutakddim	162

Proud Citizen	157
El Corredor	156
Gulf Storm	155
Honour and Glory	152
Full Mandate	151
More Than Ready	151

Of these, four are first-season sires, namely Hold That Tiger, Proud Citizen, Gulf Storm and Full Mandate.

Commercial breeders should look more closely at the fertility of a stallion that covers in excess of 130 mares per season and consider monetary consequences of much larger representation of his yearlings offered to buyers at the same sales venue.

I encourage breeders to be alert and do some homework. At least calculate the percentage of foals resulting from all mares covered. From this simple analysis one can discover actual fertility rates. Breeders have a right to expect a reasonable chance of getting their mares in foal, but with huge numbers, even with professional veterinary care and excellent management, many mares will end up barren. Big numbers put pressure on staff.

Each stallion's fertility should always be a serious factor for the breeder to consider. If a mare goes barren too often, it will cause a mare's value to decline sharply; therefore, one must be made aware of all risks involved.

It is my belief breeders should study basic statistics, especially the percentage of foals born of all mares covered by a stallion. In previous years we came to expect higher than 80 percent fertility from commercial stallions, but with larger books, we need to be re-educated. For example, figures on page 5946 of *The Blood-Horse* October 30, 2004 issue shows in 2002, Kentucky Derby winner Fusaichi Pegasus covered 191 mares resulting in only 110 foals while in 2003, the same sire covered 125 mares resulting in 92 foals. Understandably, stallion fertility statistics will be affected by the actual fertility of broodmares (some mares are always difficult to get in foal).

What is blatantly obvious is that any stallion with a large number of progeny to represent him in any given year gains an advantage over sires with fewer progeny, especially when we review the Sires' List by progeny earnings. Surely when a stallion has double the number of starters compared with other stallions, we should expect about double the amount of money earned by his runners. However logical this assumption may seem, in fact, the statistics so far show otherwise.

Perhaps the true essence of a stallion's superiority is highlighted by the number of his stakes winners compared with the total number of his starters. To my mind, this has always been a reliable guide, providing the stallion gets sound progeny. A tougher statistic is to compare stakes winners to the sire's total number of foals.

Even if the Thoroughbred industry requires a mix of part regulation and part self-regulation it remains entirely up to the breeder whether he wishes to support stallions covering large books of mares. Freedom of choice prevails. Needless to say, there exists high risk when commercial breeders choose to use unproven stallions with large books. While Thoroughbred racing today is just another business competing for a slice of the entertainment pie, there are still fortunate breeders who possess the luxury of enjoying it as a sport and breeding solely for the racetrack.

In the next decade, I fear opinionated people in the industry might make unwise changes to important traditional races programmed at distances of 1 ½ miles (2,400m) or more. Change is inevitable in our industry, but positive change is desired. Frustrated officials of race clubs should not tamper with traditional classics.

Designing Speed in the Racehorse was neither written to highlight juvenile racing nor to emphasize a case for brilliant short-course specialist sprinters. I wanted merely to focus attention on classic speed at a mile or more.

The very best racehorses of any generation inherit brilliance, even stayers. The evolution of racehorse speed is intriguing and I sincerely hope young horse breeders find my research of interest. Knowing information about specific ancestors in the fourth, fifth and sixth generation of international pedigrees is helpful in determining how to select the most compatible sire for a broodmare.

A superior racehorse needs to be able to accelerate at any moment during a Group 1 or Grade 1 race. Jockeys value extra "gear changes." Three-year-old classic heroes and winners of prestige events like the Prix de l'Arc de Triomphe Gr-1, Breeders' Cup Classic Gr-1, King George VI & Queen Elizabeth Stakes Gr-1 and Australia's W.S. Cox Plate Gr-1 require the ability to accelerate, sometimes more than once and sometimes to avoid traffic jams. Any horse with a genetic constitution comprising a blend of brilliant speed with stamina, soundness, the will-to-win (motivation), clean airflow and decent temperament is to be respected.

During the past decade I enjoyed researching information about the energy of the racehorse because energy (including nervous energy) is a key factor to consider when designing racehorse matings. What makes the mind and body of a racehorse work? How does ATP (adenosine triphosphate), the molecule carrying phosphate electricity (via thousands of mitochondria within cells), affect athletic performance? How might the amount of ATP in equine athletes vary and how quickly can it be resupplied for the body's use?

Nearco was champion racehorse of Europe, unbeaten winner of the Grand Prix de Paris (defeating Canot and English Derby winner Bois Roussel) who became the leading sire in England. He won all 14 starts and was bred, trained and raised by the illustrious Federico Tesio. What made Nearco a superior performer? Why did Tesio choose to alter the colt's usual training method and set the horse for France's premier 15 furlongs stamina test? Surely it was a risk Tesio need not have taken?

Federico Tesio once remarked that Nearco (Pharos-Nogara by Havresac II) was not a natural stayer and was amazed at his bay colt's racing class, speed and acceleration. Nearco transmitted high-class speed to many of his progeny and I regard him as a "genetic giant" who improved the modern racehorse. Some of his progeny carried their speed up to or beyond the mile and a half distance.

Nearco's most celebrated son Nasrullah, champion juvenile colt of his year in England, made a game effort in his attempt to win Epsom's 1943 English Derby for owner-breeder the Aga Khan. Although Nasrullah failed in his classic mission, he was gallant in defeat when third to Straight Deal.

MOTHER GOOSE, granddam of Almahmoud and fourth dam of Halo and Northern Dancer.

Buckpasser as a 3-year-old in 1966

Nasrullah (Nearco-Mumtaz Begum by Blenheim) inherited excessive nervous energy. He was a very temperamental horse to train, loaded with electricity and yet of all the sons of Nearco, it was Nasrullah who became one of three important sons to carry on his father's male line and spread his DNA to distant shores.

Tesio believed in and observed "nervous energy" in racehorses. He would sit and watch stallions for hours, absorbing their characteristics and personality before deciding whether any should be used for his Dormello Stud breeding operation. Tesio also studied many of the best racehorses in training. In 1952, although his eyesight was failing, he gazed upon a homebred foal that would develop into another unbeaten champion. The little highly-strung bay colt was Ribot who would win for Italy the coveted Prix de l'Arc de Triomphe not once, but twice. Sadly, Federico Tesio never lived to see Ribot rise to become champion of the world. Tesio passed away before the little energized colt with such a huge girth made his debut in Italy.

I always wondered why Tesio made a point about nervous energy in one of his books. Obviously he believed it was an important consideration when he mused over how he would design Dormello Stud's mare matings.

There is a mix of fact, interpretation, legend and subjective opinion in this book, plus carefully selected pedigree research I wanted to share with the reader.

I hope my explanation of how speed evolved in the racehorse is informative and interesting for breeders who don't have the time to look back in Thoroughbred history and discover those great ancestors who really shaped the breed.

Today's Group or Graded stakes winners rely on the quality and strength of their ancestry, made possible by the craftsmanship and selection skills of men and women who were devoted to improving speed, stamina, temperament and soundness. We owe a great debt to them. For more than 50 years I studied the pedigrees of the most outstanding racehorses bred in various countries and tried to comprehend why a specific stallion was chosen for a specific broodmare.

I learned valuable information by extending the pedigrees of champion racehorses bred by famous breeders like Federico Tesio, Lord Derby, Marcel Boussac, William Hall-Walker, His Highness the Aga Khan III, Lord Astor, Arthur B. "Bull" Hancock II of Claiborne Farm, Harry Payne Whitney, C.V. Whitney, Colonel E. R. Bradley, Edward P. Taylor and more recently the exploits of His Highness the Aga Khan IV, Maria Niarchos, the Phipps family, Josephine Abercrombie, Lord Howard de Walden, Daniel Wildenstein, Prince Khalid Abdullah (Juddmonte Farms), Frank Stronach (Adena Springs Farm), Arthur B. Hancock III (Stone Farm), the Maktoum family, Coolmore Stud and partners, Three Chimneys Farm, Taylor Made Farm, Arrowfield Stud and Kirsten Rausing (Lanwades Stud) etc.

I must have read more than a thousand books, magazines and catalogs on racing and breeding and on our travels, inspected breeding stock in eight countries.

Pedigree research is enlightening and informative. There are reasons why certain strains successfully blend to produce upgraded racing class. A difficulty is to identify the main players and make use of information gained. Apart from a lack of opportunity, there are reasons why sire lines and families rise and fall.

Today, breeding journalists and companies abuse the real meaning of genetic affinities and "nicks." What they call a "nick" is plain nonsense! Computerized information about rating one sire line with another sire line is generalized rubbish in my opinion because for all the winners mentioned, there are many more losers. In my book I refer to real nicks and real genetic affinities.

However, no matter how much we may research, no matter how hard we try to select the right stallion for a specific mare, in the end all matings are governed by what portion of the parents' gene pool is actually inherited by a foal. A mating repeated several times will always produce a variety of mixed results.

To really learn from pedigree and conformation research, I forced myself to think out of the box, use common sense, and conduct research with an open mind. I assumed details shown in the Stud Books of the world are fairly accurate, knowing full well that future mitochondrial DNA tests might disclose a small number of anomalies.

Knowledge of the laws of inheritance (genetics) guided me and helped explain why Mill Reef was a champion performer and his brother well below average. Nature provides an essential process for all species to survive – genetic variation.

It is nothing new.

Once we accept this fact we may proceed with pedigree and conformation research knowing that "chance" will affect every mating designed specifically for the racetrack. No matter how hard we try to select for soundness and stakes performance, in the final analysis, genetic probability will determine the genes that will be inherited by a Thoroughbred foal.

THE ENERGY MACHINE OF THE RACEHORSE

"The body may have plenty of energy and capacity to perform some action, but if the brain is tired or asleep, or if you do not have sufficient motivation to perform the action, it may not happen." - Dr. Guy Brown Ph. D.

Many times have I walked around the picturesque grounds of Keeneland and Fasig-Tipton to chat with breeding and racing folk and inspect yearlings, weanlings, and broodmares offered for sale. Early in September, Keeneland holds the largest yearling sale in the world. Heat from the sun's energy beats down on buyers, sellers and horses alike. September is the beginning of Kentucky's beautiful "fall" when the leaves finally decide to turn red and gold, when the locals glow with healthy tans and visitors from all around the world mingle together. Breeders' expectations run high hoping this year's sale will be even better than previous years. Depth of quality in the sale books creates keen demand from buyers.

If I don't wear a hat, by afternoon the sun's energy infiltrates the top of my skull and I feel heat being absorbed. Solar energy is the giver of life on earth. Without it we would not exist, nor would the racehorse.

Having researched and observed Thoroughbred racehorses around the world since I was a boy, I never fully appreciated the importance of energy in the scheme of things. Listening to trainers about various successful techniques of conditioning, learning about families that consistently transmit desirable genetic qualities, learning about nutrition and how to correctly raise an athlete were foremost on my agenda. Often I would fall asleep after studying pedigrees and their patterns, but during my studies I neither focused on energy nor understood how it works.

Energy is the vital force required for the miracle of motion. The only time I seriously examined or questioned this force was when I competed in athletic events at school. Later, I studied topics about energy – articles about muscle fiber, increased muscle mass, strength training, anabolic steroids, mitochondria, ATP (adenosine triphosphate), etc. We all know what happens when our energy reserves are low, and we all know how to live life when our energy reserves peak. Some people are never motivated enough to reach out and fulfill their goals, while others are driven with ambition, so much so that their energy levels need to be replaced in a hurry.

There are limits to physical exercise and athletic performance.

We know what happens when our energy levels are exceeded because key regulators of body energy have a ceiling. Our mind and body use energy to control stress and fatigue. Let's say you are about to compete in a road race or an athletic event beyond a mile. Emotions rise up in the body as adrenaline surges through your veins at the starting line. You become anxious. Your mind races, your stomach feels squeamish, muscles twitch and you begin to sweat. At last the starter's gun is fired and your nervous system reacts quickly because a wave of neurotransmitters hits your muscles.

With muscles activated, your calcium levels rise. You are running!

Contraction of the nerve fibers occurs simultaneously with an abundant flow of ATP providing you with energy. Phosphocreatin kicks in, but you need to start breaking down your muscle glycogen into glucose and use it to make more ATP. The high carbohydrate foods you ate at breakfast will ensure your muscles are full of glycogen for distance running.

The blood supply to your muscles increases dramatically, supplying plenty of oxygen to fuel the thousands of mitochondria in cells that are producing ATP. Your oxygen level increases ten-fold along with energy turnover. Adrenaline abounds in body and mind. Eventually body fat is burned in preference to glucose, while glucose is produced for the brain (by the liver using amino acids supplied by your muscles). You remain focused and assess your position with other competitors.

You are now more than three-quarters of the way and all of a sudden you start feeling the beginnings of fatigue. Your muscles don't seem to be working as well now and they begin to hurt. Gradually a burning sensation is felt and you stress a little. You know lactic acid is building up and pervading your system and other competitors are beginning to run past you. Sure enough, you reach the finish but you collapse in a heap, even though you have given your best. Dripping with sweat, you know recovery for your body will take time to make the necessary metabolic repairs.

Now imagine yourself as a racehorse!

Take a moment to comprehend the massive effort required by a racehorse during competition. Imagine the energy that will be expended! The racehorse needs to be fit and highly motivated if it is to have any chance for victory.

What stops us from going faster? How might we overcome fatigue? Antoine Lavoissier discovered (in the 18th century) oxygen consumption of our body increases with intensity of exercise and if we keep increasing the intensity of exercise required we eventually reach a "limit" which corresponds to the maximal energy production or maximum metabolic rate of the body.

This rate is 10 times the resting rate in trained athletes. Our lungs can work faster, but use of available energy and the performance of our heart (pumping blood around our body) place limitations on what we are able to achieve. The heart rate of a trained marathon runner can increase by 40 percent mainly because the heart has increased in size and the chambers inside grow bigger so that for each heartbeat, the heart is able to pump more blood. The heart rate of an untrained person averages about 75 beats per minute at rest, whereas the heart rate of a fit athlete is about 50 beats per minute. Power exercise and endurance exercise use different body fuels and have different limitations.

By increasing the blood's hemoglobin level you can increase the maximal energy production of the body by five percent or more. Hemoglobin carries the oxygen required by an athlete. Blood-doping through use of EPO (erythropoietin) stimulates the body to make more red blood cells, but EPO is now a banned substance. You might recall it was the drug that disrupted the 1998 Tour de France. (EPO is an illegal drug that if given in slightly higher than recommended doses can cause fillies and colts to drop dead during morning workouts.)

Training has the potential to increase the maximal metabolic rate by up to 20 percent and the potential to increase endurance by hundreds of percent. Special training and careful conditioning by athletes encourages the quantity of mitochondria per muscle cell to double. Yes, potentially it can double! Therefore, "interval training" is one of the better techniques athletes should seriously consider.

Interval training stimulates an increase in the number of mitochondria per muscle cell (thereby boosting energy levels). Mitochondria represent the cell's powerhouse – the factory producing energy. Mitochondria generate ATP much more efficiently than glycolysis from glucose and glycogen. However, it is the depletion of carbohydrate stores that corresponds to exhaustion during endurance exercise and this explains why marathon runners use a high carbohydrate diet beforehand as it fills up the carbohydrate stores of muscle and liver. On a high fat diet, carbohydrate depletion and exhaustion is likely to occur around about an hour and a half of running, whereas on a high carbohydrate diet it is possible to run for another two hours before the pangs of exhaustion are felt.

Although our main fuel at rest is fat, during high-intensity exercise 95 percent of the fuel comes from carbohydrate. We begin to burn fat again only when carbohydrate levels run down. There are two ways carbohydrate is used to produce ATP (energy), either by breaking it down and burning it in the mitochondria, or by breaking down glucose to release lactic acid, the latter not requiring the use of oxygen.

The type of muscle fiber present in an athlete may be changed slightly by training, as well as by the type of fuel used. There are two distinct types of muscle fiber – fast (but rapidly fatiguing) and slow (high endurance). Fast fiber muscle is white, whereas slow fiber muscle is red, brown or gray. Slow fiber muscle is rich in mitochondria and blood vessels – quite different to fast fiber muscle (e.g. that of a 100 meter human sprinter or a five furlongs equine sprinter) containing fewer mitochondria and blood vessels. Instead, it relies on anaerobic glycolysis to supply ATP rapidly, but at an unsustainable rate. Racehorses who are brilliant up to five furlongs or 1,000 meters but unable to sustain their speed rate a little further to six furlongs or 1,200 meters tend to produce progeny with similar failings unless they are matched with partners able to deliver a larger supply of slow fiber muscle.

Probably this is the reason why short-course specialist sires find it difficult to make the top 10 sires' list. A short-course sprinter's forte is really to get quick maturing, useful juvenile winners and older short-course performers. Muscle fibers inherited by a five furlongs sprinter are almost exclusively the fast twitch type.

Matching a brilliant five-furlong winner with another brilliant five-furlong winner is not the way to go if one seeks a six or seven furlongs performer. Since these parents were unable to sustain speed the extra furlong, why should their progeny? The DNA blueprint is not that generous! Matching a short-course stallion or mare with a partner who excelled at a mile makes more sense.

Why? Because the mile performer has a combination of slow and fast fiber muscles and as such, provides the opportunity for progeny to extend their speed rate further than five furlongs. Naturally there are other factors to be considered, such as clean airflow, large heart etc., but let's not cloud the issue for the moment. From research of pedigrees of Group and Graded stakes winners I discovered influence from short-course stallions (essentially five furlong specialists) gradually disappears after a couple of generations.

Please understand, the outstanding mile specialist requires a combination of about 50 percent fast fiber and 50 percent slow fiber muscle compared with a sprint specialist with about 100 percent fast fiber muscle whereas a middle distance specialist (1¼ miles or 2,000 meters) will have a higher proportion of slow fiber muscle compared to a miler.

A true stayer at a distance of two miles or 3,200 meters has an even higher proportion of slow fiber muscle – probably in the vicinity of 90 percent or more.

SUNDAY SILENCE (Halo-Wishing Well) winning the Santa Anita Derby Gr-1 on his way to Kentucky Derby glory.

The Cheveley Park Stakes – Steve Cauthen surging DESIRABLE to go through a gap between Pebbles (partly hidden) and Prickle, to win by a neck.

Matching an Ascot Gold Cup winner with a stoutly-bred mare is likely to produce a plodder, i.e. a tough endurance animal lacking in the speed desirable for stakes competition. I admit this practice was successful a hundred years ago, but no longer is it advisable in the 21st Century. Besides, yearlings bred along exclusive stamina lines no longer appeal to yearling buyers.

However, if two classic winners such as an English Derby hero and an English or Irish Oaks winner are matched, this union can supply enough speed to produce a potential Group winner over a distance. Classic-winning parents inherit enough fast fiber muscle to support stamina derived from a large quantity of slow fiber muscle. In other words, the foal should inherit enough fast fiber muscle to develop into a decent stakes runner.

In Europe, English Derby and Oaks winners represent the cream of the crop over the distance of a mile and a half. Classic performers inherit a valuable ratio of speed and stamina to enable them to run the distance faster than their rivals.

Tesio respected winners of the English Derby and supported Derby-winning stallions even when they fell out of fashion. History reveals Tesio chose wisely for he bred numerous high-class performers sired by English Derby winners. The reader should be reminded that Tesio never possessed a lot of money to support his breeding operation. Any decision he made to send a mare from Dormello Stud in northern Italy to a French or English-based sire would cost him fees, board, plus shipment. He needed to be convinced about any "special" matings he felt warranted enough potential to produce a stakes runner. My research of Tesio's pedigrees indicates he sought use of stallions with quite specific ancestors in mind. His aim was to reinforce their influence in a foal and he duplicated ancestors via male and female channels.

Part of the success of private owner-breeders in Europe and North America is due to the fact they employed exceptional trainers, patient men who opted to train the "individual" and knew the value of a protein-rich diet. Leading trainers have a habit of attracting top jockeys, and if a trainer has practical hands-on experience with an owner-breeder's homebreds, he or she would be familiar with strengths and weaknesses in the ancestry of those homebred horses. In other words, they would have a fair idea about the characteristics of parents and grandparents, etc.

Famous racing connections that come to mind are Lord Derby (the 17th Earl of Derby) with trainer George Lambton, His Highness the Aga Khan III with private trainer Richard C. Dawson, Marcel Boussac with private trainer C. M. Semblat, Robert Sangster with Vincent O'Brien, Francois Dupre with F. Mathet, Calumet Farm with Ben Jones, William T. Young with D. Wayne Lukas, the Phipps family with Claude "Shug" McGaughey, and the Australian brothers Jack and Bob Ingham with John Hawkes.

The relative proportions of different fibers in muscle can be slightly altered by training technique. A sprinter may have 80 percent fast fibers and 20 percent slow fibers but special conditioning can actually increase the amount of slow fiber muscle. It is important a racehorse receives the right type of training otherwise it could end up with the wrong type of fibers. Successful trainers study the pedigree of horses to be conditioned because pedigrees indicate the amount of speed and stamina in the horse's immediate ancestry. Increasing the amount of muscle is directly related to power output. Anabolic steroids, now banned in most sports, were used to improve muscle mass. More recently, human growth hormone was used until racetracks tested for it. Special training techniques are able to build muscle mass.

The introduction of "interval training" involves a series of repeated periods of exercise and rest, and was developed by German cardiologist Dr. Hans Reindell. He wanted to find a way to strengthen the hearts of human patients so he began a series of tests and measured the heart's performance. The most effective test was what he termed "interval training" whereby patients were asked to run repetitive short distances with short rest periods in between. This technique resulted in not only an increase in the size of the heart but also an increase in the quantity of blood pumped per heartbeat. To Dr. Reindell's surprise, he noticed a definite increase in the total oxygen consumption of the body during exercise. Changes had taken place in the skeletal muscle.

At the time (the early 1930's), Dr. Reindell would not have been aware that the quantity of mitochondria per muscle cell (in patients tested) would have increased. For a short period at the beginning of exercise, the mitochondria within muscle cells work hard and experience "stress." The muscle cell will thereupon react to make more mitochondria so as to supply more energy. During intense exercise, lactic acid and other fatigue-inducing molecules are produced, but the rest period flushes out these unwanted molecules from the muscle and prevents fatigue.

The key is repetition. Intensities of exercise within the intervals will stress parts of the body and effectively train those parts. Let's now examine something called noradrenaline. The sympathetic system is the body's alarm system. When the brain detects a threatening situation it sends a message via this system to all parts of the body for immediate action. Impulses via a network of tiny nerves work quickly throughout the body and at the end of these tiny nerves is a "messenger molecule" that is released. It is called noradrenaline.

Noradrenaline and its cousin adrenaline are alarm messengers of the body and brain. Together they communicate with the body to prepare for strenuous physical and mental activity. They are factors involved in activating the "sympathetic nervous system" and require the release of instant energy. Noradrenaline reacts faster in the body than adrenaline and is classified a "neurotransmitter" whereas adrenaline is classified a hormone. They both tell the heart to pump faster and direct attention to the muscles and brain. They order the muscles to contract. As expected, the heart beats very fast in flight animals, especially a racehorse, when threatened.

The brain controls the body via "motor nerves" acting on muscles. Stress is unavoidable for athletes. Stress saps energy levels, something the racehorse is well acquainted with, and prolonged stress causes painful stomach ulcers. Other effects from stress on the body include a decrease in the ability of the immune system to function properly and enlargement of the adrenal gland. The three main "stress" classifications are exhaustion, resistance and alarm. Unfortunately, chronic stress will decrease resistance to infections and disease.

The temperament of a racehorse is, of course, important. Trainers dislike entire colts that misbehave and cause trouble in the mornings. Throughout turf history many of the great racehorses were colts and fillies described as being highly-strung and falling into this category are champions and successful sires such as St. Simon, Flying Fox, Nasrullah, Ribot, Alleged and Nijinsky II.

It took three strong men to bring Prix de l'Arc de Triomphe Gr-1 winner Alleged to the breeding shed at Walmac Farm in Lexington, Kentucky, and great care was needed to handle Ribot when he was in one of his aggressive moods at Darby Dan Farm.

In England, Nasrullah was like a coiled spring in training. Initially he was sold for stud duties in Ireland before being purchased by a syndicate and shipped to Kentucky. The lads handling him had to be careful and always alert because Nasrullah manufactured plenty of adrenaline! Excitable racehorses

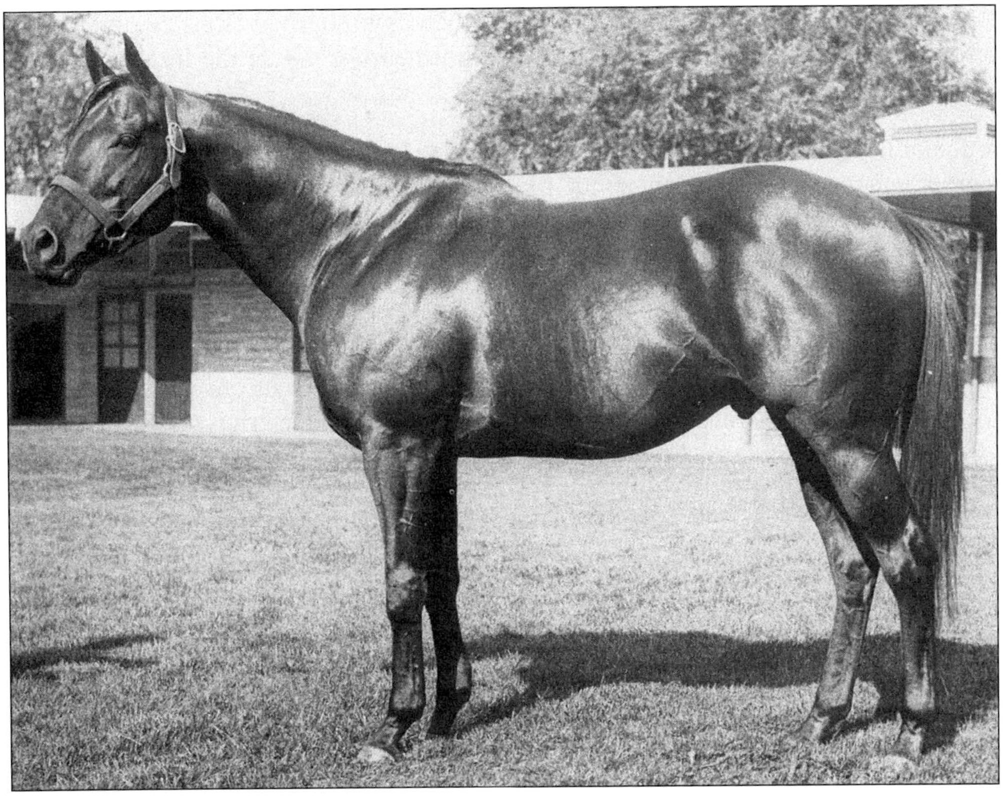

NEVER BEND (Nasrullah-Lalun by Djeddah) Champion 2YO colt out of a Kentucky Oaks winner.

HAIL TO REASON (Turn-To-Nothirdchance by Blue Swords), Champion 2YO colt and sire of Roberto (English Derby) and Halo.

possess explosive proton electricity – positively charged energy inherited from the unique union of their parents. Electrical nerve impulses pass down to the end of neurons where the impulse causes the release of a chemical called a "neurotransmitter."

Each particular neuron normally releases only one type of neurotransmitter to many different neurons. A single neuron integrates information about the electrical activity of many input neurons and this influences its own electrical activity sent to many other output neurons. Readers should be made aware that a neuron (or network of neurons) can integrate information from a variety of sources.

Yes, the body and mind work on electricity. Different types of electricity drive tiny machines and chemical factories to provide a wide electric field – electrically charged molecules. All matter is made up of electrons (negatively charged), protons (positively charged) and neutrons (neutral, with no charge). Within the cells of our body and the body of the racehorse, electricity is carried by electrons, protons, phosphate and sodium ions. An "ion" represents an atom or molecule with a charge.

So where does the electricity come from?

It comes from the food we eat and the air we breathe.

Electrons are collected from our food intake, fed to oxygen and pass down an electron transport chain (consisting of a tiny wire of copper and iron atoms housed in a membrane comprised of proteins). An electric current flows through this wire and is controlled by a "start or stop" action.

Electron electricity is used to generate proton electricity via the mitochondria. Positively charged ions are produced by mitochondria acting within a cell. This explains why mitochondria are referred to as the "powerhouses" of cells. Electrons burn food and are converted to protons that provide proton electricity (energy). Proton electricity generates large amounts of ATP (adenosine triphosphate) plus small amounts of phosphate electricity.

Occasionally electrons leak out of the mitochondrial electron transport chain to produce "free radicals," a group of dangerous toxic chemicals. Most stable molecules possess electrons in pairs, but molecules with a loose, unpaired electron end up being a free radical and seek one extra electron by snatching it from a nearby molecule, thereby starting a nasty chain reaction that destroys cells. Among the free radicals are superoxide and a hydroxal radical, the latter sometimes responsible for mutations.

To negate the impact of free radicals, three important antioxidants, namely betacarotene, vitamin C and vitamin E, are recommended because they are molecules that can prevent toxic effects. Natural antioxidants are found in vegetables (especially broccoli), red wine and tea. These are able to supply the extra electrons required to halt a chain reaction. Chinese Green Tea is a very effective antioxidant and regular consumption of broccoli helps neutralize cancer-causing enzymes should they ever become activated. Vitamin E helps, too.

Another leak occurs when proton electricity escapes from the mitochondrial membrane, thereby lessening (according to the size of the leak) the amount of ATP produced in the cell. It is important to remember that proton electricity drives the motor to make ATP, so if leakage occurs, energy is lost.

Specific female families can be affected by "proton leakage" via multiple cells, causing family members to inherit wastage of energy. We know mitochondria possess a small amount of DNA (MtDNA) representing the only source of DNA found outside the cell's nucleus and we know mitochondrial DNA can only be inherited via direct female descent. Therefore, a number of cells may constitute inefficient users of energy. Perhaps Group or Graded stakes winners are racehorses exempt from proton leakage?

If you believe the Thoroughbred as a breed has reached or almost reached its peak of improvement, why do many of our best racehorses even fail to transmit their own ability to their progeny? People tell me the breed reached its peak nearly 50 years ago and only improvement of racetracks, the environment, different jockey styles and improved veterinary assistance actually enable today's horses to lower track records. However, contrary to popular belief, in my opinion improvement is still possible using careful selection of quality individuals (by reinforcing superior ancestors common to both parents). Opportunities do exist for breeders to manipulate the genes of a future foal, but probability or "chance" will eventually determine the outcome.

Now that the importance of energy is covered, it's of no use racing a colt or filly with enormous energy if he or she is unsound and unable to get to the races.

In the past 10 years I observed a much higher incidence of yearlings sold at various public sales that have weak front sesamoids. OCD lesions were prevalent decades ago when owners, trainers and veterinarians were ignorant of their existence. Now they seem to be in the spotlight. Clean airflow has always been a major concern (hence we scope yearlings) but the increasing number of yearlings with poorly shaped front sesamoids (especially the near fore) should be of real concern to trainers, owners and breeders. Weak sesamoids cause unsoundness. Perhaps blame for any weakness can be shared by commercial sellers who want their yearling's sale catalog page to look pretty with lots of nice black type (matings not really designed for sound conformation) and by the method of frequently duplicating popular ancestors who transmit weak sesamoids via recessive genes.

With the number of stallions standing at stud on the increase, we should identify brilliant performers who remained sound versus those who are unsound. In 2004, the top 12 leading sires based on progeny earnings in North America were:

1. Elusive Quality (Gone West-Touch of Greatness by Hero's Honor)
2. El Prado (Sadler's Wells-Lady Capulet by Sir Ivor)
3. A. P. Indy (Seattle Slew-Weekend Surprise by Secretariat)
4. Storm Cat (Storm Bird-Terlingua by Secretariat)
5. Saint Ballado (Halo-Ballade by Herbager)
6. Smart Strike (Mr. Prospector-Classy'n Smart by Smarten)
7. Pleasant Colony (His Majesty-Sun Colony by Sunrise Flight)
8. Awesome Again (Deputy Minister-Primal Force by Blushing Groom)
9. Alphabet Soup (Cozzene-Illiterate by Arts and Letters)
10. Tale of the Cat (Storm Cat-Yarn by Mr. Prospector)
11. Unbridled's Song (Unbridled-Trolley Song by Caro)
12. Grand Slam (Gone West-Bright Candles by El Gran Senor)

Of particular interest is the presence of stamina in most of the broodmare sires shown above. Smarty Jones helped put Elusive Quality at the top of the list.

DANEHILL (Danzig-Razyana by His Majesty), leading sire in Australia, inbred 3 x 3 to Natalma. His progeny include Danzero, Rock of Gibraltar, Redoute's Choice, Danewin etc.

Europe's leading sire SADLER'S WELLS (Northern Dancer-Fairy Bridge by Bold Reason). He is the sire of many champions including Barathea, High Chaparral, and Galileo. He is a brother to Fairy King.

What male lines do these 12 sires represent?

1. Native Dancer, by Polynesian (Elusive Quality)
2. Northern Dancer, by Nearctic (El Prado)
3. Bold Ruler, by Nasrullah (A .P. Indy)
4. Northern Dancer, by Nearctic (Storm Cat)
5. Turn-To, by Royal Charger (Saint Ballado)
6. His Majesty, by Ribot (Pleasant Colony)
7. Native Dancer, by Polynesian (Smart Strike)
8. Northern Dancer, by Nearctic (Awesome Again)
9. Grey Sovereign, by Nasrullah (Alphabet Soup)
10. Northern Dancer, by Nearctic (Tale of the Cat)
11. Native Dancer, by Polynesian (Unbridled's Song)
12. Native Dancer, by Polynesian (Grand Slam)

Four of the above sires belong to Native Dancer's male line of Sickle (Phalaris-Selene by Chaucer), brother to Pharamond II and half-brother to Hyperion. Four sires belong to Northern Dancer's male line of Pharos (Phalaris-Scapa Flow by Chaucer) he being a brother to Fairway, bred on the same Phalaris/Chaucer nick as Sickle, Pharamond II and Colorado.

Two sires belong to Nasrullah's male line of Pharos (sire of Nearco) and one belongs to Turn-To's male line of Royal Charger (three-parts brother to Nasrullah). The remaining male line represented on the list belongs to unbeaten Ribot, a descendant of undefeated Cavaliere d'Arpino (by Havresac II), a horse Tesio believed was one of his superior homebreds.

From the above list we discover the male line of Hyperion (Gainsborough-Selene by Chaucer) is not represented, nor are the male lines of Teddy (via his sons Bull Dog or Sir Gallahad III) or Blandford, the best son of Swynford.

Looking at the results in Europe, the top 12 sires on the 2004 Sires' List by progeny earnings were:

1. Sadler's Wells (Northern Dancer-Fairy Bridge by Bold Reason)
2. Danehill (Danzig-Razyana by His Majesty)
3. Linamix (Mendez-Lunadix by Breton)
4. Pivotal (Polar Falcon-Fearless Revival by Cozzene)
5. Night Shift (Northern Dancer-Ciboulette by Chop Chop)
6. Selkirk (Sharpen Up-Annie Edge by Nebbiolo)
7. Marju (Last Tycoon-Flame of Tara by Artaius)
8. Kingmambo (Mr. Prospector-Miesque by Nureyev)
9. Barathea (Sadler's Wells-Brocade by Habitat)
10. Sri Pekan (Red Ransom-Lady Godolphin by Son Ange)
11. Efisio (Formidable-Eldoret by High Top)
12. Cape Cross (Green Desert-Park Appeal by Ahonoora)

Once again we find no male line representatives of Teddy or Blandford.

In fact, the majority of sires shown above belong to Northern Dancer's male line tracing back to Nearco. The 12 influential sires of 2004 are descendants of the following male lines:

1. Northern Dancer, by Nearctic (Sadler's Wells)
2. Northern Dancer, by Nearctic (Danehill)
3. Northern Dancer, by Nearctic (Pivotal)
4. Northern Dancer, by Nearctic (Linamix)
5. Northern Dancer, by Nearctic (Night Shift)
6. Native Dancer, by Polynesian (Selkirk)
7. Northern Dancer, by Nearctic (Marju)
8. Native Dancer, by Polynesian (Kingmambo)
9. Northern Dancer, by Nearctic (Barathea)
10. Turn-To, by Royal Charger (Sri Pekan)
11. Hyperion, by Gainsborough (Efisio)
12. Northern Dancer, by Nearctic (Cape Cross)

Eight of the top 12 sires descend from Northern Dancer, two come from Native Dancer's male line while Hyperion has one representative, Efisio.

Efisio won eight of 26 starts and excelled at seven furlongs and a mile. His successes include the Premio Emilio Turati Gr-1 (8f), Premio Chiusura Gr-2 (7f), Bisquit Cognac Challenge Stakes Gr-3 (7f) and Horris Hill Stakes Gr-3 (7f 60 yds). He was runner-up in the Queen Anne Stakes and finished third in the Queen Elizabeth II Stakes and Prix Jacques le Marois. Efisio is the sire of brilliant filly Attraction.

In summary, two ancestors are "standouts." On the list of leading sires in North America and Europe, Nearco and Native Dancer feature most noticeably and it should come as no surprise because both were champions on the racetrack and both were influential sires. Only once was Native Dancer defeated in his career – by Dark Star in the Kentucky Derby. Native Dancer is of course the broodmare sire of champion Northern Dancer. In Europe, Blandford's best male descendant on the 2004 Sires' List is Monsun, descending from Persian Gulf's line. Standing at stud in Germany, Monsun was ranked 15th on the Sires' List while Tourbillon's best male descendant is Indian Ridge (by Ahonoora), ranked 19th.

The dominance of champion racehorse Native Dancer (grandsire of Mr. Prospector, as well as maternal grandsire of Northern Dancer) is phenomenal when one studies the pedigrees of recent Group or Graded stakes winners. Native Dancer's influence now rivals that of Nearco.

Native Dancer is a son of Preakness Stakes Gr-1 winner Polynesian, a champion sprinter linebred four times to a very special brother and sister combination, namely Sainfoin (English Derby winner) and his full sister Sierra (dam of champion English sprinter Sundridge).

Geisha, the dam of Native Dancer, was a winner at three and is by Discovery from Miyako by John P. Grier from La Chica by Sweep from La Grisette by Roi Herode. This is an extraordinary female line. La Chica produced 12 winners including Planetoid (dam of the smart filly Grey Flight) and El Chico (a brilliant two-year-old colt whose wins include the Hopeful Stakes, Great American Stakes and Saratoga

Special). Obviously Geisha inherited (perhaps via many recessive genes) substantial genetic impact from Domino, North America's champion sprinter and leading sire.

Native Dancer won 21 of 22 starts from two to four years and earned $785,240. He is renowned as the sire of Dan Cupid (sire of European champion Sea Bird II), Natalma (dam of Northern Dancer), Raise A Native (U.S. Champion 2YO colt and sire of Mr. Prospector and Exclusive Native) and Kauai King (Kentucky Derby).

Native Dancer (1950)	Polynesian	Unbreakable	Sickle	Phalaris **(Polymelus/Sainfoin)**
				Selene
			Blue Glass	Prince Palatine
				Hour Glass by Rock Sand by **Sainfoin**
		Black Polly	Polymelian	**Polymelus**
				Pasquita by **Sundridge** (ex **Sierra**)
			Black Queen	Pompey by Sun Briar by **Sundridge**
				Black Maria
	Geisha	Discovery	Display	Fair Play
				Cicuta ex Hemlock by Spearmint
			Ariadne	Light Brigade
				Adrienne
		Miyako	John P. Grier	Whisk Broom II
				Wonder by Disguise by **Domino**
			La Chica	Sweep ex Pink Domino by **Domino**
				La Grisette

Polynesian is linebred 5 x 5 x 5 x 6 to siblings Sainfoin and Sierra.

From two to five years, Polynesian won 27 races, earned $310,410 and five of these were won as a juvenile. At three, he won five races including the Preakness Stakes, Withers Stakes, Saranac Handicap and Valorous Handicap. At four, he won eight races including the Toboggan, Roseben, Pageant and Rumson Handicaps. At five, he won nine races including the Long Branch, Fighting Fox, Wilmington, Oceanport, Omnibus and Camden Handicaps.

Polynesian set a new track record for six furlongs in the Rumson Handicap and equaled the world record for six furlongs in the Pageant Handicap, going a swift time of 1:09.2. He equaled the track record in the Long Branch Handicap over 1 1/8 miles and set a new track record in the Omnibus Handicap over the same distance. This is the record of a brilliant racehorse. Polynesian's dam Black Polly was a winner at two years and is a daughter of Polymelian, a sprinter bred on a similar cross to Phalaris.

Notice how Polymelian and Phalaris act like genetic cousins (similar DNA). Black Polly only produced two foals, i.e. Polynesian (classic winner) and Black Shot, winner of 10 races. The second dam of Polynesian is Black Queen, stakes-placed winner at two and dam of seven winners including two stakes winners. The third dam of Polynesian is the outstanding mare Black Maria, 18 wins $110,350 Kentucky Oaks, Metropolitan Handicap, Whitney Stakes and Ladies Handicap, twice.

Now let's briefly examine Native Dancer's dam, Geisha, a winner at three who produced four winners including Orientation (three wins and dam of six winners, three being stakes winners) and Performance (winner of nine races).

Fortunately, Geisha also produced the unraced filly Tea House, dam and ancestress of stakes winners. I have a feeling Tea House might figure in the pedigrees of future Graded stakes winners because at some stage someone is going to breed a top performer with Tea House and her brother Native Dancer featured in its pedigree. Geisha is by Discovery, U.S. Champion Handicap Horse and an exceedingly sound, tough racehorse that carried big weights. Discovery (by Display) was an influential broodmare sire and one of his daughters, Miss Disco, produced champion Bold Ruler.

One of Geisha's powerful ancestors is English Derby winner Spearmint (Carbine-Maid of the Mint), sire of Display's second dam Hemlock. The presence of Spearmint is most interesting because his father Carbine has close genetic links with Polymelus, the sire of Phalaris. They both carry valuable impact from Brown Bess.

Nearco's granddam Catnip is a daughter of Spearmint. Nearco is of course by Pharos, a son of Phalaris by Polymelus. ***Spearmint always has a genetic affinity with Polymelus***. Reinforcement of Polymelus and Spearmint will inevitably boost racing class and pedigree research confirms Nearco's strain mixes successfully with Native Dancer's genotype. (This mix is responsible for champion Northern Dancer.)

Discovery won 27 of 63 starts and set a new world record for 1 3/16 miles in the Rhode Island Handicap. His successes include the Brooklyn Handicap three times, Arlington Handicap, Hawthorne Gold Cup, San Carlos Handicap, Saratoga Handicap and Whitney Stakes (three times). Discovery is linebred to St. Simon three times, and linebred to the brothers Laveno and Orvieto (products of the Bend Or/Macaroni nick) plus their genetic cousin Fairy Gold, a mare by Bend Or from a granddaughter of Macaroni. Furthermore, Bona Vista, the grandsire of Polymelus, is by Bend Or from Vista by Macaroni. In addition, there is another important genetic force for speed since the third dam of Discovery happens to be by Hamburg (Hanover-Lady Reel) and Hamburg's dam is half-sister to champion Domino.

Native Dancer's granddam Miyako, stakes winner of five races, won the Autumn Handicap and was runner-up in the Fashion Stakes, Demoiselle Stakes and Adirondack Handicap.

Miyako is a daughter of high-class middle distance performer John P. Grier, by Whisk Broom II. The third dam of Native Dancer is La Chica, unraced dam of seven winners, four being stakes winners. Miyako would have inherited tremendous impact from Domino. Her father, John P. Grier, is out of a mare by Disguise (by Domino) while her dam La Chica is by champion Sweep (out of Pink Domino, by Domino). Thus, we discover a genetic build-up of several strong speed elements via Native Dancer's second dam. Native Dancer is a "genetic giant" and represents all the best things one seeks in an ancestor to supply speed up to a middle distance.

By duplicating Native Dancer via both sexes, racing class was upgraded. Matching Mr. Prospector (by a "son" of Native Dancer) with the strain of Northern Dancer (out of Natalma, a "daughter" of Native Dancer) produced a plethora of major stakes winners on both surfaces and took advantage of any valuable sex-linked genes.

In the next chapter, I especially ask the reader to be patient and absorb details about ancestors because the information lays a foundation for what follows in other chapters. At what point in time did English breeders begin to concentrate more on sprinter-milers rather than stayers? The answer is not clearly identifiable, but if we go back through history, certain ancestors need to be mentioned.

The evolution of speed in the racehorse probably began with the famous mare Pocahontas and her sire, Glencoe, American-bred Domino, ancestors bred on the nicks of Bend Or with Macaroni mares, Phalaris with Chaucer mares, St. Simon and his sister Angelica (dam of Orme) plus the very special combination of Sainfoin and his sister Sierra (dam of Sundridge). Pocahontas produced three great sons: Stockwell, Rataplan and King Tom.

All these celebrated ancestors imparted brilliant speed to their descendants. I have singled out these famous ancestors from many thousands of colts and fillies who had the same chance and opportunity to influence and upgrade speed.

THE IMPACT AND EVOLUTION OF SPEED

"This shift from the dominance of the late maturing, staying horse to the earlier maturing, speedier horse, was foreshadowed in England by the success of the sprinter Sundridge (1898) in the stud of J. B. Joel, and then by the success of the sprinter Phalaris (1913) in the stud of Lord Derby." - Abram S. Hewitt

Races of four-mile heats were common in England and North America during the early development of the racehorse. The establishment of classic races for three-year-olds proved to be a directional change. The English Derby, first run at Epsom racecourse in 1780 over a mile and a half on turf would set a new standard. Diomed, a chestnut three-year-old colt bred by Mr. Richard Vernon, won the initial English Derby and was later shipped to the United States where he became a very influential sire. Diomed was by Florizel from Sister To Juno by Spectator and his pedigree showed two crosses of Partner and Godolphin Arabian, major sources of high-class stamina. Thereafter, a tradition would blossom. In Europe today, the important turf classic races for three-year-olds are as follows (with the French Derby likely to be reduced in distance from 2005 onwards):

England - English Derby Gr-1, over 1½ miles for colts and fillies
English Oaks Gr-1, over 1½ miles for fillies
Two Thousand Guineas Gr-1, 1 mile for colts and fillies
One Thousand Guineas Gr-1, 1 mile for fillies
St. Leger Gr-1, 1¾ miles for colts and fillies

France - Prix du Jockey Club Gr-1 (French Derby) 1½ miles for colts and fillies (2,400m) distance up until 2004
Prix de Diane Gr-1 (French Oaks) 1¼ miles for fillies (2000m)
Prix Vermeille Gr-1, 1½ miles for fillies (2,400m)
Poule d'Essai des Pouliches (French Two Thousand Guineas) Gr-1, 1 mile for colts (1600m)
Poule d'Essai des Poulains (French One Thousand Guineas) Gr-1, 1 mile for fillies (1600m)

Ireland - Irish Derby Gr-1, over 1½ miles for colts and fillies
Irish Oaks Gr-1, over 1½ miles for fillies
Irish Two Thousand Guineas Gr-1, 1 mile for colts and fillies
Irish One Thousand Guineas Gr-1, 1 mile for fillies

The St. Leger is the oldest classic, first run in England in 1776, won by Alabaculla, a filly bred by the Second Marquis of Rockingham. The English Oaks did not commence until 1783. In North America, all traditional classic races are run on dirt.

North America's valuable "Triple Crown" comprises the Kentucky Derby Grade 1 ($1\frac{1}{4}$ miles) at Churchill Downs, the Preakness Stakes Gr-1 ($1\ ^{3}/_{16}$ miles) at Pimlico, and the Belmont Stakes Gr-1 ($1\frac{1}{2}$ miles) at Belmont Park. These classics are open to three-year-old colts and fillies. Major Grade 1 classics for three-year-old fillies include the Kentucky Oaks, Matron Stakes, Acorn Stakes, Mother Goose Stakes and Coaching Club American Oaks. In Australia, the premier classics (all Group 1 races) are the Victoria Derby, AJC Australian Derby, Queensland Derby, South Australian Derby, Caulfield Guineas, VRC Oaks, AJC Australian Oaks, QTC Queensland Oaks, Wakeful Stakes and the One Thousand Guineas.

We all need heroes in our lives and from time to time a truly outstanding classic winner will emerge – super athletes such as American Triple Crown winners Secretariat and Seattle Slew, and memorable English Derby winners like Sea-Bird II, Mill Reef, Nijinsky II and Sinndar. I will never forget the New Zealand-bred Tulloch, Australia's champion three-year-old colt that smashed track records, or the brilliance of Australian champions Todman and Vain. Racehorses with superior ability and courage promote racing as an entertainment medium by attracting large crowds to the racetrack. The media loves champions in any sport, but sadly, gone are the days when a Seabiscuit challenges a War Admiral in a special match race.

Australia and New Zealand are countries where there are many opportunities for horses with stamina to earn big purses. Valuable handicaps are even run over two miles. The VRC Melbourne Cup is a prime target. However, in 1957 the Sydney Turf Club, under the guidance of George Ryder, decided to introduce a valuable stakes event for juvenile colts and fillies. The race club introduced the richest two-year-old race in Australia and called it the Golden Slipper Stakes (Gr-1).

Star Kingdom's brilliant son Todman, a brother to Noholme II, won the inaugural Golden Slipper Stakes. Of course, George Ryder had an agenda – he happened to stand an imported son of Fair Trial named Newtown Wonder who was the leading sire of juvenile winners when the stakes race was introduced. The irony is George's stallion never did sire a Golden Slipper winner.

Few people knew a little chestnut stallion rated England's second best two-year-old called Star King (renamed Star Kingdom) would become a sensational sire in Australia and play a dramatic role in siring many Golden Slipper winners.

When Todman won the initial Golden Slipper Stakes at Rosehill racetrack in 1957, I failed to understand how this juvenile event would change the status quo.

The "magic" of the Golden Slipper altered the way breeders in Australia planned mare matings. It affected the selection process of homebred and imported stallions. Whereas big money for yearlings had been concentrated on youngsters bred to be potential classic or cup runners, by 1960 the Australian market did a backflip! All of a sudden there was keen demand for yearlings bred for speed – yearlings that matured early enough to compete in the million-dollar Golden Slipper Stakes. Pedigrees abounding with speed became ultra-fashionable.

Over time, the Golden Slipper Stakes would be won by famous colts – Sky High, Vain, Pago Pago, Baguette, Tontonan, Luskin Star, Marscay and Danzero – and by outstanding fillies such as Magic Night, Reisling, Sweet Embrace, Storm Queen and Toy Show. Australian breeders began to support sprinting lines, especially those of Nasrullah and Royal Charger in preference to imported sons of European Derby winners, and by the mid-1950's, British breeders also experienced the shift from stamina to speed.

With the cost of English training fees on the increase, owners preferred to concentrate on early-maturing colts and fillies, hoping to redeem part of their investment as soon as possible. By 1960, juvenile colts rated by Timeform at 115 or more were in demand and soon commercial stallion operators found it easier to fill a sprinter-miler's book of mares in England and Ireland than middle-distance stayers. North American breeders always respected early maturing horses even though purses for two-year-olds developed slowly. American buyers knew to own a possible Triple Crown contender, any prospective yearling had to be bred on a combination of speed plus stamina. The Kentucky Derby Gr-1, run in early May for three-year-olds, is usually won by a colt or filly able to win a stakes race as a juvenile.

The evolution of classic speed began in England around the time a handsome chestnut colt named Bend Or sired his first runners. Bred by the First Duke of Westminster and foaled in 1877, Bend Or was a high-class juvenile by influential sire Doncaster from Rouge Rose, a non-winning mare by the fast horse Thormanby. He was Rouge Rose's eighth foal. Bend Or was undefeated at two years with five wins – among them the Chesterfield Stakes, Richmond Stakes, Princes of Wales' Stakes and Rous Memorial Stakes. He was a well-muscled horse with strong hindquarters and could successfully carry heavy weights.

At three, his preparation for the 2,000 Guineas was affected by sore shins, thus his progress was quite gradual, but Bend Or gained enough fitness to make his debut in the English Derby, winning by a head from Robert the Devil, the only other superior colt of his generation.

Bend Or's rider, Fred Archer, remarked later he thought the colt's class, not stamina, earned him victory at Epsom. However, within two weeks Bend Or was not showing his best in workouts, being slightly tender in his shins. He lined up at Royal Ascot for the St. James' Palace Stakes and although he won, his trainer John Porter was displeased with the performance and was granted permission to rest the colt. During the weeks that followed, the Duke of Westminster implored John Porter to set Bend Or for a tilt at the unsuitable distance of the St. Leger. Unfortunately, it rained the night before the classic. Bend Or started as favorite despite the heavy ground and as Porter suspected, the test of stamina proved too much for the flashy colt who weakened in the final furlongs to finish unplaced. The victor was Robert the Devil who two weeks later would again defeat Bend Or by a head in the Great Foal Stakes at level weights. Yet another defeat by his archrival came in the Champion Stakes.

At four, Bend Or was a physically stronger individual and was primed to prove he could handle a middle distance. He won the City and Suburban Handicap, the Epsom Gold Cup (defeating Robert the Devil by a neck over 1½ miles) and took revenge in the Champion Stakes. Retired to Eaton Stud, Bend Or was runner-up twice on the General Sires' List, third twice and led the Broodmare Sires' List on two occasions. He died at age 26 in 1903.

Oddly enough, Bend Or was not really a dominant sire. His superior progeny were mainly out of mares by Macaroni. There was evidence of a genetic affinity or "nick" between these two strains and a major winner bred on the Bend Or/Macaroni nick was Champion 3YO colt Ormonde, undefeated in 16 races including the English 2,000 Guineas, Derby and St. Leger.

From his first crop, Ormonde sired a brilliant son named Orme, a colt out of a mare named Angelica, sister to champion St. Simon. Orme sired a Triple Crown winner from his initial foal crop, the high-class but temperamental Flying Fox.

Flying Fox was the leading sire in France and his male line flourished via Ajax's son Teddy, Champion 3YO colt in France, sire of the influential brothers Bull Dog and Sir Gallahad III, also Asterus, Sun Teddy and the "elite" mare La Troienne.

Bend Or's chestnut son Bona Vista (born 1889) was out of Vista, a daughter of Macaroni. Bona Vista is a vital link in the evolution of speed. At two, he won three times from seven starts including an impressive victory in the Woodcote Stakes (6f).

At three he won the English 2,000 Guineas defeating the high-class St. Angelo, but in the Derby, Bona Vista failed to impress and finished unplaced behind Sir Hugo and the remarkable filly La Fleche. The next morning it was discovered Bona Vista had injured a tendon and he was retired to stud. After some success as a sire in England, he was purchased to stand in Hungary where he led the Sires' List in that country five times. Fortunately, before his export he sired an influential son named Cyllene, a symmetrical chestnut colt foaled in 1895 from Arcadia, a daughter of Isonomy. Like most of the Bend Or tribe, Cyllene inherited a wonderful temperament. He was not entered for the classics but won nine of 11 starts including the National Breeders' Foal Plate, the Jockey Club Stakes, Newmarket Stakes and the Ascot Gold Cup. Cyllene was inbred 4 x 4 to Stockwell and proved to be a prolific sire in England with eight crops before he was sold for a huge sum of money to stand in Argentina.

Cyllene sired four English Derby winners – Cicero, Minoru, Lemberg and the filly Tagalie. He was the leading sire in England in 1909 and 1910 and also led the Sires' List in Argentina. Here was a horse that could accelerate more than once during a race and he was able to pass this gift to many of his progeny, especially to his tall son Polymelus.

Polymelus (Cyllene-Maid Marian by Hampton) was a bay colt foaled in 1902. Owned by S. B. "Solly" Joel, he won 11 of 31 starts, including the Richmond Stakes, Criterion Stakes (both at six furlongs) and Rous Memorial Stakes (5f) at two years. At three, Polymelus bypassed the 2,000 Guineas won by St. Amant, finished second at Ascot in the St. James' Palace Stakes behind English 1,000 Guineas and Oaks winner Cherry Lass and the following day won the Triennial Stakes (7f). Next, he ran unplaced in the Eclipse Stakes, the race in which Cicero met his first defeat at the hands of French raider Val d'Or. Later, in a field of 17 runners, Polymelus finished third in the Goodwood Stewards' Cup. He managed to win three races at three years, among them the Duke of York Stakes at a mile and a half. At four, Polymelus won the same event again as well as the Champion Stakes and Cambridgeshire Stakes. At five, from only two starts, he won the Princess of Wales' Stakes over 1½ miles.

"Solly" Joel was a brother to Jack Joel, the owner-breeder of 11 classic winners (his homebred fillies won the English Oaks four times). The Joel brothers were connected with the De Beers Diamond syndicate in South Africa.

J. B. Joel was extremely fortunate to be able to make use of two outstanding sires – his brother's stallion Polymelus and his own champion sprinter Sundridge. Polymelus was an outstanding stallion, the leading sire in England five times and runner-up three times. His pedigree contained ancestors with early-maturing speed, allied with stamina. His dam, Maid Marian, was impeccably bred being by the stayer Hampton from classic winner Quiver, a member of the famous Brown Bess family responsible for champion Carbine (sire of English Derby winner Spearmint).

Quiver was half-sister to classic-winning fillies La Fleche and Memoir. La Fleche won four classics and was runner-up in the English Derby.

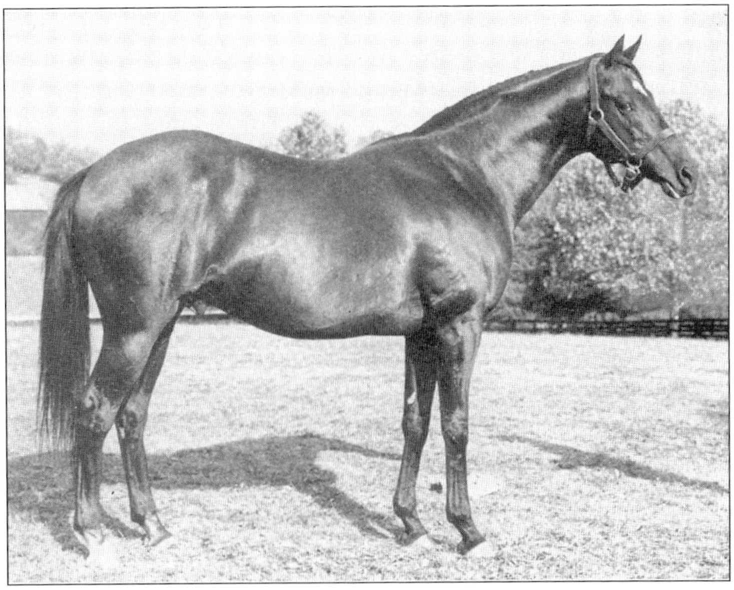

NASRULLAH (Nearco-Mumtaz Begum by Blenheim) sire of champions.

PHALARIS (Polymelus-Bromus by Sainfoin), Champion Sprinter in England. Sire of Pharos, Fairway, Sickle, Pharamond II, Colorado etc. He was bred by Lord Derby and was a huge influence for speed.

Although of moderate ability herself, Maid Marian produced three foals that would have lasting influence – Polymelus, his sister Lady Cynosure (ancestress of Wild Risk, the broodmare sire of Blushing Groom) and Grafton, a son of Galopin that was injured and never raced. Grafton was exported to Australia where he headed the Sires' List four times.

Cyllene and his son Polymelus have pedigree patterns skewed towards stamina whereas their male descendants Phalaris and Pharos have pedigree patterns reflecting a lot more fast fiber muscle, muscle type essential for early-maturing speed.

Polymelus (1902)	Cyllene	Bona Vista	Bend Or	Doncaster	**Stockwell** (**Pocahontas**)
					Marigold
				Rouge Rose	Thormanby (to **Touchstone**)
					Ellen Horne
			Vista	Macaroni	Sweetmeat
					Jocose
				Verdure	King Tom (**Pocahontas**)
					Maybloom
		Arcadia	Isonomy	Sterling	Oxford
					Whisper
				Isola Bella	**Stockwell** (**Pocahontas**)
					Isoline
			Distant Shore	Hermit	**Newminster** by **Touchstone**
					Seclusion
				Land's End	Trumpeter
					Faraway
	Maid Marian	Hampton	Lord Clifden	**Newminster**	**Touchstone**
					Beeswing
				The Slave	**Melbourne**
					Volley
			Lady Langden	Kettledrum	**Rataplan** (**Pocahontas**)
					Hybla
				Haricot	Lanercost
					Queen Mary
		Quiver	Toxophilite	Longbow	Ithuriel
					Moss Bowe
				Legerdemain	**Pantaloon**
					Decoy
			daughter of	Young Melbourne	**Melbourne**
					Clarissa by **Pantaloon**
				Brown Bess	Camel
					daughter of Brutandorf

Notes: 1) St. Leger winner Lord Clifden is out of a daughter of Volley who is sister to English Derby and St. Leger winner Voltiguer (grandsire of Galopin). Volley and Voltiguer are half-siblings to Eulogy, third dam of champion Carbine, winner of the Melbourne Cup.

2) Stockwell is a brother to Rataplan and they are half-brothers to King Tom. All three are sons of the "elite" mare Pocahontas, by Glencoe.

3) Arcadia, dam of Cyllene, is a product of the nick between Isonomy with a daughter of Hermit.

4) Hampton's grand-dam Haricot is half-sister to champion filly Blink Bonny, winner of the English Oaks and Derby. Blink Bonny was by Melbourne, whereas Hampton's sire is out of a daughter of Melbourne.

5) Macaroni, winner of the English 2,000 Guineas, Derby and Doncaster Cup, is out of Jocose, a half-sister to champion Touchstone (sire of the duplicated ancestor Newminster). Of special interest, Native Dancer's father, Polynesian, traces in direct female line to Jocose.

6) Polymelus carries tremendous maternal strength in his ancestry, especially via the influence of Pocahontas, Brown Bess, Banter, Beeswing, Queen Mary, Volley, Seclusion and Ellen Horne.

7) Brown Bess' second dam is half sister to the influential sire Tramp.

Since Polymelus descends in female line from Brown Bess, I need to show the relationship he has with Carbine, sire of English Derby winner Spearmint. The genetic connection is quite important. When the strains of Polymelus and Spearmint were united, it produced outstanding stakes winners, among them the Tesio-bred champion Nearco, the father of Nearctic, Nasrullah, Royal Charger and Dante.

Carbine	Musket	**Toxophilite**	Longbow
			Legerdemain by **Pantaloon**
		daughter of	West Australian
			Brown Bess
	The Mersey	Knowsley	**Stockwell** (**Pocahontas**)
			unnamed daughter of **Brown Bess**
		Clemence	**Newminster**
			Eulogy (half-sister to **Volley**)

Toxophilite was a sound, genuine stayer of high-class ability and son of talented mare Legerdemain, winner of the Cesarewitch Handicap. Legerdemain was a sister to successful sire Windhound (Pantaloon-Phyryne by Touchstone). Why do I mention this fact? Because Bend Or's dam is by Thormanby, a son of English Derby winner Windhound.

Thormanby	Windhound	**Pantaloon**
		Phryne by **Touchstone**
	Alice Hawthorne	Muley Moloch by **Muley**
		Rebecca

The famous mare Pocahontas is by Glencoe from a daughter of Muley. This means, of course, Polymelus is linebred to Muley via a son (Muley Moloch) and a daughter. It is quite rare to find Muley represented by one of his sons. As a result, I consider Thormanby's biochemistry to be extremely valuable. (Thormanby is one of the major reasons why The Tetrarch was a champion racehorse and an influential sire.)

Pharos is a brother to classic winners Fairway and Fair Isle, products of the successful Phalaris/Chaucer nick.

Pharos (1920)	Phalaris	Polymelus	Cyllene	Bona Vista	Bend Or by son of **Stockwell**
					Vista by Macaroni
				Arcadia	Isonomy
					Distant Shore by **Hermit**
			Maid Marian	Hampton	Lord Clifden by **Newminster**
					Lady Langden
				Quiver	Toxophilite
					daughter of Brown Bess
		Bromus	Sainfoin	**Springfield**	St. Albans
					Viridis
				Sanda	Wenlock (dam by **Rataplan**)
					Sandal by **Stockwell**
			Cheery	**St. Simon**	**Galopin**
					St. Angela
				Sunrise	**Springfield**
					Sunray
	Scapa Flow	Chaucer	**St. Simon**	**Galopin**	Vedette
					Flying Duchess
				St. Angela	King Tom (**Pocahontas**)
					Adeline
			Canterbury Pilgrim	Tristan	**Hermit by Newminster**
					Thrift
				Pilgrimage	The Palmer
					Lady Audley
		Anchora	Love Wisely	Wisdom	Blinkhoolie by **Rataplan**
					Aline by **Stockwell**
				Lovelorn	Philammon
					Gone
			Eryholme	Hazlehatch	**Hermit by Newminster**
					Hazledean
				Ayrsmoss	Ayrshire by **Hampton**
					Rattlewings by **Galopin**

Notes: 1) Ayrshire, winner of the English 2,000 Guineas and Derby, is by Hampton from Atalanta by Galopin from Feronia by Thormanby from Woodbine by Stockwell from Honeysuckle (sister to Newminster) and fuels more genetic influence from great mares Beeswing and Pocahontas. As well, Ayrshire supplies a valuable "daughter" of Galopin, the sire of St. Simon.

2) Rattlewings is a sister to successful sire Galliard, winner of the English 2,000 Guineas. Rattlewings is by Galopin from Mavis by Macaroni.

3) Wisdom's sire Blinkhoolie is by Rataplan from Queen Mary, and is therefore half-brother to champion filly Blink Bonny. Wisdom is inbred 2 x 2 to the brothers Stockwell and Rataplan, sons of the great mare Pocahontas.

4) Chaucer is a son of Oaks winner Canterbury Pilgrim.

5) Sainfoin's dam Sanda is inbred to the brothers Stockwell and Rataplan.

Scapa Flow, winner of four races over 1½ miles during World War I, produced Pharos (by Phalaris), winner of 16 races, among them the Chesham Stakes, Bedford Stakes at two years, the Royal Stakes and March Stakes at three, and the Champion Stakes and Duke of York Handicap at four. Pharos was a gallant runner-up to Papyrus in the English Derby and became a very influential speed sire in Europe.

Scapa Flow did not exhibit speed at less than a mile yet produced two classic winners, Champion 3YO colt Fairway (St. Leger) and Fair Isle (English 1,000 Guineas). Lord Derby's manager Walter Alston, a very clever pedigree analyst, recommended Scapa Flow visit Lord Derby's sprinter Phalaris (Polymelus-Bromus by Sainfoin) who was a big, muscular horse with a long back. Phalaris was endowed with plenty of bone. He was a horse of substance but fairly long in his pasterns. A striking feature of his conformation was an upright shoulder angle so typical of sprinters.

Lord Derby purchased Phalaris' dam Bromus (winner of the Seaton Delaval Plate for two-year-olds) on the advice of his trainer, George Lambton, and pedigree advisor Walter Alston.

Bromus was a highly-strung daughter of Sainfoin, by champion sprinter Springfield (son of the temperamental St. Albans) out of Viridis by Marsyas (also temperamental). As a yearling, Springfield was electrically charged and fractured his pelvis in a paddock accident. Not until the York meeting was he exposed in public. The stable lads supported him and Springfield had a facile victory in the Prince of Wales' Stakes (5½ f) for juveniles. Surprisingly, the following day in a field of five starters, he won the Gimcrack Stakes (6f), and scored again in the First October 2YO Stakes (6f). Next time out, giving 12 pounds weight to the winner, he was second by a head to Clanronald in the Criterion Stakes, and at the end of the season was runner-up to Kisber in the Dewhurst Stakes (7f). (Kisber went on to win the next year's Derby.) In 1876, Springfield's owner J.H. Houldsworth was a proud man after his three-year-old colt put together a string of sprint successes. Springfield won the Fern Hill Stakes (5f), Stockbridge Cup (6f) and July Cup (6f), scoring in the latter race by 12 lengths. Springfield was crowned England's champion sprinter. At four, he won five races including the Queen's Stand Plate (5½ f), July Cup for a second time and the Champion Stakes (1¼ miles) defeating Silvio, winner of the Derby. At his final start, Springfield won the All-Aged Stakes (6f) by 15 lengths. Never a leading sire, he nonetheless was a consistent sire of winners before he died in 1898. His son, the royally bred Sainfoin (Springfield-Sanda by Wenlock), was born in 1887.

A small chestnut colt bred by Her Majesty Queen Victoria, he won his only start at two. The following season Sainfoin captured the Dee Stakes at Chester and the English Derby at Epsom for his new owner, Sir James Miller. Possessing a kind temperament, Sainfoin was inbred 3 x 4 x 4 to champion Stockwell and his brother Rataplan (the broodmare sire of Wenlock). Thus, he inherited genetic impact from the dominant mare Pocahontas. Although never patronized much by commercial breeders, Sainfoin sired the dams of Phalaris and unbeaten Hurry On, but he is best remembered as the father of England's Triple Crown winner Rock Sand (English 2,000 Guineas, Derby, St. Leger), a colt considered to be a "smasher" who in turn sired champion Tracery.

Sainfoin is an unsung hero in turf history. He was a vital link in the development of classic speed and went unnoticed by English breeding journalists. The chestnut mare Sierra, an unraced sister to Sainfoin, produced English champion sprinter Sundridge, one of the most important ancestors in the evolution of speed.

Sundridge was absolutely brilliant! He was ahead of his generation. His 17 wins include the prestigious July Cup three times as well as the King's Stand Stakes twice, and Snailwell Stakes. The handicapper was forced to give him nine stone seven pounds or more in nearly all his sprint races when five and six years old. Sundridge led the General Sires' List in 1911, was runner-up in 1913, third in 1914 and 1915 and was the leading broodmare sire in 1923. He stood in England before finally ending up in France. At the dispersal of J. H. Houldsworth's stud, Lord Derby purchased Bromus on the recommendation of his clever manager, Walter Alston, who was impressed by the plain mare's inbreeding 2 x 3 to Springfield. Walter Alston wanted desperately to introduce more speed into Lord Derby's broodmare band, hence he sought Lord Derby's approval to mate Bromus with the outside stallion Polymelus. In 1913 Bromus produced a colt by Polymelus that would become England's champion sprinter. His name was Phalaris, a smart colt, but not quite as fast as Sundridge.

Winner of 15 of 24 starts, two to five years, Phalaris showed natural speed and won two of three starts as a juvenile including the Newmarket Stud Produce Stakes (5f). At three, he was successful in the Beaufort Stakes (7f), St. George Handicap (6f) and Royal Stakes (1¼ miles) but disappointed his owner in the English 2,000 Guineas, won by Clarissimus. At four, Phalaris progressed and won the Bretby Handicap, Chesterfield Stakes, Snailwell Stakes and Challenge Stakes but disappointed when finishing unplaced in the Cambridgeshire Handicap. At five, he won the Abingdon Plate (5f), June Stakes (1 mile), Lanwades Plate (7f) and had a walkover for the Challenge Stakes. Phalaris was retired to his owner's Side Hill Stud, Newmarket, after Lord Derby failed to sell him privately. A sprinter with a pleasant disposition, Phalaris proved popular with commercial and private breeders and attracted quality mares. Between 1923 and 1933 in England, he was among the leading sires and in 1925 and 1928 topped the General Sires' List. In addition, he led the 2YO Sires' List three times and the Broodmare Sires' List three times.

Phalaris died aged 18 years. Among his superior progeny were Manna, Colorado, Caerleon, Pharos, Fairway, Fair Isle, Silver Grass, Moabite, Warden of the Marshes and Priscilla. He sired the brothers Pharamond II and Sickle who were exported to the U.S. Phalaris had a fair amount of fast fiber muscle judging by his photographs and sired most of his superior runners from daughters of Chaucer, a stakes performer of almost 15.3 hands high. Chaucer was impeccably bred being by St. Simon from Oaks winner Canterbury Pilgrim and possessed a lovely sloping shoulder angle. Chaucer was short-coupled. These desirable features obviously helped correct Phalaris' upright shoulder angle and long back. Probably the four best sons of Phalaris, in terms of conformation, were Manna (English Derby winner inbred to St. Simon three times), Pharos, Fairway and Colorado.

In 1926, Pharos (Phalaris-Scapa Flow by Chaucer) retired initially at the Woodlands Stud, Newmarket, at a fee of 250 guineas. Later he was transferred to France when Lord Derby became British ambassador, based in Paris. Lord Derby would never allow Pharos to cover maiden mares. Italy's leading owner-trainer Federico Tesio wanted to send Nogara (Havresac II-Catnip by Spearmint) to Lord Derby's stallion Fairway at Newmarket, but the request was denied because Fairway's book was full. Desperately wanting to get a foal with a special pedigree pattern, Tesio resorted to using Fairway's brother Pharos in France. The result was the colt Nearco, Champion 2YO and 3YO of Italy and undefeated winner of 14 races.

As a juvenile, Nearco won seven races including the Criterium Nazionale, Grand Criterium, Premio Tevere and Premio Chiusura. At three, Nearco won the Premio Parioli (Italian 2,000 Guineas) by six lengths, Premio Principe Filiberto, Italian Derby, and Grand Premio di Milano by three lengths (over 3,000m), etc. On his final appearance in France he won the valuable Grand Prix de Paris by 1½ lengths and soon afterwards Tesio was offered a tempting price for Nearco to stand in England. With much at risk in 1938 owing to Hitler's rise to power in Germany, Tesio decided it would be safer for his unbeaten bay colt to move across the English Channel and so he sold Nearco to English bookmaker Martin Benson. Nearco was an exceptional sire of stakes winners and classic winners. A neat, symmetrical horse of 16 hands, he was wide between the eyes and had beautiful sloping shoulders. He was leading sire in England three times, 1947, 1948 and 1949, second in 1951, third in 1945 and 1950 and became an influential broodmare sire. Among Nearco's progeny were Nasrullah, Royal Charger, Nearctic, Amerigo, the English Derby winners Dante and Nimbus, and English Oaks winners Neasham Belle and Masaka.

We have now arrived in turf history when Nearco's son Nasrullah would dramatically influence the breed for speed. Nasrullah was bred by His Highness the Aga Khan III. Born in 1940, Nasrullah was by Nearco from Mumtaz Begum by Blenheim from Mumtaz Mahal by The Tetrarch out of Lady Josephine by Sundridge. Rated England's Champion 2YO colt of his generation, he won five of 10 starts as a juvenile including the Coventry Stakes and Great Bradley Stakes and was second to the top filly Ribbon, beaten a neck, in the Middle Park Stakes. At three, Nasrullah won the Chatteris Stakes, Cavenham Stakes and Champion Stakes, but in between these victories he displayed some shocking antics and was a difficult horse to train. He might have been genuine when fourth to Kingsway in the English 2,000 Guineas but he was rather fractious and moody when third to Straight Deal in the Derby at Epsom. Nasrullah stood initially in Ireland before being purchased by an American syndicate in 1951 for the sum of $350,000. He was shipped to Claiborne Farm, Kentucky, in the same year he led the General Sires List in England. Nasrullah proved to be an immediate success and led the Sires' List in North America five times, viz. 1955, 1956, 1959, 1960 and 1962.

His most celebrated sons were Never Bend, Never Say Die (English Derby), Nearula (English 2,000 Guineas), Grey Sovereign, Noor, Nashua and Bold Ruler. Other sons who were successful sires include Princely Gift, Bald Eagle, Indian Hemp, On-And-On, Fleet Nasrullah, Coronation Boy, Nasram II, Rego, Orgoglio, Nadir and Red God. Nasrullah had two sisters, Rivaz and Malindi, who perpetuated Mumtaz Mahal's influence for speed. What should be of interest to readers is Nasrullah's close genetic association with Nearco's grandson, Northern Dancer, whose second dam Almahmoud is by Mahmoud, a three-parts brother to Nasrullah's dam. Every time Nasrullah meets up with Northern Dancer in the same pedigree the mix reinforces Nearco, Blenheim and Mumtaz Mahal and upgrades racing class. In my opinion, Nasrullah's most influential sons were Never Bend and Bold Ruler. Never Bend was U.S. Champion 2YO colt in 1962 and is half-brother to Bold Reason, the broodmare sire of Sadler's Wells and Fairy King. Never Bend won 13 of 23 starts for earnings of $641,524. From 10 starts at two years, he won the Futurity Stakes (defeating Outing Class), Champagne Stakes (by eight lengths from Master Dennis and Outing Class), Cowdin Stakes (by three lengths) and four other races. He was runner-up in the Arlington-Washington Futurity to Candy Spots (defeated a half length), third in the Sapling Stakes (beaten by Delta Judge), and third in the Garden State Stakes on a very sloppy track. By late January, Never Bend was ante-post favorite for the Kentucky Derby. At three, he won the Flamingo Stakes by five lengths, Yankee Handicap by four lengths and four other races. He was runner-up in the Kentucky Derby (to Chateaugay),

Woodward Stakes (to champion Kelso) and finished third in the Preakness Stakes and Long Island Handicap. Thereafter he was syndicated and retired to Spendthrift Farm. Never Bend's classic-winning dam, Lalun, carries three lines of Teddy, and Teddy's second dam Doremi is bred on the Bend Or/Macaroni nick just like Bona Vista whose male line extends to Phalaris.

Never Bend	Nasrullah	Nearco	Pharos	Phalaris (dam by Sainfoin) Scapa Flow
			Nogara	Havresac II Catnip
		Mumtaz Begum	Blenheim	Blandford Malva by Charles O'Malley
			Mumtaz Mahal	The Tetrarch Lady Josephine by Sundridge
	Lalun	Djeddah	Djebel	Tourbillon ex **Durban*** Loika, dam by **Teddy**
			Djezima	Asterus by **Teddy** **Heldifann***
		Be Faithful	Bimelech	Black Toney La Troienne by **Teddy**
			Bloodroot	Blue Larkspur Knockaney Bridge

Never Bend's dam, Lalun, won the Kentucky Oaks, Beldame Handicap, Pageant Stakes and two other races, was runner-up in the Coaching Club American Oaks and finished third in the Matron Stakes. Lalun was a powerfully built filly with short cannons. She is linebred 5 x 4 x 4 to French champion Teddy (from Flying Fox's male line) and her dam, Be Faithful, was an exceptionally tough racemare.

Be Faithful won 14 races including the Vanity Handicap, Hawthorne Gold Cup, Beverly Handicap twice, and was runner-up in the Alabama Stakes. She is sister to Frizette Stakes winner Bimlette.

Among Never Bend's standout progeny were Mill Reef (English Champion 3YO colt, English Derby, Eclipse Stakes, King George VI & Queen Elizabeth Stakes, Queen Elizabeth II Stakes, Prix de l'Arc de Triomphe), Riverman (French 2,000 Guineas, Prix d'Ispahan, Prix Jean Prat), J. O. Tobin (Laurent Perrier Champagne Stakes, Richmond Stakes, Malibu Stakes, Swaps Stakes), Iron Ruler (Cowdin Stakes, Jerome Hcp., Tyro Stakes), Proudest Roman (Hopeful Stakes, National Stallion Stakes), Never Bow (Widener Hcp.) and Courtly Dee, dam of Althea, Native Courier and Foreign Courier, the latter being the dam of Green Desert.

Lalun, dam of champion Never Bend, is an "elite" mare by stakes winner Djeddah (Djebel-Djezima). Lalun produced six winners including Bold Reason (seven wins at three years, $304,082, American Derby, Travers Stakes, Hollywood Derby and Lexington Handicap). He finished third in the Kentucky Derby and Belmont Stakes.

MUMTAZ MAHAL, one of the fastest fillies ever seen on the British turf. She is the grand-dam of Nasrullah and Mahmoud. Her dam, Lady Josephine (by Sundridge), also produced Lady Juror, dam of Fair Trial.

FAIR TRIAL (Fairway-Lady Juror by Son in Law), who is linebred to Sainfoin and his sister Sierra. He is the sire of Court Martial and Petition.

Lalun also produced Staunch Eagle, nine wins and runner-up in the San Marcos Handicap. Bold Reason, son of champion Hail To Reason, is of course the broodmare sire of Sadler's Wells and Fairy King. Sadler's Wells (Northern Dancer-Fairy Bridge by Bold Reason) sired many Group winners out of mares carrying Never Bend's strain. This match duplicated Lalun, a lovely mare with very short cannons. When Sadler's Wells covered daughters of Darshaan (by Shirley Heights, grandson of Never Bend) this mix produced many Group winners in Europe.

Never Bend's influence for speed is legendary. Breeders throughout the world are duplicating him successfully to upgrade racing class. Riverman's classic-winning son Irish River (out of Irish Star by Klairon) had a genetic affinity with Northern Dancer, which was predictable because the mix involved two similarly-bred ancestors, viz. Nasrullah and Northern Dancer – both possessing genotypes comprising Nearco, Blenheim, and Mumtaz Mahal. For example, Alhaarth, Bahri and Anabaa are high-class performers bred on this cross. Champion racehorse Daylami (Doyoun-Daltawa by Miswaki), owned and bred by His Highness the Aga Khan IV, has one of the most interesting pedigree patterns I have ever studied. He stands at Gilltown Stud in Ireland, a beautiful farm managed by Pat Downes.

Daylami's victories include the French 2,000 Guineas, Eclipse Stakes, King George VI & Queen Elizabeth II Stakes, Coronation Cup, Man o' War Stakes and Breeders' Cup Turf – all Group 1 or Grade 1 events. Daylami is by Doyoun, winner of the English 2,000 Guineas in 1988. Doyoun was never fully appreciated by commercial breeders yet he has done well as a sire of stakes winners. Doyoun is by champion Mill Reef out of French 1,000 Guineas victress Dumka, dam of six stakes winners including Dalsaan, Dafayna and Dolpour. What is of special interest to me is the presence of Prince Taj in Dumka's ancestry. Prince Taj sired Faizebad, the grand-dam of Doyoun.

Prince Taj	Prince Rose	Rose Prince
		Indolence
	Malindi	Nearco by Pharos
		Mumtaz Begum (ex Mumtaz Mahal)

Malindi is a sister to Nasrullah; thus Doyoun is linebred 3 x 4 to Nasrullah and his sister Malindi. Furthermore, Lady Josephine is reinforced via Doyoun's broodmare sire Kashmir II, a horse linebred to Lady Juror. Both Lady Juror and champion Mumtaz Mahal are daughters of Lady Josephine (by Sundridge).

The Aga Khan designed the mating that produced Doyoun, and it was a very clever pedigree pattern. Designing the mating of an English 2,000 Guineas winner would give enjoyment to any breeder. Kashmir II was a brilliant racehorse and plays a valuable role in Doyoun's biochemistry. Apart from the obvious 4 x 4 duplication of talented mare Lady Juror, Kashmir's second dam is a daughter of His Grace, stakes-winning brother to Blenheim, broodmare sire of Nasrullah and Malindi.

Blenheim won the English Derby and is a son of the dominant mare Malva. I recommend Daylami be tested with mares possessing Fair Trial's strain, thereby reinforcing Lady Josephine's daughter Lady Juror. I visualize mares with Forli (linebred 4 x 4 to Lady Juror) could play an emphatic role in the production of Daylami's best Group winners. Forli (Aristophanes-Commotion by Mieuxce) was Argentina's Horse of the Year. A nice way to test this prediction is to match Daylami with daughters of Sadler's Wells, Fairy King or Nureyev.

Results from testing these recommendations could produce Group performers or even classic winners if the right genes are inherited. Perhaps we should examine the pedigree of Forli, remembering Lady Juror is out of Lady Josephine by Sundridge.

Forli (1953)	Aristophanes	Hyperion	Gainsborough	Bayardo
				Rosedrop
			Selene	**Chaucer**
				Serenissima
		Commotion	Mieuxce	Massine
				L'Olivete
			Riot	Colorado by **Phalaris**
				Lady Juror
	Trevisa	Advocate	Fair Trial	Fairway by **Phalaris**
				Lady Juror
			Guiding Star	Papyrus (by Tracery)
				Ocean Light (by Sunstar)
		Veneta	Foxglove	Foxhunter
				Staylace (by Teddy)
			Dogaresa	Your Majesty
				Casiopea

Note: In the above pedigree, Colorado and Fairway are bred on the same cross, i.e. by Phalaris out of daughters of Chaucer. Sunstar is a "son" of champion sprinter Sundridge whereas Lady Josephine, dam of Lady Juror (and of Mumtaz Mahal), is a "daughter" of Sundridge.

At this stage, I need to emphasize the progression of speed accumulating from reinforcement of brother and sister, Sainfoin and Sierra (dam of Sundridge). Phideas, winner of the Irish 2,000 Guineas, was an early example of this reinforcement, but the colt who caused pedigree researchers to sit up and take notice was Lord Dewar's homebred Fair Trial (Fairway out of Lady Juror by Son-in-Law out of Lady Josephine by Sundridge). Fairway's sire Phalaris is out of a daughter of Sainfoin. In Forli's pedigree shown above, Fair Trial represents a surprisingly dominant source of speed. Genetically, Fair Trial is a cousin to Nasrullah and Royal Charger who inherited similar genes from the same mix of Sainfoin and Sierra.

A chestnut horse born in January 1932, Fair Trial was not a stayer despite the fact he was by Fairway, a St. Leger winner, from a mare by the stoutly bred Son-in-Law. However, Sundridge dominated these strains and Fair Trial inherited speed not stamina and failed to win beyond $1\ \frac{1}{8}$ miles.

From nine starts, Fair Trial won seven times at three and four years. Lord Dewar requested he be put away to develop, assuming the colt was bred to be a stayer and perhaps a classic hopeful. Hence, the colt never ran at two years. At three, Fair Trial made a fine impression when capturing the Queen Anne Stakes (7f 155 yards) at Royal Ascot. He also won the Select Stakes and two other events. (This was the year the Aga Khan's Bahram won the English "Triple Crown.")

In 1936 at age four, Fair Trial opened his account by easily taking the Newmarket Spring Plate (one mile) from Lord Derby's colt Bobsleigh. Next, he was set for the mile and a half March Stakes and was made favorite at odds-on. He proved conclusively that day he was not a genuine stayer, for when challenged by Plassy in the final furlong, his courage and energy failed. He weakened but still finished second. (Later in the season, Plassy would win the Coronation Cup.) Returned to a mile for the Rous Memorial Stakes, Fair Trial won with something to spare.

In the Lingfield Park Plate, Fair Trial had scared away rivals, even though he was asked to carry top-weight with nine stone one pound. On race day, only the three-year-old Boswell lined up against him and Fair Trial won easily by six lengths. (Boswell would go on to win the St. Leger.) The very next day, Fair Trial was painfully sore in his back and Lord Dewar's hope of running his colt in the Eclipse Stakes was shattered. Fair Trial had in fact run his final race and was forced into retirement. He proved a consistent sire of winners with speed up to a mile, heading the English 2YO Sires' List three times – 1940, 1946 and 1949 – and was third on the List in 1945.

Fair Trial led the General Sires' List in 1950, was runner-up in 1945 and third in 1948. In addition, he proved to be an influential broodmare sire and led this category in 1951. Rather than just show Fair Trial's pedigree, I prefer to show the pedigree of one of his best sons, Champion 2YO colt Court Martial (winner of the English 2,000 Guineas). It involves not only the combination of Sainfoin and Sierra but also impact from an extra source of Sainfoin, via the dam of unbeaten Hurry On.

Court Martial (1942)	Fair Trial	Fairway	Phalaris	**Polymelus**
				Bromus by **Sainfoin**
			Scapa Flow	Chaucer
				Anchora
		Lady Juror	Son-in-Law	Dark Ronald
				Mother-in-Law
			Lady Josephine	Sundridge ex **Sierra**
				Americus Girl
	Instantaneous	Hurry On	Marcovil	Marco
				Lady Villikins
			Tout Suite	**Sainfoin**
				Star
		Picture	Gainsborough	Bayardo
				Rosedrop
			Plymstock	**Polymelus**
				Winkipop

Fair Trial's strain was a huge success in Australia. His son Newtown Wonder headed the Australian 2YO Sires' List before Hyperion's grandson Star Kingdom took it away from him. Fair Trial was represented by numerous successful sons at stud including Court Martial, Petition, Palestine, Newtown Wonder, Fair's Fair (leading sire in New Zealand twice), Fairthorn (leading sire in South Africa six times), Advocate, Confessor, Drum Beat (leading sire in South Africa twice), The Solicitor and Ballyogan. Although Fair Trial toed out in both forefeet it was considered a trivial fault. Many stakes-winning progeny inherited this toe-out including Court Martial and his influential son Wilkes, leading sire in Australia.

Wilkes sired champion Vain, one of the fastest sprinters I have ever seen in the past 50 years. Goofed, a daughter of Court Martial, produced Lyphard who was leading sire in France in 1978 and 1979 before his export to the U.S. Lyphard won the Prix de la Foret and Prix Jacques le Marois (defeating High Top). A small, elegant horse of only 15.2 hands high, Lyphard was typical of the Northern Dancer physique and not at all like Court Martial who was a fairly tall horse with substance.

A kind horse to train, Court Martial was unbeaten at two years. From eight career starts he won six including the English 2,000 Guineas (defeating Dante by a neck), Whepstead Stakes and Champion Stakes, but he was only able to finish third to Dante and Midas in the English Derby, a distance way beyond his scope. (The 1945 Derby was run at Newmarket owing to the war.) Court Martial led the General Sires' List in England twice, 1956 and 1957, before he was purchased to stand at stud in Kentucky. Of his 96 stakes winners mention should be made of Above Suspicion, Wilkes, Epaulette, High Treason, King's Bench, Major General, Ratification, Star of India, Victoria Cross and Full Dress.

By the 1930's, winners of the English 2,000 Guineas were exceedingly popular with commercial breeders. I suppose the trend started with Colorado when his first crop won major juvenile stakes events. Bred by Lord Derby in 1923, Colorado was a brilliant colt who won nine races including the 2,000 Guineas, Coventry Stakes, Richmond Stakes, Princess of Wales' Stakes and Eclipse Stakes. He transmitted speed to most of his progeny. Unfortunately he died in the prime of his life.

Colombo, winner of the English 2,000 Guineas in 1934, was another popular stallion with commercial breeders. Bred by Sir Alec Black, he was sold at the Doncaster yearling sales for 510 guineas.

Colombo won nine of 11 starts and was undefeated Champion 2YO colt in England. He was the sire of Happy Knight (English 2,000 Guineas), Claro (Irish 2,000 Guineas), Dancing Time (English 1,000 Guineas) and British Empire, a leading sire in Argentina. Here is his pedigree (the asterisk denoting ancestors bred on the Bend Or/Macaroni nick):

Colombo (1931)	Manna	Phalaris	Polymelus	Cyllene by Bona Vista*
				Maid Marian
			Bromus	**Sainfoin**
				Cheery by **St. Simon**
		Waffles	Buckwheat	Martagon*
				Sesame
			Lady Mischief	**St. Simon**
				Vain Duchess
	Lady Nairne	Chaucer	**St. Simon**	**Galopin**
				St. Angela
			Canterbury Pilgrim	Tristan
				Pilgrimage
		Lammermuir	Sunstar	Sundridge (ex **Sierra**)
				Doris
			Montem	Ladas
				Kermesse

Colombo weakened over the concluding stages when third to Windsor Lad in the English Derby. His father Manna (inbred to St. Simon) inherited a tremendous amount of nervous energy and although a difficult horse to train, had the speed and stamina to win the English 2,000 Guineas and Derby in 1925.

The evolution of speed in the racehorse continued with the appearance of a sensational colt named Tudor Minstrel (Owen Tudor-Sansonnet by Sansovino from Lady Juror). An athletic, lightly framed horse, Tudor Minstrel seemed to float over the ground. His high Timeform rating puts him in the top 10 racehorses of all time in Europe. Tudor Minstrel was undefeated Champion Two-Year-Old in England and progressed to win the 1947 English 2,000 Guineas for his owner-breeder, Lord Arthur Dewar. Tudor Minstrel also won the St. James' Palace Stakes and Knights Royal Stakes and represents another product of combining brother and sister, Sainfoin and Sierra. His pedigree reveals duplication of Gondolette 5 x 3 and English Oaks winner Canterbury Pilgrim 5 x 4 via her best sons Chaucer and Swynford.

Tudor Minstrel (1944)	Owen Tudor	Hyperion	Gainsborough	Bayardo
				Rosedrop
			Selene	**Chaucer** (ex **C'bury Pilgrim**)
				Serenissima (ex **Gondolette**)
		Mary Tudor	Pharos	Phalaris (dam by **Sainfoin**)
				Scapa Flow by **Chaucer**
			Anna Bolena	Teddy
				Queen Elizabeth II
	Sansonnet	Sansovino	Swynford	John O'Gaunt
				Canterbury Pilgrim
			Gondolette	Loved One (ex **Pilgrimage**)
				Dongola
		Lady Juror	Son-in-Law	Dark Ronald
				Mother-in-Law
			Lady Josephine	Sundridge (ex Sierra)
				Americus Girl

In the pedigree above, classic mare Pilgrimage is duplicated three times via her daughter Canterbury Pilgrim, plus a son, Loved One. When Tudor Minstrel's strain was mixed with Northern Dancer or Nasrullah it usually produced stakes runners. Blushing Groom is an example, being by Nasrullah's son Red God out of Runaway Bride by Wild Risk out of Aimee by Tudor Minstrel, and successful Irish sire Be My Guest is by Northern Dancer from What A Treat by Tudor Minstrel. England's Champion 2YO colt Tudor Melody (Tudor Minstrel-Matelda by Dante) has the Tudor Minstrel link with Nearco just like Will Somers (Tudor Minstrel-Queen's Jest by Nearco), the sire of Balidar whose male line extends to Cadeaux Genereux.

Among the first matings I ever designed for William T. Young's Overbrook Farm was the match between Claiborne Farm's outstanding sire Mr. Prospector and the maiden mare Blushing Promise (Blushing Groom-Summertime Promise by Nijinsky II). Mr. Prospector's season was expensive in 1986 and the team at Overbrook Farm had a right to question me on my recommendation.

Fortunately, Mr. Young listened to my justification and next spring the mare produced Carson City, a small, muscular chestnut colt with quite short cannons who grew to about 15.2 ½ hands high. Trained by Wayne Lukas, Carson City won six of 15 starts and earned $306,240 including the Sapling Stakes, Fall Highweight Handicap (six furlongs in 1:09 ⅘) and Boojum Handicap. He retired to Overbrook Farm and transmitted heaps of early-maturing speed to his progeny.

Carson City was always near or at the top of the Juvenile Sires' List and consistently high on the Sires' List. Among his 72 stakes winners (at time of writing) are State City (champion miler in UAE), Small Promises (champion older mare in Canada), Cuvee (Futurity Stakes), City Zip, Carson Hollow, Lord Carson, City Band, Flying Chevron (NYRA Mile Handicap), Pearl City, Paved in Gold, Imperfect World, Dublin and Five Star Day.

Carson City's dam is bred on the Blushing Groom nick with Nijinsky II which seems to work nicely with Mr. Prospector's strain. Years later, for Gainsborough Stud, I designed the mating that supplied Prix Saint-Alary Gr-1 winner Nadia (Nashwan-Nazoo by Nijinsky II) and Hi Dubai (Rahy-Jood by Nijinsky II), winner of the Pretty Polly Stakes, runner-up in the Prix Saint-Alary and placed in the E. P. Taylor Stakes. The cross of Rahy with daughters of Nijinsky II or Storm Bird works to improve the skeletal structure, adding size and providing a balance of speed and stamina.

Using Northern Dancer-line mares with Blushing Groom's son Rahy produced champions (e.g. Serena's Song, Noverre, Tranquility Lake) and when daughters or granddaughters of Nijinsky II were matched with Rahy it produced major stakes winners such as Fantastic Light, Designed For Luck, Hawkesley Hill, Dearly, Hi Dubai, Howbaddouwantit and Royal Lodge Stakes winner Perfectperformance.

Michael Goodbody, general manager of Gainsborough Stud, purchased Shamardal for Mr. Abdulla BuHaleeba at the 2003 Houghton Sales for only 50,000 guineas. The colt came from the first crop of champion Giant's Causeway.

In 2004, Shamardal was Europe's unbeaten Champion 2YO and was rated highly by Timeform after his devastating victory in the Dewhurst Stakes Gr-1, defeating Oratorio. Shamardal is by Giant's Causeway (Storm Cat-Mariah's Storm by Rahy) from Helsinki, a stakes-placed daughter of Machiavellian, son of Mr. Prospector from Coup de Folie (linebred to Almahmoud).

Storm Cat's father, Storm Bird, is bred along very similar lines to champion Nijinsky II. They both possess Northern Dancer, Bull Page, and one of the brothers Omaha or Flares. Mark Johnston, who trains some of the Gainsborough Stud horses, liked the Giant's Causeway yearling and began to bid on Lot 151. When he saw his friend Michael Goodbody bidding too, he decided to back off. Afterwards, Mark approached Michael and asked could he train the colt, which he did up until Shamardal's final juvenile victory in the Dewhurst Stakes. By then, ownership of the champion colt had changed. His Highness Sheikh Maktoum bin Rashid al-Maktoum became the new owner and decided the Godolphin team would train Shamardal as a three-year-old in 2005.

Giant's Causeway has the potential to sire Group and Graded stakes winners from mares carrying Mr. Prospector's strain. This cross creates genetic reinforcement of superior ancestors in a clever pedigree pattern.

Moving onwards, the successful Bend Or/Macaroni nick is still being duplicated numerous times in pedigrees of modern Group and Graded stakes winners. This nick remains a vital force and represents another source of early-maturing speed.

Among important ancestors bred on the Bend Or/Macaroni nick are Kendal (sire of Tredennis), Laveno and his brother Orvieto, English Triple Crown winner Ormonde (sire of Orme), Bona Vista (sire of Cyllene), Martagon, and Doremi (grand-dam of champion Teddy). Northern Dancer sired many of his major Group winners from mares carrying Teddy, especially via Bull Dog and Sir Gallahad III.

Teddy (1913)	Ajax	Flying Fox	Orme	Ormonde (**Bend Or/Macaroni**)
				Angelica by **Galopin**
			Vampire	**Galopin**
				Irony
		Amie	Clamart	Saumur
				Princess Catherine (dam by **Macaroni**)
			Alice	Wellingtonia (two daughters of **Pocahontas**)
				Asta
	Rondeau	Bay Ronald	Hampton	Lord Clifden by Newminster
				Lady Langden
			Black Duchess	Galliard by **Galopin**
				Black Corrie
		Doremi	**Bend Or**	Doncaster by Stockwell (**Pocahontas**)
				Rouge Rose
			Lady Emily	**Macaroni**
				May Queen

Teddy is the father of La Troienne, the "elite" mare from whom champions descend. Whilst Teddy has no source of St. Simon, he does inherit similar genes via Orme, a brilliant son of St. Simon's sister Angelica. In North America, La Troienne possessed an affinity with Black Toney and Blue Larkspur, so let's compare Teddy's pedigree with Blue Larkspur to reveal genetic similarities.

Blue Larkspur (1926)	Black Servant	Black Toney	Peter Pan	Commando by Domino
				Cinderella
			Belgravia	Ben Brush
				Bonnie Gal by **Galopin**
		Padula	Laveno	**Bend Or**
				Napoli by **Macaroni**
			Padua	Thurio
				Immortelle
	Blossom Time	North Star III	Sunstar	Sundridge (ex Sierra)
				Doris by Loved One (ex Pilgrimage)
			Angelic	St. Angelo by **Galopin**
				Fota by Hampton
		Vaila	Fariman	Gallinule by Isonomy
				Belinzona
			Padilla	Macheath by **Macaroni**
				Padua

The union of Teddy's strain with Blue Larkspur produced classic speed and duplicated Galopin and the Bend Or/Macaroni nick. Examples of this cross were Miss Dogwood (third dam of Mr. Prospector), Businesslike (dam of Busanda who produced Buckpasser), Real Delight (dam of Plum Cake, also third dam of Alydar), Blue Grass (grand-dam of Ole Bob Bowers, Bluescope), Flitabout (dam of Flirtatious, also grand-dam of Broadway who produced champion filly Queen of the Stage). Nothirdchance (dam of champion Hail To Reason), Revoked, Delta Queen (grand-dam of Delta Judge), Bee Ann Mac, Spring Beauty, Alablue (grand-dam of Boldnesian), Larksnest (grand-dam of T.V. Lark), Belle of Troy (dam of Cohoes), Big Event (grand-dam of The Axe II), champion filly Twilight Tear (dam of Bardstown), Ampola (dam of Sly Pola, grand-dam of Green Dancer), Blue Grail (grand-dam of Hold Your Peace), No Strings (dam of Nail, Globemaster, Mito), Be Faithful (grand-dam of champion Never Bend, Bold Reason), Bull Page (broodmare sire of champion Nijinsky II), Bimlette (dam of No Robbery) and Rarelea (grand-dam of champion Roberto). This is an imposing list!

If two or more ancestors with the Blue Larkspur/Teddy affinity are linked together it would produce enough electricity to light up Paris or New York! Breeders should consider linking Roberto with Mr. Prospector, or Nijinsky II with Mr. Prospector, or Buckpasser with Mr. Prospector. Four stallions by Mr. Prospector from daughters of Buckpasser were highly successful – Miswaki, Seeking The Gold, Woodman and Mining. Seeking the Gold, winner of eight races from 15 starts and $2.3 million, is by Mr. Prospector from Con Game by Buckpasser from Flitabout, and has three sources of the Blue Larkspur/Teddy affinity. He won the Dwyer Stakes, Super Derby, Peter Pan Stakes and was runner-up in the Breeders' Cup Classic and Travers Stakes. To date, Seeking The Gold has sired 62 stakes winners, with more to come.

Miswaki is by Mr. Prospector from Hopespringseternal by Buckpasser from Rose Bower by Princequillo. He won six of 13 starts including the Group 1 Prix de la Salamandre in France and is the sire of 93 stakes winners. Miswaki is the broodmare sire of European champions Daylami, Dalakhani and Galileo. Woodman was Champion 2YO colt in Ireland, winning three of five starts and is the sire of 90 stakes winners including Hawk Wing, Hector Protector, Bosra Sham and Hishi Akebono. Woodman is by Mr. Prospector from Playmate by Buckpasser from Intriguing by Swaps and comes from the direct female line of La Troienne (by Teddy).

Woodman should make a successful broodmare sire. Mining won six of seven starts for $264,030 including the Vosburgh Stakes but was imperfect in his forelegs. Mining is by Mr. Prospector from I Pass by Buckpasser from Impish by Majestic Prince and carries La Troienne via her champion son Bimelech, sire of Better Self. He shows signs of becoming a fairly decent broodmare sire.

Another major ancestor who influenced early-maturing speed was Sainfoin's best son, Rock Sand, winner of the English 2,000 Guineas, Derby and St. Leger. Rock Sand sired two exceptional progeny that help balance modern pedigree patterns – English champion Tracery (Rock Sand-Topiary by Orme) and the American mare Mahubah, dam of champion Man o' War. Domino's male line of Black Toney and his grandson Blue Larkspur blended successfully with Man o' War's line to produce stakes winners with superior speed.

Federico Tesio went out of his way to use stallions or buy mares with Tracery in their pedigree and I came to the conclusion he must have appreciated unique maternal strength from both Pocahontas and Angelica (St. Simon's sister).

American-bred Tracery is found in the pedigrees of extremely important ancestors, especially Nearctic (sire of Northern Dancer), Princequillo, Alibhai and unbeaten Ribot. Frankly, I believe Tracery is one of the main reasons why Nasrullah's genotype succeeded with Princequillo's strain, forming a genetic affinity that produced champion racehorses like Mill Reef, Secretariat, Bold Lad (USA) and impressive performers such as Riverman, Natashka and Rose Bower etc.

				St. Albans by **Stockwell** (**Pocahontas**)
			Springfield	Viridis
		Sainfoin		Wenlock, dam by **Rataplan** (**Pocahontas**)
			Sanda	Sandal by **Stockwell** (**Pocahontas**)
	Rock Sand			**Galopin**
			St. Simon	**St. Angela** by King Tom (**Pocahontas**)
		Roquebrune		Hermit
			St. Marguerite	Devotion by **Stockwell** (**Pocahontas**)
Tracery (1909)				Bend Or by Doncaster by **Stockwell**
			Ormonde	Lily Agnes by Macaroni
		Orme		**Galopin**
			Angelica	**St. Angela** by King Tom (**Pocahontas**)
	Topiary			Chattanooga (dam a daughter of **Pocahontas**)
			Wellingtonia	Araucaria (daughter of **Pocahontas**)
		Plaisanterie		Trocadero
			Poetess	La Dorette

Elusive Quality, North America's leading sire in 2004, who set a world record of 1:31 1/5 for a mile on turf, is the product of reinforcing the Nasrullah/Princequillo affinity as well as the quite similar Royal Charger/Princequillo mix available through Sir Gaylord. Supporting these nicks are ancestors I have highlighted in this chapter, i.e. Tudor Minstrel, Hail To Reason, Polynesian and his champion son Native Dancer. Elusive Quality was North America's leading sire in 2004 and sired U.S. Champion 3YO colt Smarty Jones, winner of the Kentucky Derby and Preakness Stakes.

A. P. Indy (Seattle Slew-Weekend Surprise by Secretariat) was U.S. champion 3YO colt and Horse of the Year. He is inbred to the Nasrullah/Princequillo affinity via Poker and Secretariat and has the support of Sir Gaylord (bred on the Royal Charger/Princequillo mix) plus Buckpasser and Hail To Reason. A. P. Indy has a proven affinity with mares carrying Mr. Prospector's strain – highly predictable because Seattle Slew succeeded with Mr. Prospector's strain (thereby duplicating the fast mare Myrtlewood) and nearly always succeeded with Polynesian's strain. A member of Nasrullah's male line, Triple Crown winner Seattle Slew is out of My Charmer (by Poker from Fair Charmer by Jet Action), a mare inbred to the sisters Striking and Busher (by War Admiral) who have La Troienne as their second dam.

Identifying genetic connections within pedigrees helps us to understand why some lines are perpetuated while others disappear. If our objective is to design stakes-winning pedigrees, perhaps the next step towards achieving this goal is to identify valuable genes transmitted by influential mares – the "elite" mares in the Stud Book. I cannot emphasize enough the importance of maternal strength.

UPDATED LIST OF "ELITE" MARES

"Now, the first and most important problem of the Thoroughbred breeder is to recognize the prepotent individual, the sire or dam which is more likely to produce a high-class racer than most other sires and dams." - *Joe Estes*

In 1987, I wrote *Quest For A Classic Winner* and published a list of the most influential mares that made a significant contribution to the improvement of classic speed in the racehorse. Readers asked me to update the list. Despite an ever-increasing Thoroughbred female population, the number of mares qualifying for admission to the "elite" mare list remains quite limited.

I wrote: "By identifying these mares, I wish to recommend to all breeders that future use may be made of the (elite) charts because these special mares are worthy of either being collected in one pedigree, or duplicated in one pedigree. These mares have something special in their genotypes and while I am unable to prove it with scientific evidence, I believe they may have powerful sex-linked characteristics that are transmitted to their descendants; so powerful, their influence is inherited on a more regular basis than probability normally permits."

Those of you who have time to enjoy pedigree research will have noticed duplication of great mares in the ancestry of many Group and Graded stakes winners. This observation is not new – breeders during the past century purposely and successfully reinforced dominant mares. The evolution of the racehorse has always relied on the power of maternal strength.

English Champion 2YO filly Mumtaz Mahal is considered to be one of the most influential mares in the General Stud Book. She was a brilliant, early-maturing gray filly who produced a number of talented progeny, but her fame rests more with three descendants – three "genetic giants" who became leading sires. They were:

Mahmoud (Blenheim-Mah Mahal by Gainsborough-Mumtaz Mahal), winner of the English Derby in race record time.
Nasrullah (Nearco-Mumtaz Begum by Blenheim-Mumtaz Mahal) English Champion 2YO colt.
Royal Charger (Nearco-Sun Princess by Solario-Mumtaz Begum by Blenheim-Mumtaz Mahal) Stakes winning sprinter-miler.

Seattle Slew, unbeaten going into the Kentucky Derby, was a Triple Crown winner and a sensational racehorse, yet he was not an expensive yearling purchase. His father was Bold Reasoning (eight wins at three and four, $180,564, Jersey Derby, Withers Stakes and runner-up in the Grade 1 Metropolitan Handicap). Apart from one other high-class performer (Super Concorde), Bold Reasoning did not set the world on fire as a sire of stakes winners and I believe only Seattle Slew was able to carry on this branch of Nasrullah's male line via Bold Reasoning. So where did Seattle Slew inherit his championship speed?

Perhaps if we study the pedigree of his stakes-winning dam My Charmer (Poker-Fair Charmer by Jet Action) we might be able to solve part of the puzzle.

				Prince Rose
			Princequillo	Cosquilla by Papyrus by Tracery
		Round Table		Sir Cosmo
			Knight's Daughter	Feola
	Poker			Nearco by Pharos
			Nasrullah	Mumtaz Begum by **Blenheim**
		Glamour		**War Admiral** by **Man o' War**
			Striking	**Baby League** ex **La Troienne**
My Charmer (1969)				**Blenheim**
			Jet Pilot	Black Wave by Sir Gallahad
		Jet Action		**War Admiral** by **Man o' War**
			Busher	**Baby League** ex **La Troienne**
	Fair Charmer			Good Goods
			Alsab	Winds Chant
		Myrtle Charm		Equipoise by Pennant
			Crepe Myrtle	Myrtlewood by Blue Larkspur

At once we can see inbreeding 3 x 3 to the sisters Striking and Busher, stakes-winning fillies by champion War Admiral out of Baby League by Bubbling Over out of the "elite" mare La Troienne by Teddy. (Note: Bubbling Over comes from the male line of Sundridge). Striking and Busher are three-parts sisters to stakes winner Busanda, dam of champion Buckpasser, so one might suspect superior genes flow through their chromosomes.

My Charmer has other genetic "goodies" in her ancestry. English Derby winner Blenheim is duplicated 5 x 4 via a daughter (Mumtaz Begum) and a son (Jet Pilot) as well as duplication of French champion Teddy via a daughter (La Troienne twice) and a son (Sir Gallahad III) while the Bend Or/Macaroni nick appears further back in the pattern. Teddy's second dam Doremi is a product of this nick.

Jet Pilot's second dam brings in a son of Sainfoin via Friar Rock (Rock Sand-Fairy Gold by Bend Or) thereby complementing Nasrullah who has Sainfoin and his sister Sierra in his genotype. Furthermore, Rock Sand (son of Sainfoin) is reinforced via Mahubah, dam of Man o' War. Therefore, when My Charmer was matched with Bold Reasoning this union duplicated a son and daughter of Nasrullah, reinforced Sainfoin and his sister Sierra many times (especially via Polynesian, broodmare sire of Boldnesian), and supplied Nasrullah's three-parts brother Royal Charger who has a double of Sundridge, son of Sierra. The chance this mating might breed a champion racehorse depended entirely upon genetic probability – whether desirable genes from duplicated superior ancestors would be inherited by the foal.

As luck would have it, champion Seattle Slew was born. He excited a nation, promoted racing and became a very influential sire. His champion son A. P. Indy also has an intriguing pedigree pattern since he is 4 x 3 to Bold Ruler, linebred to Nasrullah and his three-parts brother Royal Charger, linebred to champion Turn-To (who is inbred 3 x 3 to a son and a daughter of Pharos) and linebred twice to a son and a daughter of Princequillo. Weekend Surprise, the dam of A. P. Indy, has "elite" mare Somethingroyal (Princequillo-Imperatrice by Caruso) duplicated; and the successful Nasrullah/Princequillo nick is reinforced in the pattern, supported by the Royal Charger/Princequillo mix of Sir Gaylord. Hence, very similar biochemistries united.

Reinforcement of valuable genes via great mares like Somethingroyal is a proven technique used to upgrade racing class. The sire to date of 75 stakes winners, A. P. Indy is a horse whose progeny seem to prefer dirt surfaces rather than turf. This was certainly true in the case of Mineshaft, voted North America's Horse of the Year in 2003. A. P. Indy won eight of 11 starts for career earnings of $2,979,85 and is a horse with substance, standing at Lane's End Farm in Kentucky.

Voted Champion 3YO and U. S. Horse of the Year, A. P. Indy won the Breeders' Cup Classic, Belmont Stakes, Santa Anita Derby and Hollywood Futurity etc. To the end of 2004, his progeny earned more than $60 million. So let's take a look at how A. P. Indy's male line progressed from Nasrullah. We know it's the sire line established by Bona Vista (Bend Or-Vista by Macaroni) through his son Cyllene (sire of Polymelus). Worth noting in Nasrullah's pedigree are:

a) Havresac II, the broodmare sire of Nearco, is inbred to St. Simon 2 x 3 and possesses St. Simon's sister Angelica via Flying Fox.
b) Chaucer and Swynford are half-brothers, being sons of the "elite" mare Canterbury Pilgrim.
c) The third dam of Blenheim is Marliacea, by Martagon (Bend Or/Macaroni nick) and Mumtaz Mahal's sire The Tetrarch is out of Vahren by Bona Vista (Bend Or/Macaroni nick).
d) Carbine is related to Polymelus – via the Brown Bess family.
e) Sierra (dam of Sundridge) is a sister to Derby winner Sainfoin.

Nasrullah	Nearco	Pharos	Phalaris	Polymelus (to **Bona Vista**)
				Bromus by **Sainfoin**
			Scapa Flow	Chaucer by **St. Simon**
				Anchora
		Nogara	Havresac II	Rabelais by **St. Simon**
				Hors Concours
			Catnip	Spearmint by Carbine
				Sibola
	Mumtaz Begum	Blenheim	Blandford	Swynford
				Blanche by White Eagle
			Malva	Charles O'Malley
				Wild Arum
		Mumtaz Mahal	The Tetrarch	Roi Herode
				Vahren by **Bona Vista**
			Lady Josephine	Sundridge ex **Sierra**
				Americus Girl

The pedigree above shows the combination of Sainfoin and his sister Sierra, duplication of the Bend Or/Macaroni nick, unbeaten St. Simon plus his sister Angelica, and duplication of English Oaks winner Canterbury Pilgrim.

The alternate sex line of influence (sometimes referred to as the "heart line") in Nasrullah's pedigree zigzags to Derby winner Blenheim and to his broodmare sire Charles O'Malley, a highly-strung racehorse. If Nasrullah inherited important sex-linked genes they would surely have come via Blenheim's dam, Malva.

Blenheim (1930)	Blandford	Swynford	John O' Gaunt	**Isinglass**
				La Fleche by **St. Simon**
			Canterbury Pilgrim	Tristan by Hermit
				Pilgrimage
		Blanche	White Eagle	Gallinule by **Isonomy**
				Merry Gal by **Galopin**
			Black Cherry	Bendigo
				Black Duchess
	Malva	Charles O'Malley	Desmond	St. Simon by **Galopin**
				L'Abbesse de Jouarre
			Goody Two Shoes	**Isinglass** by **Isonomy**
				Sandal by Kisber
		Wild Arum	Robert le Diable	Ayrshire, dam by **Galopin**
				Rose Bay (dam sister to **Bend Or**)
			Marliacea	Martagon (**Bend Or/Macaroni**)
				Flitters by **Galopin**

Blenheim's pedigree reflects substantial genetic impact from Galopin and his son St. Simon, plus a double of Triple Crown winner Isinglass, a triple of Hermit and speed from Wild Arum, a mare inbred to Bend Or and his sister Rose of Lancaster (the dam of Rose Bay).

Now let's study champion racehorse and sire Bold Ruler. His pedigree has the Bend Or/Macaroni nick via Fairy Gold (dam of Fair Play) and again via Orvieto and Bona Vista. Influential sire Light Brigade is by Picton (Orvieto-Hecuba by Isonomy) from Bridge of Earn (Cyllene-Santa Brigida by St. Simon).

Bold Ruler (1954)	Nasrullah	Nearco	Pharos	Phalaris (dam by **Sainfoin**) to **Cyllene**
				Scapa Flow
			Nogara	Havresac II
				Catnip (dam by **Spearmint**)
		Mumtaz Begum	Blenheim	Blandford
				Malva by Charles O'Malley
			Mumtaz Mahal	The Tetrarch (dam by **Bona Vista**)
				Lady Josephine by **Sundridge (S)**
	Miss Disco	Discovery	Display	Fair Play (ex Fairy Gold - **Bend Or**)
				Cicuta (dam by **Spearmint**)
			Ariadne	Light Brigade (dam by **Cyllene**)
				Adrienne
		Outdone	Pompey	Sun Briar by **Sundridge (Sierra)**
				Cleopatra
			Sweep Girl	Sweep On
				Dugout (dam by Disguise)

Cyllene is by Bona Vista, by Bend Or out of Vista by Macaroni. Fair Play's dam, Fairy Gold, is by Bend Or out of Dame Masham by Macaroni. Blenheim carries Martagon, another source of the Bend Or/Macaroni nick. By adding the double of Sundridge with Sainfoin, Bold Ruler's pedigree is skewed towards classic speed.

Bold Ruler won 23 of 33 starts, earned $764,204 and was leading sire in North America for seven years.

He was Horse of the Year and Champion 3YO colt, winner of the Preakness Stakes, Wood Memorial Stakes (defeating Gallant Man), Flamingo Stakes (in track record time), Vosburgh Handicap (7f in $1{:}21\ ^{2}/_{5}$), Jerome Handicap, Carter Handicap and the Futurity Stakes.

Next we should mention an important ancestor that helped Seattle Slew become a champion racehorse – Boldnesian (Bold Ruler-Alanesian by Polynesian). This chestnut horse born in 1963 won four of five starts including the Santa Anita Derby, and an allowance race over six furlongs in $1{:}09\ ^{3}/_{5}$ by four lengths.

Boldnesian's dam Alanesian was outstanding, winning nine races including the Spinaway Stakes, Astarita Stakes, Margate Handicap, New Castle Stakes etc.

Alanesian is a daughter of Preakness Stakes winner Polynesian, an ancestor with Sainfoin and his sister Sierra featured four times. Boldnesian is linebred to the brilliant sprinter Pompey via two daughters, and Pompey is a grandson of Sundridge (out of Sierra). Not often will you find Boldnesian in a pedigree, but if you do, learn to respect him because he was an exceptionally fast sprinter-miler.

Boldnesian (1963)	Bold Ruler	Nasrullah	Nearco	Pharos (**Phalaris/Chaucer**)
				Nogara by Havresac II
			Mumtaz Begum	Blenheim
				Mumtaz Mahal, dam by **Sundridge**
		Miss Disco	Discovery	Display
				Ariadne
			Outdone	**Pompey** by son of **Sundridge**
				Sweep Out
	Alanesian	Polynesian	Unbreakable	Sickle (**Phalaris/Chaucer**)
				Blue Glass
			Black Polly	Polymelian
				Black Queen by **Pompey** (to **S**)
		Alablue	Blue Larkspur	Black Servant
				Blossom Time
			Double Time	Sir Galahad III by **Teddy**
				Virginia L.

Sickle (Phalaris-Selene by Chaucer) acts like a three-quarter genetic brother to Pharos. This fact is important because Sickle's male line of Native Dancer blended successfully with Pharos's line of Nearctic (e.g. Northern Dancer) and Nasrullah (e.g. Mr. Prospector). Phalaris is out of a daughter of Sainfoin. Duplication of the sprinter Pompey builds on the biochemistry of champion sprinter Sundridge whose dam Sierra is a sister to Sainfoin. Sundridge features again via his grandson North Star III.

In 1968, Boldnesian sired a colt out of Reason To Earn by champion Hail To Reason. This match introduced Nasrullah's three-parts brother Royal Charger via Turn-To (inbred 3 x 3 to Pharos).

Boldnesian's son was named Bold Reasoning, winner of eight of 12 starts and smart enough to set a new track record for six furlongs at Belmont Park in $1{:}08\ ^{4}/_{5}$.

Bold Reasoning won the Withers Stakes and was gallant in defeat when runner-up in the Grade 1 Metropolitan Handicap to Executioner, beaten a neck in a thrilling finish. Hail To Reason, an exceptionally tough juvenile performer, is out of Nothirdchance bred on the Blue Larkspur/Sir Galahad III affinity. The female line of Bold Reasoning goes back to Knickerbocker's dam, Warrior Lass (by Man o' War-Sweetheart), thus adding more influence from Sainfoin via Rock Sand.

The combination of three-quarter siblings Nasrullah and Royal Charger brings together similar genes via a "son" and "daughter" of Mumtaz Begum. Royal Charger's dam is by Solario from Mumtaz Begum, and Solario is out of a daughter of Sundridge.

Now we arrive at the next generation – Horse of the Year and Champion 3YO colt Seattle Slew, son of Bold Reasoning. Seattle Slew sired A. P. Indy whose pedigree reveals the sisters Striking and Busher, plus their three-parts sister Busanda:

A.P. Indy (1989)	Seattle Slew	Bold Reasoning	Boldnesian	**Bold Ruler** by **Nasrullah**
				Alanesian by Polynesian
			Reason to Earn	Hail To Reason (to **Royal Charger**)
				Sailing Home
		My Charmer	Poker	Round Table by **Princequillo**
				Glamour by **Nasrullah** ex **Striking**
			Fair Charmer	Jet Action ex **Busher**
				Myrtle Charm
	Weekend Surprise	Secretariat	**Bold Ruler**	**Nasrullah**
				Miss Disco by Discovery
			Somethingroyal	**Princequillo**
				Imperatrice (to **Polymelian**)
		Lassie Dear	Buckpasser	Tom Fool (to Pharamond II)
				Busanda
			Gay Missile	Sir Gaylord (to **Royal Charger**)
				Missy Baba by My Babu

A. P. Indy has five sources of Nasrullah and Royal Charger, plus their genetic female relative Perfume II, dam of champion My Babu. Perfume II is by Badruddin (Blandford-Mumtaz Mahal) out of Turn-To's second dam Lavendula II (Pharos-Sweet Lavender by Swynford) – the same mix as Nasrullah.

Turn-To (Royal Charger-Source Sucree by Admiral Drake-Lavendula II by Pharos) is of course the father of Hail To Reason and Sir Gaylord.

A. P. Indy features three ancestors bred on the same affinity – Poker and Secretariat (with the Nasrullah/Princequillo nick) and Sir Gaylord (the Royal Charger/Princequillo mix). Weekend Surprise is inbred 2 x 4 to Princequillo's daughter Somethingroyal. The mares Striking, Busher and Busanda are all by champion War Admiral, son of Man o' War who carries Sainfoin's best son Rock Sand.

Striking, Busher and Busanda are granddaughters of "elite" mare La Troienne, by Teddy. Logically they must have affected the biochemistry of A. P. Indy in a positive way. I hope the reader understands it was no fluke Seattle Slew was a great racehorse, inheriting genetic strength from reinforcing superior ancestors, and I would guess A. P. Indy is the most likely son to extend Seattle Slew's male line.

A. P. Indy is already the sire of Pulpit, winner of the Blue Grass Stakes, Fountain of Youth Stakes and sire of swift two-year-old Sky Mesa and champion Mineshaft (10 wins, $2,283,402, Woodward Stakes, Pimlico Special Handicap, Jockey Club Gold Cup, Suburban Handicap etc.). Interestingly, both Pulpit and Mineshaft are out of daughters of Mr. Prospector, thus duplicating the fast mare Myrtlewood.

The pedigree of Sky Mesa is impressive, representing a very clever pattern. Not only do we find 4 x 4 duplication of champion Secretariat, but also the genetic female relative La Mesa, by Round Table (son of Princequillo) out of a daughter of Nasrullah. If we add Seattle Slew's broodmare sire Poker, by Round Table (son of Princequillo) out of a daughter of Nasrullah, the pedigree pattern has a triple input of the same powerful nick. Sky Mesa has two more genetic forces working in his favor. He is linebred to Round Table twice, and to Round Table's sister Monarchy, dam of State. (Monarchy belongs to the family of "elite" mare Feola.) Sky Mesa inherits fantastic speed from the similarly bred genetic cousins Nijinsky II and Storm Bird.

There are reasons why I predict Sky Mesa should make a very successful commercial sire at Three Chimneys Farm. He was undefeated at two years, winning a Saratoga 2YO Maiden Special, the Hopeful Stakes and Lane's End Breeders' Futurity. He was the logical colt to beat in the Breeders' Cup Juvenile Stakes, but on the morning of the race was found to be lame and was withdrawn. Sky Mesa has strong hindquarters and traces in direct female line to Busanda, dam of Buckpasser.

He most likely inherits valuable influence from the duplication of Busanda and her three-quarter sisters Striking and Busher, and young sires with maternal strength usually succeed at stud. When his first crop hits the racetrack it will be exciting!

Duplicating outstanding mares is a technique always worth considering because it enables a breeder to manipulate the genes of a foal and develop prepotency. The mitochondria of cells supply all the body's energy. Mitochondrial DNA (MtDNA) is passed on to mares and fillies solely via direct female descent.

It is impossible for mitochondrial DNA to be transmitted by any male. Instead, influential stallions upgrade female lines using the normal blueprint process from nuclear DNA located in the nucleus of cells. Valuable genes are located on X sex chromosomes and these genes, called "sex-linked" genes, have a huge bearing on heart size and maybe even the thickness of the heart's walls.

Over a long period of time I was able to notice how desirable genes zigzag from generation to generation via the X sex chromosome passed on by a stallion to his daughters, thence to her sons, thence to their daughters etc. Fillies sired by a stallion whose dam was an outstanding performer have a much better chance to inherit upgraded racing class than fillies by a stallion whose dam showed below average performance. Naturally exceptions will occur; however, there are certain female lines that habitually produce colts who succeed at stud, irrespective of race records, and one of the best examples is the family of Rough Shod II (Gold Bridge-Dalmary by Blandford-Simon's Shoes by Simon Square-Goody Two Shoes by Isinglass).

Rough Shod II, a winner in England, was born in 1944. Arthur "Bull" Hancock of Claiborne Farm fame purchased the filly because of her close relationship with Carpet Slipper, dam of Irish Triple Crown winner Windsor Slipper and English 1,000 Guineas and Oaks winner Godiva.

"Bull" Hancock always sought mares from the best stakes-winning families of Europe and encouraged many of his clients to buy into fashionable female lines. Hancock and his clients bred many Graded stakes winners from imported mares.

Goody Two Shoes' branch of the Number 5 Family, to which Rough Shod II belongs, was "on a roll."

Carpet Slipper's granddaughter Vali produced Val de Loir (French Derby) and Valoris (English Oaks, Irish 1,000 Guineas). Carpet Slipper's daughter Silken Princess produced Silken Glider (Irish Oaks) and another of her daughters, Coventry Belle, would become the third dam of Reform (by Pall Mall). Rough Shod II was by English champion sprinter Gold Bridge from Dalmary, a mare bred on similar lines to Blenheim. European breeders such as Maria Niarchos, John Magnier and Robert Sangster must have noticed the genetic connection between Dalmary and Blenheim because they were fans of Rough Shod's family.

		Swynford
	Blandford	Blanche
Blenheim		
		Charles O'Malley (Desmond - Goody Two Shoes)
	Malva	Wild Arum

Note: Charles O'Malley is by Desmond, by St. Simon.

compare with...

		Swynford
	Blandford	Blanche
Dalmary		
		Simon Square by St. Simon
	Simon's Shoes	Goody Two Shoes

Rough Shod II is the ancestress of Nureyev (champion miler), Fairy King and Europe's leading sire Sadler's Wells. Here is her family tree:

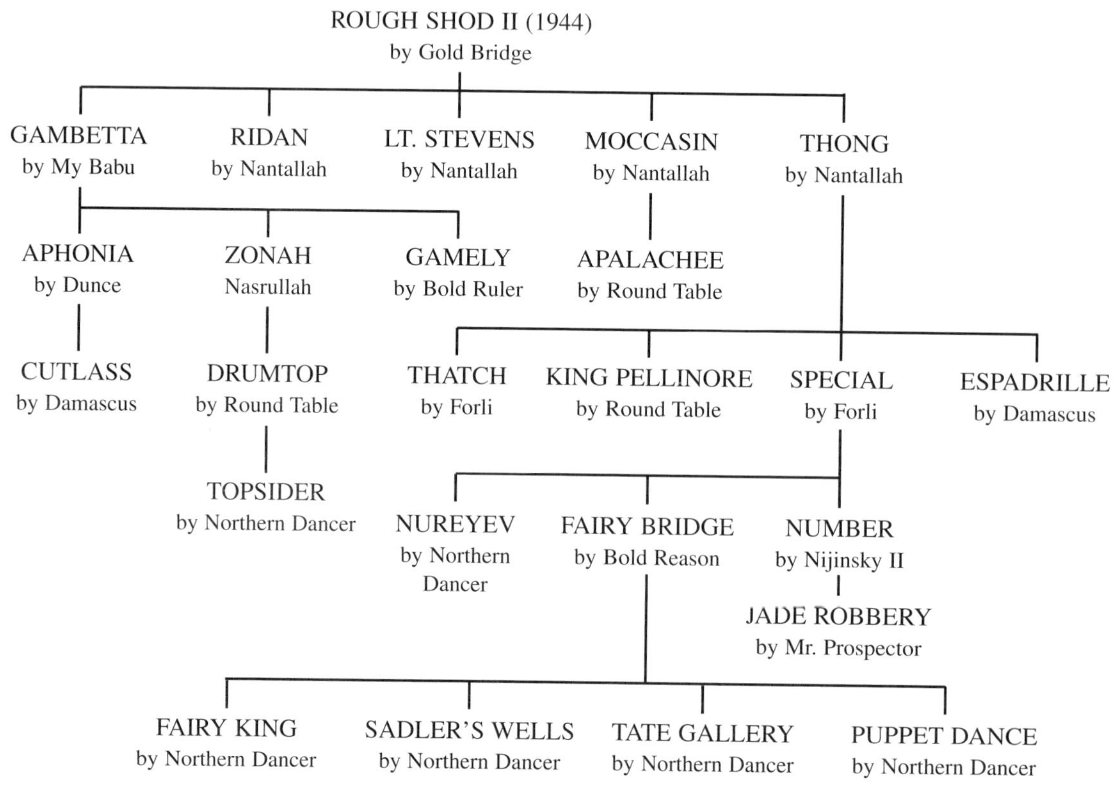

Another successful branch of Goody Two Shoes' strong family is Rough Shod's half-sister Jennydang, a mare by English 2,000 Guineas winner Colombo. Jennydang produced Erica Fragrans, by English 2,000 Guineas winner Big Game.

- JENNYDANG (1938) by Colombo
  - ERICA FRAGRANS by Big Game
    - DARRICA by Darius
      - ABELLA by Abernant
        - THATCHING by Thatch
        - GOLDEN THATCH by Thatch
    - TUDOR ERA by Owen Tudor
    - PHOENISSA by The Phoenix
      - LORENZACCIO by Klairon
      - GALLISSA by El Gallo
        - PERLA by Young Emperor
          - SOVEREIGN PEARL by Nonoalco

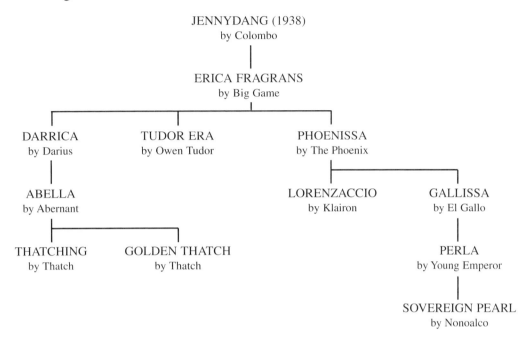

Matings whereby Lorenzaccio's strain unites with Nureyev, Fairy King or Sadler's Wells might produce stakes runners because of similar genes inherited from the half-sisters Rough Shod II and Jennydang.

Inbreeding to the mare Special (Forli-Thong) is something I believe will produce outstanding runners, although probability has to be generous for a breeder to achieve maximum results. Already for clients I have designed matings with inbreeding to Thong's daughter Special, preferring to design matings combining Nureyev with Sadler's Wells. This particular cross offers a pedigree pattern involving a "son" and a "daughter" of the mare Special. Here is an example:

			Nearctic
		Northern Dancer	Natalma
	Sadler's Wells		Bold Reason
		Fairy Bridge	**Special**
Barathea			Sir Gaylord
		Habitat	Little Hut
	Brocade		Runnymede
		Canton Silk	Clouded Lamp
			Nearctic
		Northern Dancer	Natalma
	Nureyev		Forli
with daughters of		**Special**	Thong
	xxxxx		

Even though champion Northern Dancer is duplicated 3 x 3 fairly close up (he being a small horse with short forearms and gaskins), I believe the genetic influence of Special (4 x 3 via both sexes) will provide enough size and substance to lengthen forearms and gaskins. I selected Barathea as the above example, but other good sons of Sadler's Wells should work with daughters or granddaughters of Nureyev.

There are many other ways to design matings whereby the dominant mare Special can be duplicated, for example, using a son of Nureyev with mares that possess Sadler's Wells in their make-up.

Daughters of Indian Ridge (Ahonoora-Hillbrow) might have a genetic affinity with sons of Sadler's Wells and Fairy King. The reason? Indian Ridge is a grandson of Lorenzaccio who descends from Jennydang, half-sister to Rough Shod II.

Indian Ridge is a particularly interesting stallion to me because he is free of Northern Dancer, descends in male line from champion Tourbillon, and is himself inbred 4 x 4 to Discipliner, a daughter of champion Court Martial. Indian Ridge has a "son" of English sprinter Gold Bridge in his pedigree pattern, as well as a "daughter" of Polynesian. (Note: Sadler's Wells and Fairy King have Rough Shod II, a daughter of Gold Bridge, in their make-up.)

Indian Ridge (1985)	Ahonoora	Lorenzaccio	Klairon	Clarion III by Djebel by Tourbillon
				Kalmia by Kantar
			Phoenissa	The Phoenix
				Erica Fragrans (ex Jennydang)
		Helen Nicholls	Martial	Hill Gail by Bull Lea
				Discipliner by Court Martial - **Fair Trial**
			Quaker Girl	Whistler, dam by **Fair Trial**
				Mayflower
	Hillbrow	Swing Easy	Delta Judge	Traffic Judge by Alibhai
				Beautillion by Noor - **Nasrullah**
			Free Flowing	Polynesian
				Rytina
		Golden City	Skymaster	Golden Cloud, by Gold Bridge
				Discipliner by Court Martial - **Fair Trial**
			West Shaw	Grey Sovereign by **Nasrullah**
				Irish Candy by son of **Fair Trial**

Fair Trial is duplicated four times in the above pedigree. Apart from the double via his son Court Martial, Fair Trial is represented as the sire of Farthing Damages (dam of Whistler) and that fast horse Ballyogan, sire of Irish Candy. There is clever concentration of Sainfoin and his sister Sierra in Indian Ridge's genotype, especially via the speed strains of Polynesian and Nasrullah (sire of Noor and Grey Sovereign).

Incidentally, daughters of Indian Ridge should be compatible with stallions from the line of Polynesian and his champion son Native Dancer. Why? Because Polynesian is the ancestor who sits on Indian Ridge's "alternate sex line" and any valuable sex-linked genes inherited by Polynesian should be reinforced to boost speed. Northern Dancer is out of a daughter of Native Dancer (by Polynesian) and his strain suits Indian Ridge; and alternative stallions with Native Dancer's strain can be tested, especially Raise a Native and his best son Mr. Prospector.

There are many examples of superior runners that are inbred to stallions or inbred to famous mares. One of the most interesting is Bolero who appears in the pedigree of Storm Cat and Royal Academy.

When I managed bookings for Storm Cat during his initial years at Overbrook Stud, I needed to guess what compatible strains might work successfully with his genotype. When I noticed Bolero as the sire of Bolero Rose (Storm Cat's third dam) I didn't know enough about this ancestor, so I looked him up and discovered he is a major contributor of quick-maturing speed and established two world records. Born in 1946, Bolero was a chestnut horse with a remarkable pedigree pattern. A sound racehorse, winning each year from two to five, he was the product of inbreeding to Sainfoin's champion son Rock Sand and unbeaten champion The Tetrarch. In addition, he gained speed from the duplication of Domino and family members.

Bolero won 16 of 39 starts and set a new world record of 1:08 ½ for six furlongs. His victories include the Del Mar Derby, San Jose, Pacific, Preview and Kentfield Handicaps, and when he won the San Carlos Handicap he set a new world record time of 1:21 flat for seven furlongs and defeated another crack sprinter, Your Host.

				Rock Sand by **Sainfoin**
			Friar Rock	**Fairy Gold** (**Bend Or/Macaroni**)
		Pilate		**The Tetrarch** (dam by **Bona Vista**)
			Herodias	Honora by Gallinule
	Eight Thirty			Ultimus by Commando by **Domino**
			High Time	Noonday by **Domino**
		Dinner Time		Man o' War (dam by **Rock Sand**)
			Seaplane	Bathing Girl by Spearmint
Bolero				Blackstock by **Hanover**
(1946)			Mentor	Meta
		Wise Counsellor		Russell
			Rustle	Lady Louise by Iroquois
	Stepwisely			**The Tetrarch** (dam by **Bona Vista**)
			Stefan The Great	Perfect Peach by Persimmon
		Stephanie		**Rock Sand** by **Sainfoin**
			Malachite	Miss Hanover by **Hanover**

Bolero comes from the same family as Quickly, dam of champion Count Fleet, Horse of the Year and winner of America's Triple Crown. Bolero stood at The Stallion Station in Lexington, Kentucky, and was prominent on the juvenile Sires' List. Among his progeny were Bolero U, Battle Dance, Jimmer, Bolero Rose and Frizette Stakes winner Capelet. Bolero Rose (Bolero-First Rose by champion Menow) was fast. A stakes winner, Bolero Rose won nine races including the Continental Denver Hotel Handicap. She produced four winners. Among them was Crimson Saint, a very attractive chestnut mare by Crimson Satan who carried the strain of champion Tracery, son of Rock Sand. Crimson Saint inherited brilliant speed, earned black type, and won seven races for $91,770 including the Hollywood Express Handicap and Meteor Handicap, twice. Crimson Saint produced stakes winners Alydariel, Pancho Villa and Terlingua.

By champion Secretariat (bred on the Nasrullah/Princequillo nick), Terlingua was trained by Wayne Lukas and was the best juvenile filly of her year on the West Coast. An exceedingly beautiful chestnut mare, she possessed lots of fast fiber muscle.

Terlingua was often temperamental when she had a foal by her side. She earned $423,696 from seven wins two to four years. Her successes include the Hollywood Juvenile Championship Stakes against colts, Hollywood Lassie Stakes, Del Mar Debutante Stakes, Santa Ynez Stakes, Las Flores Handicap, La Brea Stakes. She produced stakes winners Storm Cat and Chapel of Dreams. I remember she resented us whenever we entered her box – pinning both ears down – always protective of her foals. She was also impatient when on heat. I recall the times I took her to visit Alydar at Calumet Farm where we had to wait for her to be covered. Terlingua became very fractious. The Calumet crew didn't realize a "princess" was being kept waiting!

Terlingua and Hopespringseternal were by far the most intelligent mares on Overbrook Farm. Miswaki's dam Hopespringseternal (Buckpasser-Rose Bower by Princequillo-Lea Lane by Nasrullah) was a majestic mare, oozing quality, but restricted because of an injured nearside knee. She was never put into training. Her foals possessed intelligence and refinement.

Hopespringseternal produced Miswaki, Northern Eternity and Hope For All, dam of Prix Saint-Alary winner Lacovia. However, the nicest colt she ever produced died as a young foal. Her spirit will live on because I expect Miswaki to make a great broodmare sire. (Hopespringseternal's dam, Rose Bower, is an "elite" mare.)

Terlingua has a fascinating pedigree. She was the second best stakes-winning daughter of Secretariat in the Stud Book.

Terlingua (1976)	Secretariat	Bold Ruler	Nasrullah	Nearco by Pharos (**Phalaris/Chaucer**)
				Mumtaz Begum ex Mumtaz Mahal
			Miss Disco	Discovery
				Outdone by Pompey by Sun Briar
		Somethingroyal	Princequillo	Prince Rose
				Cosquilla by Papyrus by **Tracery**
			Imperatrice	Caruso by Polymelian
				Cinquepace (dam by **Teddy**)
	Crimson Saint	Crimson Satan	Spy Song	Balladier
				Mata Hari
			Papila	Requiebro, dam by **Tracery**
				Papalona
		Bolero Rose	Bolero	Eight Thirty by Pilate by Friar Rock
				Stepwisely
			First Rose	Menow by Pharamond II (**Phalaris/Ch**)
				Rare Bloom by Sir Galahad III by **Teddy**

Caruso, sire of Secretariat's second dam Imperatrice, is a son of the sprinter Polymelian (Polymelus-Pasquita by Sundridge). Champion racehorse Native Dancer is by Polynesian whose dam is by Polymelian. Whenever Secretariat's strain meets up with Polynesian's strain via Native Dancer, the dominant Sainfoin/Sierra mix is reinforced. Storm Cat is by Storm Bird, champion son of Northern Dancer whose dam Natalma is by Native Dancer. How much Bolero contributed to Storm Cat's success is anyone's guess, but it might have been substantial. Readers should note Terlingua has strong concentrations of Sainfoin, via his best son Rock Sand (Sainfoin-Roquebrune by St. Simon), especially through Rock Sand's sons

Tracery and Friar Rock. All three ancestors mentioned were absolutely high-class. Tracery is inbred to St. Simon and his sister Angelica and heavily linebred to the famous mare Pocahontas.

Phalaris (sire of genetically related stallions Pharos and Pharamond II) is out of a daughter of Sainfoin, and Bolero happens to have a triple cross of Sainfoin's son Rock Sand. In addition, Pompey is a grandson of Sundridge and Nasrullah carries Sundridge whose dam is Sainfoin's sister Sierra.

Great racehorses have powerful mares close up in their ancestry. Perhaps now is the right place to supply an updated list of "elite" mares.

"ELITE MARES" – UPDATED LIST

The taproot mares or foundation mares of each family are listed in my book *Quest For A Classic Winner.* Their descendants play a forceful role in the production of Group and Graded stakes winners and are selected solely on their ability to transmit superior genes to future generations. They are mares most worthy of reinforcement. Who knows, some may even possess special mitochondrial DNA and/or valuable sex-linked genes.

Although the list might be considered small, I can assure you these mares are quite extraordinary, quite superior and from powerful female lines.

No. 1 Family.
Sunrise, Picture Play, Canterbury Pilgrim, Matelda, Courtesy, Gas, Rouge Rose, Tillywhim, Djebellica, Sweet Lavender, Rose Red, Perfume II, Source Sucree, War Path III, La Troienne, Baby League, Intriguing, Big Event, Black Helen, Big Hurry, Businesslike and the new additions, Aspidistra and La Mesa.

No. 2 Family.
Almahmoud, Somethingroyal, Feola, Above Board, Mixed Marriage, Knight's Daughter, Sierra, Meld, Cos, Clemence, Mata Hari, Doubly Sure, Cosmah, and the new additions, Coup de Folie, State and Height of Fashion.

No. 3 Family.
Kasbah, Sanctimony, Blanche, Jean's Folly, Martine III, Gallenza, Glasalt, Poet's Star, Cinna, Uganda and the new additions Traffic Court, Tree of Knowledge and Lassie Dear.

No. 4 Family.
Flower Bowl, Baton Rouge, Marguerite, Nogara, Nella da Gubbio, Nixe, Audience, and the new additions A Wind Is Rising, Ciboulette, Golden Trail and Gay Hostess.

No. 5 Family.
Seraphine, Mother Siegel, Majideh, Masaka, Carpet Slipper, Vali, Dalmary, Rough Shod II, Erica Fragrans, Schwester, Grey Flight, and the new additions Special and Broadway.

No. 6 Family.
Selene, Composure, Myrobella, Emancipation (by Le Sage), Teresina and the new addition Lunadix.

No. 7 Family.
Dinner Partner and Sif. No new addition.

No. 8 Family.
Rare Perfume, Crimson Saint, Vaila, Barley Corn, Stolen Hour, Flaring Top, La Fresnes, Irish Lass II, Alcibiades, Erin, Violet, Belle Rose, Feronia, Pink Domino, Miss Whisk, Boola Brook, and the new additions Dancing Show, Shenanigans and Lady Be Good.

No. 9 Family.
Mumtaz Mahal, Lady Juror, Mah Mahal, Mumtaz Begum, Rivaz, Malindi, Diableretta, Alveole, Aversion, Khairunissa, Nellie Flag, Comely Nell, Escutcheon, Zariba, Likka, Lady Peregrine, Minnewaska, Dusky Evening, Saint Astra, Sunday Evening, Plum Cake, and the new additions Daltawa, Allegretta (Ger) and Eight Carat.

No. 10 Family.
Galicia, Vieille Maison, and the new additions Victoriana and River Lady.

No. 11 Family.
Angelica. No new addition.

No. 12 Family.
Nymphe Dictee, Ballade. No new addition.

No. 13 Family.
Scapa Flow, Durban, Heldifann, Myrtlewood, Valkyr, Albarelle, Tourzima, Albanilla, Licata, Delsy, My Charmer, and the new addition Natashka.

No. 14 Family.
Jocose, Satirical, Banish Fear, Deasy, Molly Desmond, Molly Adare, Sister Sarah, Delleana, Square Angel, Eastern Grandeur, Flute Enchantee, and the new additions Balidaress, Brocade, Kamar, and Jesmond Lass (Aust).

No. 15 Family – Nil.

No. 16 Family.
Plucky Liege, Friar's Daughter, Festa, Avella, Relance III, Cequillo, Derna, Lea Lark, Rose Bower and the new addition Ampola.

No. 17 Family.
La Flambee. No new addition.

No. 18 Family – Nil.

No. 19 Family.
Bloodroot, Topiary, and the new additions Lalun, Grecian Banner and Gay Violin.

No. 20 Family.
Djenne, and the new additions Bee Mac and Miesque.

No. 21 Family.
Phase, Iltis and the new addition Dumka.

No. 22 Family.
Éclair, Infra Red, Aimee, Centro, Praise, Pennon, Homage and the new addition of Royal Statute.

No. 23 Family.
Mannie Gray, Mannie Himyar, Miss Carmie and the new additions Northern Meteor and Classy Quillo.

No. 24 Family – Nil.

No. 25 Family.
Tananarive. No new addition.

No. 26 Family.
Oola Hills, and the new addition of Flying Melody.

OTHER FAMILIES:
American Family No. 1 – Friar's Carse. No new addition.
The Medley Mare – Uncle's Lassie, Judy-Rae, Iron Maiden, and the new addition of Courtly Dee.
Janus Mare – Novice, and the new addition of Silver Fog.

Darshaan, champion 3YO in Europe in 1984, became an influential sire. He won the Prix du Jockey Club (French Derby) defeating Sadler's Wells and Rainbow Quest, the Prix Greffulhe, Prix Hocquart, Criterium de Saint-Cloud and was bred by His Highness Karim, the Aga Khan. Darshaan is different to Delsy's other foals and resembles Arbar and Djebel (from Tourbillon's line). Darshaan's dam, Delsy, is inbred 3 x 4 to the prized mare Astronomie, dam of Group winners Arbar and Marsyas II.

Delsy (1972)	Abdos	Arbar	Djebel	**Tourbillon** by Ksar
				Loika by Gay Crusader
			Astronomie	Asterus by **Teddy**
				Likka
		Pretty Lady	Umidwar	Blandford
				Uganda
			La Moqueuse	**Teddy**
				Primrose Lane
	Kelty	Venture VII	Relic	War Relic
				Bridal Colors
			Rose O'Lynn	Pherozshah, ex Mah Mahal
				Rocklyn
		Manilla	Marsyas II	Trimdon
				Astronomie
			Albanilla	Pharis II by Pharos
				Tourzima by **Tourbillon**

Marcel Boussac adored the stamina transmitted by Astronomie. Boussac knew many of his best home-bred performers, be they stakes winners or classic winners, were products of combining Tourbillon's strain with Teddy and Pharos. Delsy traces to the famous mare Tourzima, she being 2 x 2 to the sisters Durban and Heldifann:

Tourzima	Tourbillon	Ksar	Bruleur	Chouberski
				Basse Terre by Omnium II
			Kizil Kourgan	Omnium II
				Kasbah
		Durban	**Durbar II**	Rabelais by St. Simon
				Armenia
			Banshee	Irish Lad
				Frizette
	Djezima	Asterus	Teddy	Ajax
				Rondeau by Bay Ronald
			Astrella	Verdun
				St. Astra
		Heldifann	**Durbar II**	Rabelais by St. Simon
				Armenia
			Banshee	Irish Lad II
				Frizette

No. 13 Family

The Aga Khan's champion DARSHAAN (Shirley Heights - Delsy), winner of the French Derby and sire of Dalakhani. He traces to the elite mare Tourzima.

DALAKHANI (Darshaan - Daltawa by Miswaki) winning the Prix Lupin Gr-1. Champion 3YO in France. He won 7 of 8 starts including the French Derby, Prix de l'Arc de Triomphe and is half-brother to champion Daylami.

"Courage is not simply one of the virtues, but the form of every virtue of the testing point" - C. S. Lewis

Members of Tourzima's family inherited courage and breeders should contemplate reinforcing this female line, especially with the availability now of using champion Dalakhani (Darshaan-Daltawa by Miswaki) who stands at Gilltown Stud in Ireland. I recently inspected Dalakhani and was impressed by his deep girth, correct forelegs and clean hocks. Dalakhani won the Criterium International, Prix des Chenes, and Prix du Pre d'Auge as a two-year-old, showing considerable promise. At three, he impressed by winning the Prix Lupin, Prix du Jockey Club (French Derby), Prix Greffulhe, Prix Niel, Prix de l'Arc de Triomphe and was runner-up in the Irish Derby, defeated narrowly by his stable mate.

Dalakhani is half-brother to champion Daylami but has more height and scope. He is an ideal replacement for his father, Darshaan, a member of Mill Reef's male line of Never Bend.

Dalakhani	Darshaan	Shirley Heights	Mill Reef	Never Bend by **Nasrullah**
				Milan Mill by **Princequillo**
			Hardiemma	Hardicanute
				Grand Cross
		Delsy	Abdos	Arbar by Djebel
				Pretty Lady
			Kelty	Venture VII by **Relic**
				Marilla
	Daltawa	Miswaki	Mr. Prospector	Raise a Native by Native Dancer
				Gold Digger by Nashua by **Nasrullah**
			Hopespringseternal	Buckpasser
				Rose Bower (**Princequillo/Nasrullah**)
		Damana	Crystal Palace	Caro by Fortino II (dam by **Relic**)
				Hermieres by Sicambre
			Denia	Crepello by Donatello II by **Blenheim**
				Rose Ness by Charlottesville

At first glance, the pedigree of Dalakhani (at least in the first four removes) appears to be an outcross mating, but in fact it is a pattern where many superior ancestors are reinforced. Consider the following:

> Mill Reef (by a son of Nasrullah from a daughter of Princequillo) is bred on the same cross as Rose Bower (by Princequillo-Lea Lane by Nasrullah) with both sexes represented by Nasrullah. Nashua, the brood-mare sire of Mr. Prospector, is also by Nasrullah; and French champion Caro (sire of Crystal Palace) is by Fortino II, a grandson of Nasrullah.
>
> It is no coincidence that Fortino II has a female ancestor called Nervesa, a "daughter" of Nogara (the dam of Nearco who sired Nasrullah). Charlottesville (winner of the Prix du Jockey Club (French

Derby), Grand Prix de Paris and Prix Lupin etc.) is bred on a similar nick to Mill Reef and Rose Bower – the original Prince Rose/Nearco nick.

Charlottesville is by Prince Chevalier (Prince Rose-Chevalerie) from Noorani (Nearco-Empire Glory) and acts like a genetic cousin to Mill Reef and Rose Bower. Crystal Palace has a pedigree pattern with two ancestors in common, viz. Nasrullah and Prince Rose.

Relic is duplicated, making use of Man o' War whose dam is by Rock Sand.

We know Dalakhani's dam, Daltawa, produced Daylami when she was matched with Doyoun (Mill Reef-Dumka by Kashmir II), so it would seem the family likes the Nasrullah/Princequillo nick. Perhaps even Sir Gaylord's line will succeed with Dalakhani, seeing Sir Gaylord is a product of the Royal Charger/Princequillo mix?

Obviously mares with Northern Dancer's strain will be bred to Dalakhani and this cross gives a chance to produce classic runners. I am hoping some breeders will even think to send daughters of Indian Ridge to Dalakhani since he is a member of Tourbillon's male line and has Fair Trial reinforced in his make-up. Fair Trial acts like a genetic cousin to Nasrullah, and Doyoun's broodmare sire Kashmir II is linebred to Lady Juror, so this cross has considerable merit.

All this objectivity is fine if a foal inherits the best genes, but one has to be pragmatic. Breeding the racehorse is an inexact science. Probability factors cause many variations, winners and losers, and luck is required for successful results.

His Highness the old Aga Khan used the bay stallion Prince Bio on many occasions, despite the fact the stallion was never considered fashionable. Bred by Alec Head's father, W. Head, and foaled in 1941, Prince Bio won six of 11 starts after the war including victories in the French 2,000 Guineas, Prix de Fontainbleau and Prix Daru. He was not handsome by any means and did not have the scope of his own sire, Belgium's champion stayer Prince Rose. Instead, Prince Bio had a plain head and was short-coupled. Prince Aly Khan and Madame Vuillier were keen supporters of the stallion. Why? Was it because Prince Bio had the right Vuillier "dosage" figures to suit specific broodmares based in France? Not until he became a proven sire was he appreciated and patronized by other French breeders.

Prince Bio is the father of Sicambre (champion racehorse, leading sire in France, winner of the Prix du Jockey Club-French Derby, Grand Prix de Paris, Prix Hocquart, Prix Greffulhe, Grand Criterium), Northern Light (Grand Prix de Paris), Le Loup Garou (Prix du Cadran, Criterium de Saint-Cloud), Sedan (Italian Derby, Gran Premio di Milano), Pres de Feu (French 1,000 Guineas), Rose Royale (English 1,000 Guineas, Champion Stakes, Prix du Moulin de Longchamp), Lovely Princess (Prix de Malleret), Alibela (Italian Oaks, Italian 1,000 Guineas), Princillon (Prix de la Salamandre) and Le Petit Prince (Prix du Jockey Club-French Derby).

What was in Prince Bio's pedigree that gave Madame Vuillier (who helped design the Aga Khan's mare matings) such confidence to use the stallion so often? There were many attractive stallions available in France during the period 1959 to 1965 that could be used.

Intuitively, I came up with three plausible reasons. First and foremost, Prince Bio is out of a daughter of the sprinter Bacteriophage (Tetratema-Pharmacie by Charles O'Malley), a horse bred for early maturing speed. Charles O'Malley was full of electricity and was the broodmare sire of the Aga Khan's English Derby winner Blenheim.

Second, Tetratema was a fast son of The Tetrarch, another brilliant horse but one who also possessed stamina. The Tetrarch was an unbeaten son of Roi Herode.

Third, Prince Rose descends from St. Simon's male line via Derby winner Persimmon. A tough stayer, Prince Rose is out of a daughter of English Triple Crown winner Gay Crusader who is inbred 3 x 3 to Galopin via two daughters, and has another son of St. Simon represented in the pedigree, namely St. Frusquin.

Thus, Prince Bio was loaded with Galopin and this might explain his value – he could improve the "dosage" figures for mares lacking in Galopin's influence (and for that matter, his son St. Simon). Prince Bio had the right "quantity" of Galopin to help adjust the standard deviation figures of the Vuillier system used by the old Aga Khan. For what it's worth, I honestly believe Charles O'Malley (by St. Simon's son Desmond) was the real dominant force in Prince Bio's genotype.

Prince Bio (1941)	Prince Rose	Rose Prince	Prince Palatine by Persimmon by **St. Simon**
			Eglantine by Perth
		Indolence	Gay Crusader (inbred 3x3 to **Galopin**)
			Barrier by Grey Leg
	Biologie	Bacteriophage	Tetratema by The Tetrarch
			Pharmacie by Charles O'Malley (to **St. Simon**)
		Eponge	Cadum by Sans Souci II
			Sea Moss by William The Third by **St. Simon**

Prince Bio is found in the pedigrees of only a few great performers but what super athletes they were – champion Sea-Bird II (English Derby, Prix de l'Arc de Triomphe), La Lagune (English Oaks, Prix Vanteaux), Kalamoun (French 2,000 Guineas, Prix Lupin, Prix Jacques le Marois), Shantung (Prix la Rochette, 2nd Grand Prix de Saint-Cloud, unlucky 3rd English Derby behind Parthia), Bikala (Prix du Jockey Club-French Derby), Kenmare (Prix Jacques le Marois), Doyoun (English 2,000 Guineas) and Daylami (French 2,000 Guineas, Coral Eclipse Stakes, King George VI & Queen Elizabeth Stakes, Breeders' Cup Turf).

Included in the new list of elite mares is Lunadix (Breton-Lutine by Alcide-Mona by Abernant), tracing to that smart filly Myrobella by Tetratema. Lunadix is the dam of Linamix (by Mendez), four wins from 10 starts in France, French 2,000 Guineas, Prix de Fontainebleau, Prix La Rochette, second in the Dubai Champion Stakes, Prix du Moulin de Longchamp (to Distant Relative) and Prix Jacques le Marois (to Priolo).

Lunadix also produced Long Mick (by Gay Mecene), Champion 2YO colt in France; Luna Wells (by Sadler's Wells), five wins in France including the Prix Saint-Alary, Prix Vanteaux, Prix de la Nonette; and Luna Blue, winning dam of Lorymaya (Prix de Psyche), Luazar (Del Mar Invitational Handicap) and Lunafairy (Prix de Sandringham). Linamix is one of the most successful sires currently standing in France.

Another important elite mare is German-bred Allegretta (Lombard-Anatevka by Espresso), dam of King's Best (English 2,000 Guineas), Urban Sea (Champion mare of Europe, Prix de l'Arc de Triomphe, Prix d'Harcourt, Prix Exbury), Allez Les Trois (Prix de Flore), Turbaine (Prix Rose de Mai) and Anzille (dam of Anzillero). King's Best (by Kingmambo) made a fine impression with his first crop of two-year-olds to race in 2004 and most of his progeny are rather attractive individuals.

Urban Sea has already produced Galileo by Sadler's Wells (Champion 3YO colt of Europe, six wins including the English Derby, Irish Derby, King George VI & Queen Elizabeth Diamond Stakes), Melikah by Lammtarra (Newmarket Pretty Polly Stakes, 2nd Irish Oaks, 3rd English Oaks), Black Sam Bellamy by Sadler's Wells (Gran Premio del Jockey Club, Tattersalls Gold Cup), and All Too Beautiful by Sadler's Wells (Salsabil Stakes, 2nd English Oaks, 3rd Blandford Stakes).

Allez Les Trois (by Riverman) is the dam of Anabaa Blue, winner of the Prix du Jockey Club (French Derby), Prix Noailles, Grand Prix de Chantilly, 2nd Prix Lupin etc., while Turbaine (by Trempolino) is the dam of Tertulian, Champion Older Sprinter in Germany, 12 wins including the Grosser Preis von Berlin, and in Italy, the Premio Chiusura.

For decades I have been studying the progress of Germany's famous "A" family tracing to the elite mare Alveole. I started to take notice when the family tree looked like this:

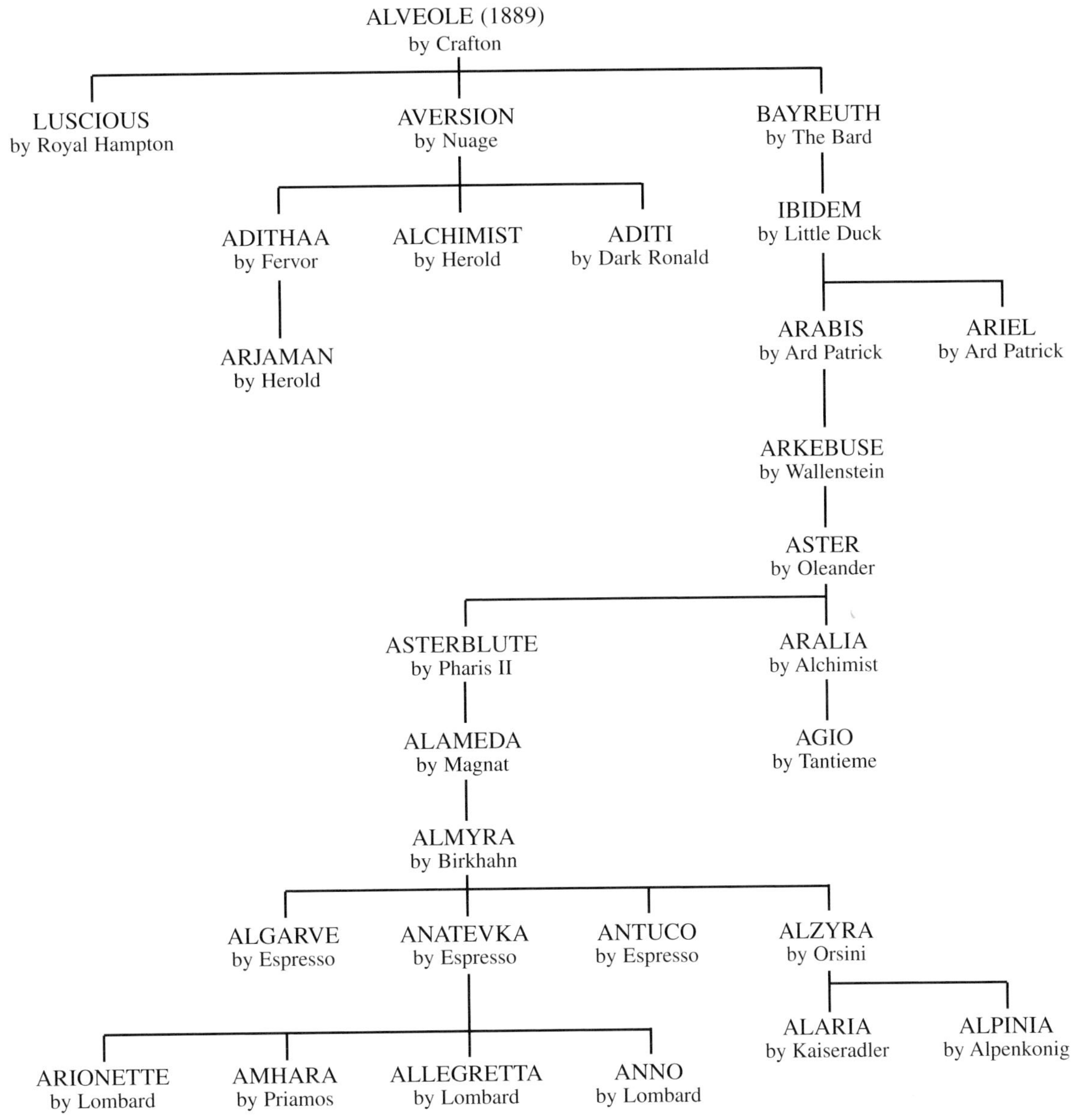

Allegretta is a sister to German Champion 3YO colt Anno. This is the female line of Germany's influential sires Aditi, Alchimist and Arjaman.

In the mid-1960's at Perringa Stud in Western Australia, I was stallion groom and mucked out the boxes of Martello Towers (Australia's champion 3YO) and Endless Honey (Never Say Die-Run Honey by Hyperion).

Endless Honey descends from Alveole via a branch of Honey Buzzard. I had especially asked Dot Parry to try and buy Endless Honey for stud duties. Eventually Dot and her son Bryan arranged the purchase through Sir Philip Payne-Gallwey, representative of the British Bloodstock Agency. Endless Honey did not disappoint us. He became the leading sire in Western Australia and over time I followed the development of Alveole's family and was always impressed by the stallion Birkhahn, a very correct, masculine horse who upgraded his mares in Germany. Unfortunately, Birkhahn was born in 1945, almost at the termination of World War II when English and French breeders were downcast on anything of German origin. Twenty-five years later, I studied the pedigree of Selkirk (1988), a robust chestnut horse by Sharpen Up from Annie Edge by Nebbiolo whose dam is by Birkhahn (a sound racehorse who can be duplicated in any matings with confidence).

Birkhahn (1945)	Alchimist	Herold	Dark Ronald	Bay Ronald
				Darkie
			Hornisse	**Ard Patrick**
				Hortensia
		Aversion	Nuage	Simonian
				Nephte
			Antwort	**Ard Patrick**
				Alveole
	Bramouse	Cappiello	Apelle	Sardanapale
				Angelina
			Kopje	Spion Kop by Spearmint
				Dutch Mary
		Peregrine (Fr)	Phalaris	Polymelus
				Bromus by **Sainfoin**
			Clotho	Sunstar by Sundridge (**Sierra**)
				Jenny Melton

Bramouse was an exceptionally well-bred mare. Her sire, Cappiello, has two fabulous grandsires, French champion Sardanapale and English Derby winner Spion Kop, son of English Derby winner Spearmint. Federico Tesio trained Apelle who developed into a high-class stayer. Bramouse's dam, Peregrine, was inbred to brother and sister Sainfoin and Sierra, dam of Sundridge. Peregrine is by a son of Polymelus who carries genetic influence from dominant mare Brown Bess, as does Carbine, the father of Spearmint. Phalaris is, of course, out of Bromus by Sainfoin. Alchimist, the sire of Birkhahn, was champion 3YO colt of Germany and one of the best German Derby winners on record.

Alchimist won the Grosser Preis von Baden-Baden, Grosser Preis von Berlin, Grosser Preis von Koln and was the leading sire in Germany. Unfortunately, when the Russians swept into Germany at the end of the war, Alchimist was slaughtered for food. He was a masculine horse and son of the elite mare Aversion.

Alveole's family is now internationally famous. Almyra (Birkhahn-Alameda by Magnat) is the granddam of Allegretta, dam of King's Best and Urban Sea. To begin to understand how the family progressed we need to study Almyra's pedigree. It reveals duplication of Bay Ronald and his son Dark Ronald, duplication of Sunstar (by Sundridge) and duplication of Phalaris (dam by Sainfoin) via a son and a daughter. I should add Almyra's dam is inbred 3 x 4 to Wallenstein, son of Dark Ronald.

When Almyra was matched with Espresso it produced Anatevka and since Espresso is inbred 4 x 3 to Blandford via two sons (Blenheim and Bahram) there was a concentration of the elite mare Black Duchess. Furthermore, Almyra's pedigree shows a daughter of Swynford (sire of Blandford) to help balance the pattern.

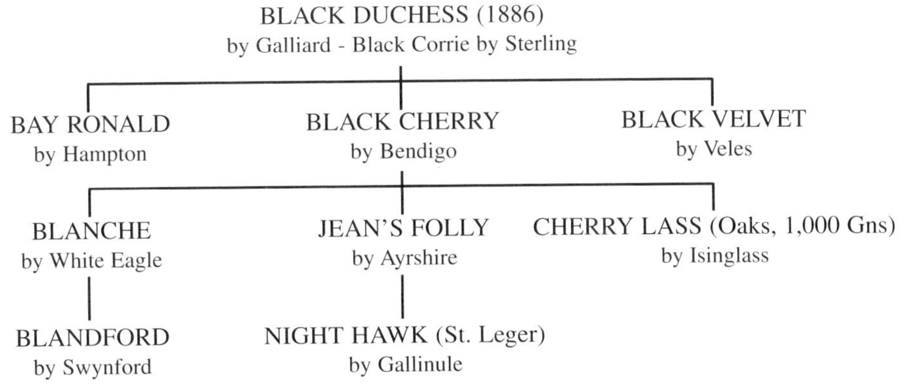

French champion Teddy (Ajax-Rondeau by Bay Ronald) adds more impact from Bay Ronald to further intensify Black Duchess. Teddy is the sire of Asterus whose son Magnat sired Alameda. When Anatevka (Espresso-Almyra by Birkhahn) was mated with German-bred stallion Lombard, it not only duplicated Aster and Alchimist, but also Bahram (son of Blandford) and Bay Ronald, thus continually building on the genetic influence of the elite mare Black Duchess.

Hyperion (who is duplicated in the pedigree of Allegretta below) also comes from Bay Ronald's sire line.

Allegretta (1978)	Lombard	Agio	Tantieme	Deux Pour Cent (to **Teddy**) Terka
			Aralia	**Alchimist** **Aster**
		Promised Lady	Prince Chevalier	Prince Rose Chevalerie
			Belle Sauvage	Big Game by **Bahram** Tropical Sun by **Hyperion**
	Anatevka	Espresso	Acropolis	Donatello II by Blenheim Aurora by **Hyperion**
			Babylon	**Bahram** by **Blandford** Clairvoyante
		Almyra	Birkhahn	**Alchimist** Bramouse
			Alameda	Magnat by Asterus by **Teddy** Asterblute ex **Aster**

Allegretta, a new addition to the "elite" mares list, is likely to become a significant force. Notice her pedigree has sons and daughters of Aster and Alchimist (balanced breeding). Perhaps daughters of Selkirk might suit King's Best or Galileo, thereby doubling up on Birkhahn?

Another new "elite" mare is A Wind Is Rising (Francis S.-Queen Nasra by Nasrullah) whose descendants include Balanchine (Champion 3YO in Europe, Irish Derby, English Oaks, 2nd English 1,000 Guineas), Romanov (Sagitta Jockey Club Stakes), Musical Chimes (French 1,000 Guineas, Oak Tree Breeders' Cup Mile, John C. Mabee Handicap) and Storming Home (Champion Stakes, Charles Whittingham Handicap, King Edward VII Stakes and one of the best turf performers seen in North America during 2003). A Wind Is Rising produced It's In The Air (by Mr. Prospector), a Champion 2YO filly who was game and genuine. It's in the Air won 16 races two to five years and earned $892,339. She captured the Vanity Handicap (twice), Ruffian Handicap, Alabama Stakes, Oak Leaf Stakes, Delaware Oaks, Arlington-Washington Lassie Stakes, Mademoiselle Stakes, El Encino Stakes and was runner-up in the Frizette Stakes, Hollywood Oaks etc. Here is her pedigree:

				Polynesian (inbred to **Sundridge** & **Sierra**)
			Native Dancer	Geisha
		Raise A Native		Case Ace by **Teddy**
			Raise You	Lady Glory
	Mr. Prospector			**Nasrullah** ex **Mumtaz Begum**
			Nashua	Segula
		Gold Digger		Count Fleet (to **Sundridge**)
			Sequence	Miss Dogwood by Bull Dog by **Teddy**
It's In The Air (1969)				**Nearco**
			Royal Charger	Sun Princess ex **Mumtaz Begum**
		Francis S.		War Admiral by Man o' War
			Blue Eyed Momo	Big Event ex La Troienne by **Teddy**
	A Wind Is Rising			**Nearco**
			Nasrullah	**Mumtaz Begum**
		Queen Nasra		Stimulus
			Bayborough	Scarborough

It's In The Air is linebred to Mumtaz Begum (Blenheim-Mumtaz Mahal) via a son (Nasrullah) and a daughter (Sun Princess). Nasrullah is duplicated twice, but of significance, his influence comes via a son and a daughter. There are many ways a breeder is able to duplicate an ancestor because different patterns may be designed. If there is concentration of a male ancestor only via his sons, it is a limiting factor and will automatically exclude any valuable sex-linked genes located on the X sex chromosome. Male ancestors can ***only*** transmit their Y sex chromosome to sons. However, by reinforcing a male ancestor via both sexes (son and daughter) it provides an opportunity for valuable sex-linked genes to be inherited in a foal because a male ancestor's X sex chromosome is ***always*** given to his daughters. This is why I preach the concept of duplicating male ancestors via sons and daughters so as to deploy similar genes on ***both*** sides of chromosomal pairings.

In the pedigree of It's In The Air, Royal Charger is a three-parts brother to Nasrullah. The quarter difference in their pedigrees is Royal Charger's dam Sun Princess who is by Solario (Gainsborough-Sun Worship by Sundridge). Thus, Royal Charger has duplication of champion sprinter Sundridge whereas Nasrullah has a single source of Sundridge. Mumtaz Begum's dam Mumtaz Mahal is out of Lady Josephine, by Sundridge. Owned by H. H. Sheikh Maktoum bin Rashid al-Maktoum, It's In The Air produced 12 foals, nine winners.

They include three stakes winners and the stakes-placed filly Sous Entendu (dam of stakes winners Slip Stream and Banafsajee). Her stakes winners are Bitooh (filly by Seattle Slew), four wins Criterium de Maisons-Laffitte, Prix Amandine, Prix du Pin – Air Dancer (filly by Northern Dancer), four wins \$123,649, Honeymoon Handicap – and Monaassabaat (filly by Zilzal), three wins Tattersalls Virginia Stakes, 2nd John Musket Stakes, Oak Tree Stakes and dam of Echo River, winner of the Milcar Star Stakes and runner-up in the May Hill Stakes. When Michael Goodbody (general manager of Gainsborough Stud) hired me in 1997 to help design matings, I recommended Try To Catch Me (Shareef Dancer-It's In The Air) visit Machiavellian.

At the time, Try To Catch Me had produced two minor winners and was considered a disappointing producer. We used Machiavellian and Try To Catch Me produced a strong colt named Storming Home. Here is the pedigree showing how Mahmoud was linked with his three-quarters sister Mumtaz Begum (dam of Nasrullah, also granddam of Royal Charger), how Mr. Prospector was duplicated via a son and a daughter, how Turn-To was reinforced using his best sons Hail To Reason and Sir Ivor, and why Natalma was duplicated even though the intention was to gain a triple of her dam, Almahmoud. Native Dancer appears four times via a son and a daughter.

				Native Dancer by Polynesian
			Raise A Native	Raise You
		Mr. Prospector		Nashua by **Nasrullah**
			Gold Digger	Sequence by Count Fleet
	Machiavellian			Hail To Reason by **Turn-To** (**R. Charger**)
			Halo	Cosmah ex **Almahmoud** by **Mahmoud**
		Coup de Folie		Hoist the Flag
			Raise the Standard	**Natalma** ex **Almahmoud** by **Mahmoud**
Storming Home				Nearctic
			Northern Dancer	**Natalma** ex **Almahmoud** by **Mahmoud**
		Shareef Dancer		Sir Ivor by **Turn-To** by **Royal Charger**
			Sweet Alliance	Mrs. Peterkin by Tom Fool
	Try To Catch Me			Raise A Native
			Mr. Prospector	Gold Digger by Nashua by **Nasrullah**
		It's In The Air		Francis S. by **Royal Charger**
			A Wind Is Rising	Queen Nasra by **Nasrullah**

Storming Home might be prepotent. He raced in England and North America and earned £594,842 winning the Champion Stakes, two Grade 1 events in California and was first past the post in the Arlington Million only to be disqualified for bearing out at the wire. Storming Home now stands at Shadwell Stud, Norfolk, U.K.

Another daughter of It's In The Air named Note Musicale retired as a three-year-old in 1998. She never ran. Michael Goodbody and I decided she should be retained because she is a daughter of Sadler's Wells and a nice type. We sent her to California to In Excess to test a special pedigree pattern and a filly foal resulted named Musical Chimes who won the French 1,000 Guineas. Later, when trained by Neil Drysdale, Musical Chimes won the John C Mabee Handicap and Oak Tree Breeders' Cup Mile, both Grade 1 events.

Thus, from both a non-stakes winning daughter and an unraced daughter of It's In The Air, Sheikh Maktoum bred two Group winners.

Machiavellian was Champion 2YO colt in France and was trained by Francois Boutin for the Niarchos family. One November day when I was inspecting breeding stock at Keeneland, Maria Niarchos happened to ask me what I thought about a match between Mr. Prospector and her valuable mare Coup de Folie. The concept had true merit because this special match reinforced Native Dancer via a "son" and a "daughter" and made use of Nasrullah's input.

Maria and her stud manager, Tim Richardson, were well aware of my fondness for Coup de Folie because of the mare's inbreeding to elite mare Almahmoud. I had written about Coup de Folie in my book *Quest For A Classic Winner* (1987) and predicted she would likely become a great producer of stakes winners.

Maria spends a tremendous amount of time analyzing pedigrees and racetrack performance. She has definite reasons for designing her broodmare matings each year and will sometimes seek advice from Tim Richardson and her racing manager, Alan Cooper. As a team, they are formidable, with an outstanding record of achievement.

Maria designed the pedigree that produced five-time champion mare Miesque (nine wins including the Breeders' Cup Mile twice, English 1,000 Guineas and French 1,000 Guineas). Miesque has produced Kingmambo (French 2,000 Guineas, St. James' Palace Stakes, Prix du Moulin de Longchamp), Miesque's Son (Prix de Ris-Orangis, 2nd Prix Maurice de Gheest), Mingun (Meld Stakes, Budweiser Celebration Stakes), Moon Is Up (Prix de Lieury) and East of the Moon, Champion 3YO filly in France (French 1,000 Guineas, Prix de Diane Hermes-French Oaks, and dam of Moon Driver and Mojave Moon). Miesque (Nureyev-Pasadoble by Prove Out) is a new addition to the list of "elite" mares.

Another outstanding female line to come into prominence is that of Kamar (Key to the Mint-Square Angel by Quadrangle), Champion 3YO filly of Canada, seven wins from 11 starts. Kamar won the Canadian Oaks, Duchess Stakes, and Yearling Sale Stakes and was stakes-placed 2nd Princess Elizabeth Stakes, 3rd Shady Wells Stakes etc. At the Warner Jones dispersal, I implored William T. Young to purchase Kamar's weanling filly by Seattle Slew. Her pedigree pattern was exceptional! Mr. Young asked me how much the weanling might bring and I told him it really didn't matter – she needed to be bought for Overbrook Farm to become a foundation mare.

Japanese bidders went to $1 million when Kamar's weanling filly was being auctioned at Keeneland and my heart sank, but Mr. Young nodded to his agent to go one more time and with another $50,000 bid, the hammer fell. Overbrook's farm manager, Jim Cannon, suggested the filly be named Seaside Attraction. She grew into a nice type and was full of electricity!

Trained by Wayne Lukas, she showed ability right from the start, earned $272,541 from four wins at two and three years, won the Kentucky Oaks, was runner-up in the Churchill Downs Budweiser Breeders' Cup Handicap and finished third in the Acorn Stakes and Beaumont Stakes.

Seaside Attraction produced five foals, all of them stakes winners except for Mercer Mill, a colt by Forty Niner that won at two and three years and is now at stud. Her best filly is Golden Attraction, U.S. Champion 2YO filly (eight wins $911,508, Frizette Stakes, Spinaway Stakes, Matron Stakes, Debutante Stakes, Turfway Breeders' Cup Stakes, Schuylerville Stakes) and already the dam of stakes winner Gold Trader.

Her best colt was undoubtedly Cape Canaveral, by Mr. Prospector, although the record books won't justify my claim. Wayne Lukas advised William T. Young that, in his opinion, Cape Canaveral was a serious Kentucky Derby prospect. Bruce Jensen, yearling manager at Overbrook, the farm who raised so many top horses in the 1990's, also believed Cape Canaveral was "something special."

Cape Canaveral sure had "extra gears" but he was one of those unlucky colts that had a few problems in training. He easily won his only start at two years in a maiden race at Santa Anita and was put away to develop. At three, Cape Canaveral won the San Miguel Stakes from Aristotle over six furlongs and ran third in an allowance. These were his only starts at three years – tendon trouble kept him away for the rest of the year. At four, he made a comeback to win a seven furlongs allowance at Santa Anita by three lengths, but his old injury flared up and he was retired to Overbrook Farm.

From four starts he won three and earned $125,640. However, it would not surprise me if he became a better sire than his three-quarter brother Cape Town. Seaside Attraction's son Cape Town by Seeking The Gold won five races, ($795,817, Florida Derby, Holy Bull Stakes, Kentucky Jockey Club Stakes and finished third in Keeneland's Toyota Blue Grass Stakes). Cape Town is the sire of Champion 3YO filly Birdtown, winner of the Kentucky Oaks, Acorn Stakes and Charon Stakes. Birdtown is a member of Cape Town's first crop to race. Overbrook Farm sold a yearling filly by Mr. Prospector out of Seaside Attraction at Keeneland, and my mate Chris Richardson bought her for Mr. and Mrs. Thompson, the owners of Cheveley Park Stud, Newmarket. Mrs. Thompson named the filly Red Carnival; she won the Cherry Hinton Stakes as a juvenile. Red Carnival produced stakes winners Carnival Dancer and Funfair. (Mrs. Thompson always creates clever names for her horses.)

Kamar (1976)	Key to the Mint	Graustark	Ribot	Tenerani by Bellini
				Romanella dam by **Papyrus** by **Tracery**
			Flower Bowl	Alibhai (**Hyperion/Tracery** nick)
				Flower Bed by Beau Pere
		Key Bridge	Princequillo	Prince Rose
				Cosquilla by **Papyrus** by **Tracery**
			Blue Banner	War Admiral
				Risque Bleu by Blue Larkspur
	Square Angel	Quadrangle	Cohoes	Mahmoud by Blenheim
				Belle of Troy ex La Troienne by **Teddy**
			Tap Day	Bull Lea by **Bull Dog** by **Teddy**
				Scurry
		Nangela	Nearctic	Nearco by Pharos
				Lady Angela (**Hyperion/Tracery** nick)
			Angela's Niece	Tim Tam (inbred to **Bull Dog** by **Teddy**)
				Great Niece

Kamar produced Key To The Moon by Wajima (13 wins, $714,536, Champion 3YO colt in Canada, winner of the Queen's Plate, Discovery Handicap, Dominion Day Handicap, Gulfstream Sprint Championship, Display Stakes, Marine Stakes etc.).

Kamar produced Hiaam by Alydar, (three wins including the Princess Margaret Stakes at Ascot and Wallis Fillies Stakes at Sandown). Hiaam is the dam of three stakes winners, viz. Munnaya, Sheer Reason and Mall Queen.

Gorgeous (Slew O'Gold-Kamar) won eight races including the Hollywood Oaks, Ashland Stakes, and Vanity Handicap, and produced stakes winner Stunning. Jood (Nijinsky II-Kamar) placed twice, produced world champion Fantastic Light (12 wins including the Breeders' Cup Turf, Irish Champion Stakes, Hong Kong Cup, Prince of Wales' Stakes), and his sister Hi Dubai won the Pretty Polly Stakes, 2nd Prix Saint-Alary etc. Last but not least is Wilayif (Danzig-Kamar), a winner at three and dam of stakes winner Morning Pride (by Machiavellian). Kamar is of course a sister to Love Smitten, dam of Swain by Nashwan, Champion Older Male in England and Ireland with 10 wins and earnings of $3,797,566.

Height of Fashion, Co-Champion 2YO filly in Europe, won five races including the Princess of Wales' Stakes, Ascot Fillies' Mile, May Hill Stakes, Lupe Stakes and is a new addition to the ranks of "elite" mares. A big mare, she is by Bustino from Highclere by Queen's Hussar from Highlight (incestuously inbred to Hyperion) and was bred by Her Majesty Queen Elizabeth II who later sold her to Sheikh Hamdan bin Rashid al-Maktoum, the owner of Shadwell Stud. Height of Fashion's dam, Highclere, won the English 1,000 Guineas. Height of Fashion produced six stakes winners and two other winners that were stakes-placed. Her stakes winners are:

Nashwan (by Blushing Groom) Champion 3YO in England, six wins 786,357 pounds, English 2,000 Guineas, English Derby, Eclipse Stakes, King George VI & Queen Elizabeth Stakes.
Unfuwain (by Northern Dancer) six wins 263,936 pounds, Jockey Club Stakes, Chester Vase, Princess of Wales' Stakes, John Porter Stakes, Epsom Warren Stakes.
Nayef (by Gulch) Champion 3YO colt in England, eight wins $3,594,157, Champion Stakes, Juddmonte International Stakes, Dubai Sheema Classic etc.
Alwasmi (by Northern Dancer) two wins 54,419 pounds, John Porter Stakes, 2nd Jockey Club Stakes.
Mukddaam (by Danzig) three wins 62,982 pounds, Fred Archer Stakes, 2nd King Edward VII Stakes, Princess of Wales' Stakes.
Sarayir (by Mr. Prospector) three wins 28,222 pounds, Oh So Sharp Stakes, Virginia Rated Stakes Handicap.

Nashwan sired champion Swain and 2004 Prix de l'Arc de Triomphe winner Bago. Unfuwain sired Europe's Champion 2YO Alhaarth who in turn sired English 2,000 Guineas and Champion Stakes winner Haafhd.

Sinndar, a truly impressive winner of the English Derby, is another Aga Khan homebred classic winner. He is by Grand Lodge from Sinntara by Lashkari and comes from Tourzima's female line, as does Darshaan. Johnny Murtagh, who rode Sinndar, described the classic colt as follows:

"He has pace, class and the most superb temperament. He's the best I've ridden without a doubt, the best we've seen in years."

I always admired the clever matings designed by France's famous breeder Marcel Boussac. Tourzima became an outstanding foundation mare for Boussac. She is three-parts sister to Djeddah and half-sister to Priam. Djeddah won the Eclipse Stakes, Champion Stakes and Criterium de Maisons-Laffitte and is the sire of Lalun, dam of champion Never Bend and Bold Reason. Obviously the Aga Khan wanted to double up on Tourzima's dam, Djezima, when he designed the mating of Sinndar's dam, Sinntara, because he used a stallion with Lalun's son Never Bend in its pedigree.

Sinndar, the latest star from Tourzima's family, won the National Stakes and the EBF Dance Design Maiden Handicap at two years, progressed through winter, and at three won the Derrinstown Stud Derby

Trial, English Derby, Irish Derby, Prix Niel and established himself as the best turf horse in the world when winning the prestigious Prix de l'Arc de Triomphe at Longchamp. His only defeat, when not quite fit enough, was in Ireland, notably the Ballysax Stakes when he finished second.

Sinndar is a well-made, symmetrical horse with perfect shoulder angle and is destined to become another successful stallion for his breeder, the Aga Khan.

				Northern Dancer
			Danzig	Pas de Nom
		Chief's Crown		Secretariat ex **Somethingroyal**
			Six Crowns	Chris Evert
	Grand Lodge			Sir Gaylord ex **Somethingroyal**
			Habitat	Little Hut
		La Papagena		Tudor Melody by Tudor Minstrel
			Magic Flute	Filigrana
Sinndar				Never Bend by **Nasrullah**
(1997)			Mill Reef	Milan Mill by **Princequillo**
		Lashkari		Right Royal by Owen Tudor
			Larranda	Morning Calm by Crepello
	Sinntara			High Top
			Top Ville	Sega Ville by Charlottesville
		Sidama		Abdos
			Stoyana	Bielka ex Tourzima

In Sinndar's pedigree, Secretariat is by a son of Nasrullah from a daughter of Princequillo and is a genetic cousin to Sir Gaylord. Mill Reef is a product of the Nasrullah/Princequillo nick and reinforces similar genes Sinndar inherits from Secretariat and Sir Gaylord. Charlottesville is by Prince Chevalier from Noorani, a "daughter" of Nearco (and therefore a product of the Prince Rose/Nearco nick). Princequillo and Prince Chevalier are sons of Prince Rose with similar linebreedings. Nasrullah is a "son" of Nearco. I recommend mares with the Nasrullah/Princequillo nick should be mated with Sinndar because he could have an affinity with these superior bloodlines. For Gainsborough Stud, I doubled up on Secretariat by recommending one of his daughters named Insijaam, be sent to Sinndar during his initial year at Gilltown Stud. This match produced Sinndar's first juvenile winner, a filly named Pictavia who was twice stakes-placed in 2004 and finished strongly when second in the Group 1 Moyglare Stud Stakes.

Balidaress (Balidar-Innocence by Sea Hawk II) is another new member to the "elite" mare list. Winner of three races, she produced eight winners, four stakes winners.

Desirable (Lord Gayle-Balidaress) won three races including the Cheveley Park Stakes, was runner-up in the Moyglare Stud Stakes and finished third in the English 1,000 Guineas. Desirable has produced Shadayid (Champion 2YO filly in Europe, winner of the English 1,000 Guineas, Prix Marcel Boussac, Fred Darling Stakes, etc, 2nd Sussex Stakes, Coronation Stakes), Dumaani (seven wins, Keeneland Breeders' Cup Mile Stakes twice, King Charles II Stakes and in Japan the Keio Hai Spring Cup), and Fath (Theo Fennell Lennox Stakes, 2nd Middle Park Stakes).

Park Appeal (Ahonoora-Balidaress) was Champion 2YO filly in England and Ireland, five wins including the Cheveley Park Stakes, Moyglare Stud Stakes and in North America at four years won the Country Queen Stakes. Park Appeal is the dam of Cape Cross (Lockinge Stakes, Royal Ascot Queen Anne Stakes, Celebration Mile), stakes-placed Lord of Appeal, as well as Arvola (winning dam of Diktat) and Pastorale (winning dam of Kareymah). Diktat won the Prix Maurice de Gheest and Haydock Sprint Cup and appears to be a promising young sire.

Other progeny out of Balidaress are the stakes winners Nashamaa and Alydaress, as well as Balistroika, dam of English Champion 3YO filly Russian Rhythm whose wins include the English 1,000 Guineas, and Perfectperformance, winner of the Royal Lodge Stakes. Russian Rhythm, a gorgeous mare with powerful hindquarters, is owned by Cheveley Park Stud and was trained by Sir Michael Stoute.

Cape Cross is the sire of English Champion 3YO filly and Cartier Horse of the Year, Ouija Board (five wins $1,671,768, English Oaks, Irish Oaks, Breeders' Cup Filly & Mare Turf Stakes, Pretty Polly Stakes etc.). Cape Cross is a powerful, masculine stallion with plenty of fast fiber muscle by the sprinter Green Desert, whose second dam Courtly Dee has been added to the list of "elite" mares. Courtly Dee was quite a small mare that won four races and placed seven times in North America. She is by Never Bend out of Tulle by War Admiral out of the elite mare Judy Rae.

Courtly Dee produced 15 winners, eight stakes winners – a truly remarkable produce record. Among her stakes-winning progeny are Althea ($1,275,255, Arkansas Derby, Santa Susanna Stakes), Ali Oop (Sapling Stakes), Native Courier (14 wins, $522,635), Aquilegia (eight wins $446,081, New York Handicap, Black Helen Handicap), Twining (five wins, Peter Pan Stakes, Withers Stakes) and Princess Oola (five wins, Whitemarsh Handicap and dam of Azzam, winner of the AJC Sydney Cup). Courtly Dee also produced the unraced mare Foreign Courier, by Sir Ivor.

Foreign Courier produced the Danzig horse Green Desert (five wins including the July Cup, Vernons Sprint Cup and Flying Childers Stakes), a successful sire in England. Among Green Desert's progeny are Oasis Dream, Desert Prince, White Heart, Invincible Spirit, Cape Cross, Sheikh Albadou, Owington, Rose Gypsy and Heat Haze. Foreign Courier is also the dam of stakes winner Yousefia, dam of Princess Margaret Stakes victress Mythical Girl.

Among new additions to the list of "elite" mares are Grecian Banner and Gay Violin. Grecian Banner was voted North America's Broodmare of the Year in 1988. She is the dam of two gifted stakes winners bred and owned by Ogden Phipps and Ogden Mills Phipps.

They are the courageous filly Personal Ensign and Personal Flag. An amazing performer, Personal Ensign was voted Champion Older Female. Her race record shows 13 wins, two to four years, for earnings of $1,579,880.

Personal Ensign's major victories include the Breeders' Cup Distaff, Beldame Stakes (twice), Frizette Stakes, Whitney Handicap, Hempstead Handicap, Shuvee Handicap and the Maskette Stakes. She was voted North America's Broodmare of the Year in 1996. To date she has produced My Flag by Easy Goer (six wins $1,557,057, Breeders' Cup Juvenile Fillies Stakes, Coaching Club American Oaks, Gazelle Handicap and dam of Storm Flag Flying [Champion 2YO filly whose wins include the Breeders' Cup Juvenile Fillies Stakes]); Miner's Mark by Mr. Prospector (six wins $967,170 Jockey Club Gold Cup, Jim Dandy Stakes); Traditionally by Mr. Prospector (five wins $495,660, Oaklawn Handicap) and stakes-placed winner Our Emblem by Mr. Prospector (five wins $366,013, 2nd Carter Handicap, 3rd Metropolitan Handicap).

My Flag's daughter Storm Flag Flying was exceptionally fast. I recall the day she ran six furlongs at Belmont Park in 1:08.4 winning by seven lengths. Later at Gulfstream Park she went seven furlongs in the sizzling time of 1:21.4, and when beaten a nose in the Carter Handicap she went seven furlongs in 1:21.2.

Here is the pedigree of the multiple Grade 1 winning filly by Storm Cat.

				Nearctic
			Northern Dancer	Natalma by **Native Dancer**
		Storm Bird		New Providence
			South Ocean	Shining Sun
	Storm Cat			Bold Ruler by **Nasrullah**
			Secretariat	Somethingroyal by **Princequillo**
		Terlingua		Crimson Satan
			Crimson Saint	Bolero Rose by Bolero
Storm Flag Flying				Raise a Native by **Native Dancer**
(2000)			Alydar	Sweet Tooth (to **Nasrullah**)
		Easy Goer		**Buckpasser** by Tom Fool
			Relaxing	Marking Time
	My Flag			Damascus (dam by My Babu)
			Private Account	Numbered Account by **Buckpasser**
		Personal Ensign		Hoist the Flag by Tom Rolfe
			Grecian Banner	Dorine (Arg)

First, we must try to understand why My Flag was such a brilliant filly. Her pedigree shows reinforcement of champion Buckpasser (Tom Fool-Busanda by War Admiral-Businesslike by Blue Larkspur-La Troienne by Teddy).

Further back we find the half-sisters Mumtaz Mahal and Lady Juror (daughters of Lady Josephine by Sundridge).

Damascus is out of a daughter of champion My Babu (Djebel-Perfume II by Badruddin-Lavendula II by Pharos) and Perfume II acts like a genetic female cousin to Nasrullah, the father of On-And-On who sired Sweet Tooth.

Private Account's dam, Numbered Account, was a small mare tracing to La Troienne, as does champion Buckpasser, so one suspects My Flag probably inherited "genetic goodies" from La Troienne – but hold your horses, that's just the beginning of the analysis.

Hoist the Flag, champion racehorse and sire of Grecian Banner, is by Tom Rolfe from Wavy Navy by War Admiral. Buckpasser is also from a daughter of War Admiral. Little champion Tom Rolfe has a superb pedigree. He is linebred to English Derby winner Papyrus (by Tracery), to Pharos and Sickle who are bred on the same Phalaris/Chaucer nick, and carries impact from unbeaten St. Simon and his sister Angelica. Further back, Tom Rolfe has a valuable double of the brilliant Orme.

			Bellini by Cavaliere d'Arpino by **Havresac II**
		Tenerani	Tofanella by Apelle
	Ribot		El Greco by **Pharos** (**Phalaris/Chaucer**)
		Romanella	Barbara Burrini by **Papyrus** by **Tracery**
Tom Rolfe			Sir Gallahad III by Teddy
(1962)		Roman	Buckup by Buchan by Sunstar by **Sundridge**
	Pocahontas (USA)		**Princequillo** dam by **Papyrus** by **Tracery**
		How	The Squaw II by **Sickle** (**Phalaris/Chaucer**)

Tracery is by Rock Sand (son of Sainfoin) from Topiary by Orme (Ormonde-Angelica). Ribot comes from the male line of Havresac II who is inbred 2 x 3 to St. Simon; and Havresac II is out of a mare by Ajax, by Flying Fox by Orme. Whenever Tom Rolfe's strain links up with Nearco (Pharos-Nogara by Havresac II) there is potential for this cross to produce graded stakes performers. Why? The combination of Havresac II with Tracery (which intensifies not only St. Simon and his sister Angelica, but also the famous English mare Pocahontas) can create classic speed. According to private research, racehorses inheriting larger than normal hearts often possess both Havresac II and Tracery in their make-up. A fine example is Nearctic, the sire of Northern Dancer. Nearctic is by Nearco (dam by Havresac II) from Lady Angela by Hyperion from Sister Sarah (by Abbot's Trace, son of Tracery).

Roman, Tom Rolfe's broodmare sire, is by Sir Gallahad III, a grandson of French champion Ajax, and Havresac II is out of a daughter of Ajax. Roman also has Sunstar in his genotype. Sunstar is by Sundridge, son of Sierra, a sister to Sainfoin (broodmare sire of Phalaris). Next, consider the unusual genetic link between Storm Cat's fourth dam First Rose (Menow/Sir Galahad III mix) with champion Tom Fool (by Menow-Gaga by Bull Dog) because they act like three-parts genetic cousins, with very similar biochemistry. Indeed, Storm Flag Flying has a strong pedigree because of reinforcement of superior runners viz. Nearco, Havresac II, Buckpasser, Princequillo, Tracery, etc., and her pedigree pattern suggests she is likely to become a Grade 1 stakes producer.

Grecian Banner's dam is Dorine, a chestnut mare born in Argentina in 1958. Dorine is by Aristophanes from Doria by Advocate and is therefore bred on the same cross as Forli (Aristophanes-Trevisa by Advocate). Perhaps someone owning a female descendant of Grecian Banner might test stallions with Forli in their make-up (e.g. Sadler's Wells, Fairy King or Nureyev) because linebreeding to Forli and his three-quarter genetic sister Dorine appeals as a worthwhile test. This match reinforces Lady Juror.

If I recall correctly, Doria (Arg), the second dam of Grecian Banner, was imported to Kentucky by Mrs. Henry Carnegie Phipps whose Wheatley Stable was feared by rival owners. Doria is linebred to Tracery (Rock Sand-Topiary by Orme). Her dam is by Argentina's leading sire Congreve, a grandson of Tracery. Thus, Doria has a classic pedigree pattern with speed enhanced via Sainfoin and Sierra.

				Phalaris (dam by **Sainfoin**) to **Cyllene**
			Fairway	Scapa Flow by Chaucer
		Fair Trial		Son-in-Law
			Lady Juror	Lady Sundridge by **Sundridge** (**Sierra**)
	Advocate			**Tracery** by Rock Sand by **Sainfoin**
			Papyrus	Miss Matty by Marcovil
		Guiding Star		Sunstar by **Sundridge** (ex **Sierra**)
			Ocean Light	Glass Doll by Isinglass
Doria (Arg) (1949)				**Tracery** by Rock Sand by **Sainfoin**
			Copyright	Rectify by William The Third
		Congreve		Perrier by Persimmon by **St. Simon**
			Per Noi	My Queen
	Donatila			**Cyllene** by **Bona Vista**
			Saint Emilion	Albilla by **Gay Hermit**
		Dona Ines		Pietermatitzburg by **St. Simon**
			Dona Cecilia	Rivera by **Gay Hermit**

Notes: William The Third is another son of St. Simon. Tracery is linebred to unbeaten
St. Simon and his sister Angelica. Sierra is a sister to Sainfoin.
Cyllene is the sire of both Polymelus and Saint Emilion.

Probably Mrs. Henry Carnegie Phipps realized Advocate's second dam Ocean Light was three-parts sister to successful sire North Star III. Mrs. Phipps happened to be a close friend of Olin Gentry, manager of Edward R. Bradley's Idle Hour Farm where North Star III was domiciled; or perhaps a reason for purchasing Doria was because Princequillo dominated pedigrees of major stakes winners in the 1950's. Princequillo is out of a daughter of Papyrus, son of Tracery. Once again we discover speed genes transmitted by Sainfoin and his sister Sierra as well as St. Simon and his sister Angelica (a high-class combination). We should be able to now appreciate why the dam of Storm Flag Flying was so compatible with Storm Cat – here are some genetic connections:

a) Secretariat is out of a daughter of Princequillo whose dam is by Tracery's best son Papyrus.

b) Northern Dancer's sire, Nearctic, carries Tracery via Abbot's Trace.

c) Crimson Satan carries Tracery via the dam of Requiebro.

d) Tom Rolfe's second dam is by Princequillo (adding more Tracery).

e) Dorine is linebred to Tracery.

There are people in the horse industry who believe pedigree research is a waste of time and prefer to remain ignorant. Fortunately researchers like Anne Peters, Phyllis Allen, John Prather, Les Brinsfield, Robert Keck and Alan Porter would disagree. These dedicated pedigree analysts seriously study pedigree patterns and use clever but different techniques to design mare matings. One of the most knowledgeable pedigree analysts I have ever met is John Prather.

In the past, I admired Olin Gentry Sr. who managed the great stallions Ribot, Graustark, His Majesty and Roberto at John Galbreath's Darby Dan Farm. Olin designed the matings of four Kentucky Derby winners as well as European champion Roberto, winner of the English Derby. Olin was a great mate of mine and I miss him.

Strange as it may seem, not many commercial stud operators employ or use professional pedigree consultants as part of their business strategy. For example, in Europe, successful breeders like Maria Niarchos, H. H. Karim the Aga Khan IV, Prince Khalid Abdullah, Sheikh Hamdan, Alec Wildenstein, Cheveley Park Stud and Moyglare Stud spend a considerable amount of research time selecting suitable sires to test with individual broodmares. In North America, some farms hire or employ pedigree analysts (e.g. Winstar Farm, Three Chimneys Farm), but not as many as one would expect. Times have changed. Statistical data seems to be more important than genetic compatibility between sire and dam. Commercial breeders are transfixed by yearling prices and many of them breed purely for the sale ring with almost total disregard for the racetrack. Hence, I admire owner-breeders like Josephine Abercrombie (Pin Oak Stud), Arthur B. Hancock III (Stone Farm), Maria Niarchos (Haras Fresnay-Le-Buffard), Sheikh Hamdan bin Rashid al-Maktoum (Shadwell Stud), Kirsten Rausing (Lanwades Stud) and Prince Khalid Abdullah (Juddmonte Farms) who breed Group and Graded stakes winners on an ongoing basis using their own skills of pedigree research.

These breeders would get to know each mare's family strengths and weaknesses as did great breeders like Marcel Boussac, Lord Derby, the Aga Khan, William Woodward, Colonel E. R. Bradley, "Bull" Hancock, Harry Payne Whitney, the Phipps family and Eddy Taylor.

Another family being upgraded is that of the new "elite" mare Gay Violin (Sir Gaylord-Blue Violin by First Fiddle). Born in 1964, Gay Violin won twice at three and produced six winners, three stakes winners, namely Gay Fandango (Jersey Stakes, Waterford Crystal Mile), Cellist (Senorita Stakes, 2nd Hollywood Oaks and dam of Concert Hall) and Happy Strings (Speed To Spare Championship Stakes). Gay Violin also produced Violino (by Hawaii), dam of Italy's Champion 2YO filly Lasting Lass, and Minstrelette (by Round Table), winner at three and dam of 10 winners including Punctilio and Carduel (by Buckpasser).

Probably champion Buckpasser (Tom Fool-Busanda by War Admiral) is responsible for upgrading racing class in Carduel's descendants. Carduel produced six winners, three stakes winners. She is the dam of Always Fair (Prix Quincey, Coventry Stakes, 2nd Lanson Champagne Stakes, Hungerford Stakes), Asassy (Weidenpescher Meile in Germany), Faithful Son (Prince of Wales' Stakes, Festival Stakes, 2nd Coral Eclipse Stakes, Juddmonte International Stakes, 3rd Queen Elizabeth II Stakes), as well as Golden Digger (dam of Group winner Naheef) and Lailati (dam of Copper Carnival and the classic filly Lailani, seven wins $600,000 plus earnings, Irish Oaks, Nassau Stakes and Flower Bowl Invitational Stakes etc).

Lailani is by Unfuwain (Northern Dancer-Height of Fashion), six wins from 10 starts and £263,936. Unfuwain was ranked fourth top three-year-old in Europe in 1988. He won the Princess of Wales' Stakes (defeating Undercut and Infamy), Chester Vase and Warren Stakes, was runner-up to Mtoto in the King George VI & Queen Elizabeth Stakes at Ascot and finished fourth to Tony Bin in the Prix de l'Arc de Triomphe. At four years, he won the Jockey Club Stakes and John Porter Stakes. His best son to date is Alhaarth.

For Gainsborough Stud, I purposely designed the pedigree of Irish Oaks winner Lailani to incorporate duplication of two elite mares, Feola and Mumtaz Mahal. Nasrullah, Royal Charger (sire of Turn-To) and Mahmoud are all descendants of champion Mumtaz Mahal (see Lailani's pedigree below).

Lailani (1998)	Unfuwain	Northern Dancer	Nearctic	**Nearco**
				Lady Angela by **Hyperion**
			Natalma	**Native Dancer**
				Almahmoud by Mahmoud
		Height of Fashion	Bustino	Busted by Crepello
				Ship Yard by Doutelle (to **Feola**)
			Highclere	Queen's Hussar
				Highlight (to **Feola**)
	Lailati	Mr. Prospector	Raise a Native	**Native Dancer**
				Raise You by Case Ace
			Gold Digger	Nashua by **Nasrullah** by **Nearco**
				Sequence by Count Fleet
		Carduel	Buckpasser	Tom Fool by Menow by Pharamond II
				Busanda by War Admiral
			Minstrelette	Round Table (to **Feola**)
				Gay Violin by a son of Turn-To (**R.Ch.**)

Unfuwain's dam, Height of Fashion (a new addition to the "elite" mares list), has a double of Feola in her ancestry. Doutelle is by Prince Chevalier from Above Board by Straight Deal out of Feola, whereas Highlight is by Borealis out of English 1,000 Guineas winner Hypericum by Hyperion out of Feola. Seeing as Lailani's dam Lailati carries Round Table (grandson of Feola), it made sense to test Unfuwain.

Round Table	Princequillo	Prince Rose
		Cosquilla by Papyrus
	Knight's Daughter	Sir Cosmo
		Feola

Round Table was a "super" tough champion who can be duplicated with confidence. He won 43 races (31 of them stakes) for earnings of $1,749,869 in days when purses were much lower than they are today. He was voted Champion Handicap Horse twice, Champion Grass Horse and Horse of the Year in North America. Doutelle is bred along similar lines to Round Table:

Doutelle	Prince Chevalier	Prince Rose
		Chevalerie
	Above Board	Straight Deal
		Feola

Lailani is not big but she has quality. Michael Goodbody and I decided Lailani should be sent to A. P. Indy whose dam, Weekend Surprise, is inbred to Somethingroyal by Princequillo. We repeated the mating to thoroughly test its potential because within the pedigree pattern are two closely-related ancestors, Prince Chevalier and Princequillo, who act like genetic cousins with similar biochemistry. Lailani produced two nice colts by A. P. Indy at Gainsborough Farm in 2003 and 2004. Time will tell if either inherits racing class. Carduel's daughter Golden Digger is bred on the same lines as Miswaki, Woodman, Mining and Seeking The Gold.

Golden Digger is by Mr. Prospector from a daughter of Buckpasser and as a test, we sent her to Marju to duplicate Round Table (to reinforce Feola) and the result was multiple Group 3 winner Naheef (five wins including the Strensall Stakes, Winter Hill Stakes, Champagne Lanson Vintage Stakes, Al Rashidya Stakes, 2nd National Stakes, La Coupe, and Ernst and Young Euro Cup). Always Fair (Danzig-Carduel by Buckpasser) initially stood in France before his export to North America. Already his French-bred daughters are proving to be stakes producers.

Another new addition to the ranks of "elite" mares is Gay Hostess who hails from the female line of Boudoir II (by Mahmoud). Graustark and His Majesty descend from Boudoir II via Flower Bowl's branch.

Gay Hostess (1957)	Royal Charger	Nearco	Pharos	Phalaris (dam by **Sainfoin**)
				Scapa Flow by **Chaucer**
			Nogara	Havresac II
				Catnip by Spearmint
		Sun Princess	Solario	**Gainsborough**
				Sun Worship by **Sundridge** (**Sierra**)
			Mumtaz Begum	**Blenheim**
				Mumtaz Mahal (dam by **Sundridge**)
	Your Hostess	Alibhai	Hyperion	**Gainsborough**
				Selene by **Chaucer**
			Teresina	Tracery by Rock Sand by **Sainfoin**
				Blue Tit
		Boudoir II	Mahmoud	**Blenheim**
				Mah Mahal (**Gainsborough**-**Mumtaz Mahal**)
			Kambala	Clarissimus
				La Soupe by Prince Palatine

Mumtaz Begum is three-parts sister to English Derby winner Mahmoud. Gay Hostess has three strains of champion Gainsborough (Bayardo-Rosedrop), winner of the English 2,000 Guineas, Derby and St. Leger. Once again we find Sainfoin and his sister Sierra, Havresac II and Tracery, and Charles O'Malley (the broodmare sire of Blenheim). Gay Hostess was an unraced sister to stakes winner Royal Clipper and half-sister to successful sire T.V. Commercial. Her dam, Your Hostess, was sister to brilliant stakes winner Your Host (13 wins $384,795) and half-sister to Flower Bed, grand-dam of Graustark and His Majesty.

Gay Hostess produced two outstanding colts, one in England, the other in North America. Majestic Prince (by Raise a Native) was a refined, flashy colt with tremendous hindquarters that was purchased as a yearling for $250,000. His nine wins from 10 starts include the Kentucky Derby, Preakness Stakes, Santa Anita Derby, Los Feliz, San Vincente and San Jacinto Stakes, but he broke down after finishing second to Arts and Letters in the Belmont Stakes. He was slightly unsound during his tough three-year-old campaign but certainly inherited the "will-to-win."

Majestic Prince was a success at stud and a useful broodmare sire. He is the father of Majestic Light (11 wins including the Man o' War Stakes, Amory L Haskell Stakes), who became the sire of talented stakes winner Wavering Monarch.

Majestic Prince's younger brother Crowned Prince was physically different, being built like a sprinter-miler with pronounced forearm muscles. Crowned Prince was Champion 2YO colt of England, winner of the Dewhurst Stakes and Champagne Stakes. Unfortunately he inherited weak ankles from his father, Raise a Native, and was only a moderate success as a sire of black type winners.

Gay Hostess also produced Lovely Gypsy (12 wins $95,198, Miss Chicago Stakes, Bangles and Beads Handicap), stakes-placed Our Queen, Rollabout (dam of Lady Face) and stakes-placed Betty Lorraine.

Betty Lorraine (Prince John-Gay Hostess) was short-coupled with a deep girth and possessed plenty of substance. A small mare, she was fairly genuine on the racetrack winning seven races at two and three years, $33,865 and earned black type when third in the Junior Miss Stakes. She produced Caracolero (by Ribot's son Graustark), Co-Champion 3YO colt in France, four wins and $331,588 earnings whose major victory came in the Prix du Jockey Club (French Derby) in which he defeated Dankaro, Mississipian and Mount Hagen.

Betty Lorraine was matched with champion Secretariat, resulting in Betty's Secret, a heavy-bodied mare with a short, thick neck. Edward P. Taylor liked the pedigree of Betty's Secret and purchased this daughter of Secretariat especially for his homebred stallion, Northern Dancer, and in 1981 at Windfields Farm, a future English Derby winner was born. His name was Secreto.

Gay Hostess also produced Meadow Blue, a refined mare by Believe It, who produced U.S. Champion 3YO colt Real Quiet. Really Blue won three races at three and four years and is also the dam of Mining My Business, dam of Real Cozzy ($464,840 1st Fair Grounds Oaks, 2nd Mother Goose Stakes, Kentucky Oaks, 3rd Acorn Stakes).

Real Quiet (by Quiet American) earned $3,271,802 from six wins, five seconds, and six thirds and almost won the Triple Crown. Trained by Bob Baffert, Real Quiet won the Hollywood Futurity at two years defeating Artax, and progressed the following year when second in the San Felipe Stakes and Santa Anita Derby (always finishing fast) before victory in the Kentucky Derby and Preakness Stakes (defeating Victory Gallop on both occasions). However, he went down by a nose to his arch-rival in the longer Belmont Stakes after leading all the way, caught in the final few strides. At four, Real Quiet added the

Hollywood Gold Cup (defeating Budroyale and Malek), Pimlico Special Handicap (defeating Free House) and was stakes-placed three times carrying high weights.

Meadow Blue's daughter Mangala is the dam of Allied Forces, Champion Older Male in the United Arab Emirates. Allied Forces earned $682,417 in England, the U.S. and the UAE. His wins include Royal Ascot's Queen Anne Stakes, the Jamaica Handicap and Pegasus Breeders' Cup Handicap.

We now come to one of my equine favorites – Swaps, a most courageous, fleet-footed world champion. The pedigree of Swaps (Khaled-Iron Reward by War Admiral) is cleverly constructed, but before going into brief details about his ancestry, let's first consider his race record:

Swaps, chestnut colt 1952 - race record:

25 starts, 19 wins, two seconds, two thirds and $848,900 career earnings.

Voted U.S. Horse of the Year and Champion Handicap Horse, Swaps captured the Kentucky Derby, Hollywood Gold Cup, Santa Anita Derby, American Derby, Californian Stakes, American Handicap, Sunset Handicap, Will Rogers Stakes, San Vincente Stakes, Inglewood Handicap etc., and established the following speed records:

New world record for 8 ½ furlongs at Hollywood Park, 1:40.2
New world record for 8 ½ furlongs at Hollywood Park, 1:39.0
New world record for 8 furlongs at Hollywood Park, 1:33.1
New world record for 13 furlongs at Hollywood Park, 2:30.1
New world record for 8.32 furlongs at Gulfstream, 1:39.3
Equaled the world record for 9 furlongs, Hollywood Park, 1:46.4
New Track record for 10 furlongs at Hollywood Park, 1:58.3
New Track record for 8 furlongs at Washington, 1:33.2

What racehorse in the recent past could be truly compared with Swaps's blazing speed? Perhaps Secretariat might come close. We must consider an important fact – the times shown above were accomplished 50 years ago!

Swaps (1952)	Khaled	Hyperion	Gainsborough	Bayardo by **Bay Ronald**
				Rosedrop
			Selene	Chaucer by St. Simon
				Serenissima by Minoru
		Éclair	Ethnarch	The Tetrarch
				Karenza by William The Third
			Black Ray	Black Jester by **Polymelus**
				Lady Brilliant by Sundridge
	Iron Reward	Beau Pere	Son-in-Law	Dark Ronald by **Bay Ronald**
				Mother-in-Law
			Cinna	**Polymelus**
				Baroness La Fleche
		Iron Maiden	War Admiral	Man o' War (dam by Rock Sand)
				Brushup by Sweep
			Betty Derr	Sir Gallahad III by Teddy
				Uncle's Lassie

Swaps is linebred to unbeaten St. Simon via various ancestors and other ancestors to influence speed are Cinna, Black Ray, War Admiral, and the mix of Sainfoin and Sierra (via Rock Sand and via Sundridge).

We know Polymelus is a common denominator in the pedigrees of Black Ray and Cinna, so let's look into Iron Maiden's pedigree. She is by War Admiral from Betty Derr by Sir Gallahad III whose dam Plucky Liege is by Spearmint (son of Carbine, a close relative of Polymelus). English 1,000 Guineas winner Cinna (dam of Beau Pere) sits on the alternate sex line, the zigzag that might carry valuable sex-linked genes, and although Cinna is by Polymelus, more significant is her inbreeding to Hampton (3 x 3) and Quiver (3 x 3), thereby reinforcing two powerful strains.

Quiver is the granddam of both Polymelus and Baroness La Fleche:

			Bona Vista
		Cyllene	Arcadia
	Polymelus		**Hampton**
		Maid Marian	**Quiver**
Cinna (1917)			**Hampton**
		Ladas	Illuminata
	Baroness La Fleche		St. Simon
		La Fleche	**Quiver**

The person who designed Cinna's pedigree was Sir Robert Jardine who enjoyed researching Thoroughbred pedigrees and knew the value of classic-producing female lines. Cinna possessed acceleration. She won the English 1,000 Guineas, Coronation Stakes and produced Beau Pere, Balloch and Mr. Standfast, very successful sires in New Zealand. Quiver is a granddaughter of Brown Bess, the mare cleverly duplicated in the pedigree of champion Carbine.

Thus, whenever you find Cinna's son Beau Pere in pedigrees, learn to respect him because his genotype is highly compatible with Fairway, Pharos and Nearco, the strongest members of Polymelus' male line. Beau Pere features in the ancestry of the brothers Graustark and His Majesty. Danehill, a remarkable sire, is out of a daughter of His Majesty. Even though Danehill is inbred to Natalma he transmits many of His Majesty's characteristics to his progeny. Natalma was of course slightly back at the near knee, a trait Danehill inherited, but the strength from His Majesty's parents, Ribot and Flower Bowl, both exceptional athletes, maintained soundness.

One of the most competent judges of breeding and racing stock I have ever met was George Blackwell who not only knew the best bloodlines in the world, but also knew where the best racehorses were raised. He kept records of the farms that consistently raised stakes winners. George sure did have an eye for a horse and was respected by his peers at the British Bloodstock Agency. George Blackwell was responsible for helping many American breeders acquire well-bred English mares.

At the 1952 Tattersalls December Sales, Edward P. Taylor was in attendance, and sought the advice of Blackwell. Eddy Taylor was still developing his Windfields Farm in Canada and knew if his yearlings were to compete with Kentucky bred yearlings, he needed to acquire mares from successful families.

He asked George which was the best mare in the sale catalog. The answer came without hesitation – Lady Angela, by champion Hyperion from Sister Sarah by Abbot's Trace, tested in foal to unbeaten Nearco. Blackwell pointed out the strength of the female line which traced to champion mare Pretty Polly.

Quoting from page 210 of Abram S. Hewitt's book, *The Great Breeders and their Methods*, here is what transpired.

"Very well," Taylor told Blackwell. "I'll buy the mare, but only if I can breed the mare back to Nearco again in 1953."

George Blackwell approached ex-bookmaker Martin Benson, who had bought Nearco from breeder Federico Tesio and still largely controlled the syndicate. Benson grumbled that he had only a few shares left etc. etc. etc. but finally said: "Look here, I like to go to Palm Beach, Florida, in the winter and there are currency restrictions on taking money out of England. If Mr. Taylor will pay me $3,000 in Palm Beach (U. S. currency), he can have the nomination." Taylor, when informed of this, said: "I will do it. He just might be breaking the law, but I am not!"

In the spring of 1953, Lady Angela foaled a miserable-looking chestnut colt by Nearco, then was covered by him again and shipped to Canada. In 1954 she foaled a splendid dark brown colt by Nearco whom Taylor named Nearctic. The next year this colt was offered with all Taylor's other yearlings at his "one price" auction with $35,000 as the reserve price. No one bought him, and he went into Taylor's training stable."

Nearctic won 21 of 47 starts and earned $152,384. Eddy Taylor thought enough of his juvenile colt to ask trainer Horatio Luro to send Nearctic down to Saratoga where the colt won the Saratoga Special. At three, Nearctic established a new track record at Fort Erie for 6 ½ furlongs and the following year when trained by McCann, equaled the track record at Fort Erie for 8 ½ furlongs and set new track records for six furlongs at Woodbine and a mile at Detroit.

In 1960, Nearctic began stud duties at Windfields Farm, Canada. In May, Taylor was forced to retire his stakes-placed three-year-old filly Natalma who went sore in her left knee. A small bay filly, Natalma had been purchased as a yearling because of her bloodlines. She was by Native Dancer from stakes winner Almahmoud by Mahmoud. Taylor sent Natalma to Nearctic (the last mare covered in 1960) and she duly foaled a small bay colt supposedly on May 27, 1961. Offered for sale to some of Taylor's friends, the colt did not attract anyone's attention.

I recall a conversation with the late Jack Kent Cooke, owner of Elmendorf Farm, for whom I designed mare matings. He told me Taylor offered him a half-share in Natalma's yearling colt, which he graciously declined.

"Ken, it was the biggest mistake I ever made concerning the horse business," Mr. Cooke said. "I should have given the idea more thought – but understand, at the time, those Canadian-breds were way behind our best Kentucky-breds."

E. P. Taylor named the bay colt Northern Dancer and he would become a legend. Among the Windfields Farm broodmares was Victoriana, now added to the "elite" mare list. Victoriana produced seven winners including Victoria Park (the first Windfields horse specifically aimed at the Kentucky Derby), Northern Queen (Canadian Oaks), Bull Vic (Coronation Futurity, Display Stakes), and Victoria Regina (eight wins including the Princess Elizabeth Stakes, My Dear Stakes, Star Shoot Stakes. etc., and dam of Viceregal and Vice Regent).

Victoria Park ran third in the "Run for the Roses" at Churchill Downs and was second at Pimlico in the Preakness Stakes. He is best remembered as the broodmare sire of The Minstrel, winner of the English

Derby. Although unraced, Victoriana is half-sister to Canadiana, 20 wins $173,116, Canada's Horse of the Year. Victoriana is by Windfields out of Iribelle by Osiris II from Belmona by King James. When her daughter Victoria Regina was matched with Northern Dancer (who carries the strains of Tracery and St. Simon) it produced Vice Regal, Canada's Horse of the Year. Osiris (Papyrus-Most Beautiful by Great Sport) was an exceptional sire of stakes runners and a great broodmare sire in Canada. Vice Regal's brother Vice Regent sired Deputy Minister, Champion 2YO colt in the U.S. and Canada, and voted Canada's Horse of the Year. Deputy Minister is linebred to Polynesian and Bunty Lawless while his granddam's sire Jabneh is out of a mare by Beau Pere, son of Cinna.

NORTHERN DANCER'S DOMINANT MALE LINE

"There is something fascinating about science. One gets such wholesale returns of conjecture out of such a trifling investment of fact." - *Mark Twain*

Maternal strength is a primary consideration if we aim to breed Group or Graded stakes winners, but maternal strength is limited to only a small percentage of stallions and mares comprising the world's Thoroughbred population. By reinforcing brothers and sisters or very closely-related ancestors of superior ability, it is actually possible to upgrade racing class and manipulate genes, and sex-linked genes play a hidden role in the puzzle. In preceding chapters I have identified specific ancestors who upgraded speed. While a breeder must set achievable goals when designing matings for each broodmare, the selection process is critical and the cost of stallion fees a constant constraint. Of supreme importance, the breeder must select sires that are "genetically compatible" with individual mares.

Living things are specified in detail at the level of atoms and molecules, with incredible delicacy and precision. Genetic information is carried in one of two closely-related families of giant chain molecules – the nucleic acids, DNA and RNA.

The genetic language has only four letters, the components of base-pairs, namely A (adenine), T (thymine), G (guanine) and C (cytosine) which I call DNA's secret structure. To replicate DNA, RNA (the copying machine) is needed. When a gene is coded, adenine always pairs with thymine (A-T) and cytosine always pairs with guanine (G-C). Both DNA and RNA easily form a two-chain structure in which the two chains lie together, side by side, twisted around one another to form a double helix and linked together by their bases. The genetic message is conveyed by the exact base-sequence along one chain. Given this sequence, the sequence of its complementary companion can be read off, using the base-pairing rules of A with T, G with C.

The genetic information is thus recorded twice, once on each chain, useful if ever the chain is damaged since it can be repaired using the information of the other. The chains are antiparallel, i.e. sequences run up one side and down the other side. Each living cell contains a nucleus in which DNA, the blueprint of life, is stored. Outside the nucleus but within the cell are many organelles including the mitochondria with their small amount of MtDNA (mitochondrial DNA). It is from mitochondria that the cell receives energy to work the bio-machine. Mitochondrial DNA (inherited only via the direct female line) is a hundred times more prone to mutate than nuclear DNA. Mutations rarely occur, but when they do, they may be caused by molecular accidents or more likely by changes directed by mitochondrial DNA. Consider this fact – when we comment upon the pedigree of a racehorse we are really describing a total package; however, only "part" of the ancestry is inherited by an individual. That's why brothers and sisters are so different to each other.

The ancestry of a racehorse comprises a mixture of dominant, co-dominant and recessive genes inherited via the pairs of normal chromosomes (called autosomal chromosomes) and the sex chromosomes, XX for female, XY for male.

Nearctic, sire of Northern Dancer, was a brilliant racehorse inheriting most of the best genes from his parents. However, his chestnut brother, born a year earlier, inherited many weak genes from his parents – but we never hear about him.

The pedigree of a racehorse reveals the names and sex of its ancestors, but what does a pedigree really tell us unless we know something about each ancestor? We need background information about conformation, temperament, soundness and athletic performance of parents, grandparents, great grandparents, etc. Only a DNA test will tell us what "portion" of its ancestry a colt or filly really inherited. Years ago I met a man with 10 children – a nice guy, a sportsman who loved the outdoors. His wife played no sport and preferred the indoors. Here was a case of "opposites attract." Anyway, of their 10 children, six were boys and four were girls and none of the kids were alike (and no identical twins were involved). Some of the children inherited red hair and blue eyes (via the union of recessive genes), whereas the majority inherited brown hair and brown eyes (via dominant genes). Half of the children were athletic, half of them were not – yet all were from the same parents. Yes, Mother Nature is truly amazing. Nature ensures the survival of a species by building in a factor called "genetic variation," a safeguard against genetic mistakes – a safeguard for some members of a species to better adapt to ever-changing environments and be able to survive. When we design racehorse matings we hope to improve upon the existing physical, mental and athletic attributes of each parent. Even if the selection of stallion with mare seems highly suitable and compatible, we are still delving into probability factors of genetic variation. This means we may not get the desired result the first time around. A sensible mating should be repeated (as happened with Lady Angela's second match with Nearco to produce Nearctic). Knowing about genetic variation helps explain why the same matings produce good, bad and indifferent results.

There are hundreds of thousands of hidden recessive genes lurking in the genotypes of Thoroughbreds. Whilst some recessive genes are valuable, by far the majority are not. Accepting the fact a tremendous amount of genetic variation exists in the breed, I decided long ago to identify traits and remember specific characteristics handed down from generation to generation by individual stallions and mares. At my age, I can recall details about ancestors up to the seventh generation in racehorse pedigrees. Pedigree research is a never-ending task and I must admit, the more one learns, the more complex it all seems – that is, until you reach the stage where you finally begin to understand the real ancestors that supply strength and speed. Suddenly, research becomes clearer and you can understand why bad matings (using incompatible or weak sires) cause previously good families to run out of steam and decline. St. Simon was born in 1881, but from photographs and information gained from books, I gather he was one of the earliest stallions to have inherited sickle-shaped hocks. Over time, this prepotent stallion had a dynamic affect on the skeletal structure (and probably the nervous system) of the modern breed.

Not until St. Simon's progeny won major races and classics did English and Irish breeders accept St. Simon's modified shape of hocks, quite common in his colts and fillies. When did the altered shape occur? Well, nobody knows the answer to that question although it may have commenced with Voltaire who may have passed this trait on to his son Voltiguer.

However, with time to reflect, I think perhaps Glencoe's daughter Pocahontas is most probably the origin of sickle-shaped hocks in Europe. Pocahontas is the dam of King Tom, the maternal broodmare sire of St. Simon.

St. Simon (1881)	Galopin	Vedette	Voltiguer by **Voltaire**
			Mrs. Ridgeway
		Flying Duchess	The Flying Dutchman
			Merope by **Voltaire**
	Merope	King Tom	Harkaway
			Pocahontas by Glencoe
		Adeline	Ion
			Little Fairy

Pocahontas produced three influential sons – her best was Stockwell, often referred to as the "Emperor of Stallions." Stockwell's brother Rataplan was also a success at stud and their half-brother King Tom was a leading broodmare sire. Stockwell is one of the greatest sires on record. His male line via Doncaster is now the dominant sire line in the world today, thanks to Northern Dancer, Nasrullah and Royal Charger. Major male lines Stockwell firmly established are –

Doncaster-Bend Or-Bona Vista-Cyllene-Polymelus-Phalaris-Fairway-
Fair Trial - to his son Court Martial-Wilkes-Vain
to his son Petition-Petingo-Pitcairn-Ela Mana Mou
Doncaster-Bend Or-Bona Vista-Cyllene-Polymelus-Phalaris-Pharos-
Nearco- to Nasrullah (and all his many male descendants)
to Royal Charger-Turn-To-Hail To Reason (to Halo and Roberto)
to Nearctic (to Northern Dancer and Icecapade)
to Dante-Darius II-Derring Do-Dominion-Primo Dominie
Doncaster-Bend Or-Ormonde-Orme-Flying Fox-Ajax-Teddy-
to Sun Teddy-Sun Again-Sunglow-Sword Dancer-Damascus
to Deiri-Deux Pour Cent-Tantieme
Doncaster-Bend Or-Bona Vista-Cyllene-Polymelus-Phalaris-Sickle-
Unbreakable-Polynesian-Native Dancer
Doncaster-Bend Or-Bona Vista-Cyllene-Polymelus-Phalaris-Pharamond II-
Menow-Tom Fool-Buckpasser (to Egg Toss, Silver Buck)

At the present time, Nearco's male line via his sons Nasrullah and Nearctic (sire of Northern Dancer) dominate modern pedigrees. But if history is to be repeated, a different male line will eventually rise to power – a sire line that is genetically compatible with mares inbred or linebred many times to Nasrullah, Nearctic and Northern Dancer whose genotypes are being saturated everywhere.

Native Dancer's male line through Mr. Prospector is quite successful when crossed with strains of Northern Dancer and Nasrullah, but it, too, is from the same source, i.e. Doncaster by Stockwell. Teddy's male line which was so prominent after 1930 through the deeds of Sir Gallahad III and his brother Bull Dog, is instead represented today by Sun Teddy-Sun-Again-Sword Dancer-Damascus and his male descendants, or via Aethelstan-Deiri-Deux Pour Cent-Tantieme to his sons Tanerko and Reliance or via Deiri-Bay-Beigler Boy-Matun-Mat Boy-Festin.

What about other sire lines? If sire lines rise and fall (the wave effect) as shown by the history of sire lines, then one or two different male lines should soon begin to shine. Among the possibilities are the following alternatives:

Touchstone-Newminster-Lord Clifden-Hampton-Bay Ronald-Bayardo-
Gainsborough-Hyperion-
to his sons ... Khaled-Swaps-No Robbery
Aristophanes-Forli-
to Formidable
to Thatch-Thatching-Puissance-Mind Games
Aureole-Vienna-Vaguely Noble
Owen Tudor- to Abernant
to Tudor Minstrel-Will Somers-Balidar
Stardust-Star Kingdom
to Noholme II-Nodouble
to Biscay-Bletchingly
-Marscay

Touchstone-Newminster-Lord Clifden-Hampton-Bay Ronald-Dark Ronald-
Son in Law-Bosworth-Plassy-Vandale II-Herbager
to Grey Dawn II
to Big Spruce

Touchstone-Newminster-Lord Clifden-Hampton-Bay Ronald-Dark Ronald
-Herold-Alchimist-Birkhahn-Literat-Surumu-Acatenango-Lando
Flying Dutchman-Dollar-Androcles-Cambyses-Gardefeu-Chouberski-
Bruleur-Ksar-Tourbillon-Djebel-Clarion III-Klairon-Lorenzaccio-
Ahonoora-Indian Ridge

Blacklock-Voltaire-Voltiguer-Galopin-St. Simon-Chaucer-Prince Chimay-
Vatout-Bois Roussel-Migoli-Gallant Man-Gallant Romeo-Elocutionist

Blacklock-Voltaire-Voltiguer-Galopin-St. Simon-Persimmon-
Prince Palatine-Rose Prince-Prince Rose-Princequillo
to his son Round Table-
to Apalachee-Indian Trail
Flirting Around-Wolf Power
Illustrious
Knightly Manner-Stonewalk
to his son Prince John
to Speak John-
Hold Your Peace
John Alden
Thunder Puddles
Verbatim
to Stage Door Johnny-Southern Sultan
to Transworld-Zie World

Blacklock-Voltaire-Voltiguer-Galopin-St. Simon-Persimmon-Prince Palatine-
Rose Prince-Prince Rose-Prince Bio-
to his son Prince Taj-Petrone-Silveyville
to his son Sicambre-Roi Dagobert-On The Sly-Playfellow

Blacklock-Voltaire-Voltiguer-Galopin-St. Simon-Rabelais-Havresac II-
Cavaliere d'Arpino-Bellini-Tenerani-Ribot-
to his son Tom Rolfe-Hoist The Flag-Alleged-Shantou
to his son Graustark-Key to the Mint-Java Gold
to his son His Majesty
to Pleasant Colony
Pleasant Tap
Behrens
Pleasantly Perfect
to Cormorant-Go For Gin-Albert The Great

Isonomy-Isinglass-John O' Gaunt-Swynford-
to his son St. Germans-The Rhymer-Vertex-Vertee
to his son Blandford-
Blenheim to his sons-
Mahmoud-
to Cohoes-Quadrangle-Quadratic
to The Axe II-
to Al Hattab
to Hatchet Man
Donatello II-Crepello-Busted-Bustino-Labus-Akarad
Bahram to his son Persian Gulf (thence to the male line of Konigsstuhl in Germany)

Melbourne-West Australian-Australian-Spendthrift-Hastings-Fair Play-
Man o' War-War Relic-
to his son Relic-Olden Times-Full Pocket
to his son Intent-Intentionally-
to In Reality
to Judge Smells
to Known Fact-Warning
to Relaunch-Skywalker-Bertrando-Officer
to Valid Appeal

Melbourne-West Australian-Solon-Barcaldine-Marco-Marcovil-Hurry On-Precipitation-
Sheshoon-Sassafras-Saros

Touchstone-Orlando-Eclipse-Alarm-Himyar-Domino-Commando-Colin-Neddie-Good
Goods-Alsab-Armageddon-Battle Joined-Ack Ack-Broad Brush (to his sons)

Touchstone-Orlando-Eclipse-Alarm-Himyar-Plaudit-King James-Spur-Sting-Questionnaire-
Free For All-Rough'n Tumble-Minnesota Mac-Great Above-Holy Bull-Macho Uno

Certainly the American male line of champion Man o' War is making some progress, especially via his male descendant In Reality. Could this be the male line to flourish, or might it stem from Germany, Australia or South America?

WAR CHANT (Danzig - Hollywood Wildcat by Kris S.), winner of the Breeders' Cup Mile Gr-1. His dam was U.S. Champion 3YO filly.

NORTHERN DANCER, a great sire of sires. His sons include Sadler's Wells, Nureyev, Danzig, Nijinsky II, Northern Taste and The Minstrel.

Northern Dancer's male line has captured a sensational share of market! In Europe, nearly three out of every four commercial stallions belong to his sire line.

There are too many to mention in this chapter, but I would like to highlight Northern Dancer's most popular sons, my top 20 list:

1. Sadler's Wells (Northern Dancer-Fairy Bridge by Bold Reason)
2. Nureyev (Northern Dancer-Special by Forli)
3. Danzig (Northern Dancer-Pas de Nom by Admiral's Voyage)
4. Nijinsky II (Northern Dancer-Flaming Page by Bull Page)
5. Storm Bird (Northern Dancer-South Ocean by New Providence)
6. Northern Taste (Northern Dancer-Lady Victoria by Victoria Park)
7. Vice Regal (Northern Dancer-Victoria Regina by Menetrier)
8. Lyphard (Northern Dancer-Goofed by Court Martial)
9. Unfuwain (Northern Dancer-Height of Fashion by Bustino)
10. Fairy King (Northern Dancer-Fairy Bridge by Bold Reason)
11. Dixieland Band (Northern Dancer-Mississippi Mud by Delta Judge)
12. Night Shift (Northern Dancer-Ciboulette by Chop Chop)
13. Northfields (Northern Dancer-Little Hut by Occupy)
14. Shareef Dancer (Northern Dancer-Sweet Alliance by Sir Ivor)
15. Try My Best (Northern Dancer-Sex Appeal by Buckpasser
16. El Gran Senor (Northern Dancer-Sex Appeal by Buckpasser)
17. The Minstrel (Northern Dancer-Fleur by Victoria Park)
18. Be My Guest (Northern Dancer-What A Treat by Tudor Minstrel)
19. Fabulous Dancer (Northern Dancer-Last of the Line by The Axe II)
20. Ajdal (Northern Dancer-Native Partner by Raise A Native)

Many of the best-performed sons of Northern Dancer carried French champion Teddy (Ajax-Rondeau by Bay Ronald) in their dam's pedigree. Storm Bird and Nijinsky II are similarly bred as their dams have in common the ancestors Bull Page with one of the brothers Omaha or Flares. Sadler's Wells, Fairy King and Nureyev have Lady Juror featured in their dams, as does Lyphard and Be My Guest.

Inbreeding up close to Northern Dancer has been partially successful, particularly if it is supported by another source of Almahmoud (granddam of Northern Dancer), Nasrullah or Mahmoud, but I much prefer to linebreed to Northern Dancer using his best sons and daughters. The reader should be made aware of the similarities between Northern Dancer and Nasrullah.

Northern Dancer	Nearctic	Nearco by Pharos
		Lady Angela by Hyperion
	Natalma	Native Dancer by Polynesian
		Almahmoud by Mahmoud by Blenheim

Note: Mahmoud is by Blenheim from Mah Mahal by Gainsborough - Mumtaz Mahal.

Nasrullah	Nearco	Pharos by Phalaris
		Nogara by Havresac II
	Mumtaz Begum	Blenheim
		Mumtaz Mahal

When these strains meet up with each other they reinforce the same Nearco-Blenheim-Mumtaz Mahal mix which includes the Sainfoin/Sierra combination.

Two of the most successful sires in England were Nearco and Hyperion. Breeders sent daughters of Hyperion to Nearco and vice versa thinking the cross would be a match in heaven, but the results proved disappointing even though unbeaten St. Simon was duplicated. No English classic winner was ever bred on this cross. However, the Hyperion/Pharos cross did work for Owen Tudor (Hyperion out of Mary Tudor II by Pharos), winner of the English Derby in 1941.

The most successful representative of the Nearco/Hyperion cross is Nearctic, and the bottom quarter of Nearctic's pedigree gives a clue as to why it was successful when others failed. Nearctic is out of Lady Angela by Hyperion from Sister Sarah by Abbot's Trace (son of Tracery) from Sarita by Swynford.

Sister Sarah possessed maternal strength from Tracery's dam Topiary, and from Swynford's dam Canterbury Pilgrim. Lord Derby, owner-breeder of Hyperion, repeatedly duplicated Canterbury Pilgrim and her dam Pilgrimage and bred classic winners using this technique. Tracery's dam Topiary is by Orme (son of Angelica, the sister to St. Simon) from Plaisanterie by Wellingtonia. Perhaps here lies the key.

Although Orme and his dam Angelica gave the pedigree pattern upgraded speed, a further boost was inherited from Wellingtonia, a great broodmare sire inbred to two "daughters" of the elite mare Pocahontas, by Glencoe. Pocahontas' "sons" are Stockwell, Rataplan and King Tom, the latter being broodmare sire of St. Simon. Nearctic inherited sickle-shaped hocks and transmitted this trait to his son Northern Dancer who passed it on to many of his sons.

Danzig, a fast sprinter, unsound in his near knee, never won a stakes race. By Northern Dancer from Pas de Nom, he only started three times and won them all. At two, Danzig won a Maiden Special at Belmont Park over 6 ½ furlongs in 1:03 3/5 by 8 ½ lengths. The time was only 3/5ths second off the track record. At three, he won an allowance race at Belmont Park going seven furlongs in 1:22 flat by 5 ½ lengths and another allowance race at Aqueduct over six furlongs in 1:09 2/5 by 7 ½ lengths. Retired to Claiborne Farm, Danzig surprised everyone with quality speed runners. He is one of the leading sires by Average Earnings Index, sire of 109 stakes winners and 21 champions.

Among Danzig's progeny are Danehill, Chief's Crown, Anabaa, Yamanin Paradise, Polish Precedent, War Chant, Danzig Connection, Lure, Green Desert, Century City, Belong To Me, Elnadim, Langfuhr, Golden Snake, Maroof, Polonia, Chimes at Midnight, Dispute, Brahms and Pas de Response.

Chief's Crown sired Grand Lodge, sire of champion Sinndar (English Derby).

Danehill is the sire of Redoute's Choice (Caulfield Guineas), Elvstroem (VRC. Derby, Caulfield Cup, Dubai Duty Free Stakes), Flying Spur (Golden Slipper Stakes), Danewin (Rosehill Guineas, Spring Champion Stakes), Exceed and Excel (VRC Newmarket Handicap), Dane Ripper (W. S. Cox Plate), the fillies Merlene and Ha Ha (winners of the Golden Slipper Stakes) and Danzero (Golden Slipper Stakes).

Green Desert is the sire of champion Oasis Dream, Invincible Spirit, Desert Prince, Cape Cross, Sheikh Albadou, Heat Haze and Owington.

The pedigree of Redoute's Choice shows the genetic compatibility of Danzig's strain with that of Nijinsky II. This cross (involving duplication of Northern Dancer) reinforces the brothers Sir Gallahad III and Bull Dog, sons of the elite mare Plucky Liege by Spearmint. Furthermore, it brings in Hyperion's line again via his grandson Star Kingdom (leading sire in Australia). Star Kingdom was second best two-year-old colt (to Abernant) in England when he raced under the name Star King.

Star Kingdom's line is genetically compatible with Northern Dancer's strain and the Hyperion link with Tracery (dam by Orme) should be noted. Here is his pedigree:

Star Kingdom (1946)	Stardust	Hyperion	Gainsborough	Bayardo
				Rosedrop
			Selene	Chaucer (**Canterbury Pilgrim**)
				Serenissima
		Sister Stella	Friar Marcus	Cicero
				Prim Nun
			Etoile	**Sunstar** by **Sundridge** (**Sierra**)
				Princess de Galles
	Impromptu	Concerto	Orpheus	Orby by **Orme**
				Electra
			Constellation	**Sunstar** by **Sundridge** (**Sierra**)
				Stop Her
		Thoughtless	Papyrus	Tracery by Rock Sand by **Sainfoin**
				Miss Matty by Marcovil
			Virgin's Folly	Swynford (**Canterbury Pilgrim**)
				Widow Bird (to **Canterbury Pilgrim**)

The female line of Star Kingdom traces back to Oaks winner Canterbury Pilgrim as follows: Widow Bird by White Eagle from Entebbe by Bridge of Canny - St. Victorine by St. Serf from Canterbury Pilgrim. St. Victorine is actually a three-quarter sister to Chaucer.

Star Kingdom sired many great sons including Star of Heaven, Columbia Star, Sky High, Skyline, Star Affair, etc. but his strongest speed line is via his son Biscay whose dam carries reinforcement of similar superior strains. Here is the pedigree of Biscay's dam Magic Symbol – her sire Makarpura is linebred to Orby, by Orme.

Magic Symbol (Aust) (1956)	Makarpura	Big Game	Bahram	Blandford by **Swynford** (**Cb'y Pilgrim**)
				Friar's Daughter by **Friar Marcus**
			Myrobella	Tetratema by The Tetrarch
				Dolabella by White Eagle
		Cap d'Or	Gold Bridge	Golden Boss, grandson of **Orby**
				Flying Diadem by son of **Orby**
			Lady Madcap	Solario - dam by **Sundridge** (**Sierra**)
				Hasty Sister by Hurry On (to **Sainfoin**)
	Magic Wonder	Newtown Wonder	Fair Trial	Fairway by Phalaris (dam by **Sainfoin**)
				Lady Juror - dam by **Sundridge** (**Sierra**)
			Clarapple	Apple Sammy
				Racla
		Conveyor	Pylon II	Pharos by Phalaris (dam by **Sainfoin**)
				Pyramid by **Papyrus** by **Tracery**
			Baringo	Flamingo by Flamboyant by **Tracery**
				Middle East

Apart from the brother and sister combination of Sainfoin and Sierra, the triple of Tracery in Biscay's pedigree must have provided him with maternal strength. Speed was inherited from Orme and his son Orby. Orme is of course out of a sister to St. Simon. Tracery's dam Topiary is a "daughter" of Orme.

Biscay sired two outstanding sire sons, Bletchingly and Marscay. It is a great pity Europeans failed to import Group-winning sons of either of these sires from Australia where speed lines are world-class. The new "hot" sire in Australia is Redoute's Choice by Danehill from Shantha's Choice by Canny Lad, from the new "elite" mare Dancing Show by Nijinsky II. Redoute's Choice won five of 10 starts for A$1,567,850 including the valuable Blue Diamond Stakes, C.F. Orr Stakes and Caulfield Guineas, all Group 1 races.

Canny Lad was Australia's Champion 2YO colt, earner of A$2,096,050 and winner of the Golden Slipper Stakes and VRC Sires' Produce Stakes. Canny Lad is a son of Bletchingly by Biscay. Redoute's Choice was voted Champion 3YO Miler and has commenced his stud career at Arrowfield Stud in great style. He stands 16.2 hands high and puts plenty of substance into his stock. His father Danehill sired 26 Graded stakes winners in 2004, two more than Japan's leading sire Sunday Silence.

Another successful son of Danehill is Danzero, winner of the Golden Slipper Stakes, Blue Diamond Prelude and sire of Australia's Champion 2YO colt of 2003-2004 Dance Hero, earner of over A$3 million. Danzero is out of Confidentially by Kaoru Star, a son of Star Kingdom.

Sadler's Wells, Champion Miler and winner of the Irish 2,000 Guineas and Eclipse Stakes never ever shuttled from Ireland. He led the General Sires' List 14 times during the period 1992 to 2004 and is a phenomenal sire of Group winners. A medium-sized horse with an athletic frame, he gets down on his front pasterns suggesting he would perform best on soft ground. His male progeny include Montjeu, El Prado, Galileo, High Chaparral, Barathea, Fort Wood, Carnegie, In The Wings, Scenic, Cloudings, Dolpour, Kayf Tara, Runyon and Sonus.

El Prado led the North American Sires' List and his progeny handle both dirt and turf. He stands at Adena Springs Farm in Kentucky and at time of writing his progeny have earned $45 million. El Prado is the sire of Medaglio D'Oro ($4.2 million), Kitten's Joy ($1.7 million), Senor Swinger, Mi Pradera, Quimera, and Nite Dreamer. Of interest, El Prado's dam, Lady Capulet, is inbred 4 x 3 to Mahmoud, 4 x 4 to Pharamond II and possesses a double of elite mare Alcibiades.

Storm Cat (Storm Bird-Terlingua by Secretariat) was North America's leading sire of two-year-olds for the seventh time in 2004. His progeny so far have earned $91 million. Storm Cat was leading sire in North America in 1999 and 2000 and stands at a fee of $500,000 live foal. Bred by William T. Young, Storm Cat won the Young America Stakes, World Appeal Stakes and two other races and was second to Tasso, beaten a nose in the Breeders' Cup Juvenile Stakes. His progeny include Giant's Causeway, Hennessy, Storm Flag Flying, Cat Thief, High Yield, Forest Wildcat, Forestry, Tabasco Cat, November Snow, Denebola, Black Minnaloushe, Aljabr, Catrail, Munaaji, Silken Cat, Tale of the Cat and Sweet Catomine.

Nureyev was Champion Miler in France and is the sire of 137 stakes winners including Miesque, Polar Falcon, Sonic Lady, Zilzal, Reams of Verse, Flagbird, Mehthaaf, Spinning World, Peintre Celebre, Soviet Star, Fasliyev, Vilikaia, Great Commotion, Diableneyev, Stravinsky and Theatrical.

Northern Dancer became a legend.

DESIGNING SPEED IN THE RACEHORSE

"There was a young lady named Bright,
Whose speed was far faster than light;
She set out one day in a relative way,
And returned home the previous night."
- Arthur Henry Reginald Buller

Reflecting on the methods and techniques used by great racehorse breeders such as Lord Derby, Marcel Boussac, the old Aga Khan, Lord Dewar, William Hall-Walker, Jack Joel, Lord Astor, Federico Tesio, Colonel Edward R. Bradley, William Woodward, Arthur "Bull" Hancock, Cornelius V. Whitney, the Phipps family and Edward P. Taylor, they all chose to blend speed with stamina. Breeders who concentrated on putting speed to speed (short-course sprinting strains) left nothing of lasting consequence. Conversely, breeders who concentrated solely on matching stamina with stamina are rarely remembered.

A racehorse destined for the three-year-old classics, the Breeders' Cup, the Prix de l'Arc de Triomphe or prestige races over a mile like the Metropolitan Handicap and Sussex Stakes, requires a blend of fast and slow fiber muscle as well as all those other things necessary for a sound, superior athlete. The proportion between fast and slow fiber muscle and the amount of energy available for use will determine how far the athlete will carry its speed. In England, the majority of mares owned by Lord Derby (the 17th Earl of Derby) were bred on stout lines for he wanted to win the Oaks and Derby. His trainer and pedigree advisor urged him to either breed to sires that transmitted speed, or purchase new mares from sprinting families. Lord Derby eventually rectified the balance of speed and stamina in his homebred colts and fillies. First, he purchased the mare Bromus, bred on sprinting lines and mated her with the proven stayer Polymelus.

The result was Phalaris, a fast sprinter who would supply plenty of fast fiber muscle to future foal crops. Using Phalaris, Lord Derby bred Fairway, Pharos, Fair Isle, Sickle, Pharamond II and Colorado. Using the "outside" stallion Gainsborough, a Triple Crown winner, he bred champion Hyperion.

Admittedly, Lord Derby designed some very clever matings, repeatedly reinforcing unbeaten St. Simon. He achieved tremendous success and became leading owner-breeder in England by designing matings using sons of Phalaris and experimenting with inbreeding to classic-winning mare Pilgrimage and her Oaks-winning daughter Canterbury Pilgrim. However, the apple of Lord Derby's eye was his champion colt Fairway (Phalaris-Scapa Flow by Chaucer), a highly-strung horse that covered some of the best mares in the British Isles. Fairway won 12 of 15 starts. As a juvenile he won the Coventry Stakes, July Stakes and Doncaster Champagne Stakes while at three, he won the Eclipse Stakes, Newmarket Stakes, St. Leger and Champion Stakes. (He ran a "shocker" when unplaced to Felstead in the English Derby.) At four, his wins include the Jockey Club Cup and the Champion Stakes again. Fairway was expected to transmit a fair amount of speed to his progeny, and although he led the General Sires' List four times, he was more renowned for stamina.

His influence survives mainly via his sons Fair Trial (in England), Fair Copy (in France) and Full Sail (in South America). Any high expectations for other sons of Fairway, namely Blue Peter, Airway and Watling Street, never quite came to fruition. Gradually their lines diminished over time.

On the other hand, Fairway's brother Pharos became a "genetic giant" among sires and proved his worth as an influential broodmare sire. In retrospect, Pharos imparted a higher percent of fast twitch muscle fiber to his progeny than did Fairway. Descendants of Pharos would make their mark on the three-year-old classics in every major Thoroughbred breeding region of the globe. Let's now look at the pedigree of Pharos, who was a more compact physical type than Fairway (although both had imperfect knees). Federico Tesio used Pharos to boost speed with his Italian classic-winning filly Nogara whose granddam Sibola won the English 1,000 Guineas and was runner-up to Musa in the Oaks. Note: Orme is out of Angelica, sister to St. Simon.

Nearco (1935)	Pharos	Phalaris	Polymelus	Cyllene
				Bona Vista
				Arcadia
			Maid Marian	Hampton
				Quiver
		Bromus	Sainfoin	**Springfield**
				Sanda
			Cheery	**St. Simon**
				Sunrise by **Springfield**
		Scapa Flow	Chaucer	**St. Simon**
				Galopin
				St. Angela
			Canterbury Pilgrim	Tristan by **Hermit**
				Pilgrimage
			Anchora	Love Wisely
				Wisdom
				Lovelorn
			Eryholme	Hazlehatch by **Hermit**
				Ayrsmoss
	Nogara	Havresac II	Rabelais	**St. Simon**
				Galopin
				St. Angela
			Satirical	Satiety
				Chaff
			Hors Concours	Ajax
				Flying Fox by Orme
				Amie
			Simona	**St. Simon**
				Flying Footstep
		Catnip	Spearmint	Carbine
				Musket
				Mersey
			Maid of the Mint	Minting
				Warble
			Sibola	The Sailor Prince
				Albert Victor
				Hermita
			Saluda	Mortemer
				Perfection

Readers should take notice of the way St. Simon was duplicated. In the pedigree of Pharos, we find a son (Chaucer) and a daughter (Cheery) while in Havresac's make-up we find a son (Rabelais) and a daughter (Simona) as well as St. Simon's full sister Angelica, dam of Orme.

Other ancestors hyping up the electrical system are Sainfoin, Canterbury Pilgrim, unbeaten French champion Ajax and English Derby winner Spearmint. Bromus (dam of Phalaris) carried intense inbreeding to Springfield, one of the fastest horses of his era in England.

Nearco carried his speed up to the 15 furlongs distance of the Gran Premio di Milano as well as at Longchamp in the valuable Grand Prix de Paris – the latter victory being a remarkable piece of training on Tesio's part because Nearco was essentially a middle distance runner, not a true stayer. In a previous chapter I already mentioned Nasrullah and Royal Charger, the two sons of Nearco with the Sainfoin/Sierra mix for speed, as well as Nearco's son Nearctic, the father of Northern Dancer, but as yet we have not studied the pedigree of North America's Horse of the Year, champion Native Dancer.

Native Dancer is a primary source of superior speed – early maturing superior speed. He was an attractive gray horse with a slightly upright shoulder angle and was bred and raced by Alfred G. Vanderbilt. Native Dancer traced back to imported mare La Grisette, a daughter of French stayer Roi Herode who sired unbeaten champion The Tetrarch. When La Grisette was mated with the brilliant horse Sweep (Ben Brush - Pink Domino by Domino) it produced a filly named La Chica.

La Chica was unraced but she produced seven winners from eight foals, among them Miyako (by John P. Grier) and Planetoid (by the short-course sprint specialist Ariel). Whereas Planetoid would produce Grey Flight and a wonderful stakes-winning branch of the family, Miyako would produce Geisha, the dam of champion Native Dancer. Miyako only produced three foals after five wins as a juvenile. She inherited early maturing speed, won the Autumn Day Stakes and was runner-up in the Adirondack Handicap and Fashion Stakes.

Miyako's daughter Geisha was by the tough handicapper Discovery, a horse that supplied stamina. Despite the merit of putting speed mare Miyako to a stayer like Discovery, it did not result in a stakes runner. Geisha had limited ability, winning one race as a three-year-old, and we can assume whatever valuable genes she inherited from her parents were latent, waiting patiently to be exploited with the right mating.

The most influential speed ancestor in Native Dancer's pedigree is without doubt champion sprinter Polynesian (27 wins $310,410, 1st Preakness Stakes, Withers Stakes, Toboggan Handicap, Oceanport Handicap etc) who is linebred twice to Sainfoin and twice to his sister Sierra, with a double of the stayer Polymelus.

Polynesian never received the opportunities he truly deserved when he retired to Gallagher Farm, Lexington, Kentucky. Most mares that visited him were from average families. Nevertheless, he sired brilliant progeny, among them Native Dancer, Imbros (15 wins $340,550, set a new world record for seven furlongs in 1:20 $\frac{3}{5}$ in the Malibu Sequet Stakes, set a new track record for 1 $\frac{1}{8}$ miles in the William P. Kyne Handicap, equaled the world record for 1 $\frac{1}{16}$ miles in the Californian Stakes, Saranac Handicap, Withers Stakes and equaled the track records at Hollywood Park and Santa Anita for six furlongs in 1:09 flat), Barbizon (seven wins, Champion 2YO colt, Garden State Stakes), Alanesian (five wins, Champion 2YO filly, Spinaway Stakes, Astarita Stakes), the brilliant Poly Hi (nine wins at two, 1st Astoria Stakes, Colleen Stakes, Fashion Stakes, Rosedale Stakes), Tahitian King (United States Hotel Stakes, National Stallion Stakes, 2nd to Native Dancer in the Futurity Stakes), Polly's Jet, Banquet Bell and Bureaucracy (Dwyer Stakes, National Stallion Stakes, 2nd Travers Stakes).

Native Dancer won 21 of 22 starts for $735,240 and was voted champion of his division every year he raced. He equaled the world record for 6 ½ furlongs when he crossed the wire first in the Futurity Stakes, and won all nine juvenile starts. At three, he won the Preakness Stakes, Belmont Stakes, American Derby, Arlington Classic, Gotham Stakes, Wood Memorial Stakes, Travers Stakes, Withers Stakes, Dwyer Stakes and was narrowly defeated in the Kentucky Derby. At four, he won three times including the Metropolitan Handicap with topweight. (It is worth mentioning that at the end of his juvenile career, Native Dancer's front ankles were pin-fired.) He was retired to his owner's Sagamore Farm, Glyndon, Maryland.

Native Dancer is the sire of Raise A Native (Champion 2YO colt, undefeated, 1st Great American Stakes in new track record time, Juvenile Stakes equaling his own track record set earlier, and an Aqueduct 2YO Handicap over 5 ½ furlongs in new track record time by eight lengths), Kauai King (nine wins $381,397, Kentucky Derby, Preakness Stakes, Governor's Gold Cup), Native Street (10 wins $236,808, won Kentucky Oaks, Interborough Handicap, Sorority Stakes, Astoria Stakes), Native Charger (five wins $278,893, Florida Derby, Flamingo Stakes, Tyro Stakes), Hula Dancer (Champion 2YO in France, French 1,000 Guineas, Prix du Moulin de Longchamp, Prix Jacques Le Marois), Dan Cupid (sire of champion Sea Bird II), Silver Cloud (Champion 2YO filly in France, Grand Criterium) and Native Prince (five wins, Juvenile Stakes, Great American Stakes).

Raise A Native broke down after his juvenile career, was retired to Spendthrift Farm, Lexington, and was syndicated by Leslie Combs II. A chestnut horse built like a Quarter horse with massive forearm development, Raise A Native sired sound and unsound progeny – it all depended on luck – i.e. genetic probability being kind or cruel. His best performers on the racetrack were Mr. Prospector, Exclusive Native, Majestic Prince, Raise A Cup, American Native, Native Royalty, Crowned Prince, Raise Your Glass, Princely Native and Laomedonte.

Mr. Prospector and Raise A Cup were fleet-footed sprinters out of daughters of the very sound champion Nashua (by Nasrullah). Mr. Prospector comes from the family of Myrtlewood, a filly who once held the world record for six furlongs. An athletic bodied horse with mild rotation on the axis of his near fore cannon bone, Mr. Prospector is in my opinion one of the greatest sires in North American history. He was prepotent for speed that was sustained over a middle distance.

The leading sire in North America in 1987 and 1988, he was among the leading sires 15 times and was leading broodmare sire seven consecutive years, 1997 to 2003. Bred by Leslie Combs II, Mr. Prospector was sold as a yearling in the Spendthrift draft and won seven of 14 starts for $112,171. He never ran as a juvenile. At three, he set a new track record at Gulfstream Park going six furlongs in 1:07.8 and was second in the Derby Trial Stakes at Churchill Downs. At four, he won the Gravesend Handicap at Belmont Park, the Whirlaway Handicap at Garden State Park in new track record time of 1:08.6 for six furlongs, and finished 2nd Carter Handicap, Firecracker Handicap, Royal Poinciana Handicap and 3rd Paumonok Handicap. Mr. Prospector had intelligent eyes and was a masculine horse with a placid temperament. Structurally, he had almost perfect knees although he toed out in his left front foot.

Originally retired to stud in sunny Florida, Mr. Prospector was transferred to Claiborne Farm in Paris, Kentucky, where better quality mares were made available to him. He sired 25 crops, 1,195 foals of racing age, 16 champions, 182 stakes winners of which 110 were Graded black type winners, plus 11 stakes-placed runners.

Mr. Prospector (Raise A Native-Gold Digger by Nashua) sired 752 winners (63 percent winners to foals of racing age) and his progeny earned a whopping $97,517,390. His lifetime average earnings index was 3.95. These are impressive statistics for a stallion with a strictly limited book of mares to cover each year. Here is a list of some of his best progeny:

Gulch (colt ex Jameela by Rambunctious) U.S. Champion Sprinter, $3,095,521 13 wins, 1st Breeders' Cup Sprint, Metropolitan Handicap twice, Carter Handicap, Futurity Stakes, Wood Memorial Invitational Stakes, Hopeful Stakes etc.

Forty Niner (colt ex File by Tom Rolfe) U.S. Champion 2YO colt, $2,726,000 11 wins, 1st Futurity Stakes, Champagne Stakes, Travers Stakes, Fountain of Youth Stakes, Haskell Invitational Stakes, Breeders' Futurity, Sanford Stakes, 2nd Kentucky Derby, 3rd Breeders' Cup Classic etc.

Aldebaran (colt ex Chimes of Freedom by Private Account) U.S. Champion Sprinter, $1,682,926, 1st Metropolitan Handicap, Forego Handicap, San Carlos Handicap, Churchill Downs Handicap, Tom Fool Handicap etc.

Dancethruthedawn (filly ex Dance Smartly by Danzig) Champion 3YO filly of Canada, five wins $1,609,643, 1st Queen's Plate, Woodbine Oaks, Go For Wand Stakes, Doubledogdare Stakes, Princess Elizabeth Stakes etc.

Rhythm (colt ex Dance Number by Northern Dancer) U.S. Champion 2YO colt, six wins $1,592,532, 1st Breeders' Cup Juvenile Stakes, Travers Stakes, Colin Stakes, 2nd Champagne Stakes, Dwyer Stakes etc.

Afleet (colt ex Polite Lady by Venetian Jester) Horse of the Year in Canada, Champion 3YO colt of Canada, seven wins $995,235, 1st Jerome Handicap, Pennsylvania Derby, Plate Trial Stakes, Friar Rock Stakes, Queenston Stakes, 2nd Metropolitan Handicap, Carter Handicap, Queen's Plate, 3rd Breeder's Cup Sprint etc.

Golden Attraction (filly ex Seaside Attraction by Seattle Slew) U.S. Champion 2YO filly, six wins $911,508 1st Frizette Stakes, Spinaway Stakes, Matron Stakes, Schuylerville Stakes, Turfway Breeders' Cup Stakes, Debutante Stakes, 2nd Sorority Stakes, 3rd Breeders' Cup Juvenile Stakes etc.

Ravinella (filly ex Really Lucky by Northern Dancer) Champion 2YO in England and France, Champion 3YO filly in France, eight wins $893,230, 1st Cheveley Park Stakes, English 1,000 Guineas, French 1,000 Guineas, Prix d'Arenberg, Prix Imprudence, and in North America, 1st All Along Stakes, Hialeah Budweiser Breeders' Cup Handicap etc.

It's In The Air (filly ex A Wind Is Rising by Francis S.) U.S. Champion 2YO filly, 16 wins $892,339, 1st Vanity Handicap twice, Alabama Stakes, Ruffian Handicap, Oak Leaf Stakes, Arlington-Washington Lassie Stakes, Delaware Oaks, El Encino Stakes etc.

POLYNESIAN in the winner's circle after a brilliant victory in the Preakness Stakes.

MR. PROSPECTOR (Raise A Native - Gold Digger by Nashua), leading sire and broodmare sire whose sons include Miswaki, Seeking The Gold, Machiavellian, Fusaichi Pegasus, Gulch, Woodman and Aldebaran.

Eillo (colt ex Barbs Dancer by Northern Dancer) U.S. Champion Sprinter, 12 wins $657,670, 1st Breeders' Cup Sprint, Hialeah Sprint Championship Handicap, Tallahassee Handicap, Kendall Stakes etc.

Queena (filly ex Too Chic by Blushing Groom) U. S. Champion Older Mare, 10 wins $565,024, 1st Maskette Stakes, Ruffian Handicap, Ballerina Stakes, First Flight Handicap, Vagrancy Handicap etc.

Conquistador Cielo (colt ex K D Princess by Bold Commander) U.S. Horse of the Year, U.S. Champion 3YO colt, nine wins $474,328 1st Belmont Stakes, Metropolitan Handicap, Dwyer Stakes, Jim Dandy Stakes, etc.

Tersa (filly ex Konafa by Damascus) Champion 3YO filly in Italy, five wins $81,223, 1st Premio Umbria, Prix de Seine-et-Oise, Prix de Voulogne etc.

Woodman (colt ex Playmate by Buckpasser) Champion 2YO colt in Ireland, 1st Anglesey Stakes, Curragh Futurity Stakes, 3rd Mill Ridge Stakes etc.

Coup de Genie (filly ex Coup de Folie by Halo) Champion 2YO filly in France, four wins $402,372, 1st Prix Morny Agence Francaise, Prix de la Salamandre, Prix de Cabourg, Prix Imprudence, 3rd English 1,000 Guineas etc.

Machiavellian (colt ex Coup de Folie by Halo) Champion 2YO colt in France, four wins $355,790 1st Prix Morny Agence Francaise, Prix de la Salamandre, Prix Djebel, Prix Yacowlef.

Distant View (colt ex Seven Springs by Irish River) Champion 3YO Miler in England, two wins $238,374, 1st Sussex Stakes, 2nd St. James' Palace Stakes.

Fusaichi Pegasus (colt ex Angel Fever by Danzig) six wins $1,994,400, 1st Kentucky Derby, Wood Memorial Stakes, San Felipe Stakes, Jerome Handicap, 2nd Preakness Stakes etc.

Kingmambo (colt ex Miesque by Nureyev) five wins $734,804, 1st French 2,000 Guineas, St. James' Palace Stakes, Prix du Moulin de Longchamp, etc.

Seeking The Gold (colt ex Con Game by Buckpasser) eight wins $2,307,000, 1st Super Derby, Dwyer Stakes, Peter Pan Stakes, Swale Stakes, 2nd Breeders' Cup Classic, Travers Stakes, Metropolitan Handicap etc.

Plus ... Gold Beauty (U.S. Champion Sprinter), Faltaat (Champion Older Male UAE), Proskona (Champion 3YO filly in Italy), Gone West (Gotham Stakes), Miswaki (Prix de la Salamandre) and Fappiano (Metropolitan Handicap).

Mixing the strains of Mr. Prospector with Northern Dancer is a very successful strategy. It worked to produce Fusaichi Pegasus, the son of Mr. Prospector who won the Kentucky Derby in 2000. Bred by Arthur B. Hancock III in partnership with Stonerside Farm, Fusaichi Pegasus won six of nine starts for $1,994,400 and was trained on the West Coast by Neil Drysdale. He stands at Coolmore-Ashford Stud and has commenced his stud career by siring Roman Ruler (1st Del Mar Futurity, Best Pal Stakes), South Bay Cove (Shady Well Stakes by 12 ½ lengths, Ontario Debutante Stakes), Bandini and some other promising stakes runners including Scandinavia (2nd Royal Lodge Stakes in England). Here is the classic winner's pedigree showing his dam's duplication of Almahmoud via Natalma and Cosmah:

Fusaichi Pegasus (1997)	Mr. Prospector	Raise A Native	**Native Dancer**	Polynesian
				Geisha
			Raise You	Case Ace by **Teddy**
				Lady Glory by American Flag
		Gold Digger	Nashua	Nasrullah by **Nearco**
				Segula by Johnstown
			Sequence	Count Fleet (to Sundridge)
				Miss Dogwood by Bull Dog by **Teddy**
	Angel Fever	Danzig	Northern Dancer	Nearctic by **Nearco**
				Natalma (**Native Dancer** - **Almahmoud**)
			Pas de Nom	Admiral's Voyage
				Petitioner by Petition by Fair Trial
		Rowdy Angel	Halo	Hail To Reason by Turn-To
				Cosmah (ex **Almahmoud**)
			Ramhyde	Rambunctious
				Castle Hyde by Tulyar (dam by **Nearco**)

Fusaichi Pegasus' ancestry contains substantial impact from Sainfoin and his sister Sierra, especially via Phalaris and Mumtaz Mahal. This combination of full siblings comes via Polynesian, American Flag, Nearco, Nasrullah, Count Fleet, Fair Trial, Turn-To, Almahmoud and Castle Hyde.

Angel Fever is linebred 4 x 4 to Almahmoud by Mahmoud who is three-parts brother to the dam of Nasrullah and Sun Princess (dam of Royal Charger). Fair Trial's dam, Lady Juror, is half-sister to Mumtaz Mahal. Champion racehorse Tulyar is out of a daughter of Nearco. Hence, there are three sons of Nearco in the Kentucky Derby winner's pedigree, plus one daughter. (Turn-To is by Royal Charger by Nearco.)

Seeing as how Fusaichi Pegasus has "balanced breeding" to Nearco (three sons plus one daughter) and "balanced breeding" to his sire Pharos (Turn-To's second dam is a daughter of Pharos and Rambunctious carries a daughter of Pharos), one can predict with confidence that Fusaichi Pegasus will sire his share of stakes winners out of mares with Nasrullah and/or Royal Charger in their genotype. Almahmoud appears via Natalma and Cosmah, therefore Fusaichi Pegasus can take Northern Dancer's strain again. Foals bred along these lines would have a triple of the elite mare Almahmoud. "Balanced breeding" simply means duplicating an ancestor via both sexes, i.e. son and daughter, to ensure similar genes are deployed on both sides of the chromosomes.

I know I am sticking my neck out when I say I believe one of the best matings to test with Fusaichi Pegasus is to introduce the Nasrullah/Princequillo nick or introduce Sir Gaylord (Turn To-Somethingroyal by Princequillo). Tracery's strain of Papyrus (broodmare sire of Princequillo) might be just the thing to boost racing class in progeny by the Kentucky Derby winner. Princequillo is a very important link with Nasrullah and Royal Charger, yet he is absent in the Fusaichi Pegasus pedigree. Other strains likely to be compatible with the stallion are sources of Seattle Slew (from the same female line as Mr. Prospector, tracing to Myrtlewood), Prince John who is by Princequillo from a daughter of Count Fleet (thereby duplicating Count Fleet), Affirmed who is bred on the cross of Raise A Native with Crafty Admiral, and mares that have a "daughter" of Mr. Prospector in their pedigree.

Norfolk Stakes Gr-2 winner Roman Ruler, from the first crop of Fusaichi Pegasus, is out of a mare by Silver Deputy (Deputy Minister-Silver Valley by Mr. Prospector) from a mare by Quack (T.V. Lark - Quillon by Princequillo). A smart juvenile in 2004, Roman Ruler is inbred 2 x 4 to a son and daughter of Mr. Prospector. Significantly, Quack is bred on the Nasrullah mix with Princequillo. Quack is by T.V. Lark by Indian Hemp, son of Nasrullah. Roman Ruler's pedigree pattern reinforces all the Sainfoin/Sierra and Phalaris/Mumtaz Mahal elements to increase speed.

In 1997, I inspected Fusaichi Pegasus as a weanling at Stone Farm. Arthur Hancock invited Bobby Spalding and myself to look at weanlings owned by the partnership of Stone Farm and Stonerside Farm. Bobby is farm manager at Stonerside. He used to be farm manager at Elmendorf Farm owned by Jack Kent Cooke. (Bobby and I designed the mating that produced Arazi's best son Congaree, earner of $3,267,490.) Arthur knew he had something special to show us. When I clapped eyes on Fusaichi Pegasus I was an immediate admirer. He was one of the nicest weanlings I had ever seen, with tremendous "presence" although I did notice he was slightly long in his pasterns. After inspecting the colt, I told Arthur he should double the colt's insurance lest anything go amiss before the colt went to the Keeneland sales.

Arthur keeps his young horses out in the fresh air longer than most other farms and takes risks with little bumps or cuts. Arthur's policy is to breed athletes. Fusaichi Pegasus traces in female line to Bold Irish (Fighting Fox-Erin by Transmute) and therefore carries Tracery's strain. Transmute is out of Traverse, a daughter of Tracery. It might be interesting to reinforce this female line with mares that possess the lines of Icecapade, Buckfinder, Blue Ensign or Bold Irishman. Daughters of Storm Cat should be genetically compatible with Fusaichi Pegasus.

Lane's End Farm stands Gulch, successful sire of Graded stakes winners. A champion racehorse, he is linebred to Pharos and his brother Fairway, with a daughter of Pharos via the dam of English Derby winner Owen Tudor. Gulch's second dam is Asbury Mary, by Seven Corners who is bred on the Teddy/Tracery mix. Gulch is the sire to date of 56 stakes winners with progeny earnings already exceeding $64 million. Among his progeny are Thunder Gulch (dam by Storm Bird), Nayef (dam by Bustino), Harayir (dam by Shareef Dancer), The Cliff's Edge (dam by Danzig), Wallenda (dam by Liloy), Eagle Café (dam by Nureyev) and Golden Gear (dam by Lypheor). Obviously he is compatible with Northern Dancer's strain.

Seeking The Gold, based at Claiborne Farm, is extremely compatible with mares carrying the strains of Nasrullah, Royal Charger and Northern Dancer. His best colt to date was the very talented Dubai Millennium (dam by Shareef Dancer).

Seeking The Gold's best fillies are Seeking The Pearl (dam by Seattle Slew), Heavenly Prize (dam by Nijinsky II) and the brilliant filly Flanders (dam by Storm Bird), winner of the Breeders' Cup Juvenile Fillies Stakes and voted Champion 2YO filly. Flanders defeated Serena's Song in the Grade 1 Juvenile Fillies Stakes and is bred on a similar cross to Thunder Gulch.

In 1989, Joanne Nor (Norfields) asked me to recommend a suitable sire for her mare Breezy Stories (Damascus-New Tune by New Providence). Storm Cat was suggested as a worthwhile test, knowing a foal by him would be inbred to Bull Page's son New Providence. However, we believed Damascus had all the right things in his ancestry to nick with Storm Cat, in particular Sun Teddy and My Babu's dam, Perfume II, who is by the sprinter Badruddin (son of Mumtaz Mahal) from Lavendula II by Pharos. We liked this match so much that Joanne decided to repeat the mating.

This is how Grade 1 Breeders' Cup Sprint winner Desert Stormer evolved, along with her sister Desert Stormette who also showed ability until injured. When the time came for Desert Stormer to be mated, we settled on Seeking The Gold whose genotype was compatible. This match created a special pedigree pattern.

Joanne is like a private detective because she spends hours investigating the most compatible sires for her mares. She runs pages of computer printouts of six-generation pedigrees and deserves her success. Joanne Nor has sold many Graded stakes winners and ranks as one of the most successful consignors at Keeneland. The result of the Seeking The Gold-Desert Stormer match is Sahara Gold, winner of the Beaumont Stakes Gr-2. Earlier, we designed the mating that produced Behrens, nine wins $4,563,500, Oaklawn Handicap, Gulfstream Park Handicap (twice), Dwyer Stakes, Suburban Handicap, Massachusetts Handicap etc., and runner-up in the Dubai World Cup, Whitney Handicap, Jockey Club Gold Cup and Woodward Stakes etc.

Behrens stands at Darby Dan Farm and if you study his pedigree you will see how we purposely duplicated Double Jay and Ribot.

Sons of Storm Cat are highly compatible with daughters of Seeking The Gold, Miswaki or Woodman, all products of the Mr. Prospector/Buckpasser mix. The pedigree patterns designed from this cross seem to have the potential to supply Graded stakes runners. However, the mix of Bold Ruler with daughters of Buckpasser never worked well enough to produce sound stakes winners. Progeny bred on this match inherited physical problems. Ogden Phipps designed quite a few matings with the Bold Ruler/Buckpasser cross yet bred nothing of any consequence. On the other hand, Mr. Prospector's strain certainly blends well with Storm Cat's sons.

The sire line of Mr. Prospector is at full strength thanks to his sons Machiavellian, Gulch, Kingmambo, Seeking The Gold, Fappiano and Distant View, as well as other young sons and grandsons. Native Dancer's line is in an ideal situation to rule at least for two more decades, although there are three different sire lines in North America that warrant the attention of breeders – In Reality, Pleasant Colony and Cozzene. In Reality is a natural source of early maturing speed whereas the tough constitutions of Cozzene and Pleasant Colony can only improve soundness.

Pleasantly Perfect (by Pleasant Colony) was among the top four racehorses in the world through 2003 and 2004. He started 18 times for nine wins, and earned big bucks. His career earnings amount to $7,789,880. Conditioned by Richard Mandella, Pleasantly Perfect reached peak form when he won the Breeders' Cup Classic and Dubai World Cup (defeating Medaglia d'Oro both times). He received a Timeform rating of 130 in the Dubai race and a Beyer speed rating of 119 in the Classic.

From Ribot's sire line and essentially bred for a middle distance, Pleasantly Perfect is by Pleasant Colony (U. S. Champion 3YO, six wins, Kentucky Derby, Preakness Stakes, Woodward Stakes) from the Group 1 mare Regal State (Prix Morny, 2nd Prix Jacques le Marois, Prix de la Salamandre) by Horse of the Year and Champion 3YO colt Affirmed, winner of America's Triple Crown. Commercial breeders in Kentucky shied away from breeding to Pleasant Colony. He was a tall, leggy horse whose yearlings were unfurnished by the time they were consigned to major yearling sales and his progeny rarely won as juveniles. They required time to physically mature, but when they did, many of them won Graded stakes races.

				Bellini by Cavaliere d'Arpino
			Tenerani	Tofanella
		Ribot		El Greco by **Pharos**
			Romanella	Barbara Burrini by **Papyrus -Tracery**
	His Majesty			Hyperion
			Alibhai	Teresina by **Tracery**
		Flower Bowl		Beau Pere
			Flower Bed	Boudoir II by **Mahmoud**
Pleasant Colony				Balladier
(1978)			Double Jay	Broomshot
		Sunrise Flight		Princequillo dam by **Papyrus -Tracery**
			Misty Morn	Grey Flight by **Mahmoud**
	Sun Colony			Nasrullah ex **Mumtaz Begum**
			Cockrullah	Summerleaze by Fair Trial by **Fairway**
		Colonia		Guatan
			Nalga	Nagoya

The alternate sex line of Pleasant Colony zigzags back to Sunrise Flight and to his broodmare sire Princequillo, thence to Papyrus (winner of the English Derby). I appreciate the fact English champion Tracery is reinforced three times. Mahmoud is present via two daughters and is supported by his three quarter sister Mumtaz Begum and these strains act as speed elements in the pedigree pattern.

Cockrullah rarely appears in modern pedigrees. He is bred for pure speed and was a short-course specialist over five furlongs in England but couldn't quite sustain his speed to six furlongs.

			Pharos (Phalaris - Scapa Flow)
		Nearco	Nogara
	Nasrullah		Blenheim
		Mumtaz Begum	Mumtaz Mahal by **The Tetrarch** ex **Lady Josephine** by **Sundridge**
Cockrullah			**Fairway (Phalaris - Scapa Flow)**
		Fair Trial	Lady Juror ex **Lady Josephine** by **Sundridge**
	Summerleaze		Royal Minstrel by Tetratema by **The Tetrarch**
		Somerhill	Simnel

Pleasantly Perfect's pedigree pattern emphasizes stamina from stout ancestors, e.g. His Majesty, Ribot, Beau Pere and Double Jay. Speed elements come from Alibhai, Mahmoud, Cockrullah, Nasrullah and Fair Trial. Let's examine the pedigree of Pleasantly Perfect's dam Regal State to try to guess why she was genetically compatible with Pleasant Colony.

Regal State (1983)	Affirmed	Exclusive Native	Raise A Native	**Native Dancer** by Polynesian
				Raise You
			Exclusive	Shut Out (dam by Chicle by **Spearmint**
				Good Example by Pilate by Friar Rock
		Won't Tell You	Crafty Admiral	Fighting Fox by Sir Gallahad III
				Admiral's Lady by War Admiral
			Scarlet Ribbon	Volcanic by son of **Pharos**
				Native Valor by **Mahmoud**
	La Trinite	Lyphard	Northern Dancer	Nearctic by **Nearco** by **Pharos**
				Natalma by **Native Dancer**
			Goofed	Court Martial by **Fair Trial** by **Fairway**
				Barra II
		Promesa	Darius II	Dante by **Nearco** by **Pharos**
				Yasna by Dastur, by Solario
			Peseta	Neckar (to Nervesa ex Nogara)
				Prompt Payment

Affirmed and Lyphard inherit speed from linebreeding to Sainfoin and Sierra. Friar Rock is by Rock Sand (son of Sainfoin) from Fairy Gold by Bend Or whereas War Admiral's sire, Man o' War, is out of Mahubah by Rock Sand. Court Martial brings in Fair Trial plus daughters of Polymelus and Gainsborough. Darius II carries Sundridge via Solario. Last but not least, Germany's leading sire Neckar traces back to Nervesa (half-sister to Nearco), a "daughter" of Nogara. What is not obvious in the immediate pedigree is the gradual build-up of influence from English Derby winner Spearmint whose sire Carbine is closely related to Polymelus, the grandsire of brothers Pharos and Fairway. Nearco, Neckar, Sir Gallahad III and Bull Dog all possess Spearmint's strain. In summary, there is clever reinforcement of superior ancestors in Pleasantly Perfect's pedigree and of significance is his broodmare sire of Affirmed who possesses Crafty Admiral. Why is this so special you might ask?

Well, Crafty Admiral inherits tremendous speed from his 2 x 3 inbreeding to brothers Sir Galahad III and Bull Dog (by Teddy from Plucky Liege by Spearmint) and most probably additional speed from his dam, Admiral's Lady, a mare inbred 4 x 4 to Pink Domino. Admiral's Lady is linebred to Pink Domino's sire, Domino, four times, twice via Commando. Crafty Admiral won 15 of 39 starts, was a sound racehorse and retired to stud at Mare's Rest Farm, Kentucky, when he was a six-year-old. His wins include the Palm Beach Handicap in new track record time of 1:22 flat for seven furlongs, Gulfstream Park Handicap twice, Brooklyn Handicap easily by six lengths, Whirlaway Handicap, New York Handicap and Empire City Gold Cup by 10 lengths. He was runner-up in the Suburban and Carter Handicaps. His dam, Admiral's Lady, was a juvenile winner but died shortly after foaling Crafty Admiral.

				Ajax by Flying Fox
			Teddy	Rondeau (dam Doremi by **Bend Or**)
		Sir Galahad III		**Spearmint**
			Plucky Liege	Concertina by **St. Simon**
	Fighting Fox			Commando by **Domino**
			Celt	Maid of Erin
		Marguerite		Radium by **Bend Or**
			Fairy Ray	Seraph by St. Frusquin by **St. Simon**
Crafty Admiral (1948)				Fair Play ex Fairy Gold by **Bend Or**
			Man o' War	Mahubah by Rock Sand by Sainfoin
		War Admiral		Sweep ex **Pink Domino** by **Domino**
			Brushup	Annette K dam by **Spearmint**
	Admiral's Lady			**Teddy**
			Bull Dog	**Plucky Liege** by **Spearmint**
		Boola Brook		Peter Pan by **Commando** by **Domino**
			Brookdale	Sweepaway ex **Pink Domino** by **Domino**

Admiral's Lady is half-sister to Spring Run, dam of Irish sprinter Red God, sire of champion Blushing Groom. Crafty Admiral is of course the sire of Admiral's Voyage, broodmare sire of Danzig. This raises the question as to whether mares by Danzig or his sons would suit Pleasantly Perfect? Perhaps Danzig's strain might be highly compatible with Pleasantly Perfect? It would reinforce Crafty Admiral.

Inbreeding to a superior ancestor is a technique used by great breeders to upgrade racing performance, or at least maintain a certain level of performance. Any ancestor duplicated fairly close up in a pedigree must be free of genetic weakness and, if possible, display high-class performance at a mile or more. Inbreeding to short-course sprinters is rarely successful and tends to produce horses with very upright shoulder angle (causing the forelegs to hit the ground too hard). Strange though it may seem, a number of outstanding sprinter-milers were inbred to ancestors with stamina. Intense inbreeding (very close inbreeding) to an ancestor sometimes reduces the size of a foal. (Hyperion's grandsons Smokey Eyes and Star Kingdom are examples.)

If similar hidden recessive genes are present in both parents of a foal, it may inherit completely different physical type and mental attitude normally expected from the family. Instead of resembling parents or grand-parents, in this instance the foal may be termed a "throwback" to an ancestor some generations back featured on both sides of the foal's pedigree. Another phenomenon can occur – what we term the "skip generation" factor – whereby a colt resembles his maternal grandsire, and a filly resembles her sire's mother. Kris S. (Roberto-Sharp Queen by Princequillo) was so much like Princequillo in physical type that you would think he was a son rather than a grandson of Princequillo. Yet another example is Mr. Prospector who definitely resembled his maternal grandsire Nashua. Mr. Prospector didn't look anything like a son of the heavy-bodied Raise A Native. Instead, he was an athletic horse with a medium skeletal frame and not long in the back like his daddy.

Cozzene is a gray horse by French 2,000 Guineas winner Caro from Ride The Trails by Prince John. He was North America's leading sire in 1996 and is the sire of 12 millionaires. When the horse retired to Gainesway Farm, Michael Hernon (Gainesway's manager) asked me to take a good look at Cozzene.

Michael had a purpose. He wanted William T. Young to use the young stallion with one of Overbrook Farm's broodmares. I inspected Cozzene and liked him as a type. He has a strong back and strong loins, lovely sloping shoulders, short cannon bones and a decent hip. I could see why he earned $978,152 from 10 wins and scored in the Grade 1 Breeders' Cup Mile. Cozzene would become the sire of two Breeders' Cup winners, viz. Alphabet Soup and Tikkanen, although even to this day he still doesn't command the respect due to him from commercial breeders.

Cozzene represents a blend of speed and stamina and is one of the soundest strains in North America. His dam is inbred 2 x 4 to Princequillo as shown in the following pedigree:

			Grey Sovereign by Nasrullah
		Fortino II	Ranavalo II by Relic
	Caro		Chamossaire
		Chambord	Life Hill by Solario
Cozzene			**Princequillo**
(1980)		Prince John	Not Afraid by Count Fleet
	Ride the Trails		Sir Gaylord - dam by **Princequillo**
		Wildwook	Blue Canoe by Jet Pilot

Caro is linebred to Sainfoin and Sierra and inherits maternal strength from Nearco's half-sister Nervesa (via Fortino's direct female line). Caro is therefore linebred to Federico Tesio's classic filly Nogara (Havresac II-Catnip by Spearmint) via a son (Nearco) and a daughter (Nervesa).

In the circumstances, with such a strong pedigree, it is understandable why Caro was such a great success at stud.

Cozzene has sired 78 stakes winners to date. Among his principal Group or Graded stakes winners are Alphabet Soup (10 wins $2,990,270, 1st Breeders' Cup Classic in new track record time, San Antonio Handicap, San Pasqual Handicap and Del Mar Breeders' Cup Handicap), Admire Cozzene (Champion 2YO colt in Japan, $3,155,715, won Yasuda Kinen), Star of Cozzene ($2,308,923, won Man o' War Stakes), Cozzene's Prince (Champion Older Male in Canada, $1,270,057), Tikkanen (won Breeders' Cup Turf, Turf Classic Invitational Handicap), Grey Way (Champion 3YO filly in Italy), Hasten To Add (Champion Turf Male in Canada), Mizzen Mast (won Malibu Stakes, Strub Stakes), Santa Amelia (Champion Older Female in Canada), Maxzene (won Sheepshead Bay Handicap twice, $1,175,259), Environment Friend (Champion 3YO colt in England, won Eclipse Stakes) and Running Stag (won Massachusetts Handicap, Saratoga Breeders' Cup Handicap, $1,663,227).

Cozzene did it the hard way, proving he could upgrade the mares he covered. Today he is recognized as an influential broodmare sire and one of his daughters produced Pivotal, England's Champion Sprinter, who is among the leading sires in Europe at the present time.

Caro is of course the sire of Winning Colors, a filly trained by Wayne Lukas that was able to defeat the colts and win the Kentucky Derby. Voted Champion 3YO filly, she is linebred to Nogara. Caro is also the sire of Nebos (Horse of the Year in Germany), With Approval (Horse of the Year in Canada), Madelia (Champion 3YO filly in France) and other Group winners such as Kaldoun, Crystal Palace, Carwhite, Theia, Turgeon and Rusticaro. Daughters of Caro seem to have an affinity with Mr. Prospector's strain, especially if Buckpasser is somehow connected.

Two examples of this cross are Taylor Made Farm's resident stallion Unbridled's Song (Unbridled - Trolley Song by Caro) earner of $1,311,800 including the Breeders' Cup Juvenile Stakes and one of the leading sires in North America today, and Pin Oak Stud's gray stallion Maria's Mon (Wavering Monarch - Carlotta Maria by Caro), U.S. Champion 2YO and already sire of 20 stakes winners including Monarchos, winner of the Kentucky Derby; High Limit, winner of the Louisiana Derby; and See How She Runs, winner of the Fantasy Stakes and Selene Stakes. Both stallions have Buckpasser in their genotype.

Monarchos stands at Claiborne Farm and was the fastest winner of the Kentucky Derby since Secretariat put up a time of 1:59.8 for the 1¼ mile classic. Monarchos was timed at 1:59.97 and defeated Congaree, Thunder Blitz and Point Given. From 10 starts he won four including the Florida Derby, was runner-up to Congaree in the Wood Memorial Stakes and finished third to Point Given in the Belmont Stakes. What is interesting about the pedigree pattern of the Kentucky Derby winner is the clever reinforcement of similar biochemistry via Majestic Light (in Maria's Mon's pedigree) and Graustark (in Regal Band's pedigree):

Majestic Light	Majestic Prince	Raise A Native	Native Dancer
			Raise You
		Gay Hostess	Royal Charger by Nearco by **Pharos**
			*Your Hostess by **Alibhai-Boudoir II**
	Irradiate	**Ribot**	Tenerani
			Romanella (to **Pharos/Tracery**)
		High Voltage	Ambiorix, dam by **Pharos**
			Dynamo by Menow by Pharamond II ex **Selene**

Compared with....

Graustark	**Ribot**	Tenerani	Bellini by son of **Havresac II**
			Tofanella
		Romanella	El Greco by **Pharos**
			Barbara Burrini by Papyrus by **Tracery**
	*Flower Bowl	**Alibhai**	Hyperion ex **Selene**
			Teresina by **Tracery**
		Flower Bed	Beau Pere
			Boudoir II by Mahmoud

Notes: * Your Hostess is three-parts sister to Flower Bowl.
Nearco's dam is a "daughter" of Havresac II whereas Bellini is by Cavaliere d' Arpino, a "son" of Havresac II. Ribot is duplicated via a daughter and a son. Tracery brings in not only St. Simon's full sister Angelica but also two "daughters" of famous mare Pocahontas, dam of the successful sires Stockwell and King Tom who feature in the ancestry of Monarchos.

Dixieland Band, the broodmare sire of Monarchos, introduces many valuable genes for classic speed. A small bay horse of 15.3 hands high, Dixieland Band is out of a mare inbred 3 x 4 to Alibhai (Hyperion - Teresina by Tracery) and is linebred to Hyperion and Mumtaz Mahal. Let's examine his pedigree.

Dixieland Band (1980)	Northern Dancer	Nearctic	**Nearco**	**Pharos** by Phalaris Nogara by **Havresac II**
			Lady Angela	**Hyperion** Sister Sarah by son of **Tracery**
		Natalma	Native Dancer	Polynesian Geisha
			Almahmoud	**Mahmoud** Arbitrator
	Mississippi Mud	Delta Judge	Traffic Judge	**Alibhai** (**Hyperion/Tracery**) Traffic Court (to **Tracery**)
			Beautillion	Noor by **Nasrullah** by **Nearco** Delta Queen
		Sand Buggy	Warfare	Determine (**Alibhai/Mahmoud**) War Whisk
			Egyptian	Heliopolis by **Hyperion** Evening Mist by Eight Thirty

Dixieland Band's ancestor Determine (Alibhai-Koubis by Mahmoud) offers reinforcement of the same Alibhai/Mahmoud mix featured in the make-up of Your Hostess and Flower Bowl, and really acts like a genetic male cousin. Tracery is of course a key ancestor in the pattern, as are Hyperion and his dam, Selene.

Dixieland Band is making a tremendously successful broodmare sire. He stood at Lane's End Farm and is the sire of progeny that earned in excess of $65 million including at least 100 stakes winners. Among his progeny are Dixie Union, Dixie Brass, Drum Taps, Cotton Carnival, Check The Band, Egyptband, Del Mar Dennis, Bowman's Band and Spinning Round.

Perhaps now we can understand why Monarchos was such a smart racehorse. It will be interesting to discover whether he will sire Graded stakes winners from mares that will reinforce either the Mahmoud/Tracery or Hyperion/Tracery elements. No doubt Nearctic's strain should be doubled up, and if possible His Majesty should be introduced. His Majesty is a brother to Graustark.

For example, daughters of Danehill might be ideal to match with Monarchos since he comes from Nearctic's sire line and is out of a daughter of His Majesty. In my opinion this match (Monarchos with a daughter of Danehill) has exceptional potential, enough to possibly produce a multiple Grade 1 performer. Another important strain suitable to test with Monarchos is Princequillo, whose dam is by Papyrus, son of Tracery.

There is no doubt in my mind Maria's Mon has the potential to sire more stakes winners out of mares by Dixieland Band, or mares by his sons. Because of the unusual structure of their pedigree patterns, both Maria's Mon and Unbridled's Song can succeed when Raise A Native's strain is reinforced, even if he is positioned on the sire line of mares.

Let's now turn our attention to Tartan Farm's sprint star In Reality (Intentionally-My Dear Girl by Rough'n Tumble), a direct male descendant of champion Man o' War. Owned by the Francis A. Genter Stable, In Reality won 14 of 27 starts and was managed by John A Nerud who made a huge contribution to Tartan Farms' breeding operation based in Florida.

				Man o' War by **Fair Play**
			War Relic	Friar's Carse by Friar Rock
		Intent		Bubbling Over by North Star III
			Liz F.	Weno
	Intentionally			Display by **Fair Play**
			Discovery	Ariadne by Light Brigade
		My Recipe		Percentage
			Perlette	Escarpolette
In Reality				Questionaire
(1984)			Free For All	Panay by Chicle
		Rough'n Tumble		Bull Dog by Teddy
			Roused	Rude Awakening
	My Dear Girl			Man o' War by **Fair Play**
			War Relic	Friar's Carse by Friar Rock
		Iltis		Balladier by Black Toney
			We Hail	Clonaslee

At two, In Reality started seven times for four wins. He won the Pimlico Futurity and was runner-up in the Sapling Stakes and Cowdin Stakes. At three, he won eight of 12 starts including the Florida Derby, Jersey Derby, Hibiscus Stakes, Choice Stakes, Rumson Handicap and Fountain of Youth Stakes and finished second in the Preakness Stakes, American Derby, Jerome Handicap and Florida Breeders' Handicap etc.

In Reality won four of eight starts as a four-year-old, taking his career earnings to $795,824. He was a convincing winner at a mile in the valuable Grade 1 Metropolitan Handicap and against stiff opposition, won the Carter Handicap and John B. Campbell Handicap. He was stakes-placed twice, 3rd Seminole Handicap, Royal Palm Handicap.

A neat bay horse standing only 15.2 hands high, In Reality had slight rotation through both front cannons causing some toe out in his front feet, a trait he sometimes passed on to his stakes winning progeny. He was full of electricity!

In Reality's pedigree shows 3 x 3 inbreeding to War Relic via a son and a daughter and a triple of the high-spirited Fair Play, a horse that could get nasty. Let's take a look at War Relic's unique pedigree:

			Hastings by Spendthrift
		Fair Play	**Fairy Gold** (Bend Or/Macaroni)
	Man o' War		**Rock Sand** by **Sainfoin**
		Mahubah	Merry Token by Merry Hampton
War Relic			**Rock Sand** by **Sainfoin**
		Friar Rock	**Fairy Gold** (Bend Or/Macaroni)
	Friar's Carse		Superman by Commando
		Problem	Query by Voter

War Relic won nine races for $89,495 including the Massachusetts Handicap in new track record time, Narragansett Special by 4½ lengths (defeating champion Whirlaway) and Kenner Stakes by three lengths. He never ran at two years. War Relic is by Horse of the Year and Champion 3YO colt Man o' War from stakes winner Friar's Carse, three wins including the Fashion Stakes and Clover Stakes.

War Relic is the product of intense inbreeding to Fairy Gold via her sons Fair Play and Friar Rock and to English Triple Crown winner Rock Sand (via a daughter and a son). Samuel D. Riddle who bred War Relic and controlled the stud career of Man o' War had taken a risk that War Relic would not inherit a hot temper from Fair Play. A pronounced success as a sire at Faraway Farms, War Relic was a brother to the brilliant filly Speed Boat, winner of the Test Stakes, Adirondack Handicap and dam of Level Best, winner of the Coaching Club American Oaks, Top Flight Handicap, Demoiselle Stakes etc.

Among War Relic's progeny were Battlefield (U.S. Champion 2YO colt, 22 wins $474,727, Futurity Stakes, Hopeful Stakes, Sapling Stakes, Youthful Stakes, Tremont Stakes, Dwyer Stakes, New York Handicap etc), Intent (eight wins $317,775, Santa Anita Maturity Stakes, San Juan Capistrano Handicap twice), Missile (Dover Stakes, Flash Stakes, Pimlico Futurity), War Tryst (Richmond Stakes, El Dorado Handicap), Relic (Hopeful Stakes, Hibiscus Stakes, Bahamas Handicap and a leading sire in France), I Offbeat (Prioress Stakes), War Age (eight wins, Maryland Sprint Handicap) etc. He was North America's leading juvenile sire in 1950.

Intent (War Relic-Liz F. by Bubbling Over) is linebred to Sainfoin and his sister Sierra, and to Domino and Mannie Grey. Intent is the sire of Intentionally, U.S. Champion Sprinter, 18 wins two to six, $652,258, 1st Futurity Stakes, Withers Stakes, Warren Wright Memorial Stakes (equaling the world record for a mile in 1:33.2), Jerome Handicap, Equipoise Mile Handicap, Pimlico Futurity, and sire of In Reality, Ta Wee (Champion Sprinter twice) and Tentam (11 wins $459,109, 1st Metropolitan Handicap, United Nations Handicap, Toboggan Handicap etc).

In Reality was a definite source of speed – speed that could be carried beyond a mile. He sired Desert Vixen (Champion Handicap mare, Champion 3YO filly, Beldame Handicap twice, Matchmaker Stakes, Alabama Stakes), Ring of Light (19 wins $792,218, Excelsior Handicap, Massachusetts Handicap), Known Fact (Champion miler in England, English 2,000 Guineas), Star Choice (10 wins $589,439, 1st Metropolitan Handicap), Truly Bound (nine wins $382,449, 1st Ashland Stakes, Arlington-Washington Lassie Stakes), Believe It, Valid Appeal, Smile (Champion Sprinter, Breeders' Cup Sprint), Image of Reality and Relaunch (Del Mar Derby).

Valid Appeal was a consistent sire of early maturing sprinters. He retired to Mockingbird Farm, Ocala, Florida, after a career spanning 36 starts for eight wins and $201,733, 1st Dwyer Handicap, 2nd Jerome Handicap, Saratoga Special, 3rd Futurity Stakes. He is the sire of 88 stakes winners including World Appeal, Nannerl, Stormy But Valid, Valid Vixen, Proud Appeal, Valid Expectations and Successful Appeal.

Valid Expectations won 12 of 27 starts for $596,092 and is a leading juvenile sire. His wins include the Derby Trial Stakes, Sport Page Handicap and Thanksgiving Handicap. Successful Appeal is a promising young sire at Walmac Farm, Kentucky. A dark brown horse of 16.1 hands high, he is by Valid Appeal from Successful Dancer by Fortunate Prospect.

Although Successful Appeal possesses a slightly upright shoulder angle, he is an athletic type out of a mare inbred 3 x 3 to Lucky Debonair (with Northern Dancer duplicated 4 x 3). From 22 starts, Successful Appeal won eight races and earned $654,681. His best performances were wins in the Withers Stakes (defeating Best of Luck) and Kentucky Cup Sprint Stakes (defeating Five Star Day). In 2004, Successful Appeal was leading freshman sire and runner-up to Storm Cat on the Leading 2YO Sires' List with 15 winners, six of them stakes winners.

The 1923 English Derby winner PAPYRUS (Tracery - Miss Matty) with owner Ben Irish and trainer Basil Jarvis. Papyrus is the broodmare sire of champion sire Princequillo.

SOLARIO (Gainsborough - Sun Worship by Sundridge), winner of the St. Leger, Coronation Cup and Ascot Gold Cup. He sired two English Derby winners, Straight Deal and Mid-day Sun, and Sun Princess, dam of Royal Charger.

Relaunch (In Reality-Foggy Note by The Axe II) is the sire of 89 stakes winners. A gray horse built like a tank with plenty of fast twitch muscle fiber, he won five races for $278,100 including the La Jolla Mile Stakes. Among his progeny are Skywalker (1st Breeders' Cup Classic), Relasure (Champion Older Female in Italy), With Anticipation (Sword Dancer Invitational Handicap, twice), Waquoit (Brooklyn Handicap, twice), Launch A Pegasus, Special Happening, Cee's Tizzy and Honour and Glory.

Bred by Overbrook Farm, Honour and Glory was sold as a yearling at Keeneland. He won six of 17 starts for $1,202,942 including the Metropolitan Handicap, San Rafael Stakes, King's Bishop Stakes (defeating Elusive Quality), San Miguel Stakes, Breeders' Futurity and finished second in the Santa Anita Derby (to Cavonnier), Vosburgh Stakes etc. and third in the Breeders' Cup Sprint (won by Lit de Justice). Honour and Glory is out of a half-sister to Ogygian.

Honour and Glory (1993)	Relaunch	In Reality	Intentionally	Intent by **War Relic**
				My Recipe
			My Dear Girl	Rough'n Tumble
				Iltis by **War Relic**
		Foggy Note	The Axe II	**Mahmoud**
				*Blackball ex **La Troienne**
			Silver Song	Royal Note by Spy Song
				Beadah by Djeddah by **Djebel**
	Fair To All	Al Nasr	Lyphard	Northern Dancer
				Goofed by Court Martial
			Caretta	Caro
				Klainia by Klairon by Clarion by **Djebel**
		Gonfalon	Francis S.	Royal Charger
				*Blue Eyed Momo ex **La Troienne**
			Grand Splendor	Correlation
				Cequillo by Princequillo (to **Mahmoud**)

Fair To All is closely related to Demure, the dam of Grade 1 NYRA Mile Handicap winner Quiet American. They come from a branch of Cequillo (Princequillo-Boldness by Mahmoud-Hostility by Man o' War-Marguerite de Valois by Teddy-Plucky Liege by Spearmint). Marguerite de Valois is a sister to Bull Dog, the broodmare sire of Rough'n Tumble.

Man o' War's son War Admiral sired Blue Eyed Momo; hence Honour and Glory is linebred to sons and daughters of champion Man o' War.

I would guess an interesting mating would be for Honour and Glory to link up with daughters of Seattle Slew or A. P. Indy, thereby aiming to reinforce La Troienne, Nasrullah, Polynesian, Princequillo and War Admiral. To my knowledge there is only one stakes winner bred on this cross, Japanese Group 1 winner Name Value, a filly who earned $1,824,603 on turf, stakes winner of the Teio Sho and TCK Jo-O Hai etc.

Honour and Glory's best American-performed filly is Caressing (dam by Majestic Prince) the Champion 2YO filly who earned $955,998. Caressing won the Breeders' Cup Juvenile Fillies Stakes and La Troienne Stakes.

Relaunch was rather upright in his front pasterns but fortunately they were short and strong and absorbed vibration. Nevertheless, he only suited mares with decent pasterns and sired many stakes winners out of mares with Nasrullah's strain.

Among the sons of Relaunch at stud is the grey horse Cee's Tizzy (Relaunch-Tizly by Lyphard) a horse whose pedigree I designed at Overbook Farm. I thought by blending the strains of War Relic and Mahmoud with those of Court Martial (by Fair Trial) and Northern Dancer it might produce a runner. Lyphard is of course bred on the affinity between Northern Dancer and Fair Trial (like Sadler's Wells).

Cee's Tizzy's dam, Tizly, was out of a very big mare named Tizna, 18 wins in Chile and North America including the Santa Margarita Invitational Handicap twice, Ladies Handicap and Santa Monica Handicap. Tizly wasn't as big as Tizna. She won four races in France on turf and slightly resembled her sire Lyphard. Her son Cee's Tizzy has a nice shoulder, short pasterns, and on the West Coast won three races from six starts, being stakes-placed third in the Super Derby. Cee's Tizzy retired to Harris Farms in California and is a surprisingly good sire with 22 stakes winners to date including America's Horse of the Year Tiznow, twice winner of the Breeders' Cup Classic. Tizly was later sold to Japan where she produced Oteomeno Inori, earner of $1,132,883.

One of the strongest male lines via In Reality today is his grandson Bertrando (Skywalker-Gentle Hands by Buffalo Lark) who stands at River Edge Farm in California. Champion Older Male in 1993, Bertrando won nine of 24 starts and earned $3,185,610. As a juvenile he won three out of four starts, blitzing his opponents by nine lengths in the Norfolk Stakes, and scored easy wins in the Del Mar Futurity and a Maiden 2YO Handicap – his only defeat came when runner-up in the Breeders' Cup Juvenile Stakes. At three, Bertrando developed into a powerful athlete but his campaign was cut short. He won the San Felipe Stakes, was runner-up in the Santa Anita Derby and finished third in the Malibu Stakes. At four, Bertrando revealed his true form, winning the Pacific Classic in new track record time of 1:59 $^{2}/_{5}$ over $1\frac{1}{4}$ miles, the Woodward Stakes by more than 13 lengths, the San Fernando Stakes by nine lengths and was runner-up in the Metropolitan Handicap, Hollywood Gold Cup, Charles H Strub Stakes and Breeders' Cup Classic. He showed tenacity and brilliance.

At five, Bertrando won the Goodwood Handicap and Wicker Stakes. His pedigree reveals linebreeding to the speed strains of Sainfoin and Sierra. His sire, Skywalker, a big horse, is out of a mare inbred to champion Polynesian.

The fastest son of Bertrando to date is Officer, a dark brown horse about 16.2 hands high that retired to Gainesway Farm. I believe this young stallion has enormous potential – I expect him to be an immediate success with his first crop to race.

Officer was undefeated in his first five starts at two years. Essentially bred for speed, he won six races and earned $804,090 before an injury caused his premature retirement. At two, he defeated Jump Start in the Champagne Stakes, won the Del Mar Futurity, scored by seven lengths in the Best Pal Stakes, by eight lengths in the Graduation Stakes, was runner-up in the California Cup Juvenile Stakes over 1 $^{1}/_{16}$ miles and third to Siphonic in the Hollywood Futurity 1 $^{1}/_{16}$ miles. His speed took him to a mile but he was vulnerable at a longer trip.

At three, Officer won the Zany Tactics Stakes by six lengths. He is a long-bodied sprinter with plenty of fast fiber muscle and is quite light on his feet. Officer is linebred to Sainfoin and Sierra multiple times – an indication his progeny are more than likely to come to hand quickly.

Officer is also linebred to the dominant mare Traffic Court via her best sons Hasty Road and Traffic Judge, as well as to the sprinter-miler Boldnesian 4 x 5 daughter and son, Polynesian five times and Native Dancer three times. Last but not least, Nasrullah features via two sons and a daughter. This is a very special pedigree pattern. Officer is destined to suit mares from the lines of Northern Dancer and Mr. Prospector.

He was bred in California by Mr. and Mrs. Marty Wygod and descends in female line from Buckpasser's dam, Busanda (the female line of La Troienne, whose granddaughters Striking and Busher appear in the pedigree of Seattle Slew's dam, My Charmer). Officer seems to suit mares by Miswaki, Woodman and Seeking The Gold as this match reinforces Polynesian, Native Dancer and Buckpasser's dam, Busanda. Gainesway Farm set Officer's fee at only $15,000 live foal. His first foals arrived in 2004 and he is in a price range to suit everyone.

Another young stallion with a great pedigree pattern is War Chant (Danzig-Hollywood Wildcat by Kris S.-Miss Wildcatter by Mr. Prospector) who stands at Three Chimneys Farm. From his first crop to race in 2004 he is the sire of 11 juvenile winners, two stakes winners.

My first impression when I inspected his yearlings in 2001 was that they will be best suited around two-turns and some are likely to succeed at the classic distance. He already has smart juveniles from his first crop – Up Like Thunder, Speciale and Pandemic. War Chant's dam is the talented stakes winner Hollywood Wildcat, U.S. Champion 3YO filly (12 wins $1,432,160, Breeders' Cup Distaff, Hollywood Oaks, Gamely Handicap, Del Mar Invitational Oaks, Sorority Stakes, Debutante Stakes etc.).

Hollywood Wildcat is inbred 4 x 4 to champion Nashua via two daughters and is already the dam of three stakes winners.

War Chant won five of seven starts for $1,130,600. At two, he won his only start, a Maiden race at Hollywood Park by two lengths. Given time to mature, he grew into an elegant athlete and at three, won an allowance race at Santa Anita by five lengths, the San Raphael Stakes, was runner-up to The Deputy in the Santa Anita Derby, bypassed the Kentucky Derby, then won the Oak Tree Breeders' Cup Mile Stakes on turf going a mile in 1:33 ¾. At his final start, War Chant won the Breeders' Cup Turf defeating North East Bound, Dansili and Affirmed Success. He showed acceleration in that valuable event. War Chant's alternate sex line zigzags back to Princequillo, a horse with a large heart and a sound constitution. If breeders are in the process of selecting a suitable mare for War Chant I would like to suggest a good strategy is to duplicate Princequillo, especially via "sons" of Princequillo such as Round Table and Prince John. Mares with Seattle Slew's strain should be highly compatible since his dam is by Poker, son of Round Table from Glamour by Nasrullah. Duplication of Mr. Prospector is another interesting test using mares by Miswaki, Seeking The Gold, Gulch, Woodman and Gone West. (The lines of Blushing Groom, Nijinsky II, Boldnesian and Hail To Reason might also suit War Chant's genotype.)

Princequillo inherited a large heart and is an ancestor I duplicate in matings to ensure good temperament and sound legs. He is a powerful ancestor who is able to correct conformational faults in other lines. Bold Ruler would never have topped the Sires' List without the help of Princequillo's daughters. Triple Crown winner Secretariat is more a Princequillo type than his daddy Bold Ruler.

The pedigree of War Chant has a fair amount of stamina, so one would want to select mares with speed for him. Nashua plays a dominant role in the pattern.

				Nearco by **Pharos**
			Nearctic	Lady Angela by Hyperion
		Northern Dancer		**Native Dancer**
			Natalma	Almahmoud by Mahmoud
	Danzig			Crafty Admiral
			Admiral's Voyage	Olympia Lou by Olympia
		Pas de Nom		Petition by Fair Trial by **Fairway**
			Petitioner	Steady Aim by Felstead
War Chant (1997)				Hail To Reason by Turn-To
			Roberto	Rarelea by **Nashua**
		Kris S.		Princequillo (dam by Papyrus)
			Sharp Queen	Bridgework
	Hollywood Wildcat			Raise A Native by **Native Dancer**
			Mr. Prospector	Gold Digger by **Nashua**
		Miss Wildcatter		Third Martini by Hasty Road
			Elizabeth K.	Baked Apple

Olin Gentry Sr., who designed the mating that produced English Derby winner Roberto, told me he purposely duplicated French champion stayer Sardanapale. Nashua possesses Sardanapale and Nashua appears again as the broodmare sire of Mr. Prospector. This means War Chant's dam has a triple cross of Sardanapale.

War Chant's ancestry receives genetic impact from the brothers Pharos and Fairway. Turn-To is of course inbred 3 x 3 to a son and a daughter of Pharos. Nashua's sire, Nasrullah, along with Nearctic, are sons of Nearco by Pharos so the pattern has a foundation of speed from Phalaris, the sire of Pharos and Fairway. Tracery appears three times in War Chant's ancestry, adding to Sainfoin's input.

Sundridge, whose dam (Sierra) is a sister to Sainfoin, is present via the male line of Count Fleet and via Lady Josephine, dam of Lady Juror and Mumtaz Mahal.

Lady Juror is the dam of Fair Trial while Mumtaz Mahal is granddam of Nasrullah and Mahmoud, and the third dam of Royal Charger (sire of Turn-To). To add further to the Sainfoin/Sierra speed mix we find Polynesian (linebred four times to Sainfoin and Sierra) as the sire of Native Dancer who is duplicated in War Chant's pedigree. A special mating worth considering because of its unique pattern is to match War Chant with well-bred daughters of Miswaki.

		Northern Dancer (dam by **Native Dancer**)
	Danzig	Pas de Nom
War Chant		Kris S. (dam by **Princequillo**)
	Hollywood Wildcat	Miss Wildcatter by **Mr. Prospector**
		Mr. Prospector (by son of **Native Dancer**)
	Miswaki	Hopespringseternal by Buckpasser ex Rose Bower by **Princequillo**
daughters of		
	Various	

Miswaki's dam, Hopespringseternal, is by Buckpasser from Rose Bower by Princequillo from Lea Lane by Nasrullah.

The War Chant/Miswaki match has the potential to supply Graded stakes winners providing genetic probability is kind enough to allow the best genes to be expressed. A foal bred this way would have Mr. Prospector duplicated 4 x 3, plus a "daughter" of Native Dancer via Natalma, reinforcement of Princequillo, and introduce into the equation the mare Lea Lane, a "daughter" of Nasrullah so as to balance input from Nashua, a "son" of Nasrullah.

By duplicating an ancestor via both sexes, i.e. son and daughter, it helps deploy similar genes on both sides of the autosomal chromosomes, at the same loci (locations) thereby establishing homologous groups of genes. Duplicating a male ancestor exclusively via sons has a somewhat limiting effect on a foal's biochemistry.

The examples so far given in this chapter comprise racehorses with a blend of speed and stamina – speed being defined as sprinter-milers, not short course specialists over five furlongs. Let's review a few basic principles I believe breeders should consider when designing mare matings:

a) Ideally, select a sire with a proven track record at Graded/Group level (or a brilliant non-stakes winner that set new track records) making certain the sire was sound enough to improve the constitution of your mare's foal.
b) Avoid sires possessing the same genetic weaknesses of your mare.
c) Select a sire with clean airflow that is genetically compatible.
d) Select a sire that will alter the ratio of fast and slow fiber muscle – to improve speed, or to improve stamina.
e) Be extremely critical of shoulder angle. Your objective is to breed foals with nice sloping shoulder angle of about 48 to 52 degrees.
f) Be extremely critical of the hind legs (the engine of propulsion).
g) First preference should be given to a proven sire of stakes winners. However, sometimes you can justify using a young unproven sire if he has the right pedigree and conformation to suit your mare.
h) Prefer a fertile horse, no matter what age, so long as he is in good health. Also consider the number of mares the stallion is likely to cover in a year.
i) Consider the temperament of the sire selected.
j) Avoid duplication of unsound ancestors.
k) Reinforce the best elements of your mare's pedigree via superior, sound ancestors – using inbreeding or linebreeding techniques. Alternately, if your mare is intensely inbred, breed away from the duplicated ancestor to gain hybrid vigor.

This list is based on common sense. One of the most serious considerations is how much one is willing to invest in stallion service fees (cost of season/nomination) as this is often a major constraint in the selection process. If statistics are important, study them, but always keep in mind racetrack performance as the goal to be achieved. On occasions it might be wise to "overbreed" a young maiden mare to an expensive stallion that is genetically compatible, with suitable conformation. By overbreeding a young mare in her first year at stud, you quickly test her ability to produce a stakes runner.

However, if you are strictly a commercial breeder, breeding solely for the sale ring, then your strategy is quite different. You won't heed the above list. Instead, you will choose any fashionable, popular stallion and cross your fingers the resulting foal will inherit decent conformation because profit is your single-minded goal.

When consigned as a yearling, of course it will need to pass veterinary inspection. A commercial breeder's primary target will be to aim to make the catalog page of the prospective yearling as appealing as possible to catch the attention of buyers. The racetrack in this instance is not your primary objective – it is making money.

I cringe when I see decent stakes-producing families ruined by commercial breeders who either insist on using first season sires (that often end up as failures) or use inexpensive, moderate sires unable to upgrade racing class. If a mare produces yearlings that fail to win races, not only is her own value affected but also the value of her future foals. Her family's integrity is easily damaged by a series of bad matings.

When searching for a suitable sire for a specific mare, there are a few pointers to look for, apart from the need to ensure genetic compatibility. The female line of a stallion is like a storyboard, detailing the performance and soundness of his relatives. Sires from strong female lines always have a better chance to succeed at stud than do sires from moderate female lines, no matter how wonderful might be the horse's race record.

Next, and I believe this is so important, study the selected sire's broodmare sire. If the broodmare sire is a Graded or Group winner that displayed ideal speed and stamina, search to see if he is out of a mare from a powerful female line. If by chance the broodmare sire has one or two superior ancestors in his make-up also present in your mare's pedigree, then chances are the match will be compatible. Remember, nine out of 10 new sires don't succeed at stud so there is more risk using an unproven sire, although I am the first to admit, sometimes I select a well-bred young sire (hoping it is the one out of 10) that suits a specific mare on pedigree and conformation.

When planning matings for maiden mares, I recommend they be matched with proven sires in preference to unproven stallions. By using a proven sire, the breeder can judge the merits of a young producing mare more accurately.

I have one golden rule to offer – there is no golden rule that applies in the Thoroughbred breeding game. Genetic probability depends entirely on "chance," i.e. on what portion of the parents' gene pool is actually inherited by a foal. After 50 years enjoying the study of breeding racehorses, I honestly believe you can reduce risk by using logic. Great breeders had a talent for selecting the right sire for a mare and they took calculated risks to upgrade families – matings that not only produced high-class performers, but also dismal failures.

Statistics show broodmares aged between seven to 12 years have the best opportunity to produce stakes winners. This finding, based on a large sample, doesn't deter me from putting in just as much time planning matings for a maiden mare or an older mare because I don't concern myself too much with general population statistics. Providing a mare is healthy and in good breeding condition, she has the opportunity to breed her best performer at any age, but for some inexplicable reason, breeders seem to invest less in stallion fees for older mares (excluding Group or Graded stakes producers). Too many breeders give up on old mares! They study statistics and decide if a mare aged more than 14 years has produced winners without any black type, they decide to use stallions with low fees because they think the mare's future yearlings will have limited appeal to buyers. This is a weak argument!

All I can say is that a mare 14 years or more that produced handicap winners (allowance winners) with no black type, still has a chance to produce a stakes winner, especially if she belongs to a stakes-producing female line.

Maybe in the past the mare was not sent to stallions that suited her genotype? Mare owners require a stout heart, deep pockets and an optimistic outlook to stay in business. I've met small breeders with limited funds who have gone to the sales to buy a mare aged more than 14 years that is the dam of winners without black type, believing they can breed the mare to different lines and produce a stakes winner. Some succeed and reach their goal, but all of them had one definable constraint – the older mare had to belong to a stakes-producing female line. If you pin your faith on maternal strength you can get lucky. Suddenly a close relative wins a Group race or one of the mare's earlier foals earns black type. It happens!

Mares that produce a series of stakes-placed winners are knocking on the door to produce a high-class Group winner and the owner must be persistent and have faith and patience. A good example is the mare Style of Life, two wins at three years who to date has produced nine foals, seven winners. Her best foal came late on the scene, the 2004 Irish Derby winner Grey Swallow (by Daylami). Style of Life (The Minstrel-Bubinka by Nashua) produced four stakes-placed winners before producing her best foal. The mare's colts, Central Lobby (by Kenmare) and Stylish Ways (by Thatching), were both Group 3 placed, and the mare's filly Rustic (by Grand Lodge) was runner-up in the Princess Margaret Stakes Gr-3. Another filly, Style For Life (by Law Society), was third in the Prix Panacee. Then along came Grey Swallow, winner of the Killavullan Stakes Gr-3 as a juvenile, an easy winner of the Leopardstown 2,000 Guineas Trial at three, a fast-finishing third in the Irish 2,000 Guineas Gr-1, and a popular winner of the Irish Derby Gr-1.

The second dam of Grey Swallow is stakes winner Bubinka, two wins including the Premio Buontalenta Gr-3 and dam of 11 foals, four winners, Seasonal Pickup being the only stakes winner. Seasonal Pickup (by The Minstrel) won five races including the Sprint Stakes, Midsummer Scurry Handicap, Ballychorus Stakes, Carna Stakes and was stakes-placed in the Athasi Stakes and Phoenix Sprint. Because of Grey Swallow's classic victory, his immediate relatives are now quite valuable, especially his half-sisters. Let's take a look at Grey Swallow's fascinating pedigree:

				Never Bend by **Nasrullah** by **Nearco**
			Mill Reef	Milan Mill by **Princequillo**
		Doyoun		Kashmir II
			Dumka	Faizebad by Prince Taj (ex **Malindi**)
	Daylami			Mr. Prospector (dam by **Nashua**)
			Miswaki	Hopespringseternal (to **Princequillo/N**)
		Daltawa		Crystal Palace by Caro (to **Nasrullah**)
			Damana	Denia by Crepello
Grey Swallow				Nearctic by **Nearco**
(2001)			Northern Dancer	Natalma by **Native Dancer**
		The Minstrel		Victoria Park
			Fleur	Flaming Page by Bull Page
	Style of Life			**Nasrullah** by **Nearco**
			Nashua	Segula by Johnstown
		Bubinka		Sadair
			Stolen Date	Stolen Hour by Mr. Busher

Grey Swallow is linebred to champion Nashua 6 x 3, to Nasrullah five times plus his sister Malindi, to Native Dancer twice, to Nearco seven times and to Mumtaz Mahal six times. This is a fairly serious concentration of superior ancestors.

Nashua (Nasrullah-Segula by Johnstown-Sekhmet by Sardanapale) was a very correct brown horse of 16.1 hands high with a near perfect shoulder angle. Joe Hirsch, senior journalist for *Daily Racing Form*, said, "Nashua was the strongest, soundest horse this writer has ever seen."

Nashua was U.S. Champion 2YO colt, Horse of the Year and Champion 3YO colt with a record of 22 wins from 36 starts and career earnings of $1,288,565. He won the Futurity Stakes, Hopeful Stakes, Grand Union Hotel Stakes, Cowdin Stakes, Preakness Stakes (set a new track record), Belmont Stakes, Flamingo Stakes, Dwyer Stakes, Wood Memorial Stakes, Arlington Classic, Jockey Club Gold Cup twice, a match race against Swaps, Widener Handicap, Suburban Handicap, etc and was second in the Kentucky Derby.

Trained by "Sunny" Jim Fitzsimmons, Nashua was by far the best juvenile colt of his generation. Prior to the running of the Florida Derby in which Nashua was a hot favorite, heavy rain changed the conditions of the track to sloppy.

Owner William Woodward knew Fitzsimmons wanted to scratch his colt, but Nashua's fans had come in droves to Gulfstream Park to admire a champion and see him win. Woodward decided he didn't want to disappoint everyone, so Nashua ran, but the result was a desperate finish, with a muddied Nashua only a neck in advance of Blue Lem. The colt's regular rider, Eddie Arcaro, was suspended before the Wood Memorial Stakes and was replaced by Ted Atkinson. Held back until mid-stretch, Nashua wore down front-runner Summer Tan to catch him before the wire.

Next came the 81st Kentucky Derby at Churchill Downs where Nashua firmed in the market to 13-10 favorite. Santa Anita Derby winner Swaps was second choice at 14-5 with Summer Tan next at 5-1. With Eddie Arcaro back in the saddle, Nashua went out onto the track looking a picture of fitness. Fitzsimmons had told Arcaro to concentrate on Summer Tan because he considered that colt to be the main threat to Nashua.

At the start, Bill Shoemaker aboard Swaps took the California-bred colt to the lead while Nashua lay about midfield. Swaps ran freely out in front and by the turn into the stretch, Arcaro became anxious and worried. He had let Swaps dictate the pace and had grossly underestimated his rival's stamina. Arcaro used the whip, but at the wire Swaps scored by a length and a half from the fast-finishing Nashua, with Summer Tan a further six lengths behind. The time was fast! William Woodward was emotionally upset. He was more than annoyed by Arcaro's poor judgement.

Swaps missed a trip to Pimlico and returned to California. In his absence, Nashua won the Preakness Stakes in track record time of 1:54 3/5 and went on to win the Belmont Stakes by nine lengths in New York. Later that year a match race between Nashua and Swaps was organized for August 31 at Washington Park over a distance of 1¼ miles. Swaps had earned a big reputation on the West Coast with facile victories in the Will Rogers, Californian and Westerner Stakes. Shipped to Chicago, Swaps won the American Derby from Traffic Judge as a "prep" for the August 31 contest.

Nashua arrived in Chicago seven days in advance of the big event.

On August 28, Swaps came up lame in both front feet. It was touch and go whether he would be scratched; however, owner Rex Ellsworth and trainer Mesh Tenney worked their magical skills and Swaps lined up against Nashua as promised.

ROUND TABLE (Princequillo - Knight's Daughter by Sir Cosmo), champion six times, Horse of the Year, 43 wins and $1,749,869. A truly great racehorse.

Nasrullah's champion son NASHUA, 22 wins, $1,288,565 and Horse of the Year at three. He is the broodmare sire of Roberto and Mr. Prospector.

Nashua was rushed at the start to gain the lead. Although Swaps tried several times to pass him, Nashua would not yield. In the final furlong, people gasped as Swaps showed signs of weakening while Nashua extended his lead. At the wire Nashua won by 6½ lengths. The crowd of 35,000 was stunned by the ease of Nashua's victory. However, the next morning came a newsflash – the discovery that Swaps was bleeding in both front feet. The morning newspaper revealed the first six furlongs of the match race was run in 1:10 ⅕.

In late October, William Woodward was accidentally shot dead by his wife. She thought he was a prowler on their Long Island estate. The circumstances were both tragic and bizarre. Hanover Bank executives began to liquidate Woodward's Thoroughbred holdings and Nashua was offered for sale by a private sealed-bid arrangement. The champion racehorse was purchased for a record amount, $1,251,200, offered by a syndicate formed by Leslie Combs II who owned Spendthrift Farm.

Nashua would win more stakes before his final appearance on the racetrack when he captured the Jockey Club Gold Cup for a second time. He was a successful sire but a more influential broodmare sire. His daughters Gold Digger and Bramalea produced the outstanding sires Mr. Prospector and Roberto. Nashua's most successful son at stud was Good Manners, a leading sire in South America.

It is incredible how sire lines rise and fall. Forty years ago the male line of Hyperion was at its zenith. Today, Hyperion's male line is dependent upon descendants scattered across the globe. In England, the biggest surprise of all is Will Somers, a handicap sprinter by champion Tudor Minstrel, grandson of Hyperion.

Bred by Mrs. D. McCall, Will Somers won two races, the Surrey Handicap at Sandown Park and the Whitehawk Handicap at Brighton. He was placed in the Rous Memorial Stakes and Mayflower Stakes at two years and was an unlucky second three times as a four-year-old in handicaps at Newmarket, York and Ayr.

Will Somers retired to stud at Ballykisteen Stud, Tipperary, at a fee of 48 pounds inclusive. His third dam Laughter was half-sister to English Derby winner Humorist, and the next dam Jest, won the English 1,000 Guineas and the Oaks.

Will Somers (1955)	Tudor Minstrel	Owen Tudor	Hyperion	Gainsborough by Bayardo
				Selene by **Chaucer** (**C'bury Pilgrim**)
			Mary Tudor	**Pharos** by Phalaris (dam by **Sainfoin**)
				Anna Bolena by Teddy
		Sansonnet	Sansovino	Swynford (**Canterbury Pilgrim**)
				Gondolette
			Lady Juror	Son-in-Law
				Lady Josephine by **Sundridge** (**Sierra**)
	Queen's Mirth	Nearco	**Pharos**	Phalaris (dam by **Sainfoin**)
				Scapa Flow by **Chaucer** (**C'bury Pilgrim**)
			Nogara	Havresac II by Flying Fox
				Catnip by Spearmint
		Mirth	Hurry On	Marcovil
				Tout Suite by **Sainfoin**
			Laughter	Pommern by **Polymelus**
				Jest by **Sundridge** (**Sierra**)

Will Somers was purely a sprinter, yet his pedigree shows linebreeding to Oaks winner Canterbury Pilgrim (dam of Chaucer and Swynford), Sundridge (sire of Lady Josephine and Jest), Sainfoin and his sister Sierra, and Polymelus.

If we study his pedigree there appears to be a number of ancestors with stamina. He came from an exceptional classic-producing female line and has unbeaten champion Nearco as his broodmare sire. Perhaps he had some physical problem? Will Somers never attracted many quality mares but when mated with a mare called Violet Bank (by Irish Derby winner The Phoenix) he sired Balidar, a colt who sold for 420 guineas as a foal and 700 guineas as a yearling.

Balidar won nine races at two to four years. As a juvenile he won the Prendergast Stakes at Newmarket by four lengths, the Peddars Cross Plate at Yarmouth by four lengths, and was unplaced in the October Nursery Handicap while in France, he was unplaced in the Prix de la Foret (seventh of 13 runners, beaten five lengths). At three, Balidar won the Old Mill Handicap at Lingfield, Matador Handicap (defeating Jukebox) and was second to Tudor Music in the Cork & Orrery Stakes at Ascot. At four, Balidar won the Bretby Handicap at Newmarket, earned black type in the Prix du Gros-Chene and Prix de Meautry in France, and put up a superb performance to win the Prix de l'Abbaye de Longchamp defeating Huntercombe and Raffingora. He was placed in the Duke of York Stakes, Ascot's King Stand Stakes and Haydock's Vernon Sprint Cup. Balidar was voted Champion Sprinter in France in 1970.

He is best remembered for three high-class progeny, Balidaress, Young Generation and Bolkonski. Balidaress (Balidar-Innocence by Sea Hawk II), winner of three races, descends from Admiration and produced Park Appeal (by Ahonoora), Champion 2YO filly in England and Ireland, four wins and unbeaten at two, won Moyglare Stud Stakes, Cheveley Park Stakes, Phoenix Park Oldtown Stud Stakes etc and in North America at four, she won the County Queen Stakes at Hollywood Park.

Park Appeal is the dam of Arvola (dam of Diktat, seven wins, Prix Maurice de Gheest, Haydock Sprint Cup) and Cape Cross, five wins including the Lockinge Stakes and sire in his first crop of Europe's champion 3YO filly Ouija Board.

Balidaress produced Balistroika (by Nijinsky II), unraced dam of Champion 3YO filly Russian Rhythm (English 1,000 Guineas, Lowther Stakes, Princess Margaret Stakes etc). Balidaress also produced the plain but brilliant filly Desirable (by Lord Gayle), winner of the Cheveley Park Stakes (defeating Pebbles), Princess Margaret Stakes, Princess Maiden Stakes, 2nd Lowther Stakes, Moyglare Stud Stakes, Nassau Stakes, 3rd English 1,000 Guineas, Petition Stakes and finished fourth in the Irish Champion Stakes behind Sadler's Wells, Seattle Song and Princess Pati. Desirable is the dam of Europe's Champion 2YO filly Shadayid, Fath (Lennox Stakes, 2nd Middle Park Stakes) and Dumaani (Keeneland Breeders' Cup Handicap twice). Shadayid won the English 1,000 Guineas, Prix Marcel Boussac, 2nd Sussex Stakes, Coronation Stakes, 3rd English Oaks, Queen Elizabeth II Stakes etc and is already the dam of stakes winners Bint Shadayid, Imtiyaz, and Alshadiyah.

Balidaress produced two more stakes winners. Alydaress (by Alydar) was Champion 3YO filly in Ireland, three wins including the Irish Oaks, 2nd Yorkshire Oaks, Premio Jockey Club a Copa d'Oro and dam of Prix Cleopatre winner Allurement. Nashamaa (by Ahonoora) won four races including the Ballymacoy Stakes and was runner-up in the National Stakes.

Young Generation was born in 1976 by Balidar out of Brig O'Doon by Shantung out of Tam O'Shanter by Tamerlane and inherited early maturing speed.

Young Generation was a smart juvenile winning the Richmond Stakes at Goodwood, runner-up in the Middle Park Stakes at Newmarket, and finished third in the Prix Morny in France. He was a decent sprinter, capturing the Lockinge Stakes and Prix Jean Prat. Among his progeny are Cadeaux Genereux, Safawan, Prince Sabo, Purchasepaperchase, Young Runaway, and Unknown Quantity. He is linebred to Nearco via two daughters and linebred to Hyperion via a son and a daughter.

Cadeaux Genereux (1985) is a big, strong, chestnut horse, and a consistent sire of stakes winners at Whitsbury Manor Stud, England. He is by Young Generation out of Smarten Up by Sharpen Up and is linebred 4 x 5 to champion Tudor Minstrel and linebred to Pharos. Voted Champion 3YO Sprinter in Europe, he won five of eight starts. His successes at three were the Ascot Diadem Stakes and Van Geest Criterion Stakes (beating Salse) and he was runner-up to Blue Note in the Prix Maurice de Gheest. At four, he was voted Champion Older Sprinter of Europe, two wins from five starts, taking his earnings to 304,326 pounds. He added the July Cup (beating Golden Opinion and Danehill) and the William Hill Sprint Championship (beating Silver Fling and Statoblest). He finished third in the Prix du Moulin de Longchamp (behind Polish Precedent) and the Temple Stakes. Cadeaux Genereux is the sire of Touch of the Blues (Atto Mile, Criterium de Maisons-Laffitte, Maker's Mark Mile), the brilliant filly Embassy (Cheveley Park Stakes), Bijou d'Inde (St. James's Palace Stakes), Bahamian Bounty (Prix Morny, Middle Park Stakes), Hoh Magic (Champion 2YO filly of Europe, Prix Morny, Molecomb Stakes), Land of Dreams (Flying Childers Stakes), May Ball (Prix Maurice de Gheest), Warning Shadows (Sun Chariot Stakes), Cairns (Rockfel Stakes) etc. He should make an influential broodmare sire.

Hyperion's male line in Australia was continued by Star Kingdom (Stardust-Impromptu by Concerto). Prominent stallions from Star Kingdom's line are Canny Lad (Bletchingly-Jesmond Lass by Lunchtime), Hurricane Sky (Star Watch-Dancing Show by Nijinsky II), Bureaucracy (Lord Ballina-Tulla Doll by Oncidium), Jetball (Marscay-Orwhina by Vain) and Reenact (Marscay-Role by Gulch).

Canny Lad, owned by Jack and Bob Ingham, was Australia's Champion 2YO colt with earnings in excess of A$2 million. He won eight races including the Golden Slipper Stakes, VRC Sires Produce Stakes, Bill Stutt Stakes, Tattersalls Stakes and finished third in the valuable W. S. Cox Plate. Canny Lad is the sire of 32 stakes winners to date, with progeny earnings of more than A$26 million. His dam Jesmond Lass is a new addition to the list of elite mares in the Number 14 Family. Beautiful Dreamer, second dam of Canny Lad, has a unique pedigree because she is inbred 3 x 3 to Dodoma (Dastur-Mumtaz Begum by Blenheim), the half-sister to Nasrullah and Sun Princess, dam of Royal Charger.

Beautiful Dreamer	Coeur Volant	Palestine	Fair Trial (ex Lady Juror)
			Una
		Diableretta	Dante by Nearco
			Dodoma ex **Mumtaz Begum**
	Adina Rose	Jambo	Felicitation
			Dodoma ex **Mumtaz Begum**
		Chevaline	Beau Cheval
			Triplane

Mumtaz Begum is by Blenheim from Mumtaz Mahal by The Tetrarch from Lady Josephine by Sundridge. Thus, Beautiful Dreamer carries three strains of Lady Josephine who is also the dam of Lady Juror, the dam of Fair Trial. Dodoma's sire, Dastur, is by Solario (Gainsborough-Sun Worship by Sundridge) and Fair Trial is a grandson of Phalaris (dam by Sainfoin) so the Sainfoin/Sierra mix is quite active.

When Beautiful Dreamer was matched with English sprinter Lunchtime it sparked tremendous speed! I believe Jesmond Lass is in the process of creating a dynasty so here is her pedigree. (She is a new addition to the list of "elite" mares.)

Jesmond Lass (Aust) (1975)	Lunchtime	Silly Season	Tom Fool	Menow by Pharamond II (**Selene**)
				Gaga by Bull Dog
			Double Deal	Straight Deal (by **Solario**)
				Nonats by King Salmon (ex **Malva**)
		Great Occasion	Hornbeam	Hyperion (**Selene**)
				Thicket by Nasrullah (**Mumtaz Begum**)
			Golden Wedding	Sunny Brae (dam by **Solario**)
				Flighty Falls (by son of **Fair Trial**)
	Beautiful Dreamer	Coeur Volant	Palestine	**Fair Trial** by **Fairway**
				Una
			Diableretta	Dante by **Nearco** by **Pharos**
				Dodoma (**Mumtaz Begum**)
		Adina Rose	Jambo	Felicitation
				Dodoma (**Mumtaz Begum**)
			Chevaline	Beau Cheval by Beau Pere
				Triplane

Jesmond Lass has a well-constructed pedigree pattern. Diableretta (dam of Coeur Volant) is a female cousin of Nasrullah. A considerable build-up of influence emanates from Sainfoin and Sierra-Lady Josephine by Sundridge is duplicated many times via her daughters Lady Juror and Mumtaz Mahal – and Dodoma is by Dastur, a son of Solario whose dam is by Sundridge. Yet another source of Sainfoin comes via Hurry On's dam in the ancestry of Flighty Falls. Malva is the dam of Blenheim (sire of Mumtaz Begum) and King Salmon. Beau Pere is a "son" of Son-in-Law whereas Lady Juror is a "daughter" of Son-in-Law. Hence there is "balanced breeding."

Lunchtime won the Dewhurst Stakes, Ascot Clarence House Stakes, Goodwood Goldings Stakes, was second in the Greenham Stakes and became a successful sire at the Thompson family's historic Widden Stud.

Jesmond Lass won seven races including the VATC Zonda Handicap and produced seven winners. Apart from Champion 2YO colt Canny Lad, she produced stakes winner Sister Canny (Laurent Perrier Stakes, Readymix Handicap, 3rd Meyer Stakes), Group 1 filly Canny Lass (nine wins $560,800 Toorak Stakes, Marlboro Cup, William Reid Stakes, 2nd Australasian Oaks, 3rd AJC Oaks) and also an unraced filly Canny Miss, dam of Group 1 stakes winner Camarena (nine wins $938,260, Queensland Derby, Queensland Guineas, 2nd Flight Stakes, L. K. S MacKinnon Stakes, 3rd Australasian Oaks). Canny Lass, by Bletchingly, produced Astute Angel, winner of the Gibson-Carmichael Stakes. She is also the granddam of stakes winner Al Jameel.

Another stakes producer inheriting speed from the important Sainfoin/Sierra mix is Cotehele House, by brilliant English juvenile My Swanee (son of Petition) from Eight Carat by Pieces of Eight from

Klairessa, tracing to Tessa Gillian, a sister to Royal Charger. This is the female line of Nasrullah's dam Mumtaz Begum.

Cotehele House produced two colts by Danehill who were Group 1 winners, namely Danewin (13 wins A$2,031,636, won Caulfield Stakes, Doomben Cup, Spring Champion Stakes, Rosehill Guineas, L.K.S. MacKinnon Stakes, 2nd AJC Derby, VRC Victoria Derby) and Commands (four wins A$417,231, won Missile Stakes, 2nd The Galaxy, 3rd Caulfield Guineas). Danewin and Commands were colts bred in New Zealand by Sir Patrick Hogan at his famous Cambridge Stud. Danewin is the sire of such good ones as Elegant Fashion, County Tyrone and Classy Dane.

Although there was a Thoroughbred population explosion in the world after 1960, the best Thoroughbreds racing today are descendants of the original genetic material produced in Europe. Queen Victoria's homebreds, Sainfoin and his sister Sierra, are exceedingly powerful ancestors. Abram S. Hewitt was correct in stating Phalaris and Sundridge had enormous impact on the breed for speed. So far we have touched on the important role of Nasrullah, Royal Charger and Mahmoud in the evolutionary process of speed, but there are other major players to be mentioned.

In North America, the dominant speed lines of Man o' War, Domino, Blue Larkspur and the brothers Bull Dog and Sir Gallahad III made huge contributions towards improving speed, as did unbeaten French champion Ajax and his son Teddy (sire of La Troienne). Classic speed was derived from two stayers with speed, namely Princequillo and Prince Chevalier who were genetically compatible with Nearco and Ribot, the two great sires bred by Federico Tesio in Italy that were never defeated.

Today, we have basically four dominant international strains – Northern Dancer, Mr. Prospector, Seattle Slew and Sunday Silence. The continuance of their lines will depend upon quality mares being matched with their descendants. A mix of all four of these sires should produce outstanding stakes winners.

To summarize, in designing matings for speed or classic speed, ideally you need access to the most influential sires. If a breeder does not have access to them, then perhaps there is an alternative – design matings that duplicate superior strains, such as brother and sister, three-parts brother and sister, etc or collect "elite" mares in a single pedigree. Maternal strength always wins in the end. Because there are hundreds of thousands of recessive genes floating around the Thoroughbred gene pool, you will need to target strains that are dominant or partially dominant to breed stakes performers. I admit the challenge is more difficult than it was 40 years ago.

These days, the difference between a Group 1 or Grade 1 winner and a Listed stakes winner may be only two lengths, so the task at hand is not going to be easy. Nevertheless, pedigree research is a valuable tool. Great breeders of the past like Federico Tesio, Lord Derby, Marcel Boussac and the Aga Khan used pedigree research. There is an art to being able to design a mating that produces a champion racehorse or classic winner, but in the breeding of racehorses, art requires "luck."

Of all the important ancestors appearing in North American pedigrees, the sire that transmitted the most dynamic, superior genes for speed was Native Dancer (Polynesian-Geisha by Discovery-Miyako). His equivalent in Europe was Tesio's unbeaten champion Nearco (Pharos-Nogara by Havresac II), sire of Nasrullah and Royal Charger. Native Dancer and Nearco are found in the pedigrees of both Northern Dancer and Mr. Prospector – two exceptional sires that shaped the breed.

THE RISING INFLUENCE OF ROYAL CHARGER

"Science is organised knowledge" - Herbert Spence

The loss of the Aga Khan's Nasrullah, first to Ireland and then to North America, seriously affected progress made by European breeders after the war (between 1946 and 1960). World War II affected all European stud farms, spoiling Marcel Boussac's program in France (Pharis II was stolen by the Germans) and causing the Aga Khan to cut back and sell valuable breeding stock. The results of the English Derby and Prix de l'Arc de Triomphe during the period 1936 to 1950 best illustrate genotypes that triumphed when American and Australasian breeders began raiding the best bloodlines of Europe.

English Derby winners -

1936 Mahmoud (Blenheim-Mah Mahal by Gainsborough)
1937 Mid-Day Sun (Solario-Bridge of Allan by Phalaris)
1938 Bois Roussel (Vatout-Plucky Liege by Spearmint)
1939 Blue Peter (Fairway-Fancy Free by Stefan The Great)
1940 Pont L'Eveque (Barneveldt-Pontera by Belfonds)
1941 Owen Tudor (Hyperion-Mary Tudor by Pharos)
1942 Watling Street (Fairway-Ranai by Rabelais)
1943 Straight Deal (Solario-Good Deal by Apelle)
1944 Ocean Swell (Blue Peter-Jiffy by Hyperion)
1945 Dante (Nearco-Rosy Legend by Dark Legend)
1946 Airborne (Precipitation-Bouquet by Buchan)
1947 Pearl Diver (Vatellor-Pearl Cap by Le Capucin)
1948 My Love (Vatellor-For My Love by Amfortas)
1949 Nimbus (Nearco-Kong by Baytown)
1950 Galcador (Djebel-Pharyva by Pharos)

Prix de l'Arc de Triomphe winners -

1936 Corrida (Coronach-Zariba by Sardanapale)
1937 Corrida (Coronach-Zariba by Sardanapale)
1938 Éclair au Chocolat (Bubbles-Honey Sweet by Kircubbin)
1939 no race
1940 no race
1941 Le Pacha (Biribi-Advertencia by Ksar)
1942 Djebel (Tourbillon-Loika by Gay Crusader)
1943 Verso II (Pinceau-Variete by La Farina)
1944 Ardan (Pharis II-Adargatis by Asterus)
1945 Nikellora (Vatellor-Niki by Palais Royal)
1946 Caracalla (Tourbillon-Astronomie by Asterus)
1947 Le Paillon (Fastnet-Blue Bear by Blenheim)
1948 Migoli (Bois Roussel-Mah Iran by Bahram)
1949 Coronation V (Djebel-Esmeralda by Tourbillon)
1950 Tantieme (Deux Pour Cent-Terka by Indus)

In North America, Cornelius Vanderbilt Whitney took control of the bloodstock inherited from his father, Harry Payne Whitney, much of which carried the strains of Broomstick, Whisk Broom II, Peter Pan, Chicle (by Spearmint) and Pennant. When Equipoise died in 1940 at a time when none of the young sires at the Whitney Farm showed enough potential to raise hopes, C.V. Whitney decided he wanted an outcross stallion and looked towards England. Equipoise had sired four crops before he died and was sorely missed. Whitney's farm manager, Major Louis Beard, was replaced by a younger man, Ivor Balding, who recommended the purchase of Mahmoud, winner of the English Derby in record time. Mahmoud sired 24 homebred stakes winners for the Whitney Farm including Champion 2YO filly First Flight. He was acquired from the Aga Khan who stood the gray stallion for four years (between 1937 to 1940) before C.V. Whitney's offer was accepted. The Aga Khan was then living in Switzerland and was keen to sell horses during the war.

In 1936, the Aga Khan mated Nasrullah's dam (Mumtaz Begum) to Solario, a St. Leger winner, in an attempt to gain more stamina. The following year, a bay filly was born in France named Sun Princess but she showed a lack of ability and was culled. For her new owner she produced 13 foals, nine winners including Alassio, Lucky Bag, Madara, Royal Charger and Tessa Gillian. Lucky Bag ended up being a successful sire in New Zealand, Madara was a successful sire in South America and Tessa Gillian established a very strong branch of her own.

Royal Charger, a golden chestnut colt born in 1942, was by Nearco from Sun Princess by Solario out of Mumtaz Begum and therefore three-parts brother to English Champion 2YO colt Nasrullah. Royal Charger received his chestnut color from Sundridge, a champion sprinter on both sides of his pedigree. A soft, muscular youngster, Royal Charger did not win any of his starts at two although he showed a glimpse of promise when second to Sun Honey in the Isleham Stakes at Newmarket and when second in the Freckenham Nursery. At three, Royal Charger won the Stockton Tees Plate, Teversham Stakes by four lengths, defeated Golden Cloud at Newmarket in the Challenge Stakes and finished third in the English 2,000 Guineas beaten a neck and two lengths by Court Martial and Dante. He was placed in several sprint races including the Duke of York Stakes.

At four, he progressed and won the Queen Anne Stakes at Royal Ascot, Coronation Plate at Chester, Ayr Gold Cup and finished with placings in the King's Stand Stakes and Challenge Stakes. Royal Charger was somewhat temperamental like Nasrullah, yet on his best behavior he could get a mile in top company. At stud for only a short time in England, he was eventually exported to North America.

Royal Charger sired 57 stakes winners including Idun (U.S. Champion 2YO and 3YO filly), Royal Orbit (Preakness Stakes), Mongo (United Nations Handicap), Royal Native (U.S. Champion Handicap Mare), Giles de Retz (English 2,000 Guineas), Happy Laughter (English 1,000 Guineas), Seaneen (San Carlos Handicap, Californian Stakes), Banri An Oir (Athasi Stakes, 3rd English 1,000 Guineas), Sea Charger (Irish 2,000 Guineas, Irish St. Leger), Royal Serenade (Hollywood Gold Cup), Francis S. (Wood Memorial Stakes, Dwyer Handicap, Bay Shore Handicap), Gay Hostess, Finnegan, Knight's Romance, Copenhagen II, Royal Gunner, Ossian II, Royal Clipper, Pride of Kildare and the best of them all, U.S. Champion 2YO colt Turn-To.

Turn-To was a short-coupled bay colt by Royal Charger out of imported French mare Source Sucree by Admiral Drake (son of Plucky Liege).

Turn-To (1951)	Royal Charger	Nearco	Pharos	Phalaris (dam by **Sainfoin**)
				Scapa Flow by Chaucer by **St. Simon**
			Nogara	Havresac II by Rabelais by **St. Simon**
				Catnip by **Spearmint** by Carbine
		Sun Princess	Solario	Gainsborough
				Sun Worship by **Sundridge**
			Mumtaz Begum	Blenheim by Blandford by **Swynford**
				Mumtaz Mahal ex dau of **Sundridge**
	Source Sucree	Admiral Drake	Craig an Eran	Sunstar by **Sundridge**
				Maid of the Mist by **Cyllene**
			Plucky Liege	**Spearmint** by Carbine
				Concertina by **St. Simon**
		Lavendula II	**Pharos**	Phalaris (dam by **Sainfoin**)
				Scapa Flow by Chaucer by **St. Simon**
			Sweet Lavender	**Swynford**
				Marchetta by Marco

Inbred 3 x 3 to Pharos (runner-up to Papyrus in the English Derby), Turn-To has superior ancestors duplicated in his ancestry, viz. St. Simon, Canterbury Pilgrim (via her sons Chaucer and Swynford), classic sire Cyllene, the siblings Sainfoin and Sierra (dam of duplicated Sundridge) and Spearmint's sire Carbine who is related to Polymelus, the sire of Phalaris. This is a brilliant pedigree! No wonder Turn-To earned the title of U.S. Champion 2YO colt and became an exciting winter favorite for the Kentucky Derby. Bred in Ireland by the partnership of Mrs. G. L. Hastings and Mr. E. R. Miville, Turn-To was trained by Edward Hayward for the Cain Hoy Stable. There is an interesting story behind his importation to North America.

Claude C. Tanner was in the twilight of his life and desperately wanted a colt classy enough to start in the Kentucky Derby. By sea-mail, he contacted Frank More-O'Ferrall, a director of the Anglo-Irish Bloodstock Agency. The agent answered saying he knew of a colt that might be purchased privately, on a farm next to his own. He explained how he watched and admired a neat yearling colt by Royal Charger out of Source Sucree glide across adjacent paddocks. The Irish sure know how to close a sale because without fuss, the bay yearling colt was shipped to the U.S. to his new owner in early April 1952. Tanner inspected his colt and although light in condition, was pleased with his purchase; but on April 22, Claude took a bad turn at his Lexington home and died the next day. The executors of his estate entered the Irish-bred colt in the Keeneland summer sales in 1952.

Registered with the name Source Royal, the colt attracted the attention of trainer Edward Hayward who touted him to his boss, Commander Harry Guggenheim, owner of Cain Hoy Stable. Guggenheim purchased the yearling for $20,000 and changed his name to Turn-To.

He thrived in training and had a few bullet workouts during his juvenile campaign. Turn-To ran five times for three wins at two, scoring in the valuable Garden State Stakes defeating the brilliant colt Correlation, the Saratoga Special (on the disqualification of Porterhouse), a Maiden 2YO Special Handicap and finished third to Artismo in the Hopeful Stakes. His two-year-old earnings came to a staggering $176,807 and he was made winter book favorite for the Kentucky Derby.

Turn-To was co-highweighted with Porterhouse on the Experimental Free Handicap of the best two-year-olds of 1953. As he developed physically, he toed-out in both front feet, but in workouts his action was not affected by this minor fault.

After a rest, Turn-To was brought back from his owner's estate at Port Washington on Long Island to commence his three-year-old campaign at Hialeah Park, in Florida.

On February 2, 1954, carrying 122 pounds, Turn-To won by 3½ lengths an overnight allowance race at 1 1/16 miles. The time for his first six furlongs was 1:10 flat and jockey Henry Moreno came back smiling. Hayward next set Turn-To for an allowance race at 1 1/16 miles on February 16 as a "prep" for the Flamingo Stakes. It proved an easy task for the colt, scoring by 3 ½ lengths.

In the Flamingo Stakes of 1 1/8 miles $100,000 added, in a field of eight starters, Turn-To would meet a smart colt named Hasty Road. This would be a real test. Along the backstretch, Turn-To took the lead from stablemate Giant Cracker. At the furlong mark, jockey Moreno gave Turn-To a few cracks with the whip which caused the colt to swerve outwards, losing momentum, but he went to the wire three lengths clear of Black Metal and Maharajah, with Hasty Road finishing a disappointing fifth. Moreno said he felt something was wrong when he pulled Turn-To up, but next morning the colt was fine.

Turn-To was shipped to Kentucky and the Cain Hoy runner remained a short-priced Kentucky Derby favorite but on the morning of March 24, Turn-To came out of his stall quite lame – he'd bowed his left front tendon. Captain Guggenheim was told his colt's career was finished and Turn-To was retired to stud.

The colt had earned $280,032 from six wins and two placings, had defeated Errard King (winner of the Arlington Classic), Hasty Road (winner of the Preakness Stakes and runner-up to Determine in the Kentucky Derby) and Correlation (winner of the Wood Memorial Stakes). At year's end, Turn-To was given highweight of 132 pounds on The Blood-Horse Handicap for the best three year olds, ahead of High Gun at 130 pounds, with Helioscope and Determine sharing third spot at 129 pounds.

Source Sucree, dam of champion Turn-To, was a winner at three in France and half-sister to Marcel Boussac's French Champion 2YO colt Ambiorix (winner of the Grand Criterium, Prix Lupin, Prix Greffulhe etc.), Babiste (22 wins in France and Belgium, including the Prix Opott, Prix Partlet, Prix de Saint-Georges etc), and the gray mare Perfume II (dam of English Champion 2YO colt My Babu, winner of the English 2,000 Guineas, Sussex Stakes, Champagne Stakes, Nell Gwyn Stakes, Norfolk Stakes and Victoria Cup). Source Sucree was by the stayer Admiral Drake, five wins including the Grand Prix de Paris, runner-up to Brantome in the French 2,000 Guineas and third to him in the Prix du Jockey Club-French Derby.

Admiral Drake was the leading sire in France in 1955 and descends in male line from English Derby winner Sunstar, a son of Sundridge.

Turn-To was an influential sire at Spendthrift Farm. Among his progeny were Hail To Reason (Champion 2YO colt, nine wins $328,434, Tremont Stakes, Youthful Stakes, Great American Stakes, Sapling Stakes, Sanford Stakes etc), Sir Gaylord (10 wins $237,400, Sapling Stakes, Great American Stakes, National Stallion Stakes, Tyro Stakes, Bahamas Stakes, etc), First Landing (Champion 2YO colt, 19 wins $79,577, Champagne Stakes, Garden State Stakes, Hopeful Stakes, Saratoga Special, Monmouth Handicap etc), Dead Ahead (Roamer Handicap), All Hands, Captain's Gig (Futurity Stakes) and Cyane (Futurity Stakes, Dwyer Stakes). Turn-To sired many outstanding fillies including Sally Ship (1st Kentucky Oaks, Ashland Stakes), Turn To Talent (Pageant Handicap, Blue Hen Stakes) and Palace Music's granddam, Come Hither Look (Blue Hen Stakes).

To my knowledge, the biggest colt ever sired by Turn-To was Best Turn, 15 wins from 28 starts, $270,339, who was 17.2 hands high. A dark brown horse with a handsome head and tremendous length from hip to hock, Best Turn was out of Sweet Clementine, a daughter of the talented Miz Clementine (16 wins, $267,100, 1st Hollywood Oaks, Vagrancy Handicap, California Derby, Cinema Handicap, Las Flores Handicap, California Oaks) who was sister to Two Lea (U.S. Champion 3YO filly, Champion Handicap mare and dam of Kentucky Derby winner Tim Tam) and Twosy (21 wins, Sagamore Stakes, Colonial Handicap and granddam of Miss Carmie who produced U.S. Champion 3YO filly Chris Evert and All Rainbows).

Best Turn was retired to Calumet Farm after a career of 15 wins and earnings of $270,339. His victories include the Vosburgh, Saranac, John B. Campbell, Paumonok, Queens County Handicaps and he was runner-up to Tyrant in the Carter Handicap and registered 1:21 $\frac{3}{5}$ for seven furlongs in the Vosburgh Handicap.

Despite a very successful stud career, Best Turn was never quite appreciated by commercial breeders. His yearlings were big and unfurnished, requiring time to develop strength. Among his best progeny were Cox's Ridge (16 wins $667,172, Metropolitan Handicap, Oaklawn Handicap), Davona Dale (U.S. Champion 3YO filly), Cathy's Reject, Gallant Best, Grant's Best and Turn and Count (nine wins $246,971, Roamer Handicap).

Cox's Ridge was one of my all-time favorite stallions. He was tall, strong, but not heavy-bodied, with a great hip and nice clean hocks. I used to admire him when I took Overbrook Farm's mares to be covered at Claiborne Farm. Although he was a tall horse his conformation was in proportion to his size. Cox's Ridge sired Life's Magic (U.S. Champion 3YO filly, Champion Older Mare), Cardmania (U.S. Champion Sprinter), Vanlandingham (U.S. Champion Older Horse), Sultry Song (Hollywood Gold Cup, Woodward Handicap), De Roche (Jerome Handicap), the brilliant filly Twilight Ridge, Pine Circle, Little Missouri and Dream Team (dam of Orientate, U.S. Champion Sprinter).

I expect Gainesway Farm's young stallion Orientate to become a successful sire of stakes winners as he has an exceptional pedigree pattern with heavy linebreeding to Sainfoin and Sierra. Bred by Antony Beck and family, Orientate (Mt. Livermore-Dream Team by Cox's Ridge) was sold as a yearling and won 10 races $1,716,950, including the Breeders' Cup Sprint, Forego Handicap (defeating Aldebaran), Indiana Derby and Commonwealth Breeders' Cup Stakes. Antony Beck repurchased the champion for stud duty and took in as a partner John Messara, owner of Arrowfield Stud, based in the fertile Hunter Valley of Australia.

During my Overbrook years, Jim Cannon and I would visit Wayne Lukas' barn in California to inspect William T. Young's horses in training and I took a special liking to Dream Team. She was an athletic filly whose race record should have been greater than her three wins with earnings of $317,410.

Dream Team won the Oak Leaf Stakes in scintillating style. Actually, I expected her to win the Kentucky Oaks the following year, but she injured herself and never made it to the classic. However, I do know Wayne Lukas had a high regard for the filly. Some years later Antony asked me to inspect his weanlings and among them was Orientate who inherited many of the characteristics of his dam. I liked him a lot.

Orientate has a deep girth, straight hind legs like so many fast dirt horses in North America and power behind the saddle. He is bred to sire both dirt and turf runners and is free of Northern Dancer's strain – a strain that should suit him.

Probably Turn-To's second best son at stud was Sir Gaylord, a horse who stood duty on two continents. Sir Gaylord sired 56 stakes winners and was second leading sire in England in 1968 when his champion son Sir Ivor won the English 2,000 Guineas, Derby, Champion Stakes and was runner-up in both the Irish Derby and Prix de l'Arc de Triomphe. Sir Ivor was Champion 2YO in Europe, winning the Grand Criterium, National Stakes etc. and sired at least 66 stakes winners including Ivanjica, Godetia, Bates Motel, Malinowski, Cloonlara, Sir Tristram, Optimistic Gal and Lady Capulet (dam of El Prado).

Sir Gaylord (1959)	Turn-To	Royal Charger	Nearco	**Pharos** by Phalaris - **Polymelus**
				Nogara by Havresac II
			Sun Princess	Solario (dam by Sundridge)
				Mumtaz Begum
		Source Sucree	Admiral Drake	Craig an Eran by Sunstar
				Plucky Liege by Spearmint
			Lavendula II	**Pharos** by Phalaris - **Polymelus**
				Sweet Lavender by Swynford
	Somethingroyal	Princequillo	Prince Rose	Rose Prince
				Indolence by Gay Crusader
			Cosquilla	Papyrus by Tracery
				Quick Thought
		Imperatrice	Caruso	Polymelian by **Polymelus**
				Sweet Music
			Cinquepace	Brown Bud by Brown Prince II
				Assignation by Teddy

Somethingroyal is a daughter of Princequillo, a phenomenal influence for soundness who has a genetic affinity with Royal Charger and his three-quarter brother Nasrullah. Princequillo had correct knees, a valuable asset seeing Nasrullah and Royal Charger had slightly weak knees. Somethingroyal produced champion Secretariat, Syrian Sea and The Bride when mated with Nasrullah's son Bold Ruler.

In Sir Gaylord's pedigree, Polymelus is duplicated along with St. Simon and his sister Angelica.

Also present is the combination of brother and sister, the speed strains of Sainfoin and Sierra. Caruso is a "son" of Polymelian (Polymelus-Pasquita by Sundridge). You won't find Polymelian often in pedigrees but he happens to be the broodmare sire of Polynesian, the father of Native Dancer. Caruso's input explains why Native Dancer's line is blending successfully with Somethingroyal's sons Sir Gaylord and Secretariat by adding a "son" of Polymelian to the pattern.

Unplaced from one start, Somethingroyal was voted Broodmare of the Year in North America. She produced 11 winners from 18 foals and among her other stakes-winning progeny were First Family (seven wins $188,040, Gulfstream Park Handicap) and Syrian Sea (six wins $178,245, Selima Stakes, Astarita Stakes, Colleen Stakes).

Somethingroyal produced five stakes-placed winners of which the best was Grand Coulee, a filly by First Landing, five wins, 2nd Matron Handicap, 3rd Pucker Up Handicap. Slightly disappointing was her colt by Northern Dancer named Somethingfabulous who finished third in the Flamingo Stakes.

I asked Penny Chenery if Somethingroyal showed any ability in training and she told me the filly was simply disappointing, but explained how the mare was much like her sire, Princequillo, with plenty of substance. Somethingroyal must have inherited valuable sex-linked genes – genes that could produce large hearts. Although the mare had limited racing ability she must have carried superior genes on one of her X sex chromosomes. Thus, on the law of averages, some of her foals would inherit the stronger X sex chromosome with genes for large heart size.

Although a stakes winner, Syrian Sea was crooked in her forelegs whereas her sister The Bride was more correct. Bold Ruler was known to sire many brilliant sons and daughters but of his lesser progeny, many developed unsound forelegs.

Sir Gaylord is the sire of Sir Ivor, Habitat, Gay Matelda, Bonnie and Gay, Sahib, Lord Gaylord, Wildwook, Gay Missile, Yes Sir, Village Square, Francine M, and Gay Meeting. His descendants are linking up with Secretariat's descendants in a positive way. Sir Gaylord sometimes transmitted upright pasterns to his progeny (caused by recessive genes) and his successful son Habitat inherited this fault.

The best sire-son of Turn-To was Hail To Reason, a tall, athletic individual who toed-out both front feet like his daddy. Hail To Reason was a light-framed, dark brown horse with plenty of spirit and the best two-year-old of his generation. He won nine races at two years for earnings of $328,434 and was out of the genuine but tough mare Nothirdchance, 11 wins $112,660, winner of the Acorn Stakes, 2nd Ladies Handicap, Comely Stakes, and 3rd San Marcos Handicap.

Nothirdchance was bred on a similar cross to Mr. Prospector's third dam Miss Dogwood, hence the success of mixing Hail To Reason with Mr. Prospector in the same pedigree. Nothirdchance is by Blue Swords (stakes winning son of Blue Larkspur) from Galla Colors by Sir Gallahad III (brother to Bull Dog) and traces in female line to Baton Rouge, ancestress of Admiral's Voyage. Very few stallions have a "son" of Blue Larkspur in their pedigree.

Hail To Reason is the sire of the following major stakes winners –

Roberto, Champion 2YO in Ireland, won English Derby, National Stakes, Anglesey Stakes, Benson & Hedges Gold Cup (defeating Brigadier Gerard), Vauxhall Trial Stakes, Coronation Cup and runner-up in the English 2,000 Guineas.

Bold Reason, seven wins $304,082 won Travers Stakes, Lexington Handicap, American Derby, Hollywood Derby, 3rd Kentucky Derby and broodmare sire of Sadler's Wells, Fairy King and Tate Gallery.

Personality, eight wins $462,603 U.S. Horse of the Year, Preakness Stakes, Woodward Stakes, Jersey Derby, Wood Memorial Stakes, Jim Dandy Stakes.

Straight Deal, 21 wins $733,020 U.S. Champion Handicap mare, Spinster Stakes, Ladies Handicap, Santa Barbara Handicap, Hollywood Oaks, Vineland Handicap, Santa Margarita Handicap, Top Flight Handicap etc.

Stop The Music, 11 wins $448,922 won Champagne Stakes, Saratoga Special, Dwyer Handicap and sire of Cure The Blues.

Hail To All, eight wins $494,150 won Belmont Stakes, Travers Stakes, Jersey Derby, Hibiscus Stakes, 2nd Florida Derby, 3rd Preakness Stakes etc.

Proud Clarion, six wins $218,730 1st Kentucky Derby, Roamer Handicap, 2nd Blue Grass Stakes, 3rd Preakness Stakes.

Mr. Leader, 10 wins $219,803 won Jerome Handicap, Oceanport Handicap, Tidal Handicap, Stars and Stripes Handicap.

Reason To Hail, four wins $191,382 won California Derby, Tyro Stakes, 2nd Travers Stakes, Hibiscus Stakes.

Good Counsel, six wins $246,554 won Widener Handicap, Longfellow Handicap, Rosemont Stakes.

Halo, nine wins $259,553 won United Nations Handicap, Tidal Handicap, Lawrence Realization Handicap, 3rd Dwyer Handicap, Jersey Derby and leading sire in North America whose sons include Sunday Silence, Saint Ballado, Devil's Bag, Sunny's Halo, Don't Say Halo and Lively One.

Hail To Reason sired a batch of high-class fillies other than Straight Deal. They include Regal Gleam (eight wins $246,793 U.S. Champion 2YO filly), Hippodamia (Champion 2YO filly in France), Cake (Champion 2YO filly in Ireland), Inca Queen (Top Flight Handicap, Demoiselle Stakes) and the brilliant Priceless Gem (Frizette Stakes, Futurity Stakes). Here is the pedigree of Halo, twice leading sire in North America and probably an important ancestor in the next few decades:

Halo (1969)	Hail To Reason	Turn-To	Royal Charger	Nearco by **Pharos**
				Sun Princess ex **Mumtaz Begum**
			Source Sucree	Admiral Drake ex dau. of **Spearmint**
				Lavendula II by **Pharos**
		Nothirdchance	Blue Swords	**Blue Larkspur**
				Flaming Swords by Man o' War
			Galla Colors	Sir Gallahad III ex dau. of **Spearmint**
				Rouge et Noir
	Cosmah	Cosmic Bomb	Pharamond II	**Phalaris**
				Selene by **Chaucer**
			Banish Fear	**Blue Larkspur**
				Herodiade
		Almahmoud	Mahmoud	**Blenheim**
				Mah Mahal ex **Mumtaz Mahal**
			Arbitrator	Peace Chance by Chance Shot
				Mother Goose by son of **Spearmint**

Halo's dam is half-sister to Northern Dancer's dam, Natalma. Apart from the son and daughter of leading sire Blue Larkspur, and the three-parts genetic siblings Pharos and Pharamond II (both Phalaris/Chaucer products), speed is reinforced via Mumtaz Mahal and the Sainfoin/Sierra mix. Stamina is reinforced via Spearmint and Blenheim. Mahmoud is three-quarters brother to Mumtaz Begum, granddam of Royal Charger.

Halo is the sire of Saint Ballado, a horse that toed-out in front like Turn-To. Saint Ballado was a different type to his brother Devil's Bag. For one thing, he had more bone and in some respects resembled Sunday Silence's type. What I admired most about him was his nice shoulder angle and strength through the hip. His main weakness was the shape of the hocks and his characteristic toe-out.

Saint Ballado won four of nine starts for $302,820 and was nowhere near as smart as Devil's Bag on the racetrack, but in the breeding shed he was able to upgrade his mares and did it the hard way. He eventually came to Kentucky to stand at Taylor Made Farms in partnership with Aaron U. Jones. He won the Arlington Classic and Sheridan Stakes.

Saint Ballado has sired 53 stakes winners to date including Ashado (Breeders' Cup Distaff Stakes, Coaching Club American Oaks), Yankee Victor (Metropolitan Handicap), Captain Bodgit (Florida Derby), Sister Act (Hempstead Handicap), Flame Thrower (Del Mar Futurity), St. Averil (Santa Catalina Stakes) and others such as Fantasy Angel, Straight Man, Freedom's Daughter and Saintly Look. Saint Ballado was fifth on the 2004 Sires' List.

Devil's Bag is the sire of 44 stakes winners and was U.S. Champion 2YO colt in 1983. His progeny have earned almost $50 million. By far his best runner is Japan's Horse of the Year Taiki Shuttle, who in France won the Prix du Jacques Le Marois, proving to the world the best in Japan can compete with the best in Europe. Devil's Bag is also sire of Devil His Due (sire of Dubai World Cup winner Roses in May), Twilight Agenda, Devil's Orchid, Evangelical, Buy The Sport and Diablo.

However, the best son of Halo was the world's leading sire Sunday Silence who led the sire's list in Japan more times than the great stallion Northern Taste. Sunday Silence has many sons at stud in Japan and is certain to make a lasting impression on a global basis.

Southern Halo (by Halo) did well in Argentina and headed the sires' list. He also shuttled to Kentucky and his stakes winning son More Than Ready might carry on his branch of the male line.

Hail To Reason's classic-winning son Roberto is a sire of sires. Bred by John Galbreath at Darby Dan Farm, Roberto's influence is gradually spreading. His sons include Brian's Time, Silver Hawk, Robellino, Lear Fan, Kris S. (sire of the English Derby winner Kris Kin), Brocco, Arch, Metropolitan Handicap winner You And I, Dr. Fong, Three Chimneys' proven sire Dynaformer, and Red Ransom, originally based in Kentucky but now standing in Europe.

Dr. Fong has a strong pedigree pattern for a sire and is likely to get classic runners, especially if the Nasrullah/Princequillo nick or Buckpasser's strain is reinforced because I predict these are ideal strains to suit him.

Dr. Fong won both of his starts as a juvenile, scoring in the Amerada Maiden Stakes at Newbury and the Listed Autumn Stakes at Ascot over a mile. A chestnut horse with scope, he was a high-class performer at three, winning the St. James' Palace Stakes at Royal Ascot (defeating Desert Prince), the Prix Eugene Adam and Newmarket Stakes, was runner-up in the Queen Elizabeth II Stakes (to Desert Prince with Cape Cross behind), 3rd Prix Jean Prat and in North America, was runner-up in the Strub Stakes and Oak Tree Derby. He is linebred to the three-parts brothers Royal Charger and Nasrullah, but probably the key elements of his pedigree involve duplication of Princequillo, extra input from Sardanapale via Nasrullah's champion son Nashua, and maternal strength from Rose Bower (a product of the Princequillo/Nasrullah nick).

Miswaki might be one of the most influential broodmare sires in the world because he imparts plenty of "electricity" to his daughters who pass it on to their progeny. I expect Daylami, Dalakhani and Galileo (all out of daughters of Miswaki) to become excellent sires of Group and Graded stakes runners.

When we lived on Overbrook Farm our house was located not far from an old converted tobacco barn that accommodated 12 foaling mares. Our daughters Kiersten and Tanya would often watch young foals frolic in the paddocks nearby. Sometimes after work I would walk into the small paddock near our house where Hopespringseternal and her foal were enjoying the cool air.

"Hope," as we called her, had a damaged left knee from injury and preferred to be on her own. She got to know me well and appreciated fresh carrots. I can't begin to tell you how much I loved this chestnut mare. She is of course the dam of Miswaki, now an influential broodmare sire.

Like most daughters of champion Buckpasser, Hopespringseternal was feminine, intelligent and a wonderful mother. I still have a set of her shoes mounted on a plaque in my office. The photograph of her shown below was taken in 1987.

Her dam Rose Bower is an "elite" mare.

It is a pity Hopespringseternal could not race because she might have become a stakes winner at a mile or more.

HOPESPRINGSETERNAL (Buckpasser - Rose Bower by Princequillo) dam of stakes winners Miswaki, Northern Eternity, stakes-placed winner Lone Secretariat, and Hope For All (dam of Lacovia who won the Prix-Alary Gr-1 and Prix de Diane [French Oaks] Gr-1.)

Dr. Fong (1995)	Kris S.	Roberto	Hail To Reason	Turn-To by **Royal Charger**
				Nothirdchance dam by **Sir Galahad III**
			Bramalea	**Nashua** by **Nasrullah**
				Rarelea by Bull Lea by **Bull Dog**
		Sharp Queen	**Princequillo**	Prince Rose
				Cosquila by Papyrus
			Bridgework	Occupy by **Bull Dog**
				Feale Bridge by Gold Bridge
	Spring Flight	Miswaki	Mr. Prospector	Raise A Native by Native Dancer
				Gold Digger by **Nashua** by **Nasrullah**
			Hopespringseternal	Buckpasser by Tom Fool
				Rose Bower (**Princequillo/Nasrullah**)
		Coco La Investment	Coco Le Terreur	Nearctic
				Ciboulette by Chop Chop
			Great Investment	Saidam by Never Say Die son of **Nasrullah**
				Modern

It is my belief Rose Bower (Princequillo-Lea Lane by Nasrullah) is the real dominating force in Miswaki's ancestry, more so than Buckpasser. A plausible reason is her inbred ancestor Nasrullah (via a son and daughter) who overpowers other genetic influences. Probably mares with Secretariat, Riverman and Poker offer ideal tests with Dr. Fong to produce stakes runners.

Red Ransom (Roberto-Arabia by Damascus) was a sensationally fast juvenile that never earned black type. Like Danzig, he showed blazing speed but went wrong after three starts, winning two of them. Those of us who witnessed Red Ransom's victories will always remember his brilliance! Unlike his sire in type, I suspect he throws back to My Babu, a son of Djebel. He belongs to the Number 6 Family, the branch established via Fair Freedom.

My Babu's dam Perfume II (Badruddin-Lavendula II by Pharos) acts like a genetic cousin to Nasrullah and Royal Charger, boosting early maturing speed. Badruddin was a fast sprinter by Blandford out of champion Mumtaz Mahal by The Tetrarch out of Lady Josephine by Sundridge. Red Ransom has duplication of the elite mare Lavendula II, the dam of Source Sucree and Perfume II.

Lavendula II provides the pattern with a "daughter" of Pharos.

Red Ransom is the sire of Perfect Sting (U.S. Champion 3YO Turf mare), Casual Look (English Oaks), Ekraah (Gran Premio del Jockey Club), China Visit (Prix du Rond-Point), Sri Pekan (Champagne Stakes), Intikhab (Champion Miler in Europe), Bail Out Becky (Del Mar Oaks), Comic Strip (Louisiana Derby) and is the sire of many smart stakes winners in Australia including Charge Forward (Galaxy Stakes Gr-1), Crimson Reign and the brilliant filly Halibery.

Red Ransom should have a genetic affinity with Lyphard and with specific sons of Mr. Prospector. In addition, he likes Native Dancer's line and input from the brothers Fairway and Pharos.

Royal Charger's line is certainly gaining in popularity.

His descendants win on dirt and turf but the big question is whether it will be Roberto's branch or Halo's branch that is most likely to continue Royal Charger's male line in the years ahead.

POLYNESIAN AND HIS SON NATIVE DANCER

"Polynesian set many track records and equaled the world record for six furlongs. Best Sprinter of 1947." - The Thoroughbred Record.

If the author believes the two most dynamic ancestors influencing speed in North America are Polynesian and his champion son Native Dancer, then surely their ancestry requires further investigation. After all, they appear in the pedigree of every Thoroughbred having Northern Dancer and/or Mr. Prospector in their pedigree. Young breeders need to know how these supersonic strains evolved.

Champion Sprinter Polynesian, born in 1942, was an athletic bay horse tracing to imported French mare Bird Loose by Sardanapale, one of the greatest stayers in French Thoroughbred history. Bird Loose produced only two foals in North America and both were stakes winners, Head Cover (Hochelaga Handicap) and Champion 3YO filly Black Maria, 18 wins $110,350 including the Kentucky Oaks, Metropolitan Handicap, Whitney Stakes, Champion Filly Stakes, Ladies Handicap twice, Aqueduct Handicap, Illinois Oaks, Continental Handicap etc.

Owned by William R. Coe, Black Maria defeated the best milers in the country when she won the Metropolitan Handicap with 116 pounds. She produced only one foal, a filly named Black Queen (by Pompey), whose pedigree is as follows:

Black Queen (1930)	Pompey	Sun Briar	Sundridge	Amphion by Rosebery
				Sierra by Springfield
			Sweet Briar	St. Frusquin by **St. Simon** by **Galopin**
				Presentation
		Cleopatra	Corcyra	Polymelus by Cyllene
				Pearmain by **Persimmon*** by **St. Simon**
			Gallice	Gallinule by Isonomy
				St. Cecelia by St. Serf by **St. Simon**
	Black Maria	Black Toney	Peter Pan	Commando by Domino
				Cinderella by Hermit
			Belgravia	Ben Brush
				Bonnie Gal by **Galopin**
		Bird Loose (Fr)	Sardanapale	Prestige
				Gemma by **Florizel*** by **St. Simon**
			Poule au Pot	Verdun by Rabelais by **St. Simon**
				Fouilleopo by Palais Royal

Her female line traces to the great mare Banter, dam of Touchstone (English St. Leger, Ascot Gold Cup twice), Jocose (dam of English 2,000 Guineas and Derby winner Macaroni) and Pasquinade (ancestress of Rabelais). Black Queen comes from a sensational female line, perhaps the strongest branch of the Number 14 Family.

Black Queen is linebred to St. Simon and his sire, Galopin, to Jocose and to the brothers Persimmon and Florizel (by St. Simon from Perdita II by Hampton). Persimmon won the English Derby, St. Leger, Ascot Gold Cup, Eclipse Stakes etc., while Florizel II captured the Goodwood Cup.

Bird Loose is linebred several times to Banter, via Rabelais, Macaroni and her direct female line. I find this interesting because later on we will see how Rabelais fits into the picture via his son Havresac II (the broodmare sire of Nearco).

Pompey, the father of Black Queen, was a brilliant racehorse but not entirely sound in his forelegs. Bred by William R. Coe's Shoshone Stud, Pompey was North America's Champion 2YO colt in 1925. His victories include the Hopeful Stakes (setting a new track record time), Futurity Stakes, East View Stakes, United States Hotel Stakes and Wood Memorial Stakes. He was runner-up in the Travers Stakes and fifth to Bubbling Over in the Kentucky Derby, with Preakness Stakes winner Display behind him.

Readers not only should be made aware of Pompey's brilliance, but also of his structural weakness in the ankles. Why? Because Pompey happens to be the ancestor responsible for unsoundness sometimes transmitted by champion Bold Ruler during his successful years at stud. Bold Ruler's second dam Outdone is a daughter of Pompey, by the brilliant Sun Briar, a son of Sundridge.

Black Queen displayed speed as a juvenile, winning a Maiden 2YO race before being stakes-placed in the Laurel Stakes and Ladies Handicap. She produced seven winners including Perida (winner of the Fashion Stakes), Adaptable (earned $122,004, winner of the Brook, Corinthian, Manly, Meadow Brook Handicaps etc.), Queen of Clubs (dam of Hen Party), Black Polly and Taj Bibi (dam of Papa Redbird, a tough stakes winner, 11 wins $131,375 including the Arlington Classic).

Black Polly, born in 1936, was a daughter of the imported English sprinter Polymelian (Polymelus-Pasquita by Sundridge), a sound racehorse with exceptional speed. Polymelian was a muscular horse with powerful hindquarters that could be described as "goose-rumped." He had a huge over-stride and won many sprints with topweight. He is the sire of Caruso, nine wins including the Toboggan Handicap, United States Hotel Stakes, California Handicap, Richard Johnson Stakes, Thomas Curran Memorial Stakes and George Washington Handicap. Caruso is best known today as the sire of Sopranist (Spinaway Stakes) and Imperatrice (dam of Somethingroyal, the dam of Secretariat and Sir Gaylord).

Black Polly, a winner at two years, only produced two foals, namely champion sprinter-miler Polynesian and Black Shot, winner of 10 races. Black Polly never produced a filly to carry on her strong female line.

Polymelian was a son of England's five-time leading sire Polymelus whose wins include the Prince of Wales Stakes, Richmond Stakes, Criterion Stakes, Duke of York Stakes and the Cambridgeshire Handicap.

Polymelian was a sound horse and sired 20 stakes winners. He was out of Pasquita by English champion sprinter Sundridge from Pasquil who was closely related to English Triple Crown winner Flying Fox, the grandsire of Teddy who sired Asterus, Bull Dog, Sir Gallahad III and La Troienne.

There is quite a resemblance between Polymelian and his maternal grandsire Sundridge. They were similar types and both very precocious horses. Incidentally, a close genetic relationship exists between Polymelian and English sprinter Phalaris – an important connection well worth highlighting.

Whereas Phalaris is by Polymelus out of a daughter of Sainfoin, Polymelian is similarly bred, being by Polymelus from a daughter of Sundridge whose dam is a sister to Sainfoin. Therefore if we examine the pedigree of Polynesian, he inherits his genotype from two almost identical sources, Phalaris and Polymelian:

				Polymelus
			Phalaris	Bromus by **Sainfoin**
		Sickle		Chaucer
			Selene	Serenissima
	Unbreakable			**Persimmon**
			Prince Palatine	Lady Lightfoot
		Blue Glass		Rock Sand by **Sainfoin**
			Hour Glass II	Hautesse II
Polynesian				Cyllene
(1942)			**Polymelus**	Maid Marian
		Polymelian		**Sundridge** ex **Sierra**
			Pasquita	Pasquil
	Black Polly			Sun Briar by **Sundridge** ex **Sierra**
			Pompey	Cleopatra
		Black Queen		Black Toney
			Black Maria	Bird Loose

In reality, Polymelian acts like a two-thirds genetic brother to Phalaris but please notice the way the genetic influence was transported to Polynesian via a "son" of Phalaris and a "daughter" of Polymelian. This means similar genes were deployed on both sides of Polynesian's chromosomes creating an opportunity for prepotency to be established. Notice, too, the presence of Persimmon (sire of Prince Palatine) – Black Queen is already linebred to Persimmon and his brother Florizel II. So, apart from the building blocks of heavily duplicated ancestor St. Simon, Polynesian offers two sources of Sainfoin and two sources of his sister Sierra – superior ancestors representing high-class speed. Polynesian's daughter Geisha produced Native Dancer (whose pedigree is shown in Chapter 1, page 37). Leaving aside Native Dancer for the moment, let's examine the pedigree structure of some of Polynesian's descendants starting with Boldnesian who is out of Alanesian, a daughter of Polynesian.

Boldnesian continued Bold Ruler's male line through his grandson Seattle Slew whereas most other sons of Bold Ruler have failed to maintain it. So what makes Boldnesian different to all the other sons of Bold Ruler? Bold Ruler dominated the sires' list in North America with sons like Secretariat, Successor, Wajima, Bold Lad (USA), Bold Lad (Ire), Vitriolic, Bold Commander, Bold Bidder, Irish Castle, Bold Hour, Bold and Brave, Stupendous, Tyrant, King of the Castle, Cornish Prince, What A Pleasure, Raja Baba, Dewan and King Emperor. Where are their commercial extensions of Bold Ruler's male line today? King of the Castle's line survives in South America, Is It True maintains Raja Baba's branch and Maudlin maintains the branch of What A Pleasure; but of the others, few can claim true commercial status. Twenty years ago, who would have believed Boldnesian would be the strongest son to represent Bold Ruler's male line into the 21st Century?

Boldnesian (1983)	Bold Ruler	Nasrullah	Nearco by Pharos (**Phalaris/Chaucer**)
			Mumtaz Begum
		Miss Disco	Discovery
			Outdone by Pompey by Sun Briar
	Alanesian	Polynesian	Unbreakable by Sickle (**Phalaris/Chaucer**)
			Black Polly by Polymelian
		Alablue	Blue Larkspur by son of Black Toney
			Double Time by Sir Gallahad III

Boldnesian ran five times as a three-year-old, won four of them and earned $107,625. His earnings were way behind those of Bold Ruler's best-performed sons. Boldnesian revealed class, winning the Santa Anita Derby by two lengths and allowance races in fast times, including a handicap by 10 lengths, exhibiting brilliance. He was a chestnut son of Bold Ruler, as was champion Secretariat, but his racing career was cut short by weak ankles. (His coat color was inherited via recessive genes from Sundridge.) He retired to Mare Haven Farm, Florida, in 1967 at $5,000 live foal.

Alanesian, dam of Boldnesian, was a tough, sound mare that won nine races at two to four years and earned $136,997. In fact she was high-class, winning the Spinaway Stakes, Astarita Stakes, Margate Handicap, New Castle Stakes, runner-up in the Interborough Handicap, Gallorette Stakes, Maskette Handicap, Vagrancy Handicap etc. and produced Amalesian, Boldnesian, Princessnesian ($332,035 11 wins, Santa Barbara Handicap, Hollywood Gold Cup, Santa Margarita Invitational Handicap, Milady Stakes) and the useful Jackal (National Stallion Stakes).

Boldnesian was a successful sire with Florida-bred mares. Among his progeny were Wing Out (13 wins $418,315, Malibu Stakes, Chicago Handicap, Lakeside Handicap, Sun Beau Handicap), Bold Reasoning (eight wins $189,564, Jersey Derby, Withers Stakes, 2nd Metropolitan Handicap who set a new track record at Belmont Park for six furlongs in 1:8¾), Moonsplash (17 wins $154,117, Phoenix Gold Cup twice), Cheriepe (13 wins $244,700, Jim Dandy Stakes, San Antonio Stakes), Brazen Brother (10 wins $138,807, Select Handicap, Jim Dandy Stakes), Bold Laddie (To Market Stakes, Arch Ward Stakes), Frankie Adams (eight wins $158,900, Hutcheson Stakes), Bold Nix (seven wins $91,992, Lamplighter Handicap, Boardwalk Handicap), Bold Bikini (Jersey Belle Handicap), Lady Herald (Schuylkill Stakes) and Bold Statement (12 wins $118,022, Woodlawn Stakes, Congressional Handicap).

Arthur B. "Bull" Hancock made a lot of money out of standing the syndicated Bold Ruler on behalf of the Phipps family at Claiborne Farm and so it was natural he would want to syndicate Bold Reasoning, a dark brown horse, 16.2 hands high. Hancock had seen the horse (aged four) set a new track record for six furlongs at Belmont Park and was impressed with Bold Reasoning's gutsy effort when runner-up to Executioner (beaten a neck) in the valuable Metropolitan Handicap. Thus, in 1973, Bold Reasoning made his home at Claiborne Farm. He resembled his broodmare sire Hail To Reason much more than his grandsire Bold Ruler.

Bold Reasoning came from a good family, tracing to Warrior Lass, a winning half-sister to the very fast sprinter Case Ace (broodmare sire of Raise a Native). Warrior Lass was by Man o' War out of Sweetheart by Ultimus, a speed machine inbred to Domino. Warrior Lass, the fourth dam of Bold Reasoning, produced Knickerbocker, winner of the Metropolitan Handicap.

The pedigree pattern below shows a genetic relationship between the mares Alablue and Nothirdchance. Nasrullah is of course three-quarter brother to Royal Charger and Man o' War brings in Rock Sand (son of Sainfoin). Admiral Drake is half-brother to French 2,000 Guineas winner Sir Galahad III (sons of the elite mare Plucky Liege by Spearmint). Blue Larkspur is reinforced via a son and a daughter and his grandsire Black Toney is represented by a daughter, Black Maria (see Polynesian's pedigree). Sun Briar is by Sundridge. All these duplicated ancestors are high-class individuals!

Bold Reasoning (1968)	Boldnesian	Bold Ruler	**Nasrullah**	**Nearco**
				Mumtaz Begum
			Miss Disco	Discovery
				Outdone by Pompey by Sun Briar
		Alanesian	Polynesian	Unbreakable by Sickle
				Black Polly
			Alablue*	**Blue Larkspur**
				Double Time by **Sir Gallahad III**
	Reason To Hail	Hail To Reason	Turn-To	**Royal Charger (3/4 br. to Nasrullah)**
				Source Sucree by Admiral Drake
			Nothirdchance*	Blue Swords by **Blue Larkspur**
				Galla Colors by **Sir Gallahad III**
		Sailing Home	Wait A Bit	Espino
				Hi-Nelli
			Marching Home	John P. Grier
				Warrior Lass by Man o' War

If memory serves me correctly it was "Bull" Hancock's son Seth who recommended My Charmer be matched with Bold Reasoning, resulting in North America's Horse of the Year and Triple Crown winner Seattle Slew.

Purchased as an inexpensive yearling by Mickey Taylor and partner, Seattle Slew was inbred 4 x 4 to Nasrullah via a son and a daughter with his three-quarter brother Royal Charger as genetic support. Nasrullah's dam, Mumtaz Begum, is a "daughter" of Blenheim and in My Charmer's pedigree we find Blenheim's "son" – Jet Pilot.

Seattle Slew's dam, My Charmer, is inbred to the sisters Striking and Busher (by War Admiral from Baby League by Bubbling Over from La Troienne by Teddy). War Admiral introduced the classic strain of Rock Sand (by Sainfoin) as well as American champion Sweep (bringing in Domino's strain). Bubbling Over is by North Star III, a grandson of Sundridge, from a daughter of Sweep.

Years ago when Mickey Taylor visited Overbrook Farm to arrange a foal share deal with Seattle Slew, he mentioned to me he had researched the pedigrees of Seattle Slew's stakes-winning progeny and discovered Polynesian and Nasrullah were two ancestors highly successful with Slew's genotype. Mickey and Karen Taylor were keen to acquire quite specific bloodlines suitable to match with their champion racehorse – mares with the right strains, especially Polynesian.

Another smart son of Bold Reasoning was Super Concorde, Champion 2YO colt in France. He won the Grand Criterium, Prix Morny, juvenile handicaps at Deauville and Chantilly, and was eventually imported by John Gaines to stand at Gainesway Farm. Super Concorde's dam was stakes winner Prime Abord, three wins in France including the Prix Chloe and Prix de Royallieu. Prime Abord is by Primera (son of My Babu) from English Oaks winner Homeward Bound.

Super Concorde's pedigree pattern involved Nasrullah, Royal Charger and their mirror image genetic relative Perfume II, dam of My Babu.

Another fast son of Polynesian was Barbizon, Champion 2YO colt in 1956. A muscular horse who matured quickly, he won seven of 21 starts for $199,460 including the valuable Garden State Stakes, defeating Federal Hill, Iron Liege and Bold Ruler.

Barbizon was an immediate success at stud – leading sire of two-year-olds in 1965, second on the leading sire's list of two-year-olds in 1962, and the leading sire by number of races won in 1970. Among his best progeny were Pams Ego (12 wins, Frizette Stakes, Comely Stakes, Mermaid Stakes), Barbizon Streak (16 wins, Longport Stakes, Patriots Stakes), Silver Bright (five wins, Arlington-Washington Lassie Stakes), Rhubarb (10 wins, Colleen Stakes, First Lady Handicap), Su Ka Wa (Youthful Stakes, Kentucky Jockey Club Stakes) and Second Bar (10 wins, including the Lincoln Special, Coral Gables Handicap, Dragoon Stakes).

Other major stakes winners by Polynesian were Polylad (15 wins $348,004, Gallant Fox Handicap, Roamer Handicap, Nassau County Handicap), Imbros (15 wins $340,550, Will Rogers Stakes, Malibu Sequet Stakes, California Stakes), the smart filly Poly Hi (nine wins, Arlington Lassie Stakes, Astoria Stakes), and Bureaucracy (11 wins including the Dwyer Handicap). Obviously Polynesian's best son was Native Dancer whose male line has thrived.

Ironically, it progressed not through either of his Kentucky Derby-winning sons Kauai King or Dancer's Image (the latter being disqualified) but via sons inheriting natural speed. Kauai King was line-bred 5 x 3 to daughters of champion Sweep, namely La Chica and Sweepesta. Kauai King won nine of 16 starts for $381,397 including the 1966 Kentucky Derby (defeating Advocator), Preakness Stakes (defeating Stupendous and Amberoid), Governor's Gold Cup, Prince George's Stakes and Fountain of Youth Stakes. He retired to stud at Alfred G. Vanderbilt's Sagamore Farm, Maryland.

Dancer's Image was typical of Native Dancer's physical type and color. A muscular gray horse with a spirited nature, he won 12 of 24 starts (not counting his Kentucky Derby disqualification by failing a drug test) and earned $236,630. At two years, Dancer's Image won eight races including the Maryland Futurity, Clarendon Stakes, Vandale Stakes and made a favorable impression at his debut, winning a Maiden 2YO Handicap at Woodbine by eight lengths.

At three, he defeated Iron Liege in the Wood Memorial Stakes, was first past the post in the Kentucky Derby (subsequently given to Forward Pass), the Governor's Gold Cup in time one-fifth of a second off the track record, the E. Palmer Heagerty Stakes and an allowance race at Bowie, after which he developed ankle problems and was retired to Glade Valley Farms in Maryland. However, he was soon after shipped to Ireland and stood at Killeen Castle Stud in County Meath.

Dancer's Image was a successful sire. Among his progeny were Lianga, Saritamer, Godswalk, Mistretta, Sherby, Smooth Dancer, Dancing Light, Lady Rushen, Dancing On, Flashy Image, Apsara and Dancing Angela. His son Saritamer sired champion English mare Time Charter. Native Dancer is also the father of Dan Cupid, stakes winner in France whose victories include the Prix du Bois, Prix de Sablonville and runner-up to Herbager in the Prix du Jockey Club (French Derby).

Dan Cupid sired European champion Sea-Bird II, one of the truly great racehorses last century, the facile winner of the English Derby and Prix de l'Arc de Triomphe. Sea-Bird II was leased by John Galbreath to stand at Darby Dan Farm.

John Galbreath and his son Dan had earlier made a deal with Mario Incisa della Rochetta to lease unbeaten Ribot for Darby Dan Farm and it came as a surprise to European breeders to learn Sea-Bird II also had been leased to the same Kentucky farm because Sea-Bird II boasted a pedigree with turf performers. Among his progeny were Gyr, Burd Alane, Pretty Puffin, Kittiwake and Arctic Tern.

Native Charger (Native Dancer-Greek Blond by Heliopolis) was a pretty smart juvenile that went on to win the Florida Derby. He won the Tyro Stakes but couldn't match Bold Lad's speed in the Futurity Stakes and finished second, just ahead of Tom Rolfe. Native Charger was runner-up to Bold Lad in the Hopeful Stakes and Sapling Stakes, beaten a half-length in the latter race. At three, he won the Flamingo Stakes, Florida Derby and finished fourth in the Kentucky Derby to Lucky Debonair and fourth in the Preakness Stakes to Tom Rolfe. He sired High Echelon and Forward Gal.

Native Dancer's daughter Hula Dancer, Champion 2YO in France, was an exceptionally fast gray filly who defeated the colts in the Grand Criterium and Prix de la Salamandre. At three, she progressed further to collect the English 1,000 Guineas, Champion Stakes and Prix Jacques Le Marois.

In 1963, North America's Champion 2YO colt was Raise A Native who made the guys at *Daily Racing Form* sit up and take notice. A heavy-bodied chestnut colt with fast fiber muscle, Raise A Native was a sensation! Undefeated at two with four wins from four starts he resembled a Quarter horse-type being long in the back with pronounced forearm development. Raise A Native was a totally different type to his daddy Native Dancer. He must have inherited his mature physique from two ancestors, namely Broomstick and Ultimus, both heavy-topped horses with abundant speed. Ultimus, inbred to Domino, was a flying machine whose racing career was cut short by unsound forelegs.

Raise A Native won a juvenile race at Hialeah in February by six lengths going three furlongs in $32\frac{4}{5}$ seconds before setting a new track record over five furlongs at Aqueduct in May, scoring by eight lengths. At his next start the colt equaled his own record of $57\frac{4}{5}$ seconds to win the Juvenile Stakes.

Raise a Native (1961)	Native Dancer	Polynesian	Unbreakable	Sickle by Phalaris (dam by **Sainfoin**)
				Blue Glass
			Black Polly	Polymelian (inbred to **Sierra**)
				Black Queen
		Geisha	Discovery	Display
				Ariadne
			Miyako	John P. Grier by **Whisk Broom II**
				La Chica by Sweep
	Raise You	Case Ace	Teddy	Ajax by Flying Fox
				Rondeau by Bay Ronald
			Sweetheart	Ultimus by Commando
				Humanity
		Lady Glory	American Flag	Man o' War (dam by Rock Sand)
				Lady Comfey
			Beloved	**Whisk Broom II** by Broomstick
				Bill and Coo (ex Padula)

His final appearance was at Aqueduct on July 17 where he produced a dazzling display of speed to win the Great American Stakes, setting a new track record time of 1:02 ⅗ for 5½ furlongs. Soon after, he developed unsound ankles and never ran again. Raise a Native was syndicated to stand at Spendthrift Farm and was supported with quality mares owned by friends and clients of "super salesman" Leslie Combs II. The female line of the stallion went back to Bill and Coo (Helmet-Padula). Raise A Native's dam, Raise You, won five races including the Colleen Stakes, Polly Drummond Stakes and New Jersey Futurity. From 14 foals, Raise You produced 11 winners. Apart from her champion son, she produced Kingmaker, 13 wins $243,205, who set a new track record when taking the Grey Leg Handicap, the Whitney Stakes, New Orleans Handicap and Kent Stakes. The third dam of Raise A Native was Beloved, an unraced daughter of Whisk Broom II (by Broomstick), a horse of considerable substance and possessing a deep girth.

Whisk Broom II was purchased by Harry Payne Whitney as a yearling. The colt was sent to England where he won several races including the Victoria Cup and finished third to Neil Gow and Lemberg in the English 2,000 Guineas. Returned to the United States, Whisk Broom II won the Metropolitan Handicap, Brooklyn Handicap and the Suburban Handicap in record time.

Although he was a successful sire, his stud record pales by comparison with his own father, Broomstick, sire of 69 stakes winners. Broomstick was a heavy-bodied horse and strange though it may seem, Raise A Native resembled his type rather than the duplicated ancestor Whisk Broom II (5 x 4). Case Ace, the broodmare sire of Raise A Native, ran for the Milky Way Stable in the same year War Admiral made his juvenile appearance. At two, Case Ace started three times for three wins, stamping his authority with a decisive victory over Orientalist in the Arlington Futurity. Unfortunately at three, he developed a few physical problems and only managed three wins from six starts – his best effort was to win the Illinois Derby. At stud, Case Ace sired 20 stakes winners including a top-class son, Pavot.

Raise A Native sired early-maturing juveniles but they came in all shapes and sizes. He was a stallion loaded with recessive genes. Breeders needed to select the right mare because of his unsound ankles. A dear friend of mine, Olin Gentry Sr., who used to manage Darby Dan Farm, once told me, "What kind of mares did we send him? Lightly framed, short-coupled mares with correct forelegs. Oh boy, you never knew what to expect from Raise A Native."

Raise A Native's best progeny were Majestic Prince (Kentucky Derby, Preakness Stakes), Exclusive Native (Arlington Classic, Sanford Stakes), Native Partner (Maskette Handicap, Woodhaven Handicap), Alydar (Champagne Stakes, Florida Derby, 2nd Kentucky Derby, Preakness Stakes, Belmont Stakes), Raise Your Glass (Tremont Stakes), Native Royalty (Gotham Stakes), Crowned Prince (Champion 2YO in England, Dewhurst Stakes, Champagne Stakes), Bundler (Frizette Stakes), Laomedonte (Champion 3YO in Italy), Barrera, Son Ange, Princely Native and his most influential son, Mr. Prospector.

Many breeders and owners anticipated Raise A Native's male line would flourish via his sons Exclusive Native and Alydar since these Kentucky-based stallions received plenty of opportunities to cover mares with exceptional quality. Meanwhile, Mr. Prospector was enjoying the sun in Florida – that is, until his runners began to shine on the racetrack – and by then it was time for him to be shipped to Claiborne Farm in Kentucky.

The Male Line of Mr. Prospector

The following sons of Mr. Prospector represent most of the commercial extensions of his male line:

Mr. Prospector (1970)

- Kingmambo
  - King's Best
  - Dubai Destination
  - Lemon Drop Kid
  - King Cugat
- Fappiano
  - Unbridled
    - Broken Vow
    - Unbridled's Song
    - Grindstone
- Cryptoclearance
  - Victory Gallop
  - Volponi
- Quiet American
  - Real Quiet
- Rubiano
- Afleet
- Aldebaran
- Cape Canaveral
- Carson City
  - Cuvee
  - Five Star Day
  - Lord Carson
- Conquistador Cielo
  - Wagon Limit
  - Marquetry
  - El Moxie
- Crafty Prospector
  - Robyn Dancer
- Distant View
  - Distant Music
  - Explicit
  - Observatory
- E Dubai
- Forty Niner
  - Distorted Humor
  - Ecton Park
  - End Sweep
  - Twining
  - Gold Fever
  - Jules
  - Sunday Break
- Smart Strike
- Souvenir Copy
- Fusaichi Pegasus
- Gone West
  - Elusive Quality
    - Smarty Jones
  - Zafonic
  - Zamindar
  - Grand Slam
  - Mr. Greeley
- Gulch
  - Nayef
  - Thunder Gulch
    - Point Given
- Hussonet
- Jade Hunter
- Machiavellian
  - Medicean
  - Storming Home
  - Street Cry
  - No Excuse Needed
- Miswaki
  - Black Tie Affair
  - Rossini
- Mojave Moon
- Northern Prospect
- Numerous
- Our Emblem
- Rhythm
- Seeking the Gold
  - Cape Town
  - Mutakddim
  - Petionville
  - Secret Savings
  - Dubai Millennium
- Silver Ghost
- Not For Love
- Two Punch
  - Smoke Glacken
- Woodman
  - Bahhare
  - Hawk Wing
  - Timber Country
  - Hector Protector
  - Hishi Akebono
- Bellotto

Raise A Native has two descendants standing at Josephine Abercrombie's picturesque Pin Oak Stud, Versailles, Kentucky – the gray stallion Maria's Mon, Champion 2YO colt, by Wavering Monarch who traces in male line to Kentucky Derby winner Majestic Prince, and Broken Vow, a fast son of champion Unbridled, from Mr. Prospector's line. Pin Oak Stud is blessed with its own marvelous training facility. An accomplished horsewoman who competed successfully at horse shows in Texas, Josephine Abercrombie now mainly breeds to race, has a critical eye for a horse and is the breeder of many Graded stakes winners. Maria's Mon has already sired a Kentucky Derby winner (Monarchos) and looks set to make his mark in the coming years.

Raise A Native's son Exclusive Native is the sire of Triple Crown winner Affirmed, yet to sire a grandson to continue his male line. Raise A Native's son Alydar is best represented by Easy Goer's son Will's Way who stands at Pin Oak Lane Farm in Pennsylvania. Will's Way won six races including the Travers Stakes.

RAISE A NATIVE (Native Dancer - Raise You by Case Ace), North America's undefeated Champion 2YO colt who sired Mr. Prospector and Exclusive Native.

Alydar's male line of Native Dancer has been quite disappointing. Saratoga Six has yet to supply a commercial son, as does Kentucky Derby winner Alysheba. At the moment, Alydar's male line is mainly dependent upon Will's Way and grandsons based in South America.

However, two other branches of Native Dancer's line are steadily making progress. I refer to Native Dancer's son Atan, and Raise A Native's son Majestic Prince. Atan is out of Mixed Marriage, a daughter of champion Tudor Minstrel.

Atan is the sire of Sharpen Up whose sons Kris, Diesis, Trempolino and Selkirk have a chance to maintain this male line. If I had to guess which one of the four will succeed long-term, probably I would select Selkirk because he was a high-class performer and son of smart mare Annie Edge. He has a nice pedigree pattern to make a sire of sires.

Although Selkirk is not quite perfect in front, he always remained sound during three tough campaigns and is a very successful sire of Group winners. He inherited plenty of fast fiber muscle to transmit to his progeny. Selkirk won six of 15 starts for earnings of 477,379 pounds. At two, he won Goodwood's Stardom Stakes and finished fourth in the Grand Criterium. At three, he was Champion 3YO Miler in Europe, defeating Kooyonga and Shadayid in the Queen Elizabeth II Stakes, won the Milcars Temple Fortune Stakes, finished second in the Bonusprint Easter Stakes and ran third in both the Lingfield Trial Stakes and Goodwood Predominate Stakes.

At four, Selkirk was Europe's Champion Older Miler and Champion Older Horse. His three victories comprised the Challenge Stakes, Lockinge Stakes and Celebration Mile. He ran second to Marling in the Sussex Stakes and finished third to Lahib in the Queen Elizabeth II Stakes before retiring to Kirsten Rausing's Lanwades Stud, Newmarket. Selkirk succeeds with a variety of strains but especially with mares from Northern Dancer's line. His alternate sex line zigzags back to Germany's champion sire Birkhahn.

Kentucky Derby hero Majestic Prince (Raise A Native-Gay Hostess by Royal Charger) sired the workmanlike, multiple Grade 1 winner Majestic Light, 11 wins $650,158. Majestic Light's wins include the Man o' War Stakes, Swaps Stakes, Monmouth Invitational Handicap, Amory L. Haskell Handicap and he was runner-up in the American Derby and Washington International Stakes.

Standing 16.1 hands high, Majestic Light was out of Irradiate, a stakes-placed winning daughter of champion Ribot who added soundness to the line.

Irradiate's dam was U.S. Champion 2YO and 3YO filly High Voltage (13 wins $362,240, Coaching Club American Oaks, Black-Eyed Susan Stakes etc) by French Champion 2YO colt Ambiorix (Tourbillon-Lavendula II by Pharos). High Voltage produced Impressive, a handsome U.S. Champion Sprinter.

Never really appreciated by commercial breeders, Majestic Light had to fight his way up the sires' list. His daughter Nishino Flower was Champion 2YO and 3YO filly in Japan earning $3,441,504 from seven wins including The Oka Sho, The Sprinters Stakes and the Hanshin Sansai Himba Stakes, while other high-class progeny include Lite Light (eight wins $1,231,596, Kentucky Oaks, Coaching Club American Oaks, Santa Anita Oaks, Fantasy Stakes), Solar Splendor (11 wins $1,386,468, Turf Classic Invitational Stakes, Man o' War Stakes twice), Christiecat (11 wins $799,745, Flower Bowl Handicap, Diana Handicap), Wavering Monarch (six wins $466,773, Haskell Invitational Handicap, Omaha Gold Cup, San Fernando Stakes), and the Grade 1 filly Hidden Light.

Maria's Mon (by Wavering Monarch) will sire his share of Group winners on turf in Europe because he has a versatile pedigree pattern and his progeny come to hand early. European buyers will surely wake up to him because he is now covering higher quality mares. His Kentucky Derby-winning son Monarchos, also a gray, stands at Claiborne Farm.

Maria's Mon blends with Northern Dancer's strain and seems to have an affinity with the Hyperion/Tracery mix (e.g. Nearctic, Alibhai). Other suitable lines worth testing with him are Roberto, the Nasrullah/Princequillo nick, Graustark, His Majesty, Better Self and as much Polynesian as you can throw at him.

Natalma is one of Native Dancer's most influential daughters. A small bay mare, rather plain and back at the near knee, she nevertheless produced champion Northern Dancer, Native Victor, Regal Dancer, Northern Native and Arctic Dancer (dam of U.S. Champion 2YO filly and Canada's Horse of the Year, La Prevoyante [25 wins $572,417]). Australia's leading sire, Danehill, is inbred 3 x 3 to Natalma via a son and a daughter.

Native Dancer's daughter Shenanigans, now on the "elite" mare list, is another influence for speed. Voted North America's Broodmare of the Year, she won three times and was stakes-placed in the Maryland Futurity.

Shenanigans produced six winners including the great filly Ruffian (U.S. Champion 2YO and 3YO filly), Buckfinder (nine wins $230,513, William duPont Jr Handicap, 2nd Metropolitan Handicap), Icecapade (13 wins $256,468) and Laughter (four wins and dam of five stakes winners including Private Terms and Blue Ensign). Icecapade's victories include the Nassau County Handicap, Longport Handicap, William duPont Jr Handicap and Saranac Stakes. He is the sire of more than 73 stakes winners, among them Wild Again (Breeders' Cup Classic) and Clever Trick (18 wins $419,787 and sire of Phone Trick). Icecapade will most likely feature in the pedigrees of future stakes winners because he is bred on the same Nearctic/Native Dancer cross as Northern Dancer and therefore acts like a three-parts genetic relative.

Shenanigans (1963)	Native Dancer	Polynesian	Unbreakable	Sickle by Phalaris
				Blue Glass
			Black Polly	Polymelian
				Black Queen by Pompey
		Geisha	Discovery	Display
				Ariadne
			Miyako	John P. Grier by a son of **Broomstick**
				La Chica by Sweep
	Bold Irish	Fighting Fox	Sir Gallahad III	Teddy
				Plucky Liege by Spearmint
			Marguerite	Celt by Commando
				Fairy Ray
		Erin	Transmute	**Broomstick**
				Traverse by Tracery by Rock Sand
			Rosie O'Grady	Hamburg ex Lady Reel
				Cherokee Rose II by Peter Pan

Before closing this chapter, a brief look at Native Dancer's direct female line should be of interest. Native Dancer belongs to the Number 5 Family (The Massey Mare) from a branch that was undistinguished until a special mating produced a mare named La Grisette.

La Grisette was the product of a match between the gray stallion Roi Herode and Miss Fiora (by Melton from Fiona by Amphion). Amphion is of course the sire of Sainfoin and Sierra – thus, maternal strength was waiting to be exploited. Roi Herode was a successful sire whose champion son The Tetrarch sired many stakes winners including Tetratema and English Champion 2YO filly Mumtaz Mahal.

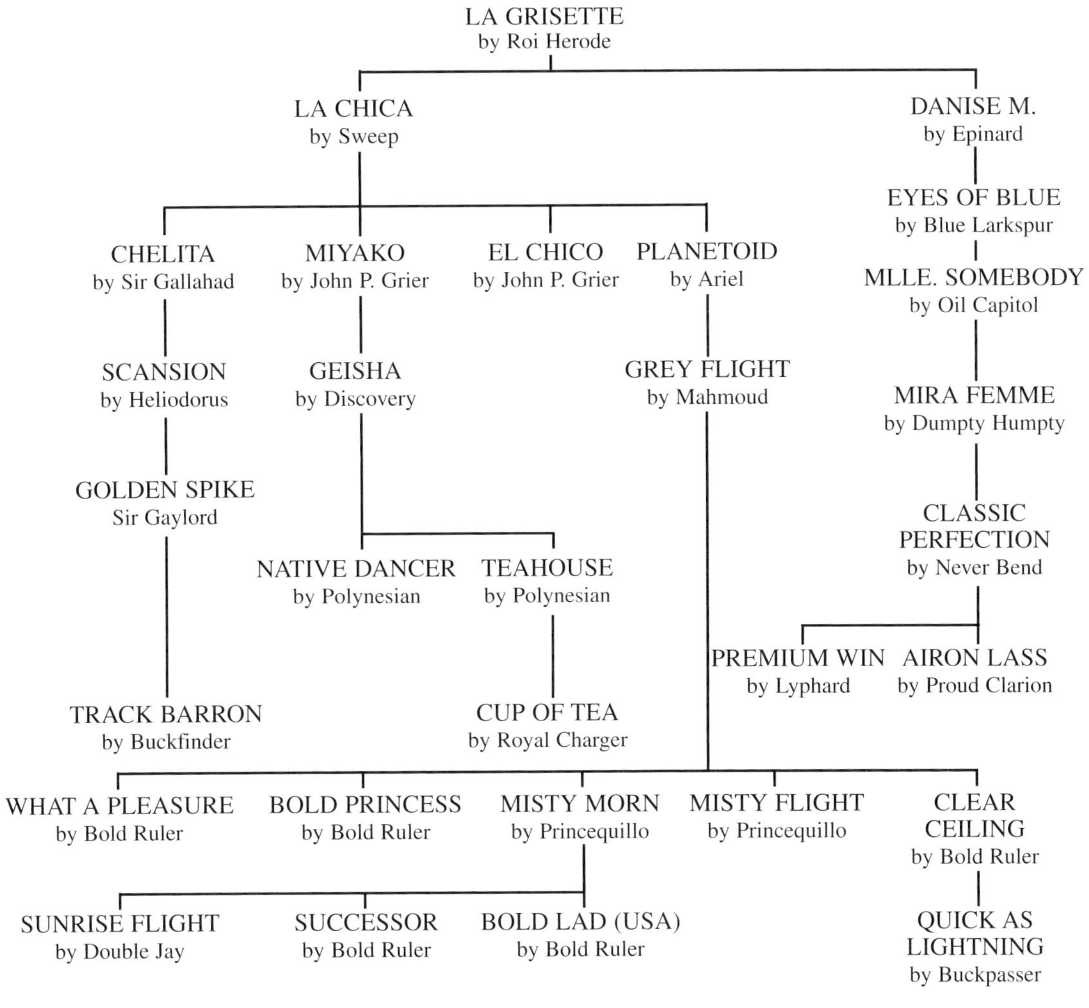

This female chart indicates Pleasant Colony's strain might suit descendants of Native Dancer since Pleasant Colony is out of a mare by Sunrise Flight (Double Jay-Misty Morn by Princequillo). Grey Flight's descendants could be tested with stallions carrying Native Dancer's strain so as to reinforce La Chica.

Teahouse, a sister to champion Native Dancer, might eventually establish a strong family in her own right. I believe female descendants of Teahouse need to be matched with stallions possessing Native Dancer so as to design pedigree patterns with input from brother and sister. Perhaps someone some day will see merit in this strategy and breed a versatile stakes performer?

THE FRENCH CONNECTION – HERBAGER AND WILD RISK

"Forgotten heroes come back to haunt us."

Genealogists come across the names of ancestors that fail to register as being anything out of the ordinary, but names in pedigrees are not just names. They represent the phenotype and genotype of real individuals and any study of their performance on the racetrack and at stud provides valuable information about racing class, soundness and temperament. Sometimes an obscure ancestor in a pedigree acts as the catalyst for brilliant speed or classic speed. Two special ancestors whose influence is rarely mentioned by breeding journalists, despite their presence in many Group 1 winning pedigrees, are the French-bred stallions Herbager and Wild Risk.

Arthur B. "Bull" Hancock made a successful pitch to buy the French stallion Herbager (Vandale II-Flagette by Escamillo) and shipped him to Paris, Kentucky, where he syndicated the stallion amongst his clients. The selection of Herbager came as a surprise to local breeders because Hancock always preferred a potential sire to have early maturing speed. It was part of his formula for choosing Claiborne Farm's sire material. Whether Hancock was a genius or simply plain lucky with his selection of stallions was inconsequential. His clients were in awe of the man's ability to select sire material and syndicating a new horse for Claiborne Farm could be finalized in a few days if Hancock was in the vicinity of a phone.

Herbager was an odd choice! He was out of an unraced mare. Yes, the horse's female line was sound and represented a well-regarded stakes-producing family developed by French breeders. Yes, New Zealand's leading sire Le Filou belonged to this branch of the family. But as a juvenile Herbager had won a minor race, the Prix Seraphine by four lengths from two starts, hardly the sort of race record Hancock would normally seek. However, Herbager made a conspicuous impact with his first French runners having sired Grey Dawn II, the only horse ever to defeat the great Sea-Bird II. Obviously Hancock was impressed.

At three, Herbager put together a string of five victories on turf and was considered one of the best stayers in Europe during 1959. He won the Prix Greffulhe by three lengths, the Prix Hocquart by two lengths, the Prix du Jockey Club (French Derby) by an impressive five lengths defeating Dan Cupid and Midnight Sun, the Grand Prix de Saint-Cloud defeating Shantung, and at his penultimate start, won the Prix du Prince d'Orange by two lengths. Herbager was the Champion 3YO colt in France. I can almost hear what "Bull" Hancock was thinking at the time. Here was a potential stallion from a different sire line that just might suit North American bloodlines. He took a calculated risk and advertised the French Derby winner at $10,000 live foal.

At the end of 1964, Grey Dawn II was rated Champion 2YO colt in France. His juvenile victories comprised the Grand Criterium (defeating Sea-Bird II), Prix Morny (defeating Carvin) and Prix de la Salamandre. At three he won the Prix de Fontainebleau by two lengths from The Marshall, a handicap at Longchamp, was runner-up to Cambremont in the French 2,000 Guineas and placed in the Prix de la Porte Maillot. Grey Dawn II was then shipped to North America to continue racing.

Herbager (Fr) (1956)	Vandale II	Plassy	Bosworth	Son-in-Law by Dark Ronald
				Serenissima by Minoru
			Pladda	**Phalaris**
				Rothesay Bay (ex **Anchora**)
		Vanille	La Farina	Sans Souci II
				Malatesta by Isinglass
			Vaya	Beppo by Marco
				Waterhen by Gallinule
	Flagette	Escamillo	**Firdaussi**	Pharos (**Phalaris/Chaucer**)
				Brownhylda by Stedfast by **Chaucer**
			Estoril	Solario (dam by Sundridge)
				Appleby by Pommern
		Fidgette	**Firdaussi**	Pharos (**Phalaris/Chaucer**)
				Brownhylda by Stedfast by **Chaucer**
			Boxeuse	Teddy by Ajax
				Spicebox by Spion Kop by Spearmint

At four, Grey Dawn II won the Brandywine Turf Handicap and an allowance race at Gulfstream Park by almost five lengths. He was retired to Domino Farm where he became a very successful sire of stakes winners. Herbager's unraced dam, Flagette, is inbred 2 x 2 to Dewhurst Stakes and St. Leger winner Firdaussi, a workmanlike dark brown horse bred by the old Aga Khan. Herbager's pedigree is of considerable interest to me because of the unique presence of Stedfast, a "son" of Chaucer. Very few individuals possess a "son" of Chaucer in their ancestry but those who do seem to be successful. Imagine all the stallions and mares that only carry daughters of Chaucer in their genotypes. Great sires out of Chaucer mares pervade modern pedigrees via Hyperion, Pharos, Fairway, Colorado, Sickle, Pharamond II etc. How then, might we balance Chaucer via a "son?" The answer is Stedfast (Chaucer-Be Sure by Surefoot), winner of 20 races including the St. James' Palace Stakes, Jockey Club Stakes, Coronation Cup and Sussex Stakes. He was runner-up to Sunstar in the English 2,000 Guineas and Derby. Stedfast happens to be the broodmare sire of Firdaussi (by Pharos) and is inbred to a son and daughter of Chaucer.

Also in Herbager's pedigree we find Spion Kop, a "son" of Spearmint. Thus, Spion Kop can help balance pedigree patterns because mares with "daughters" of Spearmint are quite commonplace thanks to the successful strains of Nearco, Niccolo dell 'Arca, War Admiral, Eight Thirty, Bull Dog, Sir Gallahad III, Bois Roussel and Admiral Drake – all with a "daughter" of Spearmint in their genotype.

Last but not least, Pladda is three-parts sister to Pharos. Herbager is the sire of Sea Hawk II (Grand Prix de Saint-Cloud, Criterium de Saint-Cloud), Grey Dawn II, The Pruner (American Derby), Dike (Wood Memorial Stakes, Gotham Stakes), Our Mims (U.S. Champion 3YO filly, Coaching Club American Oaks, Alabama Stakes, Fantasy Stakes), Loud (Travers Stakes in new track record time), Point du Jour (Palm Beach Handicap twice, Roamer Handicap), Chokri (Durazna Stakes), Appiani (Champion 3YO colt in Italy, Italian Derby), Ballade (dam of champions Devil's Bag, Glorious Song, and Saint Ballado), Fly Me First (dam of Flying Chevron), The Garden Club (dam of Nostalgia and Up The Flagpole), Gleaming (13 wins $469,245, Hialeah Turf Cup) and I Will Follow (dam of champion Rainbow Quest).

				Bosworth by Son-in-Law
			Plassy	Pladda by **Phalaris**
		Vandale II		La Farina
			Vanile	Vaya
	Herbager			**Firdaussi** by **Pharos**
			Escamillo	Estoril
		Flagette		**Firdaussi** by **Pharos**
			Fidgette	Boxeuse by **Teddy**
Grey Dawn II				Blandford by Swynford
(1962)			Blenheim	Malva by Charles O'Malley
		Mahmoud		Gainsborough
			Mah Mahal	Mumtaz Mahal
	Polamia			Case Ace by **Teddy**
			Pavot	Coquelicot by **Man o' War**
		Ampola		Blue Larkspur
			Blue Denim	Judy O'Grady by **Man o' War**

Grey Dawn II transmitted early maturing speed to his progeny and some of his stakes winners truly resembled his broodmare sire, Mahmoud. Ampola's 3 x 3 inbreeding to champion Man o' War must have had a huge influence for speed, especially at a mile or more, and made use of Rock Sand, a son of Sainfoin.

Ampola produced Sly Pola, a brilliant juvenile filly in France who was something special. Sly Pola was flighty and full of nervous energy. At two and three she won the Prix Robert Papin, Prix de l'Abbaye de Longchamp, Prix de la Grotte, and ran second in the Prix du Petite Couvert. Sly Pola is the granddam of Green Dancer (French 2,000 Guineas), Pink Valley (Prix d'Aumale), Pareo (Champion 2YO colt in Italy, Grand Criterium, Gran Premio d'Italia) and Polamia (Prix du Bois, 2nd Prix d'Arenberg, Prix de Sablonville and dam of eight winners).

Aside from champion Grey Dawn II, Polamia produced Tryptic (a colt by Tyrone that won the Prix Maurice de Gheest and was placed in the Prix du Moulin de Longchamp), Right Away (a classy filly by Right Royal V who won the French 1,000 Guineas), a Relko filly named Mia Pola (winner of the Prix La Rochette) and a filly by Timmy My Boy named Timolina (winner of the Prix Finlande).

Grey Dawn II inherited speed from Mahmoud and stamina from the clever inbreeding via son and daughter of Chaucer whose dam won the English Oaks.

Mahmoud's influence was spectacular in the United States. His colts and fillies came to hand quickly and loved turf or dirt. He led the Sires' List in North America in 1946 and sired 53 stakes winners including First Flight, a juvenile champion filly rated higher than any colt on the Experimental Free Handicap.

The gentleman who convinced C.V. Whitney to purchase Mahmoud was Ivor Balding who had taken up the position of farm manager at the Whitney farm.

Born in Leicstershire, England, Ivor Balding and his brothers came to the United States to play championship polo. In 1936, Balding was hired by C.V. Whitney to manage the farm at Old Westbury, New York, where he introduced a quality herd of Angus cattle.

Three years later he was asked to manage the Kentucky farm and persuaded his boss to introduce a speed horse unrelated to the Whitney bloodlines.

Ivor Balding admired Mahmoud's pedigree and race record and knew many of the Aga Khan's stakes-winning colts made successful sires. When the gray stallion arrived in Kentucky, some of Whitney's close friends (including trainer Max Hirsch) openly criticized Mahmoud telling everyone he was the wrong type of stallion for the Whitney broodmares. Balding quietly waited for Mahmoud's first crop to race. It was then the critics were silenced. The foreigner, the Englishman named Balding, had been right after all because Mahmoud's babies were flying! Breeders flocked to use the gray stallion after his juveniles scorched over the main tracks to win stakes races. Mumtaz Mahal's speed had prevailed yet another generation, and this time on dirt!

In 1962, Ivor Balding took over the training of C.V. Whitney's East Coast string. His first stakes winner for the boss was Honey Dear who became the fourth dam of Marylou Whitney's Champion filly Birdtown and Belmont Stakes winner Birdstone who prevented Smarty Jones from winning the Triple Crown in 2004.

Ivor Balding trained the smart horse Chompion, winner of the Travers Stakes, and Ivor's nephew Ian Balding would make a name for himself at Kingsclere with a champion colt named Mill Reef.

Grey Dawn II commanded a fee of $75,000 live foal in 1985. By that time he had sired 52 stakes winners including Vigors, Bounding Basque, Instrument Landing, Mr. Redoy, Swing Till Dawn and four champion fillies. They were Heavenly Cause (nine wins $622,481, U.S. Champion 2YO filly, Acorn Stakes, Frizette Stakes, Fantasy Stakes, Selima Stakes, Kentucky Oaks), Christmas Past (eight wins $563,670, Champion 3YO filly, Ruffian Handicap, Coaching Club American Oaks, Monmouth Oaks), Bye Bye Paris (13 wins $193,493, Champion 3YO filly in Canada, Canadian Oaks), and Dawn Deluxe (five wins, Champion 2YO filly in Canada). Grey Dawn II also sired Shy Dawn, a filly who earned $516,301 and won 19 races including the Vagrancy, Distaff, Affectionately Handicaps and the Correction Handicap twice.

Grey Dawn's daughter Grey Parlo produced the tough $2 million plus earner Waquoit, winner of 19 races from 30 starts including the Jockey Club Gold Cup, Brooklyn Handicap twice, and Jamaica Handicap. Waquoit is linebred 4 x 4 to Mahmoud. Grey Dawn II's male line continues to thrive in South America.

Herbager became an influential broodmare sire. His daughter Ballade is an "elite" mare and dam of two champions, Glorious Song and Devil's Bag. European champion Rainbow Quest owes much of his ability to Herbager's input. Rainbow Quest is by Blushing Groom from I Will Follow by Herbager. In a vintage crop of three-year-olds, he was voted Champion 3YO stayer, and at four, was ranked Co-Champion Older Horse of Europe.

At two, Rainbow Quest won twice from three starts, scoring in the El Capistrano Stakes over seven furlongs at Newmarket and the Haynes Hanson and Clark Stakes at Newbury going a mile. He was runner-up to El Gran Senor in the Dewhurst Stakes.

At three, Rainbow Quest won the Great Voltiguer Stakes, was second to El Gran Senor in the Irish Derby, and was second to Lear Fan in the Craven Stakes. He also finished third to Darshaan and Sadler's Wells in the Prix du Jockey Club (French Derby) – probably the best French Derby field seen in the last 40 years. Also, he was a fast finishing fourth to El Gran Senor in the English 2,000 Guineas.

In 1985, the son of Blushing Groom was at his peak. He won the Clive Graham Stakes, Coronation Cup and the Prix de l'Arc de Triomphe defeating Sagace and Kozana, finished second to Pebbles in the Eclipse Stakes and third to Petoski in the King George VI & Queen Elizabeth Stakes.

Rainbow Quest (1981)	Blushing Groom	Red God	Nasrullah	Nearco by **Pharos** Mumtaz Begum by **Blenheim***
			Spring Run	Menow by Pharamond II (ex **Selene**) Boola Brook by Bull Dog by **Teddy**
		Runaway Bride	Wild Risk	Rialto by Rabelais Wild Violet by **Blandford**
			Aimee	Tudor Minstrel (to **Pharos** and **Selene**) Emali by Umidwar by **Blandford**
	I Will Follow	Herbager	Vandale II	Plassy by Bosworth ex **Serenissima** Vanille by La Farina
			Flagette	Escamillo by **Firdaussi** Fidgette by **Firdaussi**
		Where You Lead	Raise A Native	Native Dancer by Polynesian (to **Selene**) Raise You by Case Ace by **Teddy**
			Noblesse	Mossborough (ex dau. of **Selene**) Duke's Delight by **His Grace*** by **Blandford**

Rainbow Quest is linebred four times to classic sire Blandford via the brothers Blenheim and His Grace, Wild Violet and Umidwar. As well, he is linebred to that great little mare Selene, dam of Hyperion, Pharamond II, Sickle (the latter being the grandsire of Polynesian) and Hyperion's three-quarter sister All Moonshine who produced Mossborough. Selene is of course half-sister to Bosworth – their dam is Serenissima, by English Derby winner Minoru.

Pharos, Pharamond II and Sickle are all by Phalaris out of daughters of Chaucer; thus Herbager with a "son" of Chaucer via Stedfast (twice through Firdaussi) provides a nice sex balance for the Chaucer duplications. Rainbow Quest's pedigree pattern is skewed towards stamina and he gets his best runners when any of the speed elements of his ancestry are reinforced. Not surprisingly, Blandford is the dominant ancestor in the pedigree, enabling most of Rainbow Quest's Group winners to run a strong mile and a half.

Rainbow Quest is a refined horse. Among his progeny are Quest For Fame (English Derby, Hollywood Turf Handicap), Nedawi (St. Leger), Fiji (Gamely Breeders' Cup Handicap), Sunshack (Coronation Cup), Raintrap (Prix Royal Oak), Spectrum (Irish 2,000 Guineas, Dubai Champion Stakes), Sought Out (Prix du Cadran), Armiger (Royal Lodge Stakes, 2nd St. Leger), Bright Generation (Italian Oaks), Saumarez (Grand Prix de Paris), Knight's Baroness (Irish Oaks), Millenary (St. Leger), Croco Rouge (Prix d'Ispahan) and Ebadiya (Moyglare Stud Stakes). He is renowned for being a sire of classic winners and is a shining star at Juddmonte Farms.

Bred along similar lines to Rainbow Quest is Rahy (Blushing Groom-Glorious Song by Halo from Ballade by Herbager) a small chestnut stallion owned in partnership by His Highness Sheikh Maktoum and Robert Clay (Three Chimneys Farm). Standing about 15.1 ½ hands high, Rahy is the sire of 10 millionaire earners, 60 stakes winners to date and progeny earnings exceeding $62 million.

He won the Bel Air Handicap by 10 lengths, Bonusprint Sirenia Stakes, finished second in the Middle Park Stakes, Goodwood Handicap etc., and third in the Mill Reef Stakes. Again, we find duplication of Blandford in Rahy's pedigree pattern.

Rahy's dam, Glorious Song, is linebred to Mahmoud who is by Blandford's son Blenheim. Rahy himself is linebred to Pharamond II (Phalaris-Selene by Chaucer) via two sons, Menow and Cosmic Bomb, adding Chaucer's impact via daughters. Of significance, there is a speed element in Rahy's pedigree absent in Rainbow Quest's pedigree – i.e. Royal Charger, grandsire of Hail To Reason. Royal Charger has two sources of Sundridge (sire of the dam of Solario, and of Lady Josephine who produced Mumtaz Mahal).

Sundridge's dam Sierra contributes speed whenever she is linked with Phalaris whose dam, Bromus, is by Sainfoin, brother to Sierra. Rahy's pedigree pattern shows two daughters of Pharos (Phalaris-Scapa Flow by Chaucer), Pharos being a genetic relative of Pharamond II, and furthermore, it must be recalled Turn-To is inbred 3 x 3 to a son and daughter of Pharos. Tudor Minstrel's sire Owen Tudor (Hyperion-Mary Tudor by Pharos) is of course linebred to two daughters of Chaucer.

Rahy	Blushing Groom	Red God	**Nasrullah**	**Nearco** by **Pharos**
				Mumtaz Begum by **Blenheim**
			Spring Run	Menow by **Pharamond II** (ex **Selene**)
				Boola Brook by Bull Dog
		Runaway Bride	Wild Risk	Rialto by Rabelais
				Wild Violet by **Blandford**
			Aimee	Tudor Minstrel (to **Pharos** and **Selene**)
				Emali by Umidwar by **Blandford**
	Glorious Song	Halo	Hail To Reason	Turn-To by **Royal Charger**
				Nothirdchance
			Cosmah	Cosmic Bomb by **Pharamond II (S)**
				Almahmoud by **Mahmoud** - **Blenheim**
		Ballade	Herbager	Vandale II
				Flagette
			Miss Swapsco	Cohoes by **Mahmoud** by **Blenheim**
				Soaring by Swaps (g'son of **Hyperion**)

A build-up of genetic influence from Pharos, Blenheim (son of Blandford) and Mumtaz Mahal is evident in Rahy's ancestry. Maternal strength from Selene is duplicated via Hyperion (sire of Owen Tudor and Khaled, the father of Swaps) and twice via Pharamond II. In addition, the gray mare Éclair is duplicated further back in the pedigree via Emali (a daughter) and Khaled (a son). Thus, Herbager's double of Stedfast, a "son" of Chaucer, is seen as a vital sex balance for all the daughters of Chaucer in Rahy's genotype.

Rahy is the sire of many outstanding Group and Graded stakes winners. His best daughter is Serena's Song, U.S. Champion 3YO filly whose wins include the Mother Goose Stakes, Hollywood Starlet Stakes and Haskell Invitational Handicap. She earned $3,283,388. Rahy's best colt is world champion Fantastic Light, out of Jood (Nijinsky II-Kamar), bred by Gainsborough Stud. Fantastic Light won 12 of 24 starts for $8,486,957 including the Breeders' Cup Turf, Prince of Wales' Stakes, Irish Champion Stakes, Tattersalls Gold Cup, Man o' War Stakes, Hong Kong Cup, Great Voltiguer Stakes, Dubai Sheema Classic, and was runner-up twice in the King George VI & Queen Elizabeth Stakes and third in the Japan Cup. He won twice as a juvenile in England. Fantastic Light stands at Dalham Hall Stud and shuttles to Australia.

				Nasrullah
			Red God	Spring Run by **Menow**
		Blushing Groom		Wild Risk (dam by **Blandford**)
			Runaway Bride	Aimee by Tudor Minstrel
	Rahy			Hail To Reason by Turn-To
			Halo	Cosmah (ex **Almahmoud**)
		Glorious Song		Herbager
			Ballade	Miss Swapsco by **Cohoes**
Fantastic Light				**Nearctic**
(1996)			Northern Dancer	Natalma (ex **Almahmoud**)
		Nijinsky II		Bull Page by Bull Lea
			Flaming Page	Flaring Top by **Menow**
	Jood			Graustark (dam by Alibhai)
			Key to the Mint	Key Bridge by Princequillo
		Kamar		Quadrangle by **Cohoes**
			Square Angel	Nangela by **Nearctic**

Mahmoud features strongly in Fantastic Light's pedigree. He is the sire of duplicated ancestors Almahmoud (5 x 5) and Cohoes (5 x 5) and his sire, Blenheim, is present in the pedigrees of three-quarter brothers Nasrullah and Royal Charger. Nijinsky's dam, Flaming Page, is bred on a similar cross to Red God's dam, Spring Run (the Menow/Bull Dog mix). Fantastic Light's dam, Jood, is linebred to Tracery (by Rock Sand) four times.

Rahy is also the sire of Mariah's Storm ($724,895 Arlington-Washington Lassie Stakes, Turfway Park Budweiser Breeders' Cup Stakes, Falls City Handicap and produced Giant's Causeway), Noverre ($1,429,344 Champion 3YO in England, Sussex Stakes), Tranquility Lake ($1,662,390 Yellow Ribbon Stakes, Gamely Breeders' Cup Handicap), Early Pioneer ($1,156,815 Hollywood Gold Cup), Exotic Wood ($890,695 Santa Maria Handicap), Tates Creek ($1,471,674 Yellow Ribbon Stakes), Designed For Luck ($915,500 Shoemaker Breeders' Cup Mile Stakes), Hawksley Hill ($1,730,922 San Francisco Mile Handicap) and Perfectperformance (Royal Lodge Stakes). Giant's Causeway (Storm Cat-Mariah's Storm by Rahy) was Europe's Horse of the Year. He is a product of the successful Northern Dancer/Blushing Groom cross. In his first crop he sired 2004 European Champion 2YO colt Shamardal (facile winner of the Dewhurst Stakes, Veuve Clicquot Vintage Stakes), Footstepsinthesand and Rockfel Stakes winner Maid's Causeway.

Giant's Causeway won nine of 13 starts and more than $3 million in earnings. At two, he won the Prix de la Salamandre and King of Kings EBF Futurity. At three, he won the Sussex Stakes, Coral Eclipse Stakes, Juddmonte International Stakes, St. James' Palace Stakes, Irish Champion Stakes, Gladness Stakes and finished second to King's Best in the English 2,000 Guineas, second to Bachir in the Irish 2,000 Guineas, second to Observatory in the Queen Elizabeth II Stakes and was a courageous runner-up to Tiznow in the Breeders' Cup Classic.

The dam of Giant's Causeway is inbred 4 x 3 to champion Hail To Reason.

HERBAGER (Vandale II - Flagette by Escamillo), winner of the French Derby, whose dam was inbred to St. Leger winner Firdaussi. Herbager was imported to Claiborne Farm by "Bull" Hancock.

WILD RISK (Rialto - Wild Violet by Blandford), leading sire in France. He is the sire of Le Fabuleux and Runaway Bride, dam of champion Blushing Groom.

Giant's Causeway (1997)	Storm Cat	Storm Bird	Northern Dancer	Nearctic Natalma ex **Almahmoud**
			South Ocean	New Providence by Bull Page Shining Sun by Chop Chop
		Terlingua	Secretariat	**Bold Ruler** by **Nasrullah** Somethingroyal by **Princequillo**
			Crimson Saint	Crimson Satan Bolero Rose by Bolero
	Mariah's Storm	Rahy	Blushing Groom	Red God by **Nasrullah** Runaway Bride by Wild Risk
			Glorious Song	Halo by **Hail To Reason** (to **Almahmoud**) Ballade by Herbager
		Immense	Roberto	**Hail To Reason** (g'son **Royal Charger**) Bramalea by Nashua by **Nasrullah**
			Imsodear	Chieftain by **Bold Ruler** (to **Princequillo**) Ironically by Intent

The elite mare Almahmoud (by Mahmoud) is represented via two daughters in the pedigree above. She is the dam of Natalma and of Cosmah, who produced Halo. While Bold Ruler features 4 x 5, real impact comes via his sire, Nasrullah, and his three-quarter brother Royal Charger, the sire of Turn-To (father of Hail To Reason).

Mahmoud is three-quarter brother to Nasrullah's dam, Mumtaz Begum. There is not only a concentration of Blenheim and Mumtaz Mahal but also Sainfoin and Sierra. Tracery is another important element in the pattern and appears via Abbot's Trace (in Nearctic's pedigree), Requiebro (in Crimson Satan's pedigree) and Papyrus, the broodmare sire of Princequillo. Probably the most interesting genetic connection in Giant's Causeway's ancestry is the combination of Secretariat with Chieftain since both are bred on a similar Nasrullah/Princequillo cross.

Europe's Champion 2YO colt Shamardal is by Giant's Causeway from a daughter of Machiavellian. Machiavellian's stakes-winning dam, Coup de Folie, is inbred to Almahmoud, therefore Shamardal has Almahmoud represented four times in his pedigree – confirming the successful technique of duplicating maternal strength.

Up to now we have briefly studied the French-bred stallion Herbager. Now our attention will focus on Wild Risk, an ancestor with a most unusual pedigree – a unique strain working extremely well with Nearco's descendants.

Wild Risk (Rialto-Wild Violet by Blandford-Wood Violet by Ksar) was born in France in 1940 when Hitler was sweeping across Europe. He was a medium-sized brown horse with slightly upright shoulders, strong hindquarters and an over-stride. His right forefoot was a bit "clubby" but it never hindered his action. Racing in France during 1942-1945 was a frustrating period and trainers had to place their runners when and where they could. Stakes winner Wild Risk won nine races in France on the flat and over hurdles including the Prix de Fontainebleau, Prix Le Sancy, Prix Fould and Prix Edgard Gillois. Wild Risk was runner-up in La Coupe and the Prix Jean Prat and tried successfully over jumps. He proved to be versatile, hailed as one of the best hurdlers in France during the years of German occupation.

Wild Risk led the Sires' List in France in 1955 and 1961 and was among the leading sires in Europe in 1964.

Wild Risk's progeny include Le Fabuleux (Champion 3YO colt in France, Prix du Jockey Club-French Derby, Prix Lupin, Criterium de Saint-Cloud), Fils D'Eve (Italian Derby), Worden II (Washington D.C. International Stakes, Prix du Conseil Municipal, Premio Roma, 3rd Prix de l'Arc de Triomphe), Vimy (King George VI & Queen Elizabeth Stakes, Prix Noailles, 2nd French Derby), Runaway Bride (dam of champion Blushing Groom), Waldmeister (Prix du Cadran, La Coupe, Prix Gladiateur, 2nd Ascot Gold Cup), Balto (Grand Prix de Paris, Ascot Gold Cup), and Almyre (Prix Omnium, dam of Ashmore, winner of the Grand Prix de Deauville).

Why should I highlight Wild Risk? What makes him so special?

He is often found in the pedigrees of Group 1 winners. Racing journalists failed unjustly to praise Wild Risk's achievements. At this point, we need to take a journey back in time, to the family of the elite mare Quiver, ancestress of John O'Gaunt (sire of Swynford), Cinna (dam of Beau Pere), Uganda (dam of Umidwar) and Maid Marian (dam of Polymelus). Descendants of famous mare Brown Bess are:

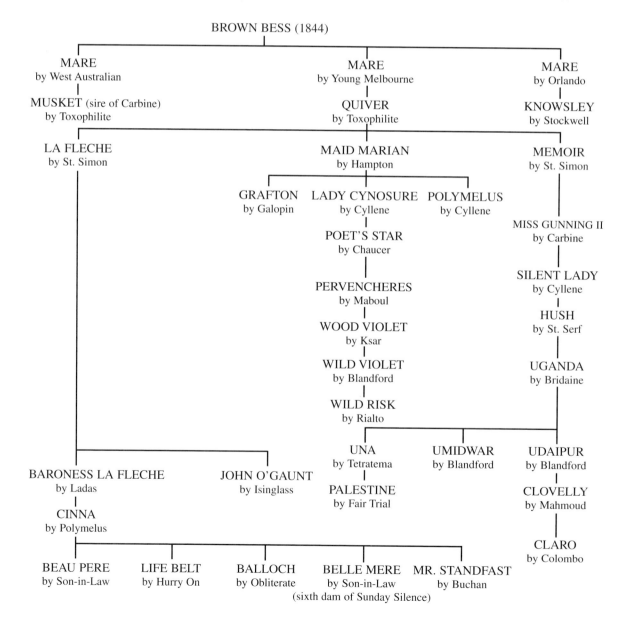

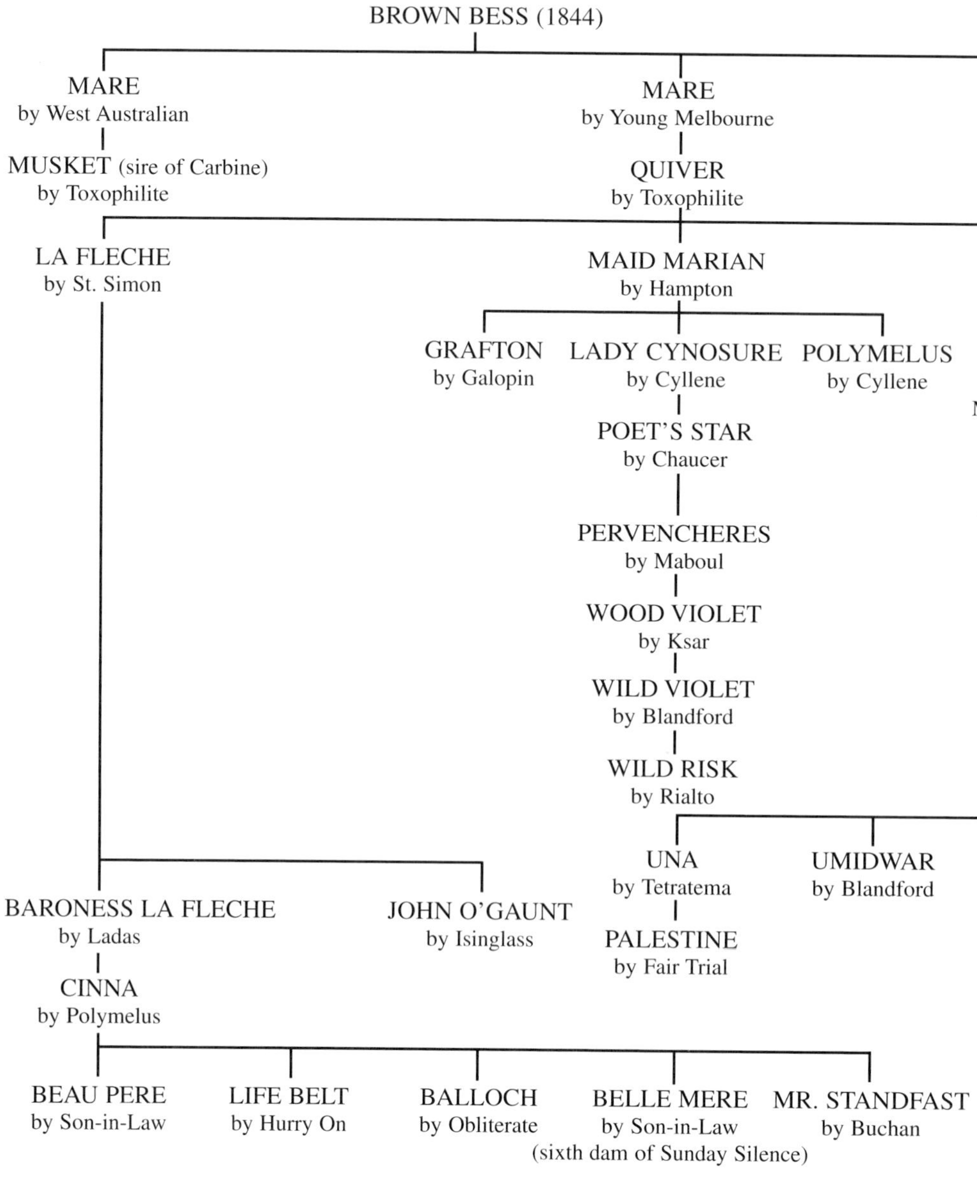

Carbine is by Musket (Quiver's three-parts brother) from The Mersey by Knowsley and is therefore inbred to the wonderful mare Brown Bess. Carbine sired English Derby winner Spearmint and features in the pedigrees of many Group and Graded stakes winners, especially when aligned with Polymelus and his son Phalaris.

Of particular interest is the pedigree of Wild Risk's granddam Wood Violet. Ksar is inbred to Omnium II who carries the strain of Wellingtonia (with two "daughters" of Pocahontas in his genotype). Most important of all, Lady Cynosure is a sister to Polymelus.

Wood Violet (1928)	Ksar	Bruleur	Chouberski	Gardefeu
				Campanule
			Basse Terre	**Omnium II** (dam by Wellingtonia)
				Bijou
		Kizil Kourgan	**Omnium II**	Upas by Dollar
				Bluette by Wellingtonia
			Kasbah	Vigilant
				Katia
	Pervencheres	Maboul	Perth	War Dance by Galliard
				Primrose Dame
			Mad	Le Sancy
				Crowflower
		Poet's Star	Chaucer	St. Simon
				Canterbury Pilgrim
			Lady Cynosure	Cyllene
				Maid Marian

Now compare Poet's Star with the pedigree of the brothers Fairway and Pharos, as it confirms Poet's Star is actually a very close genetic relative:

Pharos and Fairway	Phalaris	Polymelus	Cyllene
			Maid Marian
		Bromus	Sainfoin
			Anchora
	Scapa Flow	Chaucer	St. Simon
			Canterbury Pilgrim
		Anchora	Love Wisely
			Eryholme

When Poet's Star meets up with either Pharos or Fairway, the mix reinforces Polymelus and his sister Lady Cynosure as well as Chaucer.

A great example of this mix is French Champion 2YO and Champion Miler Blushing Groom, but there are other interesting examples. For instance, it happened when Vimy (Wild Risk-Mimi by Black Devil) covered the Court Martial mare Martial Loan to produce Sans Le Sou, dam of Busted (King George VI & Queen Elizabeth Stakes, Eclipse Stakes, Coronation Stakes etc.) and when Worden II covered the mare Commemoration whose dam is by Fair Copy, a son of Fairway, to produce Armistice (Grand Prix de Paris).

It happened when Le Fabuleux covered the mare Cymbale whose dam is by Pharis II, by Pharos, to produce Beau Charmer (Gran Premio di Milano).

It happened when Worden II covered the mare Fair Share whose dam is by Fair Trial by Fairway, to produce the good stayer Karabas (Prix du Conseil Minicipal, La Coupe, Hardwicke Stakes, Washington D.C. International Stakes), and when Le Fabuleux covered the mare Nalee by Nashua, from the male line of Pharos, to produce Meneval (Irish St. Leger, Nijinsky Stakes, Gallinule Stakes). It happened when Vimy covered the mare Upadee by Fairfax, a son of Fairway, to produce Vimadee (Irish St. Leger) and when Wild Risk covered Santa Isabel by Dante, grandson of Pharos, to produce Waldmeister (Prix du Cadran, La Coupe, Prix de l'Esperance).

				Galopin
			St. Simon	St. Angela by King Tom ex **Pocahontas**
		Rabelais		Satiety by **Isonomy**
			Satirical	Chaff
	Rialto			Cyllene
			Helicon	Vain Duchess by **Isinglass** by **Isonomy**
		La Grelee		Kilglas by **Isinglass** by **Isonomy**
			Grignouse	Simber
Wild Risk (1940)				John O'Gaunt by **Isinglass** - La Fleche
			Swynford	**Canterbury Pilgrim**
		Blandford		White Eagle by Gallinule
			Blanche	Black Cherry (ex Black Duchess)
	Wild Violet			Bruleur
			Ksar	Kizil Kourgan (to **Pocahontas**)
		Wood Violet		Maboul
			Pervencheres	Poet's Star by Chaucer (ex **Canterbury Pilgrim**)

In Wild Risk's pedigree the triple of Isinglass must not go unnoticed. Isinglass was one of the great racehorses of the turf winning the Triple Crown (i.e. English 2,000 Guineas, Derby and St. Leger) as well as the Eclipse Stakes and Ascot Gold Cup. When I study pedigrees of international stakes winners I often look for ancestors that carry a "daughter" of Blandford because only a limited number of superior ancestors possess a "daughter" of Blandford. Wild Risk is one of them.

Even though an ancestor may be well back in a pedigree pattern, if it is a dominant ancestor it will maintain its effectiveness for many generations, especially if close relatives reinforce similar biochemistry. Blushing Groom (Red God-Runaway Bride by Wild Risk) is the strongest representative of Wild Risk's input, closely followed by Rahy, Saint Ballado, Devil's Bag and Rainbow Quest. All these stallions should make wonderful broodmare sires because of their special biochemistries.

Eclipse Champion 3YO filly Ashado (2004) has a remarkable pedigree pattern and could become an "elite" mare of the future. At time of writing, Ashado has earned $2,870,440 from nine wins including the Kentucky Oaks, Coaching Club American Oaks, Breeders' Cup Distaff, Spinaway Stakes, Demoiselle Stakes, Schuylerville Stakes, Fair Grounds Oaks, Cotillion Handicap, 2nd Breeders' Cup Juvenile Fillies Stakes, Mother Goose Stakes etc. Trained by Todd Pletcher for Starlight Stables, Paul H. Saylor and Martin Johns, Ashado carries Wild Risk and Herbager in her ancestry.

Ashado is linebred 3 x 5 to stakes winner Cosmah and 4 x 5 x 6 to her famous dam, Almahmoud. The pedigree shows duplication of Turn-To whose sire, Royal Charger, is three-quarters brother to Nasrullah, thus providing a "son" and "daughter" of Mumtaz Begum who is of course three-parts sister to Mahmoud. This means there is valuable concentration of the brilliant mare Mumtaz Mahal and the English Derby winner Blenheim. Pharos (Phalaris-Scapa Flow by Chaucer) appears many times in Ashado's ancestry and the strains of Herbager, Stedfast ("son" of Chaucer) and Wild Risk (with Pharos's genetic female relative Poet's Star) help balance Ashado's pedigree pattern.

Ashado was bred by Aaron U. Jones and Marie Jones and it would not surprise me in the least to learn their breeding advisor Frank Taylor encouraged this clever match. Frank Taylor and his brothers do a lot of homework and they believe in duplicating dominant mares like Cosmah and her mother, Almahmoud.

				Turn-To by **Royal Charger**
			Hail To Reason	Nothirdchance by Blue Swords
		Halo		Cosmic Bomb by Pharamond II
			Cosmah	**Almahmoud** by **Mahmoud**
	Saint Ballado			Vandale II by Plassy (ex Pladda)
			Herbager	Flagette by Escamillo
		Ballade		Cohoes by **Mahmoud**
			Miss Swapsco	Soaring by Swaps
Ashado				Nearctic by **Nearco**
(201)			Northern Dancer	Natalma ex **Almahmoud** by **Mahmoud**
		Mari's Book		Maribeau ex **Cosmah** ex **Almahmoud**
			Mari Her	Hem and Haw
	Goulash			Red God by **Nasrullah** (**Mumtaz Begum**)
			Blushing Groom	Runaway Bride by Wild Risk
		Wise Bride		Smarten by son of **Turn-To**
			Wising Up	Hardly

Blushing Groom's strain always does well with Mahmoud's strain, clearly evident by the success rate of matching his descendants with Northern Dancer's strain. This genetic mix reached its zenith in 2004 by producing North America's Eclipse Champion Older Male and Horse of the Year, Ghostzapper.

Bred by Frank Stronach at his Adena Springs Farm, Ghostzapper was unbeaten as a four-year-old and climaxed his 2004 campaign with an impressive victory over two high-class performers, Roses in May and Pleasantly Perfect, in the Breeders' Cup Classic. Ghostzapper to date has earned $2,996,120 with eight wins from 10 starts. He recorded brilliant speed ratings and went 1:59.02 in the 1¼ mile Classic to break Skip Away's race record. At three, Ghostzapper won the Vosburgh Stakes and finished third in the King's Bishop Stakes. At four, from four starts, he won the Breeders' Cup Classic, Woodward Stakes, Tom Fool Handicap and Philip H. Iselin Breeders' Cup Handicap. He stays in training in 2005 for Stronach Stables.

His sire, Awesome Again, also won the Breeders' Cup Classic. Awesome Again is by Deputy Minister from Primal Force by Blushing Groom. The dam of Ghostzapper is stakes winner Baby Zip, bred by Kentuckian J. Robert Harris, Jr.

Ghostzapper (2000)	Awesome Again	Deputy Minister	Vice Regent	Northern Dancer (to **Mahmoud**)
				Victoria Regina
			Mint Copy	Bunty's Flight
				Shakney by Jabneh by Bimelech
		Primal Force	Blushing Groom	Red God by **Nasrullah**
				Runaway Bride by Wild Risk
			Prime Prospect	Mr. Prospector (to **Nasrullah**)
				Square Generation by Olden Times
	Baby Zip	Relaunch	In Reality	Intentionally
				My Dear Girl
			Foggy Note	The Axe II by **Mahmoud**
				Silver Song
		Thirty Zip	Tri Jet	Jester by Tom Fool
				Haze
			Sailaway	Hawaii (to **Mahmoud** & **Uganda**)
				Quick Wit by Shannon II

The alternate sex line of Ghostzapper zigzags back to The Axe II (Mahmoud-Blackball by Shut Out-Big Event by Black Toney-La Troienne).

Big Event's brother Bimelech (Black Toney-La Troienne) is found in Deputy Minister's ancestry since Bimelech is the father of Jabneh.

Blushing Groom traces back in direct female line to Emali by Umidwar, "son" of French Oaks winner Uganda. I find it interesting that Uganda is reinforced via a "daughter" named Una, dam of Mehrali, broodmare sire of South African champion Hawaii, so let's compare these strains:

Mehrali	Mahmoud	Blenheim by **Blandford**
		Mah Mahal (ex Mumtaz Mahal by **The Tetrarch)**
	Una	Tetratema by **The Tetrarch**
		Uganda

Emali is the third dam of Blushing Groom.

Emali	Umidwar	**Blandford**
		Uganda
	Éclair	Ethnarch by **The Tetrarch**
		Black Ray

Uganda was certainly a talented racemare! She won the Prix de Diane (French Oaks), Prix La Rochette, Prix Royal Oak and was placed in the Grand Prix de Paris. Was it a coincidence Emali and Mehrali, with very similar biochemistry, form a part of Ghostzapper's pedigree? Do these dominant ancestors actually affect the DNA of Frank Stronach's Horse of the Year?

If we examine the race records of Ghostzapper's four grandparents we might be able to ascertain the racing class of the pedigree. Awesome Again's sire, Deputy Minister, was a champion at two and a very influential sire. Awesome Again's dam, Primal Force, is a winning daughter of champion Blushing Groom.

Primal Force is the dam of Macho Uno, U.S. Champion 2YO colt. Let's now examine the bottom half of Ghostzapper's pedigree. Relaunch won the Del Mar Derby, La Jolla Mile Stakes and was second in the San Antonio Stakes Gr-1 and San Luis Rey Stakes Gr-1. Ghostzapper's second dam Thirty Zip was a hard-knocking mare that won 13 races worth $585,970 including the Gardenia Stakes, Melaleuca Stakes, Virginia Handicap and Begonia Stakes etc.

Baby Zip has already produced the brilliant City Zip (by Carson City), the mare's third foal who won nine races $818,225, including the Hopeful Stakes, Saratoga Special, Sanford Stakes, Amsterdam Stakes and Tremont Stakes. City Zip carries Blushing Groom's strain and therefore possesses both Wild Risk and Uganda in her pedigree because Carson City is by Mr. Prospector from Blushing Promise by Blushing Groom.

In 2002, Baby Zip produced another colt by Awesome Again. Named Aristocrat, what chance does this colt have of being half as good (or even as good) as his champion brother? Surely everything will depend upon whether he inherits the best genes (the right portion of his ancestry). Genetic variation is either kind or cruel and only time will tell us if Aristocrat becomes a stakes winner.

Frank Stronach was North America's Eclipse Award Breeder in 2004. An entrepreneur and risk taker, he deserves all the success that comes his way. Many of his critics envy him. Frank Stronach, who has invested multi-millions of dollars in the breeding and racing industry, has a positive outlook on life and is not afraid to speak his mind. He thinks out of the box and is imaginative. Stronach's runners are raised on three farms in Kentucky, Florida and Canada, and he presently owns more than 400 broodmares. In 2004 his runners earned more than $14 million.

Frank Stronach is the driving force behind Magna International, a major manufacturer of automobile parts based in Canada. He also established Magna Entertainment, a company that presently owns 10 racetracks in North America.

Dan Hall, Adena Springs' farm manager, is a quietly spoken horseman for whom I have the utmost respect. I met Dan some 15 years ago and identified him as being a loyal, hardworking guy with loads of patience and a keen eye for detail. Dan is a true professional in the game – a very flexible person – and one of his most valued assets is his ability to listen to people. Stronach chose well when he hired Dan Hall.

Stallions at Adena Springs include Awesome Again and one of my favorites, Cozzene's best son Alphabet Soup, a horse that appeals to those who breed to race. Perhaps quite soon, commercial breeders will also learn to appreciate this gray stallion because Alphabet Soup's statistics are truly impressive.

Ghostzapper will be a worthy addition to Adena Springs after he campaigns in 2005. His performance in the Breeders' Cup Classic was a memorable victory. International assessors ranked Ghostzapper the best racehorse in the world in 2004.

In summary, the French connection of Herbager and Wild Risk is rather important. Herbager and Wild Risk are unique individuals whose strains succeed with today's commercial bloodlines. Arthur B. "Bull" Hancock did Americans a favor when he imported Herbager from France. He might have been a genius after all.

I visualize Rahy and Rainbow Quest becoming two great broodmare sires in the next two decades, mainly because both possess Herbager and Wild Risk in their genotypes.

PRINCEQUILLO, ROUND TABLE AND RIBOT

"When the going gets tough,
The tough get going."

The hybrid racehorse comes in all shapes and sizes, despite selective breeding.

Some of the best two-year-olds are small and agile, in a range of 14.3 to 15.2 hands high, yet their speed carries them over a short course to victory ahead of much bigger rivals. If a small horse has courage, a large heart and a willingness to win, these factors overcome small size. Among famous small performers were Hyperion, Star Kingdom, Ribot, Northern Dancer, Lyphard, Blushing Groom and El Gran Senor.

A large, functional heart with strength through the heart's walls is one of the most desirable assets for any athlete, especially a racehorse. I happen to believe a cluster of genes located on the X sex chromosome might regulate and influence heart size and heart strength. These genes are termed "sex-linked genes."

According to texts, English stallions known to have been able to transmit above average heart size include Highflyer, King Tom, Stockwell, Newminster, Hermit, Polymelus, Dark Ronald and Bayardo. Ireland had The Tetrarch, Blandford, The Phoenix and has Sadler's Wells. France had Ksar, Tourbillon, Pharos and Teddy. North America had Glencoe, Broomstick, Domino, Rock Sand, Sweep, Blue Larkspur, War Admiral and Princequillo. Others came from Italy (namely Nearco and Ribot), Germany (Alchimist), South America (Congreve), New Zealand (Carbine and Le Filou), and Australia (Heroic, Magpie and Midstream) – all very influential sires.

When English stakes runners find the rising ground in the final furlongs at Newmarket we often see early leaders weaken. Horses who go on and win are those best able to control energy levels for a longer time period and possess the will-to-win. In Australia, any racehorse that can lead all the way to win the Caulfield Cup over a mile and a half has to be an exceptional athlete because this handicap, above all others, is always run at a very fast tempo from start to finish. Only high-class performers win a Caulfield Cup leading all the way.

Winners of Europe's championship event, the Prix de l'Arc de Triomphe (at weight-for-age), require strong, large hearts, as do winners of the classics and winners of all valuable events on Breeders' Cup day; but what do we know about the mind of a racehorse? Rarely is anything published about energy of the mind, stress factors or the brain activity of a racehorse. A horse's hypothalamus (located just above the roof of its mouth) is the drive center of the brain, controlling hunger, thirst, anxiety, lust, stress and arousal. The hypothalamus measures the body's activity and monitors the contents of the blood that flows through it, and will make adjustments to the body when required. For example, it adjusts the level of arousal and sleep.

The hypothalamus keeps track of the mind. Sensory details are picked up and communicated through the thalamus at the center of the brain with an option of taking one of two pathways, either the rational mind or the emotional mind. At the same time it compares notes with experience so that any threat of danger will activate the flight mechanism causing adrenaline to surge through the body.

Racehorses can't handle long periods of stress. Racehorses are fine-tuned, refined animals with a complicated nervous system. Being flight animals by nature, they use their speed to run away from danger.

Horse trainers monitor and try to limit the amount of stress each racehorse experiences during training. Stomach ulcers are so easily caused by stress and harm the health of a well-bred colt or filly. Stomach ulcers definitely affect racetrack performance and nearly all horses in training develop them.

When two-year-olds lack confidence going into the starting gate and refuse to enter, if they have a bad experience they will remember everything that happens. The experience is imprinted in their brain. Young horses can be so easily frightened – and they often become anxious, even distraught. Some of them never mentally recover from a really bad experience at the starting gate. Yet, racehorses are intelligent animals – so intelligent, some learn how to lose instead of win.

The brain is a network of neurons transmitting electrical impulses to deliver electrical messages. How does the brain function? An Austrian scientist named Otto Loewi was working in the 1920's on neural transmission to the heart. He noticed stimulation of the vagus nerve (connecting the brain to the heart) caused the heart to slow. Isolating a frog's heart with its vagus nerve intact, Loewi observed by stimulating the nerve he could cause the heart to slow down. He needed to discover how and why this happened. With further experiments he thought a chemical connection was the reason. He discovered electrical nerve impulses pass down to the end of neurons causing the nerve ending to release a chemical that crosses the narrow gap between two neurons (the synapse). This chemical connection would eventually be called a "neurotransmitter."

There are two main neurotransmitters in the brain – glutamate and GABA. Glutamate acts on the second neuron to increase the chance of its firing a nerve impulse and is described as an "excitatory transmitter" whereas GABA acts to decrease the second neuron's firing capacity. A neuron receives thousands of messages and nerve impulses and acts with tremendous speed!

Two modulators of glutamate and GABA are important neurotransmitters, viz. noradrenaline and serotonin. Central to brain arousal and attention is the "blue spot," a small, remarkable feature of the brain that reaches out to virtually the whole area of the brain. The blue spot is actually the "locus coeruleus" found in the brain stem where the spinal cord meets the brain. It is the alarm system and uses noradrenaline to instigate quick action. Serotonin, on the other hand, modulates moods, emotion and euphoria. A fit racehorse is usually on its toes in the saddling paddock. Its muscles will be well defined, its mind active and energized. An intelligent racehorse will look at its rivals and may even determine beforehand whether it can win because it will draw upon past experience. A racehorse also recalls the effect of spurs and whip and some actually resent their use and will under-perform. Unfortunately, we don't know enough about the mind energy of a racehorse. We may only observe (as did Federico Tesio) how "nervous energy" varies from one racehorse to another. Many champions have been electrically charged! Nasrullah and Ribot come instantly to mind.

Since the modern racehorse has become such a refined animal, breeders must turn to ancestors known to possess tough constitutions to maintain soundness.

In North America, the most gifted modern stallion to improve soundness was Princequillo (Prince Rose-Cosquilla by Papyrus-Quick Thought by White Eagle). He was a very tough horse, could carry weight, and often transmitted large hearts.

Although Princequillo had a few niggling problems in training, as a sire of stakes winners he could always be relied upon to put decent legs on his progeny. In fact, he is responsible for correcting the slightly calf-shaped knees transmitted via the stallions Nasrullah and Bold Ruler. There is no doubt in my mind Princequillo's daughters helped make Bold Ruler the leading sire in North America. Princequillo improved stamina, temperament, and corrected the structure of knees and ankles. His genes were dominant. When Princequillo retired to "Bull" Hancock's Ellerslie Stud, his pedigree was basically "foreign" to local breeders. His sire, Prince Rose, was unknown to Americans despite the fact he was Horse of the Year in Belgium, winner of 16 of 20 starts including the Grand International d'Ostende twice, Grand Prix de Bruxelles, and in France, winner of the Prix du President de la Republique. (Also, he finished third to Pearl Cap II in the Prix de l'Arc de Triomphe.) Prince Rose is also the father of Prince Chevalier, seven wins including the Prix de la Salamandre, Prix du Jockey Club (French Derby), Prix Lupin, Prix Greffulhe, 2nd Prix de l'Arc de Triomphe (to Caracalla II) and Grand Criterium.

Prince Rose is a son of the Cesarewitch Handicap winner Rose Prince (Prince Palatine-Eglantine by Perth), a representative of St. Simon's male line.

Ellerslie Farm was situated at the foothills of the Blue Ridge Mountains, not far from Charlottesville, Virginia. William Woodward was a close friend of "Bull's" father Arthur B. Hancock and boarded many of his mares at Ellerslie. Together they had purchased an exciting eight-year-old stallion in England named Maiden Erlegh, by Polymelus from Plum Tart by Persimmon, but lady luck turned against them. Disaster struck! The ship carrying the stallion and mares was sunk off the coast of Ireland by a German submarine. Nevertheless, William Woodward became involved with Hancock as underbidders for the famous stallion Solario when he came up for auction in England, but again, luck deserted the Americans. Lord Glanely outbid their agent (Frank Hills) and secured Solario for 47,000 guineas. The English lord was acting on behalf of a syndicate comprising himself, Lord Rosebery, Sir Laurence Phillips, the Aga Khan, Lord Woolavington, Mr. A. de Rothschild and a few other interested gentlemen. Princequillo was foaled in England in 1940 and raised in Ireland before his export to North America as a yearling. He won 12 of 33 starts including the Jockey Club Gold Cup (defeating Bolingbroke), Saratoga Cup, Saratoga Handicap, Merchants' and Citizens' Handicap and the Questionnaire Handicap. In the latter race he equaled the track record. Princequillo was runner-up to Bolingbroke in the Whitney Stakes and finished third to Vincentive in the Dwyer Handicap. He was an immediate success at stud. After Hill Prince began to collect a string of stakes races, Princequillo was moved from Virginia to Claiborne Farm, Kentucky.

Princequillo led the Sires' List in 1957 and 1958 and was Leading Broodmare Sire eight times. His progeny were tough and genuine. Of his 65 stakes winners we should mention Round Table, Dedicate, Prince John, Misty Morn, Hill Prince, Quill, Crimea II, Discipline and Firm Policy. He also sired Somethingroyal, dam of champion Secretariat and Sir Gaylord. Other important daughters were Milan Mill (dam of champion Mill Reef), Cherokee Rose II, How, Monarchy, Neriad (third dam of champion Miesque), Quillobelle, Rose Bower, Sequoia, Sharp Queen (dam of Kris S.), Stepping Stone and Key Bridge (dam of champion Key to the Mint).

A horse endowed with a fair percentage of slow fiber muscle, Princequillo was a true stayer even though he won races over short distances as a juvenile. Ironically, he ran in claiming races until it was discovered he could stay a mile and a half.

Princequillo never met Count Fleet, North America's Horse of the Year and Champion 3YO colt in 1943, but Mr. Vosburgh handicapped Princequillo next best of the three-year-olds. The third dam of Princequillo is Mindful (Minoru-Noble Martha by Noble Chieftain), unraced dam of eight winners including Quick Thought. A fairly big mare, Mindful is by English Derby winner Minoru who stood for a season in England before his export to Russia. Minoru is the sire of Serenissima (dam of Bosworth and granddam of Hyperion, Sickle, Pharamond II and Hunter's Moon) and Tillywhim (third dam of Australian champion Bernborough).

Princequillo (1940)	Prince Rose	Rose Prince	Prince Palatine	Persimmon by **St. Simon** by **Galopin**
				Lady Lightfoot by son of **Isonomy**
			Eglantine	Perth II by War Dance by Galliard
				Rose de Mai
		Indolence	Gay Crusader	Bayardo by Bay Ronald
				Gay Laura by Beppo
			Barrier	Grey Leg (dam by Bend Or)
				Bar The Way
	Cosquilla	Papyrus	Tracery	Rock Sand by Sainfoin
				Topiary by Orme (ex **Angelica**)
			Miss Matty	Marcovil
				Simonath by **St. Simon** by **Galopin**
		Quick Thought	White Eagle	Gallinule (**Isonomy/Hermit**)
				Merry Gal by **Galopin**
			Mindful	Minoru ex Mother Siegel by **Hermit**
				Noble Martha

Papyrus is of course linebred to St. Simon and his sister Angelica, whereas Quick Thought is linebred to Hermit via two daughters plus his sister Chanoinesse. This is typical of pedigree patterns designed by William Hall-Walker (Lord Wavertree), who developed Princequillo's female line.

William Hall-Walker owned the Tully Stud in Ireland and again used White Eagle (who is out of a daughter of Galopin) to breed the mare Blanche, dam of Blandford who sired four English Derby winners. Minoru's dam was a sister to Grand Marnier, granddam of English Derby winner Grand Parade (by Orby), thus the female line of Hermit's sister Chanoinesse was well respected by English and Irish breeders. Chanoinesse produced a daughter by Bend Or named Chatelaine who became the third dam of Spearfelt, winner of the VRC Melbourne Cup.

Princequillo's best son was America's Horse of the Year Round Table, born at Claiborne Farm the same morning as Bold Ruler. Round Table won 43 races (31 of them stakes), earned $1,749,869 and was voted Champion Handicap Horse twice and Champion Grass Horse three times. He sired 81 stakes winners including Apalachee (Champion 2YO colt in England and Ireland), Flirting Around (Champion Sprinter in England), Baldric II (Champion Miler in England and France, English 2,000 Guineas), Targowice (Champion 2YO colt in France), He's A Smoothie (Horse of the Year in Canada), Drumtop (17 wins $493,735, Hialeah Turf Cup), La Mesa, King Pellinore, King's Bishop, Tell, Royal Glint, Cellini, Foreseer, Artaius and Poker.

Round Table was an extremely sound, tough horse with a kind temperament. At two years he won five of 10 starts including the Breeders' Futurity and Lafayette Stakes. At three, he won the Hollywood Gold Cup, Hawthorne Gold Cup, United Nations Handicap, American Derby (defeating Iron Liege), Malibu Sequet Stakes, El Dorado Handicap, Cinema Handicap, Blue Grass Stakes etc., and finished third in the Santa Anita Derby and Kentucky Derby (to Iron Liege and Gallant Man).

At four, Round Table won the Santa Anita Handicap, Gulfstream Park Handicap, San Antonio Handicap, San Fernando Stakes, Argonaut Handicap, Arlington Handicap, Hawthorne Gold Cup, Arch Ward Handicap, Caliente Handicap etc. At five, he won the United Nations Handicap, Citation Handicap, Manhattan Handicap, Stars & Stripes Handicap, San Marcos Handicap etc. and was runner-up in the Jockey Club Gold Cup. He equaled the world record for 1 1/8 miles in 1:46 4/5 and set nine new track records. What an athlete!

After Round Table's two-year-old season, "Bull" Hancock sold the colt privately to Mr. and Mrs. Travis M. Kerr for $175,000. Bill Molter, the colt's new trainer, developed Round Table into a world-beater. Kerr's agent Dr. John Peters noticed the son of Princequillo had a huge over-stride and a deep girth, but he also pointed out to the new owners the colt's slightly clubby right front foot that would need constant attention. At the close of the horse's racing career, Travis Kerr asked "Bull" Hancock to syndicate Round Table and stand him at Claiborne Farm.

Round Table was North America's leading sire in 1972 and was nearly always in the top 10 on the Sires' List. A medium-sized horse of 15.3 hands high, he belongs to Feola's wonderful family. The elite mare Feola is linebred to Galopin, St. Simon and his sister Angelica, to Hermit and his sister Chanoinesse, Orme via a son and daughter, Persimmon via a son and daughter and to Gallinule via a son and daughter (a case of "balanced breeding"). Round Table's dam, Knight's Daughter (by the sprinter Sir Cosmo), was bred and raced by His Majesty King George VI.

Knight's Daughter won three races in England before "Bull" Hancock purchased her and shipped her to Claiborne Farm. Monarchy, a sister to Round Table, established a powerful branch of the family through her daughter State (by Nijinsky II). Among State's descendants are Johannesburg (World Champion 2YO colt, Breeders' Cup Juvenile Stakes, Prix Morny, Middle Park Stakes), Minardi (Champion 2YO colt of England, Middle Park Stakes), Tale of the Cat (five wins $360,900, King's Bishop Stakes), Pulpit (four wins $728,200, Blue Grass Stakes), Double Feint (11 wins $493,928, Hill Prince Stakes) and Region (12 wins $826,935, Bel Air Handicap).

A genetic affinity developed between Nijinsky II and Round Table. Claiborne Farm bred Caerleon (Nijinsky II-Foreseer by Round Table), a smart stayer who won four races including the Prix du Jockey Club (French Derby), Benson & Hedges Gold Cup and was runner-up in the Irish Derby. A small horse for a son of Nijinsky II, Caerleon was a successful sire in Ireland, particularly of stakes-winning fillies.

Champion juvenile Johannesburg is a product of the Storm Bird link with Nijinsky II – both genetically related since they are by Northern Dancer out of mares with Bull Page plus one of the brothers Omaha and Flares. Storm Bird and Nijinsky II possess similar biochemistry even though physically they are different types.

Johannesburg is a small horse who matured quickly and inherited fast fiber muscle. He should make a successful commercial sire at Ashford-Coolmore Stud in Kentucky. Unfortunately at three, Johannesburg became sour in training (mind energy loss) and disappointed his trainer, but as a juvenile, he was a world champion.

Nasrullah and his three-quarter brother Royal Charger appear in the pedigree below as well as My Babu's dam, Perfume II (who acts as a genetic female cousin since she is by Badruddin, by Blandford out of Mumtaz Mahal). Mahmoud adds speed since he is three-quarter brother to Nasrullah's dam, Mumtaz Begum, daughter of Mumtaz Mahal. Represented many times in the background of the pattern are Sainfoin and his sister Sierra. Princequillo's handsome son Prince John showed talent as a juvenile and is the broodmare sire of champion Riverman.

Johannesburg (1999)	Hennessy	Storm Cat	**Storm Bird**	**Northern Dancer**
				South Ocean by son of **Bull Page**
			Terlingua	Secretariat (**Nasrullah/Princequillo**)
				Crimson Saint
		Island Kitty	Hawaii	Utrillo II
				Ethane by Mehrali
			T. C. Kitten	Tom Cat by Tom Fool
				Needlebug
	Myth	Ogygian	Damascus	Sword Dancer by Sunglow
				Kerala by My Babu (dam Perfume II)
			Gonfalon	Francis S. by **Royal Charger**
				Grand Splendor
		Yarn	Mr. Prospector	Raise a Native by **Native Dancer**
				Gold Digger by Nashua by **Nasrullah**
			Narrate	Honest Pleasure by What A Pleasure
				State by **Nijinsky** by **Northern Dancer** (+ **Bull Page**)

Mill Reef was bred by Paul Mellon and trained by Ian Balding. He won 12 races in England and France including the English Derby, Eclipse Stakes, King George VI & Queen Elizabeth Stakes, Coronation Cup, Prix Ganay, Prix de l'Arc de Triomphe, Gimcrack Stakes, Dewhurst Stakes and was runner-up to Brigadier Gerard in the English 2,000 Guineas. Mill Reef's son Shirley Heights, a bay colt bred by Lord Halifax and Lord Irwin, won six races in England and Ireland at two and three years including the English Derby, Irish Sweeps Derby, Dante Stakes, Royal Lodge Stakes, etc. He sired Darshaan, another champion bred by the Aga Khan.

Mill Reef (1968)	Never Bend	Nasrullah	Nearco
			Mumtaz Begum
		Lalun	Djeddah
			Be Faithful by Bimelech
	Milan Mill	Princequillo	Prince Rose
			Cosquilla by Papyrus
		Virginia Water	Count Fleet
			Red Ray by Hyperion

Shirley Heights is out of Hardiemma by Hardicanute, a first class juvenile colt who won the Champagne Stakes and Timeform Gold Cup etc.

Hardicanute is linebred to Sainfoin's daughter Bromus, dam of Phalaris and Hainault. Sainfoin's sister Sierra is present via Admiral Drake.

Hardicanute possesses a "son" of Spearmint via English Derby winner Spion Kop, as well as two daughters of Spearmint, namely Plucky Liege (dam of Admiral Drake) and Catch Crop (dam of Hay Fever).

Hardicanute (1962)	Hard Ridden	Hard Sauce	Ardan	Pharis II by Pharos by Phalaris (**Bromus**)
				Adargatis by Asterus by Teddy
			Saucy Belle	Bellacose by Sir Cosmo
				Marmite by Mr. Jinks
		Tout Belle II	Admiral Drake	Craig an Eran by Sunstar by **Sundridge (S)**
				Plucky Liege by **Spearmint**
			Chatelaine	Casterari
				Yssel II
	Hardiemma	Umidwar	Blandford	Swynford by John O'Gaunt
				Blanche by White Eagle
			Uganda	Bridaine by Gorgos (dam by **Galopin**)
				Hush by St. Serf by **St. Simon**
		Hay Fell	Felstead	Spion Kop by **Spearmint**
				Felkington
			Hay Fever	Hainault (ex **Bromus** by **Sainfoin**)
				Catch Crop by **Spearmint**

Hay Fell is inbred 2 x 2 to English Derby winner Spearmint (by Carbine) and complements John O'Gaunt's female line of Brown Bess from whom Polymelus descends. Hardicanute, with a triple of Spearmint, should have been able to stay a mile and a half even though his ancestry shows many ancestors with speed. Possibly his broodmare sire Umidwar was a dominant influence? Umidwar traces in direct female line to Carbine's daughter Miss Gunning II and is himself linebred to Galopin and St. Simon via sons and daughters.

Darshaan's best son is the Aga Khan's champion Dalakhani whose broodmare sire, Miswaki, carries the Princequillo/Nasrullah nick via Rose Bower. This means Dalakhani has two immediate ancestors with similar genotypes, Mill Reef and Rose Bower (refer to Dalakhani's pedigree on page 80).

Princequillo sired three brothers who all became stakes winners. They were Hill Prince (U.S. Horse of the Year), Prince Hill ($98,300) and Third Brother ($310,787). Christopher T. Chenery, a utilities tycoon who owned The Meadow Farm in Virginia, bred these colts from Hildene, a daughter of Bubbling Over.

Chenery purchased Hildene as a yearling filly for $750 at the Xalapa Farm dispersal sale in 1939. She only managed to place in a maiden race, but after producing a decent colt named Mangohick, Hildene was sent to Princequillo who stood in Virginia at the Hancock's Ellerslie Farm. Chenery had no particular reason for choosing Princequillo – the stallion was located conveniently near his farm, but Chenery had a purpose when he sent Imperatrice to Princequillo, a match that produced Somethingroyal, dam of the chestnut "wonder horse" Secretariat, U.S. Horse of the Year, Champion 2YO and 3YO colt and Penny Chenery's pride and joy.

When Princequillo eventually moved to Claiborne Farm, Christopher Chenery kept supporting the stallion because he knew Princequillo sired sound youngsters.

Hill Prince was a strong bay horse born in 1947. He won 17 of 30 starts, earned $422,140 and set a new track record for 6½ furlongs at Aqueduct. At two, he won the World's Playground Stakes and developed into a high-class three-year-old with major victories in the Preakness Stakes, Withers Stakes, Wood Memorial Stakes, American Derby and Jerome Handicap.

Triangle Publications voted Hill Prince the nation's Champion 2YO colt. At three, he debuted in the Wood Memorial Stakes, a race in which he met Middleground for the first time. Hill Prince won convincingly by two lengths. On May 6, 1950, Your Host started favorite for the Kentucky Derby after winning the Santa Anita Derby and scorching over seven furlongs in 1:22 ⅖ in a handicap at Keeneland, defeating Oil Capitol and Blue Grass Stakes winner Mr. Trouble.

In the Kentucky Derby, Your Host and Mr. Trouble went out on the lead at a frantic pace and set the race up for late finishers, but it was King Ranch's Middleground who proved best, scoring by 1¼ lengths from Hill Prince, with Mr. Trouble holding on for third. Hill Prince won the Withers Stakes before he was shipped to Pimlico where he took revenge, winning the Preakness Stakes by five lengths from Middleground. However, in the longer Belmont Stakes in New York he could only manage fifth to Middleground.

At the close of the year, Hill Prince was voted Champion 3YO colt and Horse of the Year. He gained his reputation with a gutsy win over Noor in the Jockey Club Gold Cup and an impressive win in the Sunset Handicap, beating Next Move. In between, Noor (by Nasrullah) defeated him in the Hollywood Gold Cup.

Princequillo sired numerous high-class stakes-winning progeny. His son Prince John was produced from Not Afraid, a daughter of champion Count Fleet.

Prince John won three races as a juvenile before injury to a foot caused his premature retirement to Elmendorf Farm. He won the Garden State Stakes and was runner-up in both the Washington Park Futurity and Sanford Stakes. Although a successful sire of 55 stakes winners, he proved a much better broodmare sire and headed that category four times in North America. Among his famous daughters is River Lady, dam of Riverman.

Riverman was bred by Captain Harry Guggenheim. The elegant colt won five races including the French 2,000 Guineas, Prix d'Ispahan and Prix Jean Prat. Riverman was runner-up in the Champion Stakes and finished third in the valuable King George VI & Queen Elizabeth Stakes at Ascot.

He is a product of the successful Nasrullah/Princequillo mix, being by champion Never Bend (son of Nasrullah) from River Lady by Prince John and tracing to Coquelicot, dam of champion Pavot.

Riverman was the leading sire in France in 1980 and 1981 and was later syndicated to stand at Gainesway Farm, Kentucky. His progeny include Irish River (Champion 2YO colt and Champion Miler in France, French 2,000 Guineas, Prix Jacques Le Marois, Prix du Moulin de Longchamp, Prix de la Salamandre, Grand Criterium), Detroit (Horse of the Year and Champion 3YO filly in France, Prix de l'Arc de Triomphe), Gold River (Champion Older Horse in France, Prix de l'Arc de Triomphe, Prix du Cadran), Triptych (Champion 2YO filly in Europe), Policeman (French Derby) and Rousillon (Waterford Crystal Mile). Riverman's second dam Nile Lily is inbred 3 x 3 to Teddy and linebred to Sainfoin and his sister Sierra.

				Pharos by Phalaris
			Nearco	Nogara by Havresac II
		Nasrullah		Blenheim
			Mumtaz Begum	Mumtaz Mahal (ex Lady Josephine)
	Never Bend			Djebel by Tourbillon
			Djeddah	Djezima
		Lalun		Bimelech ex La Troienne by **Teddy**
			Be Faithful	Bloodroot by **Blue Larkspur**
Riverman				Prince Rose
(1969)			Princequillo	Cosquilla by Papyrus by Tracery
		Prince John		Count Fleet by Reigh Count
			Not Afraid	Banish Fear by **Blue Larkspur**
	River Lady			Sir Gallahad III by **Teddy**
			Roman	Buckup by Buchan by Sunstar
		Nile Lily		Sun Teddy (**Teddy/Sun Briar**)
			Azalea	Coquelicot by Man o' War

Riverman is the broodmare sire of Australia's greatest racemare, Makybe Diva, earner of almost $10 million. Prince John also sired Speak John, winner of the Del Mar Derby, whose sons Hold Your Peace and Verbatim succeeded in carrying on the male line. Hold Your Peace won 11 races including the Flamingo Stakes and Arlington-Washington Futurity and is the sire of Meadowlake, a big horse with early maturing speed. Verbatim is the sire of Alphabatim, earner of $1.3 million.

Princequillo had a genuine affinity with Ribot's strain. Tom Rolfe, Bowl Game, Key to The Mint, Run The Gantlet and Pleasant Colony, all champion racehorses, are examples of this cross involving duplication of English champion Tracery and his classic-winning son Papyrus. Tom Rolfe was a small bay colt by Ribot from stakes winner Pocahontas (USA) by Roman from stakes winner How by Princequillo. Tom Rolfe won 16 races, earned $671,297 and came from the family that produced Ack Ack (Horse of the Year). At two, when only 15 hands high, he showed surprising speed for a son of Ribot, winning the Cowdin Stakes, two other juvenile races and finished third in the Futurity Stakes and Christiana Stakes. Eventually he grew to 15.2 hands and was voted U.S. Champion 3YO colt.

Tom Rolfe's main victories at three and four comprise the Preakness Stakes, American Derby (in new track record time), Arlington Classic, Chesapeake Stakes, Citation Handicap, Aqueduct Handicap, Chicagoan Stakes and Salvator Mile Handicap. He finished second in the Belmont Stakes, third in the Kentucky Derby, and equaled the track record 1:21 flat for seven furlongs at Arlington Park. Retired to stand at Claiborne Farm, Tom Rolfe sired Hoist The Flag (U.S. Champion 2YO colt), Droll Role, Bowl Game (U.S. Champion Grass Horse), London Company, Rokeby Rose, French Colonial, Tom Tulle and Run The Gantlet (U.S. Champion Grass Horse). Bowl Game won 11 races $907,083, including the Man o' War Stakes, Turf Classic Stakes, Washington D.C. International Stakes, Gulfstream Handicap and was produced from a daughter of Round Table, thereby reinforcing Princequillo.

Key to the Mint (Graustark-Key Bridge by Princequillo) was a grandson of Ribot whom I much admired at Greentree Farm. He was an exceptionally well-bred stallion with clean legs, powerful hindquarters and a placid temperament.

Voted U.S. Champion 3YO colt, Key to the Mint won 14 of 29 starts for $576,015. I always admired this horse that was half-brother to Fort Marcy (Horse of the Year, 21 wins $1,109,791) and Key to Content ($354,773, won United Nations Handicap). Key to the Mint is the best son of Graustark.

Tom Rolfe (1962)	Ribot	Tenerani	Bellini	Cavaliere d'Arpino by Havresac II Bella Minna
			Tofanella	Apelle by Sardanapale Try Try Again
		Romanella	El Greco	Pharos by **Phalaris** (dam by Sainfoin) Gay Gamp by Gay Crusader
			Barbara Burrini	**Papyrus** by **Tracery** by **Rock Sand** Bucolic by **Buchan** by Sunstar
	Pocahontas (USA)	Roman	Sir Gallahad III	Teddy Plucky Liege by Spearmint
			Buckup	**Buchan** by Sunstar by Sundridge Look Up by Ultimus
		How	Princequillo	Prince Rose Cosquilla by **Papyrus** by **Tracery**
			The Squaw II	Sickle by **Phalaris** (dam by Sainfoin) Minnewaska by Blandford
Key to the Mint (1969)	Graustark	Ribot	Tenerani	Bellini Tofanella
			Romanella	El Greco by Pharos by Phalaris Barbara Burrini by **Papyrus** by **Tracery**
		Flower Bowl	Alibhai	Hyperion Teresina by **Tracery** by **Rock Sand**
			Flower Bed	Beau Pere (ex Cinna) Boudoir II by Mahmoud by Blenheim
	Key Bridge	Princequillo	Prince Rose	Rose Prince Indolence by Gay Crusader
			Cosquilla	**Papyrus** by **Tracery** by **Rock Sand** Quick Thought by **White Eagle**
		Blue Banner	War Admiral	Man o' War (dam by **Rock Sand**) Brushup by Sweep
			Risque Blue	Blue Larkspur Risque by Stimulus

As a juvenile, Key to the Mint won the Remsen Stakes at Aqueduct, a 2YO Maiden Special, two allowance races and finished second in the Cowdin Stakes and third in the Garden State Stakes.

At three, he progressed into a very high-class performer. His seven wins at this age include the Travers Stakes (defeating Tentam by a length), Withers Stakes, Whitney Stakes, Derby Trial Stakes, Brooklyn Handicap (equaling the track record in 1:54 $\frac{4}{5}$ for 1 $\frac{3}{16}$ miles) and he defeated Autobiography in the Woodward Stakes.

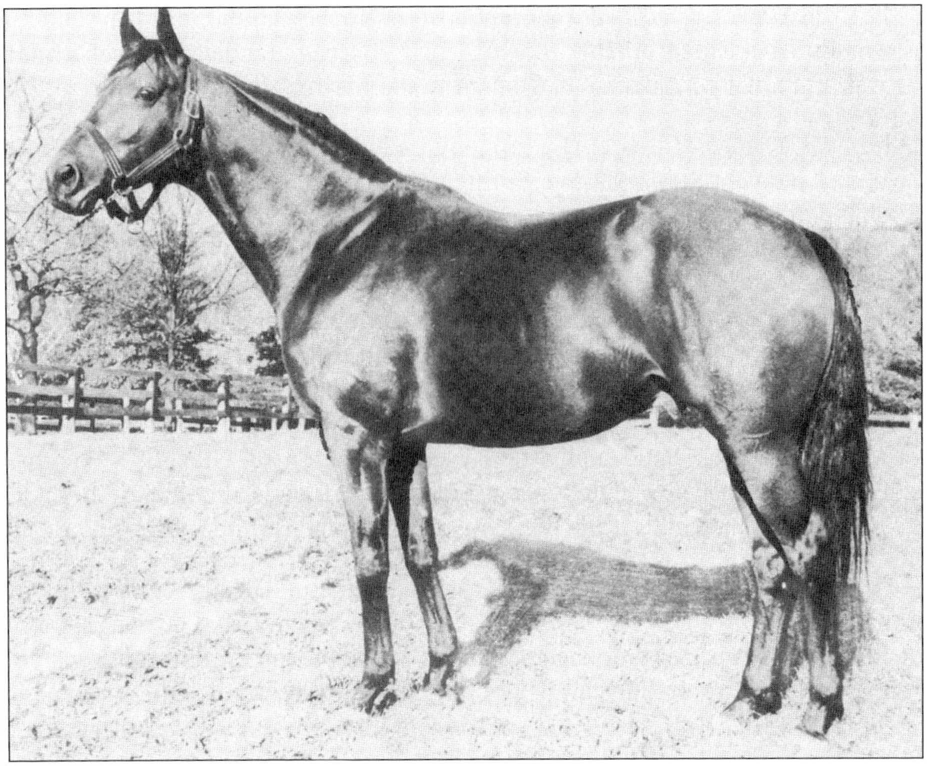

PRINCEQUILLO (Prince Rose - Cosquilla by Papyrus), leading sire and broodmare sire in North America.

ALIBHAI (Hyperion - Teresina by Tracery), a great sire of early maturing progeny.

Key to the Mint was runner-up to Autobiography in the Jockey Club Gold Cup and ran fourth in the Belmont Stakes won by Riva Ridge. At four, he won the Suburban Handicap, Excelsior Handicap, a race at Aqueduct and was an unlucky runner-up to Tentam in the Metropolitan Handicap.

Key to the Mint was a successful sire. His progeny include Kamar (Champion 3YO filly in Canada), Java Gold ($1,908,832, Travers Stakes), Love Smitten (dam of champion Swain), Plugged Nickle (U.S. Champion Sprinter), Gold and Ivory (Champion 3YO colt in Italy), Belle's Gold (10 wins, Bay Shore Handicap, Discovery Handicap), Lively Living, Sauce Boat (Arlington-Washington Futurity), Christmas Bonus, Wings of Grace, Always Mint, Sugar and Spice (Mother Goose Stakes, Ashland Stakes), Spark of Life, Key to the Bridge, Fondre, etc. He sired 62 stakes runners and 35 stakes winners. His son Java Gold stood originally at Lane's End Farm but was later sold to Germany where he has sired champion performers. Java Gold's best American-bred son was U.S. Champion Sprinter Kona Gold, winner of the Breeders' Cup Sprint. The pedigree of Key to the Mint shows a triple of Tracery (Rock Sand-Topiary by Orme), linebreeding to Rock Sand and a heavy concentration of Glencoe's daughter Pocahontas. The pattern also involves Sainfoin and his sister Sierra. Sainfoin is the sire of both Rock Sand and Bromus (dam of Phalaris) whereas Sierra is the dam of Sundridge (found in Mahmoud's make-up).

The pedigree pattern of Tom Rolfe involves 3 x 4 duplication of Tracery's best son Papyrus and 5 x 5 linebreeding to Phalaris. Tom Rolfe has a "son" of Sainfoin (Rock Sand) and a "daughter" of Sainfoin (i.e. Bromus, dam of Phalaris). To further emphasize speed, Tom Rolfe carries Sainfoin's sister Sierra, dam of Sundridge. Sundridge is the sire of Sunstar who sired Buchan (the duplicated ancestor in Tom Rolfe's pedigree) so it is probable Tom Rolfe inherited speed from this mix. He surely inherited a decent amount of fast fiber muscle.

One of the greatest racehorses in turf history was Tesio's champion Ribot, a horse with a balanced pedigree pattern (with sons and daughters of Cyllene plus St. Simon and his sister Angelica). Among Ribot's superior sons was Arts and Letters, a chestnut horse bred by Paul Mellon and raised by the mercurial Henry White.

Arts and Letters was proclaimed Horse of the Year, Champion 3YO colt and Champion Handicap Horse in North America. A versatile horse, he won 11 of 23 starts for career earnings of $632,404 and was a sound, workmanlike horse with an exceptionally deep chest. His dam, All Beautiful, was linebred 4 x 4 to stakes winner Friar Rock (Rock Sand-Fairy Gold by Bend Or-Dame Masham by Galliard).

Arts and Letters won the Belmont Stakes, Travers Stakes, Woodward Stakes, Metropolitan Handicap, Jockey Club Gold Cup, Blue Grass Stakes, Jim Dandy Stakes etc and finished second in the Kentucky Derby, Preakness Stakes and Florida Derby.

Among his progeny were Winter's Tale (Marlboro Cup, Brooklyn Handicap, Suburban Handicap twice), Codex (Preakness Stakes, Hollywood Derby, Santa Anita Derby), Cut Class (Oak Leaf Stakes), Lord Darnley (Widener Handicap, Gulfstream Park Handicap), Illiterate (Affectionately Handicap), Time and Life (Premio Lydia Tesio) and Tonzarun (Pan American Handicap).

The second dam of Arts and Letters was Parlo, eight wins $309,240, Champion 3YO filly and Champion Mare twice. Parlo was by Lord Derby's smart miler Heliopolis (Hyperion-Drift by Swynford), inbred to Canterbury Pilgrim via her sons Chaucer and Swynford. Heliopolis won the Prince of Wales' Stakes, Imperial Produce Stakes and Chester Vase before being exported to Kentucky.

All Beautiful (1959)	Battlefield	War Relic	Man o' War	**Fair Play**
				Mahubah by **Rock Sand**
			Friar's Carse	**Friar Rock** by **Rock Sand**
				Problem
		Dark Display	Display	**Fair Play**
				Cicuta
			Dark Loveliness	Traumer
				Sunny Love
	Parlo	Heliopolis	Hyperion	Gainsborough
				Selene by Chaucer
			Drift	Swynford
				Santa Cruz
		Fairy Palace	Pilate	**Friar Rock** by **Rock Sand**
				Herodias
			Star Fairy	The Satrap
				Fair Star

Riboprince (Ribot-Fiji II by Hill Prince) is another stakes winner bred on the Ribot link with Princequillo. He is the sire of German Derby winner Ako.

Run The Gantlet, America's Champion Grass Horse, has a fascinating pedigree because the link between Ribot and Princequillo was already present in his sire, Tom Rolfe. Run The Gantlet's dam merely added another source of Princequillo via Quill, Champion 2YO filly. Run The Gantlet won eight races and earned $559,079. His victories include the Garden State Stakes, Washington D.C. International Stakes (by six lengths), Man o' War Stakes, United Nations Handicap, Tidal Handicap etc., and he sired April Run (Champion 3YO filly in France), Ardross (Champion Handicap Horse in England), Swiftfoot (Champion 3YO filly in Ireland) and the redoubtable English stayer Commanche Run.

Run The Gantlet (1968)	Tom Rolfe	Ribot	Tenerani	Bellini
				Tofanella
			Romanella	El Greco by **Pharos**
				Barbara Burrini by **Papyrus**
		Pocahontas (USA)	Roman	Sir Gallahad III
				Buckup (to **Sundridge**)
			How	**Princequillo** (dam by **Papyrus**)
				The Squaw II
	First Feather	First Landing	Turn-To	Royal Charger by son of **Pharos**
				Source Sucree by Admiral Drake
			Hildene	Bubbling Over (to **Sundridge**)
				Fancy Racket by Wrack
		Quill	**Princequillo**	Prince Rose
				Cosquilla by **Papyrus**
			Quick Touch	Count Fleet (to **Sundridge**)
				Alms

Flying Water, Dactylographer, Caracolero, Cannonade, Pleasant Colony, Obratzovy, Maria Waleska, Gregorian and Arkadina are further examples of the link between Ribot and Princequillo.

Arkadina was a classy filly who won the Athasi Stakes, was runner-up in the Irish 1,000 Guineas and Irish Oaks and put up a splendid effort when third in the English Oaks. She is by Ribot from Natashka by Dedicate (son of Princequillo). Obratzovy (His Majesty-Azeez by Nashua-La Dauphine by Princequillo) won 10 races in three countries including the San Juan Capistrano Invitational Handicap, Hardwicke Stakes, Jockey Club Stakes and was runner-up in the Yorkshire Cup and San Luis Rey Stakes.

Pleasant Colony (His Majesty-Sun Colony by Sunrise Flight) was North America's Champion 3YO colt and earned $965,383. A tall, leggy horse, he won the Kentucky Derby, Preakness Stakes, Woodward Stakes, Wood Memorial Stakes etc and is by Ribot's son His Majesty from a daughter of Sunrise Flight (son of Misty Morn by Princequillo). The pedigree of Pleasant Colony is shown on page 123.

Cannonade won seven races and earned $501,164. His victories include the Kentucky Derby and Kentucky Jockey Club Stakes. He was runner-up in the Florida Derby and third in the Preakness Stakes and Belmont Stakes. Cannonade is by Bold Bidder (second dam by Princequillo) out of Queen Sucree by Ribot. Caracolero won the Prix du Jockey Club (French Derby) and is by Ribot's son Graustark out of Betty Lorraine by Prince John, son of Princequillo. Dactylographer (Secretariat-Artists Proof by Ribot) won the William Hill Futurity Stakes. Secretariat's dam is of course by Princequillo. The brilliant filly Flying Water (Habitat-Formentera by Ribot) won the English 1,000 Guineas, Prix Jacques Le Marois, Champion Stakes and Prix Maurice de Gheest. Her sire, Habitat, is by Sir Gaylord whose dam is by Princequillo.

Gregorian (Graustark-Natashka by Dedicate) won the Brigadier Gerard Stakes, Joe McGrath Memorial Stakes and finished third in the King George VI & Queen Elizabeth Stakes. Maria Waleska won the Italian Oaks and is by Ribot's son Filiberto out of Miss Protégé by Successor (dam by Princequillo). The link between Ribot and Princequillo had produced many high-class performers.

Ribot's stakes-winning sons His Majesty and Graustark stood at Darby Dan Farm. These brothers are out of Flower Bowl by Alibhai and although quite different in phenotype, both were successful sires and extremely influential broodmare sires. Australia's premier sire Danehill is out of a daughter of His Majesty. Danehill, despite being by speed sire Danzig, inherited stamina from Ribot's son His Majesty as well as from his duplicated ancestor Natalma, by Native Dancer. In Australia, Danehill had an affinity with daughters of Sir Tristram (a Sir Ivor horse inbred 4 x 3 to Princequillo); another example of the Ribot link with Princequillo.

Juddmonte Farm's young stallion Mizzen Mast interests me with his unusual pedigree pattern designed by Prince Khalid Abdullah. Mizzen Mast is by Cozzene from Kinema by Graustark and might become a sire of classic runners on dirt or turf. He has a nice ratio of speed and stamina and suits mares with Nasrullah, Royal Charger, Hail To Reason and especially Northern Dancer.

Mizzen Mast began racing in France. At two, he broke his maiden at Deauville and was runner-up in the Prix des Chenes. The following year he won the Prix de Guiche by six lengths and finished an unlucky second in the Grand Prix de Paris. Shipped to California, he won the Malibu Stakes and Bien Bien Stakes. At four he won the Strub Stakes by four lengths before retiring to stud.

				Grey Sovereign by Nasrullah
			Fortino II	Ranavalo II by Relic
		Caro		Chamossaire
			Chambord	Life Hill by Solario (dam by Sundridge)
	Cozzene			**Princequillo** (dam by **Papyrus**)
			Prince John	Not Afraid by Count Fleet
		Ride the Trails		Sir Gaylord (dam by **Princequillo**)
			Wildwook	Blue Canoe
Mizzen Mast (1998)				Tenerani
			Ribot	Romanella (dam by **Papyrus**)
		Graustark		Alibhai (dam by **Tracery**)
			Flower Bowl	Flower Bed by Beau Pere
	Kinema			Menow by Pharamond II by Phalaris
			Tom Fool	Gaga by Bull Dog
		Mrs. Peterkin		Challenger II by Swynford
			Legendra	Lady Legend

Mizzen Mast has a wonderful pedigree pattern and because his genotype is free of Northern Dancer, I sincerely hope he becomes a successful sire for Juddmonte Farms. His dam Kinema was a $2.2 million purchase and is a winning half-sister to Kentucky Oaks victress Sweet Alliance, dam of Shareef Dancer, Champion 3YO colt in England and Ireland who won the Irish Sweeps Derby and King Edward VII Stakes. Kinema is also half-sister to Dancing Champ and Whydidju, the California Oaks winner who produced Slew of Reality, Champion 2YO filly in Argentina.

Mizzen Mast's alternate sex line zigzags to Graustark and to his broodmare sire, Alibhai, a product of the Hyperion/Tracery nick. Alibhai is bred along very similar lines to Nearctic's dam, Lady Angela. For this reason I believe Mizzen Mast will be genetically compatible with Nearctic's strain via descendants of Northern Dancer and Icecapade.

Lady Angela is by Hyperion from Sister Sarah by Abbot's Trace, "son" of Tracery, whereas Alibhai is by Hyperion from Teresina, a "daughter" of Tracery. They act like genetic cousins with similar biochemistry.

Another strain that might succeed with Mizzen Mast is Blushing Groom since he carries Spring Run (Menow-Boola Brook by Bull Dog), a mare who is genetically related to champion Tom Fool (Menow-Gaga by Bull Dog). Spring Run is the dam of Red God, sire of Blushing Groom.

The clean airflow strains of Princequillo, his champion son Round Table, and the great racehorse Ribot should continue to prosper and help upgrade racing class. They are able to supply sound constitutions. Furthermore, these stallions possessed larger than normal hearts and were motivated athletes with the "will-to-win." Whereas Ribot was highly-strung, Princequillo and his son Round Table were stallions with ideal temperaments. Duplicating all three in future matings is highly recommended providing their best descendants are used in the selection process.

I trust I have done justice to Princequillo in this chapter because he is a "genetic giant" as far as I am concerned. His input in matings I designed for clients helped produce Group 1 and Grade 1 winners. His airflow was first-class – as clean as a whistle – and his knees were perfectly shaped.

SUNSTAR (Sundridge - Doris), winner of the English 2,000 Guineas and Derby.

ROYAL CHARGER (Nearco - Sun Princess by Solario), sire of champion Turn-To.

SUNDRIDGE AND HIS DESCENDANTS IN AUSTRALIA

"It is a truism that the British Thoroughbred, originally a national tribe, has been internationalised. Lines and branches thereof which were shelved in England – mainly for the reason of being dispensable – when transferred to another country developed, and in the course of time entered upon a stage of prosperity." - *Friedrich Becker*

Every sound Thoroughbred in the world can stay the distance of two miles, but few can go the pace required to win Australia's premier two-miler, the Victorian Racing Club's Melbourne Cup! There are brilliant stayers, moderate stayers and plodders, yet all can run the distance. Logic tells us the main difference between them is the time taken to cover the two miles.

A large-sized heart for an athlete is a most desirable asset, but useless if the athlete is unmotivated and lacking the will-to-win. The heart of Eclipse, according to William Youatt, weighed 14 pounds and this famous stallion (who helped establish the breed) inherited a nervous system that made him fiercely competitive. Phar Lap, the pride and joy of New Zealand, had a large heart weighing 13 pounds six ounces, and he too was a real fighter, a competitive 17 hands champion stayer able to carry huge weights. Princequillo and War Admiral are said to have had hearts weighing almost 14 pounds, but a large heart doesn't count for much if a racehorse has a defective circulatory system, a serious airflow problem, or worse still, no motivation.

Draught horses have huge hearts, but they are not athletic – they are bred purely for strength.

When we study pedigrees of stallions and mares we need to qualify performance with some recognition of time – how long it takes to complete a specific journey. Short-course five furlongs specialists, no matter how brilliant, usually make disappointing sires because they rely exclusively on explosive speed (anaerobic speed) with its definitive limits. Short-course runners do not offer the same upgrading qualities of horses that can run a fast mile or further, so when we select a suitable sire for a broodmare perhaps we should ask the question: "Do we need short or long-term energy supply in the mare's foal?"

Matching an out-and-out stayer to a mare of similar make-up will most likely breed a plodder – a one-paced athlete devoid of acceleration. Sure enough, the plodder will get two miles, but it will take longer than its faster rivals. Conversely, matching two five furlongs specialists (they being unable to win at six furlongs in top company) will nearly always breed a four to five furlongs speedball that may not be as fast as either parent. Breeders require commonsense in the selection process for a foal to have any chance of being as fast, or faster, than its parents.

Two very successful sires, Danzig and Red Ransom (both non-stakes winners), displayed brilliant speed as juveniles but both sustained injury before being able to compete in black type events. However, their pedigrees indicate they might have won beyond a mile because Danzig is a son of Kentucky Derby winner Northern Dancer whereas Red Ransom is a son of English Derby winner Roberto.

The reason why Danzig and Red Ransom were given the opportunity to stand at stud was because their owners believed them to be high-class performers, capable of winning at Grade 1 level. They ran incredibly fast times as juveniles.

Even if a racehorse has all the desirable attributes to become a super athlete, it needs to be conditioned by an experienced horseman (the trainer) and ridden by a talented jockey – a jockey who makes the least mistakes during a race. Many newcomers into the breeding and racing industry fail to identify the importance of hiring gifted, experienced people.

The trainer is the person who can either make or break an athlete. Successful trainers hire the best staff to tend to their horses on a daily basis. They also attract the best riders, hence the advantages should be obvious. Trainers need experienced track riders and capable staff to get the job done. Good staff is always hard to find.

Men and women working on stud farms who are responsible for raising young Thoroughbreds are quite important in the process of producing stakes runners. As well, we should appreciate night watchmen, foaling managers, people who prepare yearlings and the horse-breakers who educate young, immature athletes. Along the way, each Thoroughbred receives imprints of various experiences, stored in their brain. Along the way, there are many risks. Accidents can happen at any time; therefore dedicated and experienced employees are a blessing in our industry. Healthy young horses are full of energy and many are liable to accidents.

Aristotle was the first authority to use the term energia, from which the word energy is derived. How the racehorse uses its energy and how the trainer covets it is a key factor for a successful racing career. There is a relationship between respiration and physiological work – it is called energy. Today, the juvenile racehorse is trained to jump off from the start at top speed. Immature youngsters do not master their temperament – their "nervous system" masters mind and body!

Professional trainers foster young horses with obvious potential. Instance the way Sir Michael Stoute uses patience to bring along his two-year-old colts and fillies at Newmarket, or the careful approach taken with juveniles by that wonderful conditioner Charlie Whittingham in California.

The "burnout factor" of winning two-year-olds is much larger than we imagine. No wonder many of them find it difficult to show the same winning form at three years of age after a grueling campaign at two.

Australian breeders produce some of the best sprinter-milers in the world but the burnout of talented juveniles is costly to owners. Nowhere else in the world is juvenile racing held in such high esteem, not even North America. Prize money for two- and three-year-olds in Australia is so attractive and generous that Australian owners rarely consider sending stakes winners to campaign overseas until they are four or five years of age. (Australian and New Zealand horses have their birthday commencing August 1st.) This situation will change should Japan, with its lucrative prize money, open up competition to more foreign-bred runners. At the moment, Japan still enjoys protective restrictions.

Last century, healthy competition developed between racehorses bred in Australia and New Zealand. Australia's large purses for the big handicaps attracted New Zealand's best stayers. New Zealand breeders imported European stallions bred for stamina and among great sires were Night Raid, Foxbridge, Absurd, Chief Ruler and three sons of English 1,000 Guineas winner Cinna, namely Balloch, Mr. Standfast and Beau Pere (who was later exported to the U.S.).

These stallions preceded an era of influential sires like Red Mars (Hyperion-Red Garter by Knight of the Garter), the impeccably bred Nizami (Firdaussi-Mumtaz Mahal by The Tetrarch), Summertime (Precipitation-Great Truth by Bahram), the French-bred Le Filou (Vatellor-Fileuse by Casterari), English stayers Battle-Waggon (Never Say Die-Carrozza by Dante) and Mellay (Never Say Die-Meld by Alycidon), Oncidium (Alcide-Malcolmia by Sayani) as well as American-bred Sir Tristram (Sir Gaylord-Isolt by Round Table). New Zealand invaders won many coveted handicaps in Australia, viz. the Caulfield Cup, Melbourne Cup, Sydney Cup, Adelaide Cup and Brisbane Cup.

During the same era, Australian breeders relied on homebred champions like Heroic, Ajax (Aust), Matrice and successful imports such as Gay Lothario (Gay Crusader-Love in Idleness by Bachelor's Double), Magpie (Dark Ronald-Popinjay by St. Frusquin), Marconigram (Abbot's Trace-Marcia Blanche by Lemberg), Midstream (Blandford-Midsummer by Abbot's Trace), Helios (Hyperion-Foxy Gal by Sir Gallahad III), Empyrean (Hyperion-Ad Astra by Asterus), Delville Wood (Bois Roussel-Everlasting by Phalaris) and Nilo (Nearco-Dodoma by Dastur).

In the 1950's, Newtown Wonder (Fair Trial-Clarapple by Apple Sammy) followed by Star Kingdom (Stardust-Impromptu by Concerto) dominated the juvenile Sires' List, but whereas the former's progeny were mainly sprinters, Star Kingdom was able to sire brilliant milers and a few classic winners up to a mile and a half. Other successful imports include two rather small stallions, Rego (Nasrullah-Missy Suntan by Tai-Yang) and Smokey Eyes (Stardust-Celestial Light by Donatello II).

By 1960, yearling buyers in Australia preferred early maturing yearlings, although Aussie trainers still trekked to the Trentham sales at Wellington, New Zealand, for a potential classic or cup winner. English Champion Sprinter Sundridge (Amphion-Sierra) still has a profound affect on Australian breeding. From Fair Trial's male line came the sprinter Newtown Wonder. Later, the Kelly family imported French-bred stakes winner Wilkes (Court Martial-Sans Tares by Sind) who became premier sire in the country. Fair Trial (Fairway-Lady Juror) introduced brilliance via the genes of brother and sister Sainfoin and Sierra. His line made a tremendous contribution to Australian racing and breeding.

Newtown Wonder (1942)	Fair Trial	Fairway	Phalaris (dam by **Sainfoin**)
			Scapa Flow by Chaucer
		Lady Juror	Son-in-Law
			Lady Josephine by Sundridge (ex **Sierra**)
	Clarapple	Apple Sammy	Pommern
			Lady Phoebe by Orby by Orme
		Racla	Clarissimus
			Terceira by Lemberg

Newtown Wonder won the Windsor Cannon Yard Stakes, Lewes De Warrene Handicap, Offham Handicap, finished second in Goodwood's August Handicap and was placed in several other minor sprint handicaps. He sired Dubbo (Champion Australian Sprinter), Cultured (VRC Newmarket Handicap, AJC Gimcrack Stakes), New Stand and Apple Bay (Domben Ten Thousand, Challenge Stakes).

Newtown Wonder's fillies came to hand quickly, winning many early races for juveniles, but he failed to have a son extend his male line.

Wilkes (Fr), who stood at Newhaven Park Stud in New South Wales, was a more influential sire and his yearlings fetched high prices. A handsome chestnut stallion, Wilkes was half-brother to Mahan and Worden II, both winners of the Washington D.C. International Stakes. Wilkes never ran at two years. Lightly raced at three, he was unplaced on his debut, won the Prix Edgard de la Charme over 2000 meters and scored again in the Prix Sans Souci II. He is a son of Court Martial, unbeaten at two years, leading sire in Great Britain and Ireland in 1956 and 1957 and six times leading sire of juvenile winners. Court Martial won the English 2,000 Guineas (defeating Dante), Champion Stakes and finished third to Dante in the English Derby. Wilkes sired many champions in Australia. By far his best colt was Vain, Champion 2YO and Champion Sprinter, winner of the Golden Slipper Stakes, Champagne Stakes, VRC Sires' Produce Stakes, Caulfield Guineas, George Adams Handicap, Linlithgow Stakes, Freeway Stakes, Merson Cooper Stakes, etc.

The best filly Wilkes ever sired was Wenona Girl, Champion 2YO and 3YO filly, winner of the Lightning Stakes, Adrian Knox Oaks, 1,000 Guineas, Gimcrack Stakes, Rosehill Guineas, Wakeful Stakes, VRC and AJC Sires' Produce Stakes, etc.

Wilkes (1966)	Court Martial	Fair Trial	Fairway by **Phalaris** (dam by **Sainfoin**)
			Lady Juror by Sundridge (ex **Sierra**)
		Instantaneous	Hurry On (dam by **Sainfoin**)
			Picture by Gainsborough
	Sans Tares	Sind	Solario (dam by Sundridge, ex **Sierra**)
			Mirawala by **Phalaris** (dam by **Sainfoin**)
		Tara	Teddy
			Jean Gow by Neil Gow

Wilkes's champion son Vain was produced from a granddaughter of Nasrullah (bred on the Sainfoin/Sierra mix). Vain's dam, Elated, was a stakes-winning filly by Orgoglio (Nasrullah-Orienne by Sol Oriens, son of Hyperion) from Rarcamba by Helios (Hyperion-Foxy Gal by Sir Galahad III).

Sundridge transmitted a fair amount of speed when his descendants were matched with either Phalaris or Hurry On, stallions out of daughters of Sainfoin. I decided to check up on whether Sundridge's descendants succeeded as well when they were matched with outcrossed lines, in particular no presence of his dam's brother Sainfoin. The result was mediocre. The best results came when Sundridge met up with Sainfoin to reinforce explosive speed.

Thus when Star Kingdom and Smokey Eyes arrived in Australia, they brought with them Sundridge's genes to match with extensive Phalaris and Hurry On strains already existing "down under."

Star Kingdom was a small, muscular chestnut stallion. He arrived on the same ship as Big Game's son Makarpura. Star Kingdom stood only 15.1 hands high but he had pronounced forearms, a long back and typified the fast fiber muscle type. Because of his diminutive stature, commercial breeders did not flock to him during his initial years at Baramul Stud in the picturesque Widden Valley of New South Wales.

Star Kingdom was bred by Richard Ball in Ireland in 1946 and ran under the name Star King. He was ranked second best two-year-old in England behind Abernant and if he hadn't have been so small, he would never have left the shores of England. Australian-born Stanley Wootten, a trainer based at Newmarket, admired Star King and convinced his "mates" Alf Ellison and Reg Moses to import the colt to Australia.

Star Kingdom was by Stardust from Impromptu by Concerto. At two, he won the Salisbury Manton Maiden Stakes by 10 lengths, Richmond Stakes by a length, Gimcrack Stakes beating Makarpura by three lengths, Sandown Park Produce Stakes by five lengths, Hurst Park Sorrel Stakes by five lengths and was beaten a nose by champion Abernant in a photo finish for the National Breeders' Produce Stakes. For a little horse, he certainly carried big weights.

At three, Star Kingdom won Newbury's Greenham Stakes by five lengths, Ascot's Jersey Stakes, Newbury's Hungerford Stakes and finished third to Abernant in the July Cup at Newmarket. He was unplaced in the English 2,000 Guineas won by Nimbus. At four, Star Kingdom won the Coronation Stakes at Chester and was beaten a head in the Hungerford Stakes.

His pedigree reveals 4 x 4 duplication of English Derby winner Sunstar (Sundridge-Doris), linebreeding to English Oaks winner Canterbury Pilgrim and her dam, Pilgrimage (dam of Loved One), to St. Simon and his sister Angelica, and to their sire Galopin. Sainfoin, brother to Sundridge's dam Sierra, appears via Rock Sand, the sire of Tracery. Star Kingdom's dam, Impromptu, is linebred to the brilliant Orme whose dam is Angelica. Of significance, Impromptu descends in direct female line from Oaks winner Canterbury Pilgrim via her daughter St. Victorine, a three-parts sister to Chaucer.

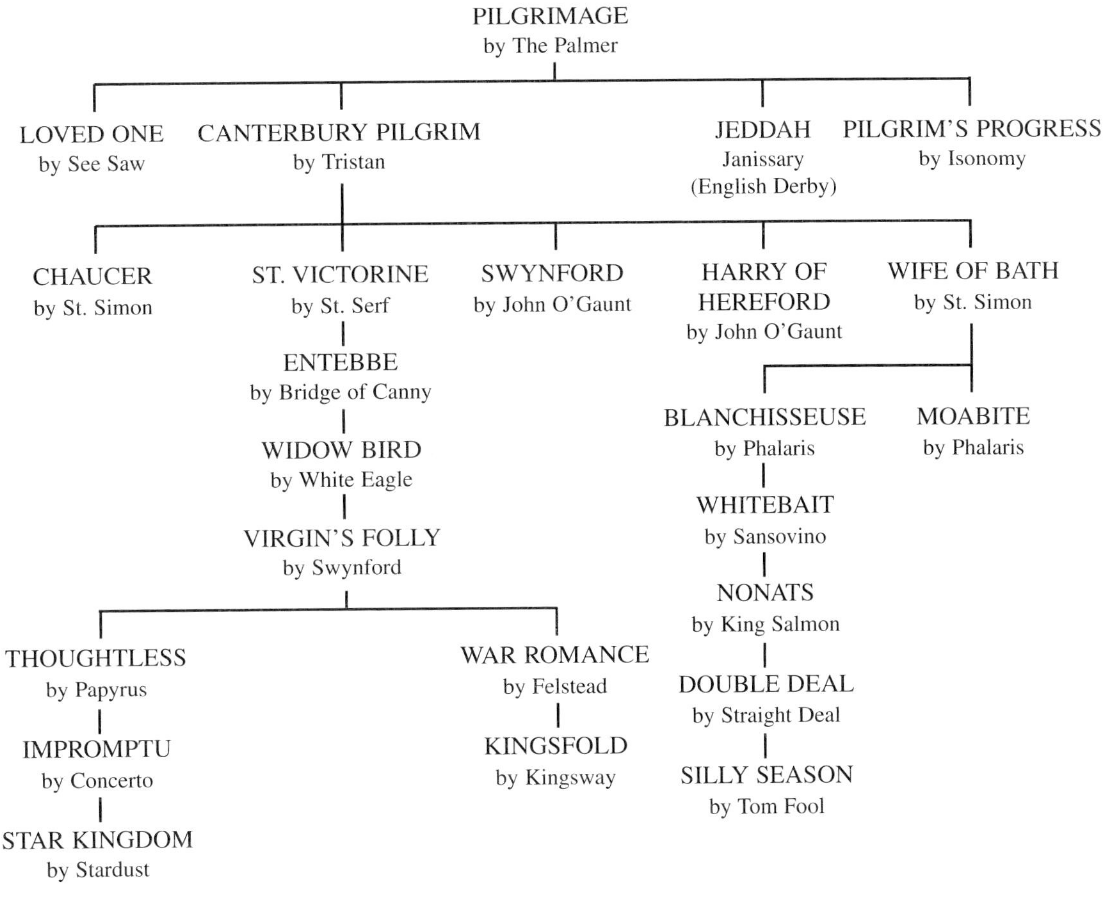

Canterbury Pilgrim also produced The Tabard (by Zinfandel), Glasconbury (by Isinglass) and Pilgrim's Way (by Frusquin), the latter mare being ancestress of North American stakes winner Lucky Mel (Olympia-Royal Mink by Royal Charger).

Star Kingdom inherited maternal strength from St. Angela (dam of St. Simon and Angelica), classic winners Pilgrimage and Canterbury Pilgrim, and speed from the dominant mare Sanda, dam of Sainfoin and Sierra. In fact, Impromptu was also linebred to the remarkable mare Brown Bess. Orme was England's Champion 2YO colt whose victories include the Dewhurst Stakes, Middle Park Stakes and Eclipse Stakes. Of course it was a "lucky dip" that Star Kingdom would inherit the best genes from his ancestry. In this instance, genetic probability was kind. However, if you analyze all the strong female elements in Star Kingdom's pedigree, perhaps "luck" was encouraged. The longest distance at which Star Kingdom won was 7 ½ furlongs. If he had been a taller colt, maybe his trainer would have tested him beyond a mile since there is middle-distance stamina in his ancestry.

Sunstar, duplicated 4 x 4 in Star Kingdom's pedigree, was born in 1908 and is by the sprinter Sundridge from Doris by Loved One, a "son" of Pilgrimage. Sunstar was a brother to White Star, a high-class two-year-old who won the Dewhurst Stakes, July Stakes, Woodcote Stakes and Doncaster Champagne Stakes. He is also half-brother to Princess Dorrie, winner of the English 1,000 Guineas and Oaks.

Bred by Jack Joel, Sunstar was a courageous colt with the ability to accelerate more than once in a race and reached peak form as a three-year-old. He inherited speed from his father, Sundridge (Champion Sprinter), and stamina from his dam, Doris, but as a juvenile he was not as brilliant as his stakes-winning brother White Star. Nevertheless, Sunstar won three of six starts at two, including the International 2YO Plate at Kempton Park, Hopeful Stakes (dead-heat for first) and Exeter Stakes (both at Newmarket), was runner-up in the Lavant Stakes at Goodwood and finished third in the Champagne Stakes at Doncaster.

At three, Sunstar grew to just over 15.2 hands high and was undefeated in three starts. He won the English 2,000 Guineas (beating Chaucer's son Stedfast by two lengths), the Newmarket Stakes by two lengths and then strained a suspensory ligament two weeks before the Derby. It was a miracle he was able to win the English Derby in which he defeated Stedfast once again by two lengths. On returning to the winner's enclosure the colt was seriously lame.

Retired to stud the following year, Sunstar was among the top 10 leading sires for seven years and runner-up leading sire in 1920 and 1921. Among his progeny were English 2,000 Guineas and Eclipse Stakes winner Craig an Eran (sire of April The Fifth who won the 1932 English Derby) and Admiral Drake, winner of the Grand Prix de Paris and placed in the French 2,000 Guineas and Prix du Jockey Club-French Derby. Admiral Drake (Craig an Eran-Plucky Liege by Spearmint) is of course the broodmare sire of America's champion 2YO colt Turn-To.

Famous French breeder Marcel Boussac thought so highly of Jack Joel's Sunstar that he sent Tourbillon's dam, Durban, across the English Channel to be mated with him. The following spring Durban produced a colt named Banstar, winner of the Prix Morny, Prix Eugene Adam and Prix La Rochette etc.

Sunstar was a sire of sires. Among his sons were Buchan (twice winner of the Eclipse Stakes), Alan Breck, North Star III (leading sire in the U.S.), Australian Sun, Comedy Star, Galloper Light and Great Star. His renowned daughters include Sunny Jane (English Oaks, 2nd English 1,000 Guineas), Lammermuir, Constellation, Sundry, Ensoleillee, Esclarmonde and Sunstep.

Star Kingdom was a phenomenal sire in Australia and dominated the Sires' List from 1958 onwards. He was leading sire five times, became a very influential broodmare sire heading that category three times, and was the leading sire of juvenile winners seven times. Among his famous progeny were Todman, Noholme II, Biscay, Citius, Columbia Star, Dark Jewel, Kaoru Star, Magic Night, Planet Kingdom,

Reveille, Ritmar, the Derby winners Skyline and Sky High, Fine and Dandy, Time and Tide, Sunset Hue, Star of Heaven, Starlit and Starquita.

Noholme II (Star Kingdom-Oceana by Columbo), Horse of the Year in Australia, was exported to Florida where he sired Nodouble (Champion Handicap Horse, 13 wins $846,749 including the Metropolitan Handicap, Santa Anita Handicap, Arkansas Derby, Brooklyn Handicap) as well as Champion Sprinter Shecky Greene. Noholme II was a brother to Todman, Champion Sprinter in Australia and winner of the Golden Slipper Stakes. Todman was a sensational sprinter!

Oceana, dam of champion brothers Todman and Noholme II, reinforces Star Kingdom's ancestry by duplicating Sunstar and Orme. The intensity of St. Simon and his sister Angelica is normally powerful for stamina, but in Noholme's case, Sainfoin and his sister dominated these strains and enhanced speed.

Noholme II (1956)	Star Kingdom	Stardust	Hyperion	Gainsborough
				Selene by **Chaucer**
			Sister Stella	Friar Marcus
				Etoile by **Sunstar** by **Sundridge**
		Impromptu	Concerto	Orpheus by **Orby** by **Orme**
				Constellation by **Sunstar** by **Sundridge**
			Thoughtless	Papyrus (g'son Rock Sand by **Sainfoin**)
				Virgin's Folly
	Oceana	Columbo	Manna	Phalaris (dam by **Sainfoin**)
				Waffle
			Lady Nairne	**Chaucer**
				Lammermuir by **Sunstar** by **Sundridge**
		Orama	Diophon	Grand Parade by **Orby** by **Orme**
				Donnetta
			Cantelupe	Amadis
				Lupercalia

Star Kingdom's line is carried on by Biscay's fast sons Bletchingly and Marscay, and by Kaoru Star's sons who include Champion 2YO colt Luskin Star.

Luskin Star was one of the greatest two-year-old colts ever seen in my lifetime. He was a commanding chestnut horse, just over 16.1 hands high with very short cannons, powerful hindquarters and strong loins. He had a huge over-stride and won 13 of 17 starts for $279,600 when prize money was nowhere near what it is today. He was ranked Champion Sprinter at three years. Luskin Star's victories comprise the Golden Slipper Stakes, Champagne Stakes, AJC Sires' Produce Stakes in record time (i.e. Australia's juvenile triple crown), Caulfield Guineas, The Galaxy and Queensland Turf Club's Marlboro Stakes (in new track record time).

Luskin Star's dam, Promising (trained by my mate Les Bridge), was by Idomeneo (linebred to Hyperion and carrying Lady Josephine by Sundridge) from Modern Touch by Fair's Fair, a son of Fair Trial, grandson of Lady Josephine. In many respects, Luskin Star is bred along similar lines to Bletchingly whose second dam is by Fair Trial. Another son of Stardust imported to Australia was the chestnut Smokey Eyes, a leading sire of two-year-olds. He was born in 1947 and like Star Kingdom was inbred 4 x 4 to Sunstar.

Smokey Eyes won 10 races in England including the Goodwood Stewards' Cup, Newmarket Crawford Handicap, July Handicap etc. His dam was Celestial Light, a half-sister to Inkling, dam of Stalino (Irish 2,000 Guineas) and Bright News (Irish Derby). This is the same branch that produced Princely Gift. Celestial Light was by the Tesio-bred stayer Donatello II from Gleam by Galloper Light, son of Sunstar.

Stardust, the sire of Smokey Eyes and Star Kingdom, was a small son of Hyperion who won the Newmarket Exeter Stakes, Sandown National Breeders' Produce Stakes and was runner-up in the Gimcrack Stakes (to Tant Mieux), English 2,000 Guineas (to Djebel) and finished sixth in the Derby won by Pont l'Eveque.

Bred by the National Stud, Stardust was purchased by Prince Aly Khan for 1,450 guineas as a yearling at the Newmarket July Sales. Unfortunately, the best race Stardust ever won was taken away from him – at three he won the Champion Stakes beating Hippius by three lengths and Pont l'Eveque by five, but was disqualified for crossing. Stardust was a more than useful sire in England and Ireland but was rarely supported by commercial breeders. Apart from Star Kingdom and Smokey Eyes, he sired Stunning, Moondust, Stalino, Bright News, Teretania and Dust Devil.

I find it most intriguing that two of Stardust's four best-performed sons were inbred to Sunstar and linebred to Canterbury Pilgrim.

Smokey Eyes (1947)	Stardust	Hyperion	Gainsborough
			Selene by Chaucer
		Sister Stella	Friar Marcus
			Etoile by **Sunstar** by **Sundridge**
	Celestial Light	Donatello II	Blenheim by Blandford by Swynford
			Delleana
		Gleam	Galloper Light by **Sunstar** by **Sundridge**
			Eagerford

Star Kingdom at one time had more than 70 sons and grandsons standing at stud in Australia and New Zealand. Today, fewer than 10 commercial sires are from his male line.

Whether a great-grandson will emerge to maintain Star Kingdom's branch of Hyperion's male line is in the lap of the gods, but no matter what happens, his name will continue to feature in the dams of future Group winners. It was a pity Bletchingly's best son Kingston Town (voted Australia's Horse of the Year) was a gelding.

Descendants of Star Kingdom and Smokey Eyes show a definite genetic affinity with Northern Dancer's line. Danehill sired some of his best stakes winners out of mares with Star Kingdom's strain and three of these are "standout" stallions:

Redoute's Choice (ex Shantha's Choice by Canny Lad) Champion 3YO Miler, 1st Caulfield Guineas, Blue Diamond Stakes, Manikato Stakes, C. F. Orr Stakes etc.
Danzero (ex Confidentially by Kaoru Star) 1st Golden Slipper Stakes, Blue Diamond Prelude, Maribyrnong Trial Stakes etc.
Catbird (ex Fitting by Marscay) 1st Golden Slipper Stakes, Black Opal Stakes.

Many years ago our good friend Norman Carlyon managed a syndicate that owned the imported mare Dancing Show (Nijinsky II-Show Lady by Sir Ivor). Norman asked me to select suitable partners for this mare and initially I advised the syndicate to test Star Watch, a sprinter with substance from Star Kingdom's line.

This match produced Hurricane Sky, six wins $893,170, winner of the Group 1 Blue Diamond Stakes (setting a race record over 6f in 1:08 flat as a juvenile), All-Aged Stakes, VATC Autumn Classic, Zeditave Stakes etc., and runner-up in the Australian Guineas.

The following year I recommended the syndicate send Dancing Show to Champion 2YO colt Canny Lad (also from Star Kingdom's line) and it produced Shantha's Choice, winning dam of Redoute's Choice and Platinum Scissors. Next, I recommended Halo's son Don't Say Halo and this match produced Show Dancing, a lovely big filly purchased as a yearling by His Excellency Nasser Lootah. Show Dancing gave every indication she would make a stakes runner when trained by Bobby Thompson. She won two races, but while resting at Emirates Park Stud injured herself in a paddock. Already she has produced two Group winners – Salameh, a brilliant filly by Secret Savings, and Al Maher, winner of the Cadbury Guineas.

Another recommendation made some years ago was a mating that produced Republic Lass, by Canny Lad out of an imported daughter of Cox's Ridge. Republic Lass won six races, earned $1,553,970 including the Australian Oaks, Adrian Knox Stakes, Rawson Stakes etc. Republic Lass finished third in the valuable Caulfield Cup and Tancred Stakes, and has the pedigree pattern of a mare that should produce Group winners. Mares carrying Star Kingdom's speed genes should succeed with Native Dancer's line because Native Dancer is by Polynesian who is inbred four times to Sainfoin and Sierra. Promising examples of this cross are Clang (Silver Slipper Stakes, Stanley Wooten Stakes, D.C. McKay Stakes, 3rd Oakleigh Plate), Zip Zip Aray (SAJC Goodwood Handicap), My Brightia (VRC Oaks), Victory Vein (Champagne Stakes, AJC Sires' Produce Stakes, Silver Slipper Stakes), Bellezevir (SAJC Goodwood Handicap, QTC Qantas Cup), Into The Night (QTC Cup), Timber Trader (South African Derby) and Reenact (QTC Sires' Produce Stakes, Grand Prix).

King's Best (Kingmambo-Allegretta by Lombard), winner of the English 2,000 Guineas who shuttles between Europe and Australia for Darley Stud, is likely to do well with mares carrying the strains of Bletchingly and Marscay. I especially like the match of King's Best with daughters of Canny Lad (by Bletchingly) because this mating reinforces speed from champion filly Mumtaz Mahal.

Sundridge made a huge impact in Victoria where his descendants continue to produce stakes winners. Imported stallion Great Star (Sunstar-Miss Matty by Marcovil) sired Ortelle's Star (Moonee Valley Gold Cup, L. K. S. MacKinnon Stakes), Donaster (SAJC Adelaide Cup, King's Cup, St. Leger), Mira Dona (Essendon Stakes), Starstone (Debutante Stakes), Matinee (Debutante Stakes) and Great Legend (Champagne Stakes). Great Star was half-brother to English Derby winner Papyrus.

In New Zealand, a son of Sundridge led the Sires' List five times. I refer to the imported stallion Absurd (Sundridge-Absurdity by Melton), a handsome chestnut horse born in England at Jack Joel's Childwick Bury Stud in 1909. Absurd was dominant for speed and enjoyed those stamina-rich broodmares based in the north and south islands of New Zealand. A brilliant juvenile, Absurd won the Middle Park Stakes and sired more than 30 stakes winners.

Martello Towers, Champion 3YO colt in Australia, was linebred to Lady Josephine (by Sundridge) and carried Sainfoin via the brothers Fairway and Pharos.

Coronation Boy, leading sire of juveniles in Australia, was dominant for early maturing speed. He stood at Colin Hayes' Lindsay Park Stud in South Australia and was inbred 3 x 3 to champion filly Mumtaz Mahal (The Tetrarch-Lady Josephine by Sundridge) and gained Sainfoin's strain via Phalaris' sons Pharos and Colorado. He sired a brilliant sprinter named Maybe Lad who inherited an extra line of Mumtaz Mahal through his dam.

Nasrullah's son Rego was imported to Australia by Carl Powell. A small brown horse with a hot temperament, Rego surprised everyone with brilliant progeny despite the fact he was a moderate performer in England. Carl Powell was a shy man who could never afford to spend big money on a stallion prospect, but Carl would do his homework and study pedigrees. He noticed Rego was linebred to Sundridge and thought Rego's temperament possibly hindered the Nasrullah colt's ability on the racecourse. In the circumstances, Carl Powell believed Rego was a good risk to stand at Brooklyn Lodge, Aberdeen.

Rego (Nasrullah-Missy Suntan by unbeaten Tai-Yang) came from the same female line as successful sires Son-in-Law and Apelle. A small horse almost 15.2 hands high, he won the Epsom Plate over 8 ½ furlongs, Beverley Etton Welter Handicap over a mile, Leicester Prince of Wales' Handicap over a mile, finished second in the Rowley Mile Nursery Handicap, third in the Falmouth Handicap at Doncaster and was placed in a few handicaps. There was nothing in his form to suggest he would make an influential sire except for the fact he was by Britain's leading sire.

Rego sired outstanding juveniles and sprinters, especially Wiggle (Caulfield Guineas, Champagne Stakes, Edward Manifold Stakes), Reisling (Golden Slipper Stakes), With Respect (Wakeful Stakes), Prince Regoli (City Tattersalls Gold Cup), Boeing Boy (VRC Sires' Produce Stakes), Megalong (Gimcrack Stakes), Flotsam (AJC Summer Cup) and Champion 2YO colt Baguette (Golden Slipper Stakes, AJC Sires' Produce Stakes, Champagne Stakes, Doomben Ten Thousand, VRC Newmarket Handicap etc). Baguette's dam was Dark Jewel, a stakes-placed winning daughter of Star Kingdom. From the pedigree shown below, Baguette was heavily linebred to Sainfoin and his sister Sierra.

Baguette (1967)	Rego	Nasrullah	Nearco	Pharos by Phalaris, dam by **Sainfoin**
				Nogara by Havresac II
			Mumtaz Begum	Blenheim
				Mumtaz Mahal, dam by **Sundridge** - **Sierra**
		Missy Suntan	Tai-Yang	Solario, dam by **Sundridge** ex **Sierra**
				Soubriquet by Lemberg
			M'selle Satan	Sardanapale
				Emille
	Dark Jewel	Star Kingdom	Stardust	Hyperion
				Sister Stella, dam by **Sunstar** by **Sundridge**
			Impromptu	Concerto, dam by **Sunstar** by **Sundridge**
				Thoughtless by Papyrus
		Red Lace	Excitement	Hurry On (dam by **Sainfoin**)
				Stefanovna by Stefan The Great
			Red Clover	Iliad by Swynford
				Redshank by Thrice

Baguette won 15 races and retired a sound racehorse. He was a brother to classic winner Heirloom, winner of the VATC 1,000 Guineas. The cross of Nasrullah with Star Kingdom was quite successful in the production of Group winners.

Occasionally, Signal Light appears in pedigrees of Australian mares. This English stallion by Pharos was out of a mare inbred to a son and daughter of Sundridge. Bred by Major L. B. Holliday, Signal Light won two races, the Craven Stakes at Newmarket beating Fox Cub and Heliopolis, and the Milton 2YO Plate at York. He was second in the Waterford Stakes at Ascot and finished third in the Midsummer Stakes at Newmarket. Signal Light's third dam Jest (by Sundridge) won the English 1,000 Guineas and Oaks and was a sister to Absurd. Therefore it was not surprising he became a successful sire in Ireland and attracted the attention of Australian breeders.

Signal Light sired Big Dipper (Champion 2YO colt in England, winner of the Coventry Stakes, Champagne Stakes, Middle Park Stakes etc), The Bug (10 wins, Newmarket July Cup, Ascot Wokingham Stakes, Diadem Stakes, Nunthorpe Stakes etc), Masked Light (Middle Park Stakes, 3rd English 2,000 Guineas), Look Ahead (Ascot Gold Vase, Newmarket St. Leger), Langis Son (Irish Cambridgeshire), Ready (Sandown Anniversary Cup), Signalman, (Chesterfield Cup), Kilbelin (Ayr Gold Cup) and successful New Zealand sire Siegfried.

Signal Light (1936)	Pharos	Phalaris	**Polymelus**	Cyllene
				Maid Marian
			Bromus	**Sainfoin**
				Cheery by **St. Simon**
		Scapa Flow	Chaucer	**St. Simon**
				Canterbury Pilgrim - **Pilgrimage**
			Anchora	Love Wisely
				Eryholme
	Ensoleillee	Sunstar	**Sundridge**	Amphion
				Sierra
			Doris	Loved One ex **Pilgrimage**
				Lauretta
		Laughter	Pommern	**Polymelus**
				Merry Agnes
			Jest	**Sundridge** ex **Sierra**
				Absurdity

Signal Light's pedigree pattern is not that dissimilar to Pay Up (Fairway-Book Debt by Buchan, son of Sunstar) winner of the English 2,000 Guineas and another example of the powerful combination of Sainfoin and Sierra. Australia's leading sire Delville Wood was out of Everlasting (Phalaris-All's Blue by Buchan, son of Sunstar) a mare bred on similar lines, as was successful sire Law Maker (Phalaris-Book Law by Buchan, son of Sunstar). These strains did not go unnoticed by breeders "down under." Sundridge's classic winning daughter Jest was the dam of the very influential stallion Chief Ruler (by The Tetrarch), leading sire in New Zealand.

Australia and New Zealand benefited greatly from Sundridge's infusion of speed. There were a couple of stallions linebred to Sainfoin and Sierra who disappointed at stud, but genetic "affinities" are governed entirely by the laws of probability, so there is no point mentioning mediocre examples.

DOMINO, WAR ADMIRAL and COUNT FLEET

"The Domino effect ... Speed, speed, and more speed.
Domino created a dynasty in North America."
- Major Daingerfield

Like all sports fans, we love a champion and Domino was certainly one of the very best sprinter-milers of all time in North America. While St. Simon, Pocahontas, Sundridge, Sainfoin and Phalaris were catalysts for early maturing speed in Europe, Glencoe, Domino and Rock Sand were their counterparts in North America.

The Blood-Horse's Silver Anniversary supplement published in August 1941 reviewed the leading American sires and made mention of the rise and fall of sire lines. I would like to quote a few passages. I found the article most interesting.

"Kingston and Hastings, both sons of Spendthrift, each led the sires' list twice, Fair Play led it three times, and Man o' War, Chatterton and Chance Play, all sons of Fair Play, led once each. The line of Bramble accounts for seven of the years at the top. Ben Brush led the list once, his son Broomstick led in three consecutive years, another son Sweep led twice, and a grandson The Porter, led as late as 1937."

"Hanover led the sire list four times and his son Hamburg led once, these being the only descendants of the Glencoe branch of Herod's line to appear at the top. In 1894, one other descendant of Herod, imported Sir Modred, was the leader, making six years of leadership for the Herod dynasty. It is not even a dynasty any longer, the Glencoe branch being represented only by Wise Counsellor and some of his young sons, and other branches being chiefly the sons of which Stefan The Great, Epinard and Royal Minstrel have left."

"Hamburg, in 1905, was the last stallion from Herod to top the list and the recession of this line is the more remarkable when it is remembered that its greatest representative in America, Lexington, led the list for 16 years. The Domino line has accounted for leadership only four times, a small number in the light of the number of prominent stallions which stem from the great speedster of the 'nineties. Himyar, Commando, Celt and High Time are the four representatives, each leading once."

"Of the imported stallions which have held leadership, all were from the Eclipse line except Sir Modred (Herod), so that the score over the five decades is Eclipse 33, Matchem 11, Herod 6. Since Lexington's reign over American sires, Star Shoot has the best record, having led the list five times. Hanover and Sir Galahad III have each led four times, and it would surprise no one if Sir Galahad III, still represented by large crops, should better his own record. Broomstick and Fair Play led three times each and Kingston, Hastings, Meddler, Sweep and Sickle have each led twice."

The writer, if alive today, would be surprised to learn Sir Galahad III's male line is almost extinct and Domino's male line has faded. To my knowledge, there are no commercial sires remaining in the northern hemisphere that descend from Herod's male line and even Man o' War's branch of Matchem's male line might be in trouble.

All Thoroughbred sire lines rise and fall like the tide, or are swept out to sea into oblivion, but does it really matter? How important are sire lines in the scheme of things? Success breeds success. If sons or grandsons of a previously successful male line fail to breed stakes runners they will be avoided and go unsupported with quality mares. They have no chance of extending their male line.

What is more important is the legacy of great stallions like Lexington, Glencoe, Domino, Broomstick, Sir Gallahad III, Bull Dog and Man o' War in the gene pool of broodmares. Their impact is far greater on the breed via broodmares than via any male line. After all, there are only about seven genes attached to the tiny Y sex chromosome that determines a male foal and history shows the survival of sire lines depends entirely on maternal strength – specific mares that produced quality sons. Two examples worth noting are the mares Canterbury Pilgrim and Brown Bess.

Canterbury Pilgrim was responsible for maintaining two male lines via her sons Chaucer and Swynford.

Chaucer kept St. Simon's line alive in England while Rabelais represented it in France, and little Chaucer had nowhere near the racing ability of other great sons of St. Simon. Swynford is the only surviving male line member of John O'Gaunt. His line continues through male descendants of Blandford and his son Blenheim.

Brown Bess is responsible for keeping three sire lines alive, as shown by the following:

John O'Gaunt	Isinglass	Isonomy
		Deadlock
	La Fleche	St. Simon
		Quiver (Toxophilite - **Brown Bess**)
Polymelus	Cyllene	Bona Vista
		Arcadia
	Maid Marian	Hampton
		Quiver (Toxophilite - **Brown Bess**)
Carbine	Musket	Toxophilite
		daughter of **Brown Bess**
	The Mersey	Knowsley (ex daughter of **Brown Bess**)
		Clemence

John O'Gaunt is the sire of Swynford, Polymelus is the sire of Phalaris, and Carbine is the sire of Spearmint. So in reality, are we impressed by these sire lines or should we value more the obvious strength from mares like Quiver and her dam, Brown Bess?

John O'Gaunt's line was extended by a handful of excellent mares. His son Swynford was produced from English Oaks winner Canterbury Pilgrim, and Swynford's best son Blandford was out of Blanche whose second dam is the wonderful mare Black Duchess. Black Duchess produced Bay Ronald, thus keeping alive another male line, that of Hampton. If Black Duchess had not been mated with Hampton we would have no Bayardo, no Gainsborough and no Hyperion!

Therefore, when studying the pedigrees of great racehorses we should not allow male lines to cloud the issue. Instead, we should analyze the whole pedigree to see how it fits together and appreciate and identify maternal strength.

Probably I am telling successful breeders of Group 1 and Grade 1 winners how to suck eggs, but for the newcomer into the industry, it is worth repeating.

The secret to breeding high-class racehorses is maternal strength. Fillies and mares from stakes-producing families have more chance to produce stakes runners than mediocre female lines. Mares from stakes-producing families are mares from sound families with no structural weakness. Their produce records abound with above average runners and if some members of the family won at Group or Graded stakes level, they represent the top six percent of the overall gene pool.

Domino (Himyar-Mannie Gray by Enquirer) was described as a whirlwind on the track and a phenomenon at stud. The last decade of the 19th century is described as a carefree, prosperous period in North American history. Born in 1891, Domino made his debut as odds-on favorite in a race at Gravesend on May 22, 1893, scoring by six lengths, then swept through five stakes races in succession before lining up at the start of the Futurity Stakes on August 29th. Domino and Dobbins shared highweight, each with 130 pounds, in a field of 20 starters. Domino raced wide and lost ground, but in the final furlong, under desperate urging by jockey Fred Taral, won by a head from Galilee and Dobbins. Two days later, the owners of Domino and Dobbins, i.e. James R. Keene and Richard Croker, organized a match race over the same distance as the Futurity but carrying 118 pounds. The race ended in a dead heat.

Domino carried 128 pounds when he won the Matron Stakes over six furlongs setting a new track record of 1:09 flat and was put away. He began his three-year-old season with a narrow victory in the Withers Stakes but disappointed when unplaced in the American Derby over 1½ miles. He returned to the enclosure with a bleeding foot. Four wins followed and he became a matinee idol, yet there remained lingering doubts about his stamina. Henry of Navarre, the three-year-old who had impressively won the Belmont Stakes, was set to run against Domino in a special match race over nine furlongs, both colts to carry 122 pounds.

This race would determine the best three-year-old in the country. Riley Grannon, owner of Henry of Navarre, offered James Keene a wager of $100,000 that his colt would defeat Domino. At the start of the race, Henry of Navarre took the lead followed closely by Domino. Rounding the first turn, Domino sprinted to a length and a half lead, but down the backstretch, Henry of Navarre moved up to share the lead. Into the final turn Henry of Navarre was a narrow leader. Under whip and spur Domino fought back and gained ground to be on equal terms with one furlong remaining. The crowd witnessing this battle was tense with excitement.

At the finish both challengers crossed the wire in a dead heat and on the rain-affected track had run 1:55 ½. The purse was divided equally. Once again, Domino's admirers doubted the colt's stamina and it was confirmed when Henry of Navarre defeated Clifford and Domino at Morris Park in a special handicap over nine furlongs in October. At four, Domino won numerous races including the Withers Stakes but failed in the Suburban Handicap. A study of his racing career of 25 starts and 19 wins shows the dark brown colt was really a sprinter-miler, nine furlongs being as far as his speed would carry him. Even so, Domino raced most of the time with bad feet. He retired with earnings of $193,550.

The inscription on his gravestone reads: "Here lies the fleetest runner the American turf has ever known, and one of the gamest and most generous of horses."

In 1897, champion Domino was found dead in his stall. He was only six years of age. He was the father of only 20 progeny, of which eight were stakes winners.

Of his nine sons, four were gelded and one died, so the odds were stacked against him that his line would ever persist. Domino's son Commando was an unimpressive-looking weanling and owner-breeder James Keene did not enter the colt for the Futurity. Commando improved rapidly as a late yearling and developed a lean, athletic body. In 1900, he was crowned Champion 2YO colt. The following year he won the Belmont Stakes over 1 ⅜ miles (the distance of the race later changed to 1½ miles). Foxhall Keene took Domino's daughter Cap and Bells to England after she proved to be among the best juvenile fillies of her year. Winner of the Spinster Stakes, Cap and Bells regained her best form in England and demoralized her opponents to win the English Oaks at Epsom by 10 lengths. English breeders were astounded by this performance! Foxhall Keene, son of James Keene, rejoiced. A year earlier, their colt named Disguise, by Domino, had finished third in the English Derby.

Cap and Bells (1898)	Domino	Himyar	Alarm	Eclipse (USA)
				Maud
			Hira	Lexington
				Hegira
		Mannie Gray	Enquirer	Leamington
				Lida
			Lizzie G.	War Dance
				daughter of Lecomte
	Ben-My-Chree	Galopin	Vedette	Voltiguer
				Mrs. Ridgway
			Flying Duchess	The Flying Dutchman
				Merope
		Ulster Queen	Uncas	Stockwell
				Nightingale
			Pirate Queen	Buccaneer
				Queen of the May

Kentucky breeders were ecstatic! The Oaks victory confirmed their belief that the best American bloodlines were no longer inferior to the best European bloodlines. Furthermore, those who studied Cap and Bells' pedigree noticed the cross of Domino with Galopin and believed Galopin and his son St. Simon would be ideal strains to bring to Kentucky. Cap and Bells traced in direct female line to Web, a sister to two English Derby winners, Whisker and Whalebone. Commando was an immediate success at James Keene's Castleton Farm. From only eight foals in his first crop there were useful winners but from his second crop emerged one of the greatest racehorses America has ever produced – undefeated Colin (Commando-Pastorella by Sterling).

Colin came from one of England's best female lines. His dam, Pastorella, traced to Nan Darrell, granddam of English 2,000 Guineas and Doncaster Cup winner Vedette. This branch of the Number 19 Family suffered in popularity when Bruce Lowe's doctrine was introduced to Europe. Bruce Lowe ranked female families according to the number of classic winners each family produced but the system had many flaws. Families numbered above No. 16 as well as non-numbered families became less appealing to commercial breeders and subsequently lost value.

Nan Darrell's direct female descendants include Bloodroot (dam of Bimlette), Puccoon (dam of The Pruner), and Be Faithful (second dam of champion Never Bend), as well as Resplendent (dam of English Derby winner Windsor Lad) and Glen Line (dam of English 2,000 Guineas winner Our Babu). Domino had a strong pedigree. He is linebred three times to influential sire Lexington and linebred 6 x 5 x 6 x 6 to the great horse Glencoe, sire of famous English mare Pocahontas who produced influential sires Stockwell, Rataplan and King Tom.

Obviously Glencoe's genes were of profound importance and since St. Simon was out of a mare by King Tom (son of Pocahontas by Glencoe) it made sense to cross Domino's strain with St. Simon's line. However, what didn't make sense was why James Keene refused to allow outside breeders to send mares to Domino. The only explanation I ever heard (from Olin Gentry Sr.) was that Domino supposedly had an infected hoof and Keene and his manager, Major Daingerfield, wanted no outsiders to know about it.

This helps explain why Domino had only six foals in his first season and 14 foals the next season. Disguise, a brilliant juvenile, came from his first crop. Disguise was out of Bonnie Gal by Galopin, bred the same way as Cap and Bells, and like her, was sent to England. He finished third in the English Derby and Eclipse Stakes before winning the Jockey Club Stakes, but the most important foal from that first crop was a filly named Pink Domino who became the dam of champion Sweep.

From the second crop, Domino sired 10 winners, five of which became stakes winners. Apart from Commando, these were Olympian, Cap and Bells, Noonday and Running Stream. Domino's second dam Lizzie G. was inbred 3 x 4 x 4 to Glencoe.

Colin (1905)	Commando	Domino	Himyar	Alarm
				Hira by **Lexington**
			Mannie Gray	Enquirer (dam by **Lexington**)
				Lizzie G. by War Dance (**Lexington**/ + 3 strains of **Glencoe**)
		Emma C.	Darebin	The Peer
				Lurline
			Guenn	Flood
				Glendew
	Pastorella	Springfield	St. Albans	Stockwell (ex Pocahontas by **Glencoe**)
				Bribery
			Viridis	Marsyas
				Maid of Palmyra
		Griselda	Strathconan	Newminster
				Souvenir
			Perseverance	Voltiguer
				Spinster

Colin (by Commando) was amazingly fast! At two, he won all 12 starts including the National Stallion Stakes, Futurity Stakes, Champagne Stakes, Saratoga Special and Great Trial Stakes and defeated Fair Play convincingly in the Matron Stakes by three lengths.

At three, he remained undefeated but was inconvenienced by sore feet.

HALO (Hail to Reason - Cosmah), sire of champion Sunday Silence.

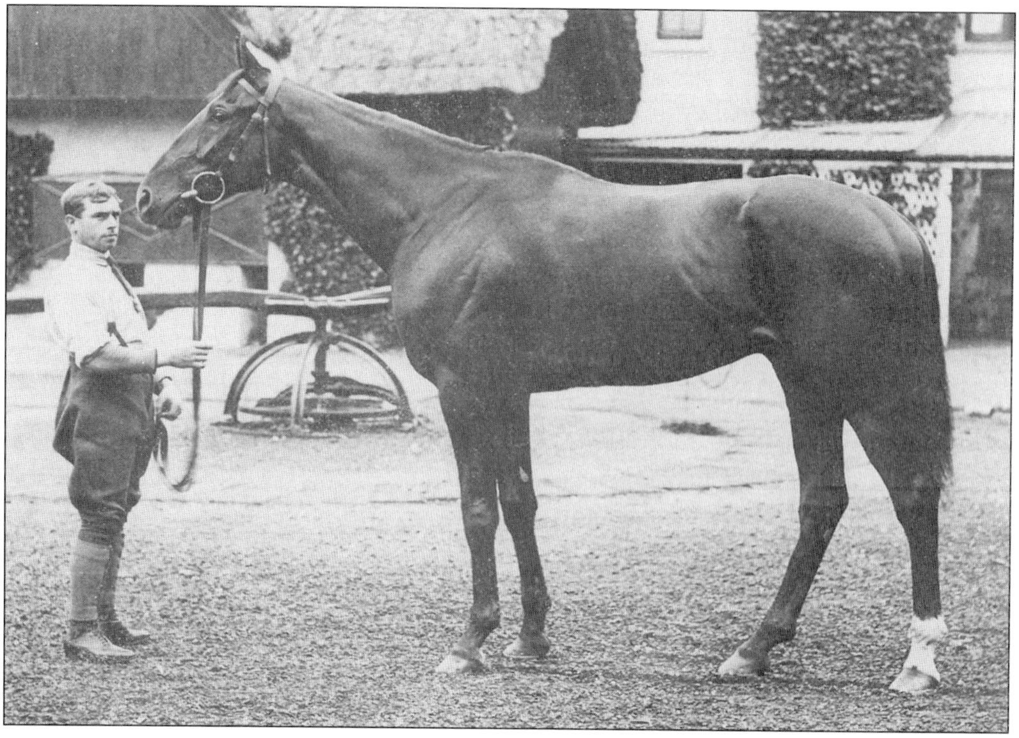

DOMINO, the champion racehorse and leading sire who was described as a "whirlwind."

At three, Colin won three races including the Withers Stakes and defeated Fair Play in the Belmont Stakes. Sent to England for a four-year-old campaign, he was never quite sound enough to race and was briefly retired to the Heath Stud at Newmarket. Unfortunately, his pedigree failed to appeal to English breeders. Returned to Kentucky, Colin was among the stallions sold at the dispersal of Keene's Estate. In 1913, James Keene passed away.

At the New York auction, Colin was purchased for $30,000, the second highest price of the day. Peter Pan, son of Commando, fetched top price at $38,000 to the bid of Payne Whitney who gave the stallion as a gift to Harry Payne Whitney. Earlier in the day, the Hancocks bought Celt for $20,000 and the young stallion Sweep was purchased by Charles Moore on behalf of a syndicate for $17,500. Sweep would become the leading sire in North America in 1918 and 1925. Highest price for a broodmare was Sweep's dam, Pink Domino, who sold for $7,100 – big money for a mare at the time. Dominant, an attractive weanling, was purchased by Harry Payne Whitney for $2,200. Nobody could guess Dominant would be the nation's Champion 2YO colt in 1915.

Incidentally, Sweep (Ben Brush-Pink Domino by Domino) was one of the soundest horses of his era and always a favorite of Colonel Edward R. Bradley who owned Idle Hour Farm, home of Black Toney. Sweep won nine of 13 starts including the Futurity Stakes, National Stallion Stakes at two, and the following year won the Belmont Stakes and Lawrence Realization Stakes.

A year behind Colin came Champion 2YO filly Maskette (Disguise-Biturica by Hamburg) inbred 3 x 4 to Mannie Gray and linebred three times to Galopin. Maskette won the Futurity and five other juvenile races. In 1910, the Keene stable raced Sweep, the nation's Champion 2YO colt. In 1911, Sweep's nephew Novelty (bred by Keene but raced by Sam Hildreth) was Champion 2YO, taking the title from Keene's smart colt Iron Mask (by Disguise).

The Domino dynasty had begun, but it was also a time when betting was outlawed in New York. In 1908 the Hart-Agnew Bill, signed by Governor Charles Evans Hughes, took effect. By 1910, betting was illegal in some states. Needless to say, West Coast tracks, plus Kentucky, Maryland and Canadian tracks, prospered during the blackout. Then to add further confusion, in 1913 the English Jockey Club passed the Jersey Act, affecting acceptance of American-bred bloodstock in the General Stud Book of England. Sam Hildreth, leading owner-trainer in the country with a large string based in New York, was disgusted by the new legislature and sold all his racing stock to Charles D. Kohler. Mr. Kohler, a wealthy piano manufacturer, decided he would send the string to race in France, providing Sam would train them. An agreement was reached and all of Mr. Kohler's horses were shipped to France.

In 1915, Broomstick's daughter Regret won the Kentucky Derby. In 1917, the Champion 2YO colt was an imported French-bred colt named Sun Briar who won the Saratoga Special from Rosie O'Grady and captured the Great American Stakes, Grand Union Hotel Stakes and Hopeful Stakes. In 1918, Eternal was the nation's leading juvenile colt. The best three-year-olds comprised Sun Briar, The Porter and Johren. Roamer was champion older horse.

Europe was engulfed in war and times were tough. However, in 1919, the American racing public was graced with the debut of a famous racehorse, Man o' War (Fair Play-Mahubah by Rock Sand). Bought as a yearling at Saratoga for $5,000 by Samuel D. Riddle, Man o' War was rated the greatest American horse since Colin!

On June 6, 1919, Glen Riddle Farms' bright chestnut two-year-old won a Maiden 2YO Special at Belmont Park by six lengths, easing up at the wire.

Man o' War proceeded to win the Keene Memorial Stakes, Youthful Stakes (defeating Colin's son On Watch both times), Hudson Stakes and Tremont Stakes. At Saratoga, Man o' War defeated Upset in the United States Hotel Stakes before an unexpected, unfortunate loss. In the Sanford Memorial Stakes, Upset took the lead while Man o' War was shuffled back in the field. Down the stretch, Man o' War flew home but was too late, beaten a half-length by Upset at the wire. Later, in the Grand Union Stakes, Man o' War reversed that form, giving Upset five pounds in weight. Next, he won the Hopeful Stakes by four lengths (with Upset unplaced) and on his final juvenile appearance defeated John P. Grier in the Futurity Stakes. Man o' War was named Champion 2YO colt. That same year, Sir Barton won the Triple Crown.

Man o' War earned his title as Champion 3YO colt in 1920. In May, Paul Jones had defeated Upset in the Kentucky Derby. Man o' War made his first start for the year in the Preakness Stakes and won easily, annihilating Upset, Wildair and On Watch. Next, he won the Withers Stakes before his hollow victory in the Belmont Stakes, winning by 20 lengths in new American record time! For the Dwyer Handicap, he had to give John P. Grier 18 pounds and although the latter made a race of it, in the end Man o' War won and set a new American record time of 1:49 $^1/_5$ for nine furlongs. John P. Grier finished second, a length and a half away.

War Admiral (1934)	Man o' War	Fair Play	Hastings	Spendthrift
				Cinderella
			Fairy Gold	Bend Or
				Dame Masham
		Mahubah	Rock Sand	Sainfoin
				Roquebrune
			Merry Token	Merry Hampton
				Mizpah
	Brushup	Sweep	Ben Brush	Bramble
				Roseville
			Pink Domino	Domino
				Belle Rose
		Annette K.	Harry of Hereford	John O'Gaunt
				Canterbury Pilgrim
			Bathing Girl	Spearmint
				Summer Girl

At his final start, Man o' War won a valuable match race against the four-year- old Sir Barton, defeating him by seven lengths. Man o' War amassed $249,465 in earnings, was named Horse of the Year, and graciously retired to stud. He was a success at stud, but not as great as Sam Riddle expected. Man o' War's three best colts were War Admiral (Champion 3YO colt, Horse of the Year), Crusader (earner of $203,261) and American Flag. War Admiral, bred and owned by Sam Riddle, was a highly-strung small colt of about 15.2 hands high, with deep girth and well-developed thighs. However, War Admiral had one vice – he nearly always played up at the starting gate. In conformation, he resembled his maternal grandsire, Sweep.

War Admiral was ranked fifth best two-year-old of 1936. The following year at three, he was unbeaten. He won an overnight allowance and the Chesapeake Stakes before lining up as an 8-to-5 favorite for the Kentucky Derby. Once in the lead he was unbeatable and won convincingly by two lengths from Pompoon with Reaping Reward third. In the Preakness Stakes, he again led all the way but had to withstand a driving finish by Pompoon, with Flying Scot third. War Admiral won the third leg of the Triple Crown by winning the Belmont Stakes in new American record time of 2:28 ⅗. After this victory he developed a slight injury, but successfully returned to racing in an allowance race. He defeated Heelfly in the Washington Handicap and then won the Pimlico Special. War Admiral's eight starts at three grossed $166,500.

That same year, Menow was named Champion 2YO colt. He was a homebred colt for Hal Price Headley who stood the colt's sire, Pharamond II, and owned the colt's dam, champion racemare Alcibiades. In the Champagne Stakes, Menow beat Bull Lea and Fighting Fox by four lengths giving them weight, and won the Futurity Stakes by four lengths from Tiger in new world record time of 1:15 ⅕ for the 6 ½ furlongs.

The leaders in 1938 were unbeaten champion juvenile El Chico (by John P. Grier), champion 3YO colt Stagehand (Sickle-Stagecraft by Fair Play), and Seabiscuit, conqueror of War Admiral in the Pimlico Special match race. War Admiral had earlier won the Widener Handicap, Queens County Handicap, Whitney Stakes, Saratoga Handicap, Saratoga Cup etc., but was unplaced in the Massachusetts Handicap. Meanwhile, Seabiscuit put a string of major stakes wins together on the West Coast and by year's end was considered the country's best handicap horse.

Bimelech (Black Toney-La Troienne by Teddy) won the 1939 Futurity Stakes and earned the title of juvenile champion for owner-breeder Colonel E. R. Bradley. It was the year the three-year-olds Johnstown (Jamestown-La France by Sir Galahad III) and champion Challedon (Challenger II-Laura Gal by Sir Galahad III) competed against each other, the former winning the Kentucky Derby and Belmont Stakes, the latter winning the Preakness Stakes and earning the most money. Eight Thirty won seven of 10 starts for George D. Widener including the Whitney Stakes, Travers Stakes, Suburban Handicap and Pimlico Special. (World War II was still in progress.) War Admiral won an allowance race in February, a "prep" for the Santa Anita Handicap. Soon after he developed laryngitis and was taken out of training. Later, when about to make a comeback, he injured an ankle and was retired.

In 1940, Our Boots (by Bull Dog) claimed the title of juvenile champion ahead of Whirlaway (Blenheim-Dustwhirl by Sweep). Bimelech was crowned Champion 3YO colt. The best older horses comprised Challedon, Seabiscuit and Eight Thirty. Although Seabiscuit became the world's leading money winner, it was Eight Thirty who in 1940 claimed the title of Champion Handicap Horse. He won the Metropolitan Handicap, Toboggan Handicap, Wilson Stakes etc., and met and defeated Challedon in the valuable Massachusetts Handicap, equaling the track record.

Eight Thirty (Pilate-Dinner Time by High Time) was inbred to Sainfoin's son Rock Sand and inbred to dominant mare Fairy Gold (by Bend Or). Eight Thirty's broodmare sire, High Time, was incestuously inbred three times to Domino. A handsome horse with sound conformation, Eight Thirty ended his racing career with 16 wins and earnings of $155,475.

His second dam Seaplane was half-sister to Annette K., granddam of champion War Admiral. Seaplane was linebred to Sainfoin and his sister Sierra.

Eight Thirty (1936)	Pilate	Friar Rock	**Rock Sand**	**Sainfoin** by **Springfield**
				Roquebrune by St. Simon
			Fairy Gold	**Bend Or**
				Dame Masham by Galliard
		Herodias	The Tetrarch	Roi Herode
				Vahren by Bona Vista by **Bend Or**
			Honora	Gallinule
				Word of Honour
	Dinner Time	High Time	Ultimus	Commando by **Domino**
				Running Stream by **Domino**
			Noonday	**Domino**
				Sundown by **Springfield**
		Seaplane	Man o' War	Fair Play ex **Fairy Gold** by **Bend Or**
				Mahubah by **Rock Sand** by **Sainfoin**
			Bathing Girl	Spearmint by Carbine
				Summer Girl by Sundridge (ex **Sierra**)

Eight Thirty retired to the Old Kenney Farm in Lexington and sired 44 stakes winners. One of them was the brilliant colt Bolero who appears in the pedigree of leading sire Storm Cat. Others were Anyoldtime, Big Stretch, Lights Up, First Nighter, Rare Perfume, Sunday Evening, Omelet Souffle, Colony Boy and Royal Coinage. Bolero held the world record for seven furlongs (in 1:21 flat) and the world record for six furlongs (in 1:08 $^1/_5$). Eight Thirty's dam, Dinner Time, chased champion 2YO filly Top Flight in several major stakes races.

Man o' War sired War Relic, winner of nine races including the Massachusetts Handicap, Narragansett Governor's Handicap and Narragansett Special (in which he defeated Blenheim's son Whirlaway). War Relic is the sire of Intent and Relic who continued Man o' War's male line.

War Relic (1938)	Man o' War	Fair Play	Hastings	Spendthrift
				Cinderella
			Fairy Gold	**Bend Or**
				Dame Masham
		Mahubah	**Rock Sand**	**Sainfoin**
				Roquebrune
			Merry Token	Merry Hampton
				Mizpah
	Friar's Carse	Friar Rock	**Rock Sand**	**Sainfoin**
				Roquebrune
			Fairy Gold	**Bend Or**
				Dame Masham
		Problem	Superman	Commando by Domino
				Anomaly by **Bend Or**
			Query	Voter
				Quesal

The mix of Ben Brush and Domino produced many high-class stakes winners, among them champions Sweep and Equipoise, but an even better mix was when Rock Sand's line met up with mares carrying Domino's strain.

Equipoise (Pennant-Swinging by Broomstick), a tough handicap horse, was a great-grandson of Domino. His sire, Pennant, was a son of Peter Pan, by Commando by Domino. Pennant was unbeaten at two, winning the Futurity Stakes. He never ran at three or four owing to weak forelegs, but made a comeback to win the Delaware Handicap. He sired 40 stakes winners.

Born in 1928, Equipoise was nicknamed "The Chocolate Soldier." He won 29 of 51 starts and earned $338,610 at that time ranking him the second top earner in the world, but he died young, getting only 74 foals. Nevertheless he led the Sires' List in 1942 and his outstanding son Equestrian sired champion Stymie.

Equipoise won the Metropolitan Handicap twice, Suburban Handicap, Toboggan Handicap, Whitney Stakes, Arlington Handicap, Havre de Grace Cup, Delavan Handicap (establishing a new world record for a mile), Stars & Stripes Handicap and Arlington Gold Cup etc. A versatile performer, he won from four furlongs to 1¾ miles.

War Admiral failed to sire a son capable of carrying on his father's sire line. At one stage it seemed Mr. Busher (War Admiral-Baby League by Bubbling Over) would do the job. This brown horse was a brother to those fast fillies Busher and Striking and although he only raced at two, winning three of four starts, was given an opportunity to succeed at Spendthrift Farm. However, he sired better fillies than colts.

				Hastings
			Fair Play	Fairy Gold by **Bend Or**
		Man o' War		Rock Sand by **Sainfoin**
			Mahubah	Merry Token
	War Admiral			Ben Brush
			Sweep	Pink Domino by **Domino**
		Brushup		Harry of Hereford
			Annette K.	Bathing Girl by Spearmint
Mr. Busher				Sunstar by Sundridge (ex **Sierra**)
(1940)			North Star III	Angelic
		Bubbling Over		**Sweep** (dam by **Domino**)
			Beaming Beauty	Bellisario by Hippodrome (to **Domino**)
	Baby League			Ajax by Flying Fox
			Teddy	Rondeau (dam by **Bend Or**)
		La Troienne		Helicon by Cyllene by Bona Vista
			Helene de Troie	Lady of Pedigree by St. Denis

Mr. Busher won the National Stallion Stakes by two lengths, the Arlington Futurity by 1½ lengths and a 2YO Maiden by six lengths. At his fourth start he broke down during the running of the Washington Park Futurity Stakes.

War Admiral's second dam Annette K. was by Swynford's brother Harry of Hereford. Kentucky Derby winner Bubbling Over was out of a mare linebred to Domino, and Hippodrome was incestuously inbred to Domino.

Mr. Busher's sister Busher was voted Horse of the Year in 1945. Her 15 victories include the Selima Stakes, Matron Stakes, Santa Susanna Stakes, Hollywood Derby, Adirondack Handicap, Santa Margarita Handicap, Vanity Handicap and she finished third in the Santa Anita Derby. Busher produced Jet Action and Miss Busher.

Her sister Striking won the Schuylerville Stakes (defeating Sunday Evening) and was runner-up to Bed O'Roses three times – the Selima Stakes (with Busanda finishing third), Spinaway Stakes and Marguerite Stakes. Striking also finished third in the Matron Stakes won by Bed O'Roses. She produced stakes winners Hitting Away, My Boss Lady, Sparkling and Glamour, the last named a filly by Nasrullah. Glamour produced Poker (by Round Table) and is the third dam of Woodman.

In the pedigree of Seattle Slew's dam, My Charmer, the sisters Striking and Busher are duplicated 3 x 3. Bred on the same cross as Striking and Busher is Busanda, dam of champion Buckpasser.

For owner-breeder Ogden Phipps, Busanda won the Alabama Stakes as a juvenile and later developed into a high-class performer. She was runner-up to Bed O' Roses in voting for Champion Handicap Mare. Busanda won the Top Flight Handicap, New Castle Handicap against her own sex and captured the Suburban Handicap and Saratoga Cup against older males.

Buckpasser (1963)	Tom Fool	Menow	Pharamond II by Phalaris
			Alcibiades by Supremus by Ultimus
		Gaga	Bull Dog by **Teddy**
			Alpoise by Equipoise by Pennant
	Busanda	War Admiral	Man o' War (dam by Rock Sand)
			Brushup by Sweep (ex Pink Domino)
		Businesslike	Blue Larkspur
			La Troienne by **Teddy**

Busanda's son Buckpasser won 25 of 31 starts and earned $1,462,014. As a two-year-old he won nine of 11 starts including the Sapling Stakes, Tremont Stakes, Champagne Stakes, Hopeful Stakes, Arlington-Washington Futurity, dead-heated for first with Hospitality in the National Stallion Stakes and was runner up to Priceless Gem in the Futurity Stakes. He was voted Champion 2YO colt. At three, Buckpasser won 13 of 14 starts with major victories in the Malibu Stakes, Flamingo Stakes, Arlington Classic, American Derby, Woodward Stakes, Brooklyn Handicap, Chicagoan Stakes and Jockey Club Gold Cup. Proclaimed the nation's Champion Handicap Horse, Buckpasser set a new world record in the Arlington Classic.

At four, he won the San Fernando Stakes, Suburban Handicap and Metropolitan Handicap (carrying 130 pounds). Damascus defeated him in the Woodward Stakes and Poker defeated him in the Bowling Green Handicap, but again he was voted North America's Champion Handicap Horse.

Buckpasser missed the Triple Crown races owing to quarter cracks and a bruised ankle. His pedigree shows linebreeding to Teddy and Domino.

He sired 36 stakes winners and five champions. Among his progeny were Numbered Account (14 wins $607,046, Champion 2YO filly, Frizette, Gardenia, Matron, Spinaway Stakes), Relaxing (15 wins $589,875, Champion Handicap Mare, Ruffian Hcp, Delaware Hcp), La Prevoyante (25 wins $572,417,

Champion 2YO and Horse of the Year in Canada, Frizette Stakes), L'Enjoleur (Horse of the Year twice in Canada, Queen's Plate), Norcliffe (Horse of the Year and Champion Handicap Horse in Canada), Balzac ($654,730 Oak Tree Invitational Hcp), State Dinner ($537,959 Metropolitan Hcp, Suburban Hcp), Silver Buck ($421,906 Suburban Hcp, Whitney Hcp), Buckfinder, Pass The Glass, Swingtime, etc. He was not perfect in the knees but it didn't seem to affect his ability. Buckpasser is one of the most influential broodmare sires of all time. His father was Tom Fool, winner of 21 races and $570,165. Tom Fool was crowned Champion 2YO colt and Horse of the Year at four, when undefeated in 10 races. A handsome, masculine horse, his wins include the Metropolitan Handicap, Suburban Handicap and Brooklyn Handicap. He was considered brilliant at a mile.

War Relic's son Intent was the product of crossing two compatible strains, Rock Sand with North Star III, thus combining Sainfoin with his sister Sierra.

Intent won eight races and earned $317,775. A high-class handicap horse, he won the San Juan Capistrano Handicap (twice), Santa Anita Maturity, Forty Niners Handicap, Lakes and Flowers Handicap (going seven furlongs in 1:21 $^{4}/_{5}$ with topweight) and also the Santa Anita Handicap but was disqualified and placed second.

		Man o' War	Fair Play by Hastings
			Mahubah by **Rock Sand** by **Sainfoin**
	War Relic		
		Friar's Carse	Friar Rock by **Rock Sand** by **Sainfoin**
			Problem by Superman
Intent (1948)			
		Bubbling Over	North Star III by Sunstar by Sundridge - **Sierra**
			Beaming Beauty by Sweep
	Liz F.		
		Weno	Whisk Broom II by Broomstick
			Rosie O'Grady by Hamburg

Intent's most important son was Intentionally, 18 wins and $652,259. At two, he won the Futurity Stakes (defeating First Landing and Dunce), Tyro Stakes, Pimlico Futurity, was runner-up to Watch Your Step in the Sapling Stakes, runner-up to First Landing in the Champagne Stakes and finished second in two other juvenile stakes.

At three, Intentionally won the Warren Wright Memorial Handicap equaling the world record for a mile in 1:33 $^{1}/_{5}$ (new track record), Jerome Handicap, Delaware Valley Stakes etc., finished second in the Gotham Stakes and third in the Arlington Classic and Discovery Handicap. At four to six years, he captured the Equipoise Mile, Toboggan Handicap, Palm Beach Handicap and Seminole Handicap (defeating Carry Back) and was runner-up to Bald Eagle in the Aqueduct Handicap. He stood as a syndicated stallion at Tartan Farms in Ocala, Florida, where he sired the good sprinter In Reality. Intentionally was out of My Recipe, an unplaced daughter of Discovery that traced in female line to Ballantrae.

We now come to one of the greatest racehorses in American history, certainly as talented as Man o' War, Colin, Swaps and Secretariat. His name is Count Fleet and, after all these years, he still ranks as the highest weighted two-year-old, assigned with 132 pounds, on the Experimental Free Handicap. Count Fleet was rated the most outstanding American juvenile of the 20th Century.

Never out of the money in 15 starts at two, Count Fleet won the Wakefield Stakes in July 1942, ran second to Occupation in the Washington Park Futurity, and startled everyone by winning the Champagne Stakes in 1:34 $\frac{4}{5}$, setting a new track record for a mile at Belmont Park and establishing world record time for a two-year-old. He won the Pimlico Futurity by five lengths from Occupation, equaling the track record of 1:43 $\frac{3}{5}$ for 1 $\frac{1}{16}$ miles, and finished the season with an easy win in the Walden Stakes (by 30 lengths). Hal Price Headley's juvenile Askmeknow was voted Champion 2YO filly that same year.

Count Fleet (1940)	Reigh Count	Sunreigh	Sundridge	Amphion
				Sierra
			Sweet Briar	**St. Frusquin**
				Presentation
		Contessina	Count Schomberg	Aughrim by Xenophon
				Clonavarn
			Pitti	**St. Frusquin**
				Florence by Wisdom
	Quickly	Haste	Maintenant	Maintenon by Le Saggitaire
				Martha Gorman
			Miss Malaprop	Meddler by St. Gatien
				Correction (ex Mannie Gray)
		Stephanie	Stefan The Great	The Tetrarch by Roi Herode
				Perfect Peach
			Malachite	Rock Sand by **Sainfoin**
				Miss Hanover by Hanover

From the early maturing speed line of Sundridge, Count Fleet carried the mix of Sierra and her brother Sainfoin. Speed emanated from other parts of the ancestry. Haste won the Saratoga Special and defeated Crusader and Espino in the Withers Stakes. Haste's granddam Correction was a sister to Domino.

The Tetrarch was unbeaten Champion 2YO of Europe and his son Stefan The Great was a flying machine over short courses. Miss Hanover was by Hanover, winner of 32 races from 50 starts. A courageous fighter, Hanover won the Belmont Stakes, Dwyer Handicap, Withers Handicap, Dixie Handicap and as well, was a very smart juvenile. Hanover was by Kentucky Derby winner Hindoo.

Count Schomberg was one of the soundest stayers you could ever wish to own and was patronized by famous breeder William Hall-Walker (Lord Wavertree). Count Schomberg won the Goodwood Cup, Jockey Club Cup, Ascot Gold Vase and Chester Cup and most likely transmitted stamina to Count Fleet.

Reigh Count (1925) won the Kentucky Derby, Saratoga Cup (two miles), Jockey Club Gold Cup, Lawrence Realization Handicap and was shipped to England where he won the Coronation Cup and finished second in the Ascot Gold Cup.

Reigh Count was a tall chestnut horse whose speed was derived from the Sundridge line and whose stamina was inherited from Count Schomberg. John D. Hertz (of Hertz Rent-A-Car fame), who bred and raced Count Fleet, purchased Reigh Count privately after seeing the colt race as a juvenile.

Reigh Count won 11 races worth $168,670 in North America. What is remarkable is that Count Fleet's stakes-winning dam, Quickly, won 32 races from two to six, set one track record and equaled two others. She produced a brother to Count Fleet that won nine races and set a world record for 1 1/16 miles in 1:41 flat. Quickly's granddam Malachite also possessed speed. She won the Alabama Stakes.

In 1943, Count Fleet was undefeated. He was voted Horse of the Year and Champion 3YO colt and was so superior, his opponents ran on sufferance. On April 13, he made his three-year-old debut winning an allowance race eased down at the wire by 3½ lengths. Next, he won the Wood Memorial Stakes and was sent out hot favorite for the Kentucky Derby which he won handily by three lengths. At Pimlico he scored an eight lengths victory in the Preakness Stakes. He won the Withers Stakes by five lengths on a muddy track and the Belmont Stakes by 20 lengths, completing the Triple Crown. When he returned to the enclosure following his Belmont Stakes victory it was discovered he had struck himself during the race – serious enough to force early retirement. We will never know what Count Fleet might have accomplished. His jockey, Johnny Longden, rated him the best racehorse he'd ever seen and recalled a morning workout when the colt, aged two, went six furlongs in the sizzling time of 1:08 1/5. Count Fleet won 10 of 15 starts as a juvenile and won all six starts at three. He earned $250,300.

Blue Swords (by Blue Larkspur) was the colt that chased Count Fleet. He was runner-up to the champion in the Champagne Stakes, Wood Memorial Stakes, Kentucky Derby and the Preakness Stakes. In any normal year, Blue Swords would have earned a championship title. He is best remembered as the sire of Nothirdchance, dam of champion Hail To Reason.

Count Fleet was a major success as a sire at Stoner Creek Stud, Paris, Kentucky. He sired two colts that were crowned Horse of the Year, Counterpoint and One Count, as well as Champion 3YO filly Kiss Me Kate, Kentucky Derby winner Count Turf, Be Fleet, Beau Gar, Count of Honor and Count Speed, who set a world record for 8 ½ furlongs. Count Fleet was the nation's leading sire in 1951.

Counterpoint (Count Fleet-Jabot by Sickle), owned by C.V. Whitney, won 10 of 21 starts and earned $284,575. He won the Peter Pan Stakes setting a new track record, the Belmont Stakes (defeating Battlefield), Lawrence Realization Handicap, Jockey Club Gold Cup (defeating Hill Prince), Empire City Gold Cup in track record time, San Fernando Stakes and was runner-up in the Preakness Stakes and third in the Blue Grass Stakes and Arkansas Derby. In 1951, a son of Count Fleet won the Kentucky Derby. His name was Count Turf.

The pedigree of Counterpoint, Horse of the Year and Champion 3YO colt, shows linebreeding to Sainfoin and his sister Sierra and duplication of Rock Sand. Sainfoin is reinforced via a son and a daughter, thus enabling similar genes to be located on both sides of Counterpoint's chromosomes.

Counterpoint's dam, Jabot, won 12 races including the Selima Stakes, Kentucky Stakes, San Carlos Handicap (in new track record time) and is a daughter of another gifted racemare, Frilette, winner of the Beldame Handicap, Beechmont Handicap etc., and runner-up in the Coaching Club American Oaks.

In 1952, the nation's Champion 3YO colt was One Count (Count Fleet-Ace Card by Case Ace), owned by Mrs. Walter M. Jeffords and trained by Oscar White. One Count ran three times as a juvenile winning a maiden race, and commenced his three-year-old campaign in January, winning an allowance race.

Counterpoint (1948)	Count Fleet	Reigh Count	Sunreigh	Sundridge (ex **Sierra**)
				Sweet Brier
			Contessina	Count Schomberg
				Pitti
		Quickly	Haste	Maintenant
				Miss Malaprop
			Stephanie	Stefan the Great by The Tetrarch
				Malachite by **Rock Sand** by **Sainfoin**
	Jabot	Sickle	Phalaris	Polymelus
				Bromus by **Sainfoin**
			Selene	Chaucer
				Serenissima by Minoru
		Frilette	Man o' War	Fair Play
				Mahubah by **Rock Sand** by **Sainfoin**
			Frillery	Broomstick
				Petticoat

One Count was a late developer who finished unplaced at his first three attempts in stakes company. In May, he was physically and mentally stronger and ran second in the Withers Stakes followed by an encouraging third to Blue Man in the Preakness Stakes. On June 7, he won the Belmont Stakes from Blue Man and progressed to capture the Travers Stakes, Jockey Club Gold Cup (defeating the older horses Mark-Ye-Well and Crafty Admiral) and the Empire City Gold Cup.

Considered to be a high-class crop of three-year-olds, One Count's rivals comprised Bull Lea's son Hill Gail, Tom Fool (who missed the Triple Crown because of a fever and cough), Cain Hoy Stable's Armageddon and the imported stakes winner Windy City II who was voted Champion 2YO colt of the British Isles. At the conclusion of his racing career, One Count had won nine races and earned $245,625. Like Counterpoint, he possessed Rock Sand's strain via Man o' War.

Count Fleet is the sire of Sequence, granddam of Mr. Prospector.

Sequence won five races at two and three years and earned $54,850 including the Princess Pat Stakes. She was a sister to stakes winner Bella Figura and produced from Kentucky Oaks winner Miss Dogwood (14 wins) by Blue Larkspur from the brilliant sprint mare Myrtlewood. Miss Dogwood was a sister to Champion 2YO filly Durazna, nine wins, a fleet filly who defeated Occupy in the Breeders' Futurity Stakes. Myrtlewood also produced Crepe Myrtle, ancestor of champion Seattle Slew.

Mr. Prospector's dam is Gold Digger, stakes winner of 10 races from two to four years, who earned $125,256. A lightly-framed mare, she won the Gallorette Handicap twice, Marigold Stakes, Columbiana Handicap, Yo Tambien Handicap, was runner-up in the Kentucky Oaks and finished third in the Matron Stakes.

Gold Digger is by Nashua (Nasrullah-Segula by Johnstown-Sekhmet by champion Sardanapale). Nashua was a sensational racehorse, Horse of the Year at three and voted Champion 2YO and 3YO colt. Those who saw him campaign say he was the best son of his famous sire, even superior to Bold Ruler and Noor.

Gold Digger would have inherited speed from the combination of Count Fleet (Sundridge line) and Nasrullah (linebred to Sainfoin and Sierra) with additional brilliance via undefeated wonder-horse The Tetrarch.

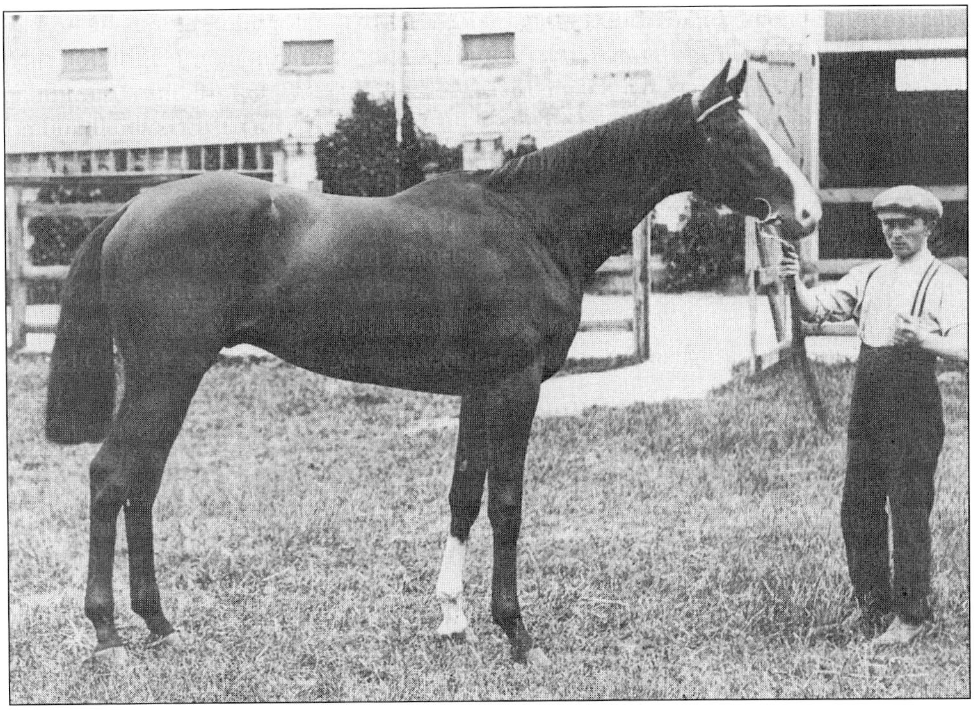

SPEARMINT (Carbine - Maid of the Mint), winner of the English Derby. He is the sire of Catnip, Spion Kop, and Plucky Liege (dam of Bull Dog, Sir Gallahad III).

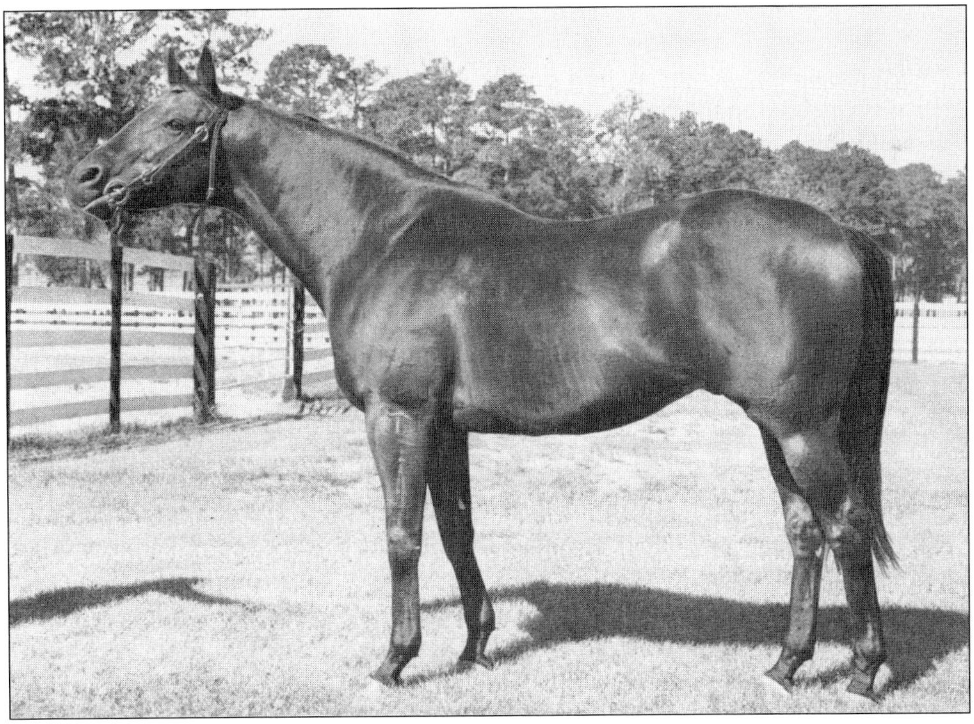

BOLDNESIAN (Bold Ruler - Alanesian by Polynesian), winner of the Santa Anita Derby and the sire of Bold Reasoning.

Gold Digger produced three stakes winners, namely Mr. Prospector (seven wins $112,171, Gravesend Handicap, Whirlaway Handicap, runner-up in the Carter Handicap, Firecracker Handicap, Royal Poinciana Stakes, 3rd Paumonok Handicap), Gold Standard (seven wins $163,542, Cortez Handicap, Los Felix Stakes, 3rd Arcadia Handicap), Lillian Russell (seven wins $144,567, 1st Cleopatra Handicap, Mint Julep Handicap) as well as stakes-placed Search For Gold, a brother to Mr. Prospector.

Gold Digger (1962)	Nashua	Nasrullah	Nearco	Pharos by Phalaris (dam by **Sainfoin**)
				Nogara (ex Catnip by **Spearmint**)
			Mumtaz Begum	Blenheim
				Mumtaz Mahal (dam by **Sundridge**)
		Segula	Johnstown	Jamestown
				La France by **Sir Gallahad III**
			Sekhmet	Sardanapale
				Prosopopee
	Sequence	Count Fleet	Reigh Count	Sunreigh by **Sundridge** (ex **Sierra**)
				Contessina
			Quickly	Haste
				Stephanie by Stefan The Great
		Miss Dogwood	**Bull Dog**	**Teddy**
				Plucky Liege by **Spearmint**
			Myrtlewood	Blue Larkspur
				Frizeur

Gold Digger was linebred to the brothers Sir Gallahad III and Bull Dog, to Spearmint three times and The Tetrarch is duplicated via a daughter, Mumtaz Mahal, and a son, Stefan The Great.

Nashua won 22 of 30 starts for $1,288,585. He won six of eight starts as a juvenile, including the Futurity Stakes, Juvenile Stakes, Grand Union Hotel Stakes and was voted Champion 2YO colt. At three, he won 10 of 12 starts including the Preakness Stakes (in new track record time), Belmont Stakes, Flamingo Stakes, Florida Derby, Wood Memorial Stakes, Arlington Classic, Jockey Club Gold Cup, defeated Swaps in a special match race and was runner-up in the Kentucky Derby.

These efforts gained him the title of Horse of the Year. At four, Nashua won six of 10 starts including the Widener, Grey Lag, Suburban and Monmouth Handicaps and the Jockey Club Gold Cup. He retired to Spendthrift Farm the property of a syndicate and sired Bramalea (Coaching Club American Oaks, Jasmine Stakes, Gazelle Handicap and dam of Roberto), Diplomat Way (Arlington-Washington Futurity, Blue Grass Stakes, Oaklawn Handicap, New Orleans Handicap), Shuvee (Champion Handicap Mare, Jockey Club Gold Cup, Mother Goose Stakes, Coaching Club American Oaks, Frizette Stakes, Acorn Stakes), Marshua (Coaching Club American Oaks, Selima Stakes, Marguerite Stakes), Shuette (Schuylerville Stakes, Liberty Belle Handicap), Bugged (Garden State Stakes), Stevward (Mayflower Stakes), Aqua Vite (Will Rogers Stakes), Nalee (Black-Eyed Susan Stakes, Santa Ynez Stakes), Tona (Alabama Stakes, Vineland Handicap), National, Exclusive Nashua and successful South American-based sire Good Manners.

Mr. Prospector resembled Nashua in phenotype and temperament. When you collect information about individuals in a stallion's ancestry you can appreciate their contribution of strengths and weaknesses in terms of racing class, airflow, soundness and temperament. European buyers were unsure about Mr. Prospector's progeny because they had small feet, suitable for firm ground rather than soft turf. Mr. Prospector inherited very short pasterns, perfect for dirt racing whereas Europeans were more accustomed to horses with longer pasterns.

Count Fleet's male line was not sustained but his name lives on through many of his descendants. He was an influential broodmare sire and his important daughters include Virginia Water (granddam of champion Mill Reef), Juliet's Nurse (dam of Gallant Romeo, Vosburgh Handicap), Run For Nurse (Chicagoan Stakes), Quick Touch (dam of Champion 2YO filly Quill who produced Caucasus and One For All), Sweet Sorrow (granddam of Timeless Moment), Fleet Rings (Hollywood Lassie Stakes and granddam of Crystal Water), Happy Go Fleet (dam of Fleet Nasrullah), Not Afraid (dam of Prince John, the sire of Speak John and broodmare sire of champions Cozzene and Alleged), Fresh As Fresh (dam of Lucky Debonair), and Home Port (third dam of Skywalker).

Skywalker (Relaunch-Bold Captive by Boldnesian) earned $2,226,750. He won the Breeders' Cup Classic and Santa Anita Derby and is linebred to Sainfoin and Sierra. His grandsire In Reality is inbred 3 x 3 to War Relic (by Man o' War). Skywalker's dam inherited speed from her 3 x 3 inbreeding to champion sprinter Polynesian plus another source of Sundridge via Count Fleet's male line.

Skywalker's best son is Bertrando, nine wins $3,185,610, Champion Older Male whose victories include the Woodward Stakes, Pacific Classic, Del Mar Futurity, Norfolk Stakes and a close runner-up in the Breeders' Cup Classic. Bertrando is the sire of Officer, a young stallion with tremendous speed now standing at Gainesway Farm. Officer's pedigree shows duplication of Boldnesian via a daughter and a son, and Nasrullah via two sons and two daughters. In particular, Officer inherits speed from a heavy concentration of Sainfoin and Sierra.

				In Reality
			Relaunch	Foggy Note
		Skywalker		**Boldnesian** (dam by **Polynesian**)
			Bold Captive	mare by Native Dancer by **Polynesian**
	Bertrando			T.V. Lark by son of **Nasrullah**
			Buffalo Lark	Chance Gauge
		Gentle Hands		Third Martini by Hasty Road
			Three Red Bells	by Beau Gar by Count Fleet
Officer				Bold Reasoning by **Boldnesian**
(1999)			Seattle Slew	My Charmer - to a daughter of **Nasrullah**
		Septieme Ciel		Green Dancer (to **Polynesian**)
			Maximova	Baracala by Swaps
	St Helens Shadow			Raise a Native by son of **Polynesian**
			Raise A Man	Delta Sal by Delta Judge
		Little Bar Fly		Ack Ack by Battle Joined
			Splendid Ack Ack	Splendid Spree (dam by **Nasrullah**)

Officer, who stands 16.1 hands high, won six of nine starts for earnings of $804,090. At two he won the Champagne Stakes (defeating Jump Start), the Del Mar Futurity, Best Pal Stakes, Graduation Stakes and was runner-up in the California Cup Juvenile Stakes. At three, he won the Zany Tactics Handicap by six lengths at his only start before injury. He is bred purely to be a sprinter-miler and should sire precocious two-year-olds. Since Officer has clever linebreeding to Polynesian he is certain to suit the lines of Northern Dancer, Nasrullah, Royal Charger and Native Dancer (a mix that would reinforce Sainfoin and Sierra). I happen to like this exciting young stallion.

Paradoxically, many Triple Crown winners in Europe and North America were highly successful broodmare sires but only moderate sires of sires. Triple Crown winners Gay Crusader, Sir Barton, War Admiral, Affirmed, Spectacular Bid and Secretariat were all quite disappointing sires of sires. Count Fleet succeeded with a number of high-class sons, but only for two generations. Bahram sired Persian Gulf, whose branch of Blandford's male line continues via Monsun, a high-class stallion in Germany. Two Triple Crown winners that bucked the trend were Rock Sand and Seattle Slew – paragons in turf history.

Man o' War's male line in North America relies solely on In Reality's male descendants, mainly through Tiznow, Cee's Tizzy, Honour and Glory, Waquoit, Bertrando, Officer and sons of Valid Appeal. Domino's male line mainly relies on sons of Broad Brush.

However, there might be male lines of Domino and Man o' War elsewhere in the world that could start a revival, but if not, it doesn't really matter because the genes of Domino and Man o' War infiltrate the Thoroughbred gene pool via many outstanding mares. Luckily, Mr. Prospector will guarantee Count Fleet's name appears in the ancestry of many future stakes winners.

When oversaturation of Northern Dancer's line occurs we can expect another male line to ascend and take his place – perhaps an entirely different branch of Nearco via Hail To Reason or Seattle Slew, or perhaps a successful male line developed in South America, Australia or Germany.

Who knows, there might even be a revival of the male lines of Hyperion or Dark Ronald?

The preceding chapters highlight the enormous contribution made by a limited number of very special male and female ancestors. Hopefully the reader will appreciate the powerful speed influence of Sainfoin and his sister Sierra (dam of Sundridge), classic speed derived from St. Simon and his sister Angelica, early maturing speed from Domino and his dam, Mannie Gray, and last but by no means least, the significant roles played by elite mares Brown Bess, Quiver, Pocahontas, Pilgrimage, Canterbury Pilgrim, Roquebrune (dam of Rock Sand), Lady Josephine via her daughters Mumtaz Mahal and Lady Juror, La Troienne and Plucky Liege (dam of Sir Galahad III, Bull Dog and Admiral Drake).

Phalaris, and to a lesser extent Hurry On, both high-class sires out of daughters of Sainfoin, relied on successful unions with mares carrying a source of Sundridge. The biochemistry of these influential ancestors was quite different to other strains and it is probable that valuable sex-linked genes were involved.

In any case, these special ancestors transmitted clusters of important genes to many of their descendants enabling them to inherit high-class speed over a mile or more. However, their influence was not necessarily transmitted in a direct line. More often, special genes would zigzag their way through the generations.

Blue Larkspur is a source of speed. From Domino's male line, Blue Larkspur was a son of Black Servant from Blossom Time by North Star III, grandson of Sundridge. One of his best sons was Blue Swords, the colt that chased Count Fleet in the Kentucky Derby and Preakness Stakes. Blue Swords is linebred to Commando and Domino, as well as to Bend Or, and carries in his make-up brilliance inherited from The Tetrarch's sire, Roi Herode, via Lady Comfey.

				Peter Pan by **Commando** by **Domino**
			Black Toney	Belgravia
		Blue Servant		Laveno by **Bend Or**
			Padula	**Padua**
	Blue Larkspur			Sunstar by **Sundridge** (**Sierra**)
			North Star III	Angelic
		Blossom Time		Fairman
			Vaila	Padilla (ex **Padua**)
Blue Swords (1940)				Hastings
			Fair Play	Fairy Gold by **Bend Or**
		Man o' War		Rock Sand by **Sundridge** (**Sierra**)
			Mahubah	Merry Token
	Flaming Swords			Ultimus by **Commando** by **Domino**
			High Time	Noonday by **Domino**
		Exalted		Roi Herode
			Lady Comfey	Snoot

Blue Swords, brother to Blue Haze (ancestress of stakes winners), is the broodmare sire of Hail To Reason, an important ancestor in the pedigree of Fairy King and Europe's leading sire Sadler's Wells. Although Blue Larkspur's male line has faded, his influence still lives on via descendants featured frequently in the pedigrees of major stakes winners.

Relic (War Relic-Bridal Colors by Black Toney) is another ancestor appearing with more frequency in the pedigrees of Group and Graded stakes winners. His dam, Bridal Colors, is bred on a similar cross to Blue Larkspur and acts like a female genetic cousin. Bridal Colors is by Black Toney from Vaila by Fariman from Padilla by Macheath from Padua.

Relic is the broodmare sire of Fortino II, sire of Caro, whose strain is effective through Unbridled's Song and Maria's Mon.

Fortino II is by Grey Sovereign, champion sire of juveniles in England and a sensational source of speed. Grey Sovereign is linebred to Bromus (dam of Phalaris and Hainault) and to Sainfoin and Sierra. In addition, he is linebred to Canterbury Pilgrim via her sons Chaucer and Swynford.

Grey Sovereign (Nasrullah-Kong by Baytown) is three-parts brother to English Derby winner Nimbus (Nearco-Kong by Baytown), but whereas the former was a brilliant "hot tempered" sprinter, Nimbus was a placid stayer. The only difference in their pedigrees is the highly-strung horse Nasrullah, an ancestor linebred to Sainfoin and Sierra. Nimbus does not have Mumtaz Begum in his pedigree, the mare that supplied Sundridge and Sierra in Grey Sovereign's make-up.

Grey Sovereign (1948)	Nasrullah	Nearco	Pharos	Phalaris ex **Bromus** by **Sainfoin**
				Scapa Flow by Chaucer
			Nogara	Havresac II by Rabelais
				Catnip by Spearmint
		Mumtaz Begum	Blenheim	Blandford by **Swynford**
				Malva by Charles O'Malley
			Mumtaz Mahal	The Tetrarch by Roi Herode
				Lady Josephine by Sundridge (**Sierra**)
	Kong	Baytown	Achtoi	Santoi
				Achray
			Princess Herodias	Poor Boy
				Queen Herodias
		Clang	Hainault	**Swynford**
				Bromus by **Sainfoin**
			Vibration	Black Jester
				Radiancy

Baytown, who won the Irish Derby and Irish 2,000 Guineas, represents a combination of speed and stamina. He was a tough, genuine racehorse.

Grey Sovereign won four of eight juvenile starts including the Sandown Rose Stakes, Goodwood Richmond Stakes, First Spring Stakes and was runner-up to champion Big Dipper in Ascot's Coventry Stakes. His successes at three and four include the Festival Stakes, Midland Handicap and Union Stakes. He was runner-up to Hard Sauce in the Challenge Stakes, runner-up to Royal Serenade in the Nunthorpe Stakes and placed second in the Kempton Park 2,000 Guineas Trial Stakes.

Grey Sovereign was England's leading sire of two-year-olds in 1958 and 1961 and second on the Sires' List in 1960. His nervous energy was passed on to some of his sons, especially Fortino II, Raffingora, Sovereign Path and Young Emperor.

Sovereign Path won eight races. His best efforts were to win the Queen Elizabeth II Stakes, The Tetrarch Stakes and Lockinge Stakes. In addition, he was runner-up in the Victoria Cup, Cork & Orrery Stakes, Wokingham Stakes and third to Venture VII in the Sussex Stakes.

His son Sovereign Edition was an outstanding sire in New Zealand.

Grey Sovereign's male line is still active, surviving in Germany via Caro's multiple Group 1 winning son Nebos, and in France via Kaldoun and the Aga Khan's grey horse Zeddaan. This line is renowned for being able to get early maturing runners. Zeddaan is of course the sire of Kalamoun and grandsire of Highest Honor.

In North America, Grey Sovereign's line is progressing well thanks to Caro's champion son Cozzene, sire of Alphabet Soup ($2,990,270 and winner of the Breeders' Cup Classic) and the young stallion Mizzen Mast.

Countess Margit Batthyany bred and raced Caro (Fortino II-Chambord) who is the broodmare sire of Kentucky's influential stallions Maria's Mon and Unbridled's Song. In my opinion, Caro is destined to feature long-term in the pedigrees of Group and Graded stakes winners because he is one of the few stallions that carries Nervesa, a "daughter" of Nogara (dam of champion Nearco). Nogara only produced one filly foal. Every time Caro's strain meets up again with Nearco and Nasrullah it balances genetic input from Nogara via a "son" and a "daughter."

THE GERMAN CONNECTION – NECKAR AND ALCHIMIST

"Conventional wisdom will tell you that the breed is not as sound today as it was 30 years ago, 50 years ago, and 75 years ago. Conventional wisdom is almost never right." - John R. Gaines

Last century, three separate regions of the world established unique bloodlines that no longer survive in England, Ireland, France or North America. These horse-breeding regions are (a) Germany and Eastern Europe, (b) Australia and New Zealand, and (c) South America. In the past 40 years, Japanese breeders established different branches of successful bloodlines that might mingle with European and North American strains, especially Roberto's line via Brian's Time and Halo's line via Sunday Silence. Before both world wars last century, German breeders acquired a considerable number of quality mares and stallions from Britain, Italy and France, and during the two wars acquired a few fillies bred by Federico Tesio.

Why Sir Abe Bailey sold Dark Ronald to Germany will never be understood – he certainly didn't need the money. English Derby winner Ard Patrick (St. Florian-Morganette by Springfield) and his half-brother Galtee More (English Triple Crown winner) were also exported to Germany and four mares established powerful families viz. Festa, Schwarzblaurot, Nella da Gubbio and Aversion. Federico Tesio's Dormello Stud in northern Italy prospered until war hindered Tesio's plans to send mares to Britain and France. During Germany's expansion through Europe, quality horsefeed was expensive and difficult to acquire. So as to cover expenses and maintain his breeding and racing program in Italy, Tesio was forced to sell a few fillies and horses-in-training to German buyers. Among them was Nella da Gubbio, a granddaughter of Catnip who established a stakes-winning family.

Catnip (Spearmint-Sibola) produced a filly named Nera di Bicci (by Tracery) that won eight of 12 starts in Italy under Tesio's supervision, including the Premio Chiusura and Premio del Sempioni. At the time, Tesio was not to know Catnip would become the granddam of two undefeated champions, Niccolo dell'Arca and Nearco. Nera di Bicci's daughter Nella da Gubbio (by Grand Parade), born in 1924, was exported to Germany as a filly out of training. For Tesio, Nera di Bicci produced Nuvolona (1920 filly by Hurry On, dam of Navarro, winner of the Gran Premio d'Italia, Gran Premio di Milano), Nannoccia (1927 filly by Michelangelo, winner of the Italian 1,000 Guineas), and Neroccia (by Harry of Hereford, winner of the Italian Oaks). In Germany, Nella da Gubbio produced Nereide, a 1933 filly by Laland, unbeaten in 10 starts, Champion 3YO filly in Germany, German Oaks, Derby and 1,000 Guineas and dam of Nordlicht (Champion 3YO colt in Germany who won the German Derby and Austrian Derby) and Nuvolari (winner of the Furstenberg Rennen, Grosser Hansa Preis, and a successful sire).

Nella da Gubbio also produced Nereda, a 1939 filly by Tourbillon, three wins and dam of Nadia (by Ticino), second best juvenile filly of her year in Germany, winner of the Herbst Stuten Preis, third in the German 1,000 Guineas; and Nizam (by Ticino), 15 wins including the Grosser Preis von Koln. The 1935 filly by Graf Isolani out of Nella da Gubbio named Nanon produced seven winners including Nixe (by Arjaman). Nixe was an important foundation mare, winner of three races and dam of Naxos (German 1,000 Guineas, Oaks) and Champion 3YO colt Neckar (six wins, German Derby, 2,000 Guineas,

Union-Rennen and Longchamp's Prix de Chantilly). Unfortunately, he injured a tendon at Longchamp and was forced to retire to stud. Neckar was leading sire in Germany five times and leading broodmare sire three times. He is inbred to Aversion via son and daughter.

Nella da Gubbio's daughter Najade (1936 filly by Oleander) produced Niederlander, a colt by Ticino that won 21 races in England and Germany and was Champion 3YO colt and Champion Older Horse. He won the German Derby, Union-Rennen, Grosser Preis von Nordrhein-Westfalen, Grosser Preis von Baden Baden etc., and was runner-up in the German St. Leger.

Neckar (1948)	Ticino	Athanasius	Ferro	Landgraf by Louviers
				Frauenlob
			Athanasie	Laland by Fels (ex **Festa**)
				Athene
		Terka (Ger)	Aditi	**Dark Ronald** by Bay Ronald
				Aversion
			Teufelsrose	Robert Le Diable by Ayrshire
				Rosanna by St. Maclou
	Nixe	Arjaman	Herold	**Dark Ronald** by Bay Ronald
				Hornisse by Ard Patrick
			Aditja	**Fervor** (Galtee More from **Festa**)
				Aversion
		Nanon	Graf Isolani	Graf Ferry by **Fervor** (ex **Festa**)
				Isabella
			Nella da Gubbio	Grand Parade by Orby by **Orme**
				Nera di Bicci by Tracery (to **Orme**)

In Neckar's pedigree, Tracery is by Rock Sand from Topiary by Orme. Neckar is linebred to Dark Ronald and to famous mares Aversion and Festa. Fervor (1906) was by Galtee Moore from Festa by St. Simon from L'Abesse de Jouarre, winner of the English Oaks. Festa was sister to influential English sire Desmond.

Festa produced the following sons:

Faust (by Saraband), winner of the Grosser Preis von Baden-Baden, Furstenberg-Rennen; Festino (by Ayrshire), winner of the Union-Rennen, Grosser Preis von Berlin; Fels (by Hannibal), winner of the German Derby, Henckel-Rennen, Grosser Preis von Berlin, Zukunfts Rennen; and Fervor (by Galtee Moore), winner of the Grosser Preis von Berlin and German St. Leger.

Festa produced 1904 filly Fabula (by Hannibal) who produced Fabella (filly by Spearmint) and Favilla (filly by Nuage), the latter dam of Faustina and Favor.

Galtee More, bred by John Gubbins in Ireland, was a bay colt born in 1892 who won the English Triple Crown (2,000 Guineas, Derby, St. Leger) as well as the Prince of Wales' Stakes, Middle Park Plate and Newmarket Stakes.

Galtee More was a very influential sire in Germany and is linebred to the high-class stallions Stockwell and Thormanby. His sire, Kendal (Bend Or-Windermere by Macaroni), was bred on the same cross as Bona Vista, Laveno and Orvieto.

Galtee More's half-brother Ard Patrick won six races including the English Derby, Prince of Wales' Stakes, Eclipse Stakes and Imperial Produce Plate. Ard Patrick was a son of St. Florian, by St. Simon.

German breeders were unafraid of duplicating high-class racehorses close up in pedigrees and Favor's pedigree indicates the type of mating tried with success (see below). St. Simon is duplicated along with his sister Angelica, and the celebrated mare Festa is duplicated 2 x 3.

Festa is a daughter of L'Abbesse de Jouarre, winner of the English Oaks.

				Bend Or
			Kendal	Windemere by Macaroni
		Galtee More		Springfield
			Morganette	Lady Morgan by Thormanby
	Fervor			**Galopin**
			St. Simon	**St. Angela** by King Tom
		Festa		Trappist by **Hermit**
			L'Abesse de Jouarre	Festive
Favor				**St. Simon**
(1922)			Simonian	Garone by Silvio
		Nuage		Flying Fox by Orme (**Angelica**)
			Nephte	Fanny by Isonomy
	Favilla			Trachenberg
			Hannibal	Zama by **Hermit**
		Fabula		**St. Simon** by **Galopin**
			Festa	L'Abbesse de Jouarre

The alternative sex line in Favor's pedigree zigzags to Flying Fox, winner of the English Triple Crown.

Between the two great wars, Dark Ronald's son Herold was one of the most influential sires in Germany. He won the German Derby and St. Leger in 1920 and the Grosser Preis von Berlin. Herold was extremely fertile and possessed a splendid temperament. He is best remembered as the sire of Alchimist, a truly outstanding racehorse, regarded by some folk as Germany's Horse of the Century.

Alchimist's victories include the German Derby, Union-Rennen, Grosser Preis von Berlin and Grosser Preis von Baden-Baden. He was inbred 3 x 3 to English Derby winner Ard Patrick.

Alchimist was a leading sire until slaughtered by the Russians at the end of the war. His dam, Aversion, comes from the same female line as Honeyway and Run Honey, tracing to Alveole (Crafton-Ste. Alvere by Hermit). Ste. Alvere was a sister to Ste. Mary, dam of English Oaks winner La Sagesse. Alchimist has been able to maintain Dark Ronald's male line whereas Dark Ronald's English-bred son, the great stayer Son-in-Law, was not so fortunate. Beau Pere managed to extend Son-in-Law's branch for two generations before it faded into obscurity.

Alchimist	Herold	Dark Ronald	Bay Ronald	**Hampton** by Lord Clifden
				Black Duchess
			Darkie	Thurio
				Insignia
		Hornisse	**Ard Patrick**	St. Florian by **St. Simon**
				Morganette by Springfield
			Hortensia	Ayrshire by **Hampton**
				Beauharnais
	Aversion	Nuage	Simonian	**St. Simon**
				Garone by Silvio
			Nephte	Flying Fox by Orme (**Angelica**)
				Fanny by Isonomy
		Antwort	**Ard Patrick**	St. Florian by **St. Simon**
				Morganette by Springfield
			Alveole	Crafton by Kisber
				Ste. Alvere by Hermit

Alchimist's male line continues through his son Birkhahn, sire of Literat and thence to his son Surumu. Birkhahn's second dam is a daughter of Phalaris – very important when studying European pedigree patterns. A masculine chestnut, Surumu won the Union-Rennen (defeating Ziethen by four lengths), the German Derby (defeating La Tour) and was runner-up to Wladimir in the Aral-Pokal. Surumu was the leading sire in Germany in 1985. (His dam is a half-sister to Tesco Boy.)

Surumu (1974)	Literat	Birkhahn	Alchimist	Herold
				Aversion
			Bramouse	Capiello by Apelle
				Peregrine by Phalaris
		Lis	Masetto	Olymp by Arjaman
				Mimosa
			Liebeslied	Ticino by Athanasius
				Liebesgottin
	Surama	Reliance II	Tantieme	Deux Pour Cent
				Terka
			Relance III	Relic by War Relic
				Polaire (dam by Papyrus)
		Suncourt	Hyperion	Gainsborough
				Selene by Chaucer
			Inquisition	Dastur by Solario
				Jury by Hurry On

Surumu's third dam Inquisition is inbred to Sierra and Sainfoin. Papyrus is by Tracery by Rock Sand (son of Sainfoin). In Birkhahn's pedigree we find Phalaris whose dam is by Sainfoin. Literat won the

Henckel Rennen (German 2,000 Guineas) and Union Rennen but could only manage fifth in the German Derby.

In Italy, Nera di Bicci's famous half-sister Nogara (Havresac II-Catnip by Spearmint) produced six winners from eight foals for Federico Tesio. Nogara was Italian Champion 3YO filly and won 13 races including the Italian 1,000 Guineas, 2,000 Guineas (against colts) and the Criterium Nazionale.

Nogara's best foal was unbeaten champion Nearco (by Pharos), 14 wins, Grand Criterium, Premio Chiusura, Criterium Nazionale, Gran Premio di Milano, Gran Premio dell'Impero, Italian Derby, Grand Prix de Paris etc. Nearco was the leading sire in England three times – 1947, 1948 and 1949.

Nogara's other foals include Naucide (by Bellini) – winner of the Premio Chiusura, Premio Ambrosiano and a successful sire in Chile; Niccolo dell'Arca (by Coronach) – Champion 2YO and 3YO colt in Italy, 11 wins, Italian 2,000 Guineas, Derby, St. Leger, Gran Criterium, Gran Premio di Milano and a leading sire in Italy; Nakamuro (by Cameronian) – Gran Premio Trivulzio, Premio Principe di Napoli, 2nd Italian Derby; Nicholaus (by Solario) – Premio Verbane; Niccolo d'Arezzo (by Ortello) – stakes-placed winner, 2nd Italian St. Leger; and the only filly Nogara ever produced, Nervesa (by Ortello) – three wins, Italian Oaks, 2nd Italian 1,000 Guineas, 3rd Premio Besana, Premio Emanuele Filiberto.

Nervesa's most important foals were:

Navarra (f. by Orsenigo), dam of Tanavar (William Hill Diamond Handicap), Marvaral (Prix de Saint-Cloud), Ranavalo II (unraced dam of stakes winners Fortino II, eight wins, incl. Prix de l'Abbaye de Longchamp, Prix de Saint-Georges, Prix de Meautry, Prix de Sablonville – Rakosi, won Prix Berteux, Prix du Pont de Flandre – Ravela, Prix de Saint Patrick, dam of stakes winners Mirkash, Riyahi), Netera (granddam of stakes winners) and Raimondo (Prix Sirtan).

Natalina da Murano (f. by Orsenigo), dam of five winners including Pinturischio.

Nerita (f. by Tenerani), dam of stakes winners Nossent (won Premio Federico Tesio) and Nardini (Gran Premio Cita di Napoli).

Nishiyama (f. by Mieuxce), granddam of Oline, won Danish Oaks.

Natura Morta (f. by Alycidon), dam of stakes winner Nigretta (won Premio ANAC, Premio Loreto, Premio Nastro d'Argento, 3rd Premio Pisa).

Fortino II and his brother Raimondo (a successful sire in Australia) were produced from Ranavalo II (by Relic) winner at two of the Prix Capiello and Prix des Villarmains. Fortino's pedigree shows a triple of Italy's leading sire Havresac II, twice via Nogara and another source via Ostana, dam of Orsenigo.

Fortino II is of course the sire of Caro, six wins including the French 2,000 Guineas, Prix d'Ispahan (defeating Crepellana, Stintino, Lorenzaccio), Prix d'Harcourt, Prix Ganay, runner-up to Mill Reef in the Eclipse Stakes and third to Sassafras in the Prix du Jockey Club (French Derby). Of significance, Caro is linebred to a "son" and "daughter" of Nogara.

Nearco's breeder, Federico Tesio, always admired Havresac II even though the stallion was owned by one of his major rivals. Purchased in France as a yearling, Havresac II won 14 races in Italy including the Premio Ambrosiano. He was very highly-strung – full of nervous energy – with a deep chest and plenty of width between the eyes. Havresac II (by Rabelais) led the Italian Sires' List 10 times and became an exceptional broodmare sire. Tesio bred one of his best sons, unbeaten Cavaliere d'Arpino, whose son Bellini sired Tenerani, the father of unbeaten Ribot.

				Vedette
			Galopin	Flying Duchess
		St. Simon		King Tom (ex **Pocahontas**)
			St. Angela	Adeline
	Rabelais			Isonomy
			Satiety	Wiley
		Satirical		Wild Oates
			Chaff	Celerrima by Stockwell (ex **Pocahontas**)
Havresac II				Orme ex **Angelica**
			Flying Fox	Vampire by **Galopin**
		Ajax		Clamart (to **Pocahontas**)
			Amie	Alice by Wellingtonia (* 2 daughters of **Pocahontas**)
	Hors Concours			**Galopin**
			St. Simon	**St. Angela**
		Simona		Doncaster
			Flying Footstep	Atlanta by **Galopin**

				Pharos by Phalaris (ex **Bromus**)
			Nearco	**Nogara** by **Havresac II**
		Nasrullah		Blenheim
			Mumtaz Begum	Mumtaz Mahal (dam by Sundridge)
	Grey Sovereign			Achtoi
			Baytown	Princess Herodias
		Kong		Hainault ex **Bromus** by **Sainfoin**
			Clang	Vibration by Black Jester
Fortino II (1959)				Man o' War (dam by Rock Sand)
			War Relic	Friar's Carse (by Friar Rock)
		Relic		Black Toney
			Bridal Color	Vaila
	Ranavalo III			Oleander
			Orsenigo	Ostana by **Havresac II**
		Navarra		Ortello by Teddy
			Nervesa	**Nogara** by **Havresac II**

The leading stud farm in Germany for more than a hundred years is Gestut Schlenderhan, currently owned by Baroness Karin von Ullmann, the mother of Baron Georg von Ullmann.

Established as far back as 1869, this privately-owned stud farm is responsible for the development of major stallion lines and currently stands Monsun, a representative of Konigsstuhl's male line, descending from Triple Crown winner Bahram (Blandford-Friar's Daughter by Friar Marcus).

Baron Georg von Ullmann races many homebreds and in 2004 his smart colt Shirocco (Monsun-So Sedulous by The Minstrel) won the German Derby and Gran Premio del Jockey Club. The Baron raced resident sires Monsun (Konigsstuhl-Mosella by Surumu) and Group 1 winner Tiger Hill (by Danehill) as well as Amarette, winner of the German Oaks.

Gestut Schlenderhan is near Cologne and among foundation mares purchased from England was Ste. Alvere (by Hermit) who produced Alveole, ancestress of Urban Sea, Galileo, King's Best, Anabaa Blue etc.

Another famous foundation mare imported by Gestut Schlenderhan was a yearling filly by Black Jester named Schwarze Kutte who became granddam of Schwarzgold, a mare who established a classic producing family in Germany. English Derby winner Slip Anchor hails from this family, as does Sagace (Luthier-Seneca by Chaparral). Sagace was co-Champion Older Horse in Europe, eight wins including the Prix de l'Arc de Triomphe, Prix Ganay, Prix d'Ispahan, Prix du Conseil de Paris, etc.

Schwarzgold produced only one filly, Schwarzblaurot by Magnat, who, when matched with leading sire Ticino, produced Scheherezade, winner at two and placed in the German 1,000 Guineas and Oppenheim-Rennen. Scheherezade produced Champion 3YO filly Schonbrunn, six wins in Germany and France, 1st German Oaks and 1,000 Guineas. She is the granddam of multiple stakes winner Steinlen.

Sagace (1980)	Luthier	Klairon	Clarion III	Djebel by Tourbillon
				Columba by Colorado (Phalaris/Chaucer)
			Kalmia	Kantar
				Sweet Lavender by **Swynford**
		Flute Enchantee	Cranach	**Coronach** by Hurry On
				Reine Isaure by **Blandford** by **Swynford**
			Montagnana	**Brantome** by **Blandford**
				Mauretania
	Seneca	Chaparral	Val de Loir	Vieux Manoir by **Brantome** by **Blandford**
				Vali
			Niccolina	Niccolo dell'Arca (ex **Nogara**)
				Light Sentence by **Pharos** (Phalaris/Chaucer)
		Schonbrunn	Pantheon	Borealis by Brumeux
				Palazzo by Dante by Nearco (ex **Nogara**)
			Scheherezade	Ticino
				Schwartzblaurot

Sagace's second dam is by the English-bred Pantheon (1958), a leading sire in Germany for Baroness Gabrielle von Oppenheim who years ago owned Gestut Schlenderhan. Pantheon won seven races including the Grosser Preis von Dusseldorf, Grosser Preis von Westfalen and finished third in the German Derby. He is half-brother to Priamos and traces in female line to Hyperion's third dam Gondolette. In 1969, the stud farm's centenary year, Schlenderhan produced its 14th German Derby winner, the talented colt Don Giovanni, half-brother to Dschinghis Khan.

Dschinghis Khan (the German spelling for Genghis Khan) was a very important stallion at Schlenderhan because he was one of the first racehorses to upgrade speed in progeny of stoutly-bred German mares.

He was a dark brown horse by Irish stallion Tamerlane (Persian Gulf-Eastern Empress by Nearco), winner of the St. James' Palace Stakes, out of Donna Diana (Neckar-Donatella). Dschinghis Khan won 12 of 33 starts and was voted Champion Miler. In Germany his successes include the Henckel-Rennen (German 2,000 Guineas) and Preis des Winterfavoriten. In France, he won the Prix Edmond Blanc and was considered a specialist on soft ground.

At the end of his five-year-old season, Dschinghis Khan was syndicated and retired to Gestut Rottgen between the years 1967-1976. He was an immediate success as a sire of early developing progeny and from his first crop sired German 2,000 Guineas winner Widschi. Within a few years he sired Germany's Triple Crown winner Konigsstuhl and the outstanding German Derby winner Orofino.

Dschinghis Khan led Germany's Sires' List in 1979 and 1981 and became a successful broodmare sire. His daughter Daun won the Grand Prix Prince Rose in Belgium before finishing fifth in the 1985 Japan Cup.

His best son is without doubt Konigsstuhl (born in 1976), whose third dam is Kaiserkrone. A high-class racehorse, Konigsstuhl won 11 races in Germany and Italy including Italy's Triple Crown and the Gran Premio del Jockey Club. His son Monsun, based at Gestut Schlenderhan, keeps Bahram's male line alive. Monsun is linebred 4 x 4 to the full siblings Kaiserkrone and Kaiseradler who are by Nebelwerfer out of Kaiserwurde. He is quite successful with mares from Northern Dancer's line and mares carrying Selene's strain.

Monsun (1990)	Konigsstuhl	Dschingis Khan	Tamerlane	Persian Gulf by Bahram by Blandford
				Eastern Princess by Nearco
			Donna Diana	Neckar
				Donatella (Ger)
		Konigskronung	Tiepoletto	Tornado by Tourbillon
				Scarlet Skies by Blue Skies
			Kronung	Olymp by Arjaman
				Kaiserkrone by Nebelwerfer
	Mosella	Surumu	Literat	Birkhahn by Alchimist
				Lis
			Surama	Reliance II by Tantieme
				Suncourt by **Hyperion**
		Monashia	Authi	Aureole by **Hyperion**
				Virtuous by Above Suspicion
			Monacensia	**Kaiseradler** by Nebelwerfer
				Motette

Monsun's German Derby-winning son Shirocco is out of So Sedulous by The Minstrel and traces to Rosemarin (Mossborough-Rose Petal). This means he is linebred four times to Hyperion (son of Selene) with support from All Moonshine (daughter of Selene) who is three-parts sister to Hyperion.

Gestut Fahrhof stood successful sire Acatenango, a son of Surumu. A bright chestnut stallion, Acatenango retired to stud in 1988. He won 16 of 24 starts two to five years and was a sound horse with nice sloping shoulders and perhaps slightly long in his pasterns. Acatenango was rated second best three-year-old of his generation in Germany. His victories include the Aral-Pokal twice (defeating Abary the first time), German Derby (from Pontiac and Lirung), Grosser Preis von Baden Baden twice, and Grosser Preis von Berlin. In France he won the Grand Prix de Saint-Cloud defeating Saint Estephe and Noble Fighter and in England finished third in the Coronation Cup at Epsom, won by that gallant mare Triptych.

Among Acatenango's best progeny is Borgia, winner of the German Derby, Grosser Preis von Baden-Baden, runner-up in the Breeders' Cup Turf and placed third at Longchamp in the valuable Prix de l'Arc de Triomphe.

Acatenango's son Lando (dam by Sharpen Up) won the German Derby, Milan Gold Cup, Gran Premio di Milano and the Japan Cup etc. Lando is bred on a similar cross to successful sire Selkirk who stands at Lanwades Stud, Newmarket.

				Alchimist
			Birkhahn	Bramouse
		Literat		Masetto
			Lis	Libeslied
	Surumu			Tantieme
			Reliance II	Relance III by Relic
		Surama		**Hyperion**
			Suncourt	Inquisition
Acatenango (1988)				Big Game (ex Myrobella)
			Combat	Commotion by Mieuxce
		Aggressor		Nearco by Pharos
			Phaetonia	Phaetusa by **Hyperion**
	Aggravate			Tetratema by The Tetrarch
			Mr. Jinks	False Piety
		Raven Locks		He
			Gentleman's Relish	Bonne Bouche

Acatenango should make a successful broodmare sire in Europe.

Gestut Fahrhof was initially the home of Lomitas (Niniski-La Colorada by Surumu), Germany's Champion 3YO colt in 1991. When Lomitas began to sire stakes winners in Europe from his first few crops, he attracted the attention of Sheikh Mohammed bin Rashid al-Maktoum who purchased the stallion for Darley's operations. Lomitas is out of a high-class mare, La Colorada, Champion 2YO filly in Germany, as was her dam, La Dorada (by Krozeuge, son of Neckar).

Lomitas won 10 of 19 starts and earned 562,060 pounds. His successes include the Grosser Preis von Baden-Baden, Der Grosse Preis der Berliner Bank, Europa Preis and Gerling Preis. He was runner-up to Temporal in the German Derby and runner-up to Journalism at Hollywood Park in the Shoemaker Handicap.

Magnat (Asterus-Mafalda by Wallenstein-Madam by Sunstar) was a decent sire in Germany at Schlenderhan and carries Sundridge in his ancestry.

Magnat ran 13 times winning six races including the Union-Rennen, German Derby, German 2,000 Guineas and Grosser Preis von Baden-Baden. Among his best fillies was Thila, winner of the German Oaks, German 1,000 Guineas and in France winner of the Prix du Conseil Municipal. Thila, who was voted Champion 3YO filly of Germany in 1957, is out of Thilde, a mare inbred 3 x 3 to Fervor and linebred three times to the dam of Ard Patrick and Galtee More.

Countess Margit Batthyany, owner of Gestut Erlenhof, was a great promoter of German bloodlines. A popular figure in Europe, the Countess stood two Kentucky Derby winners during the 1970's at her French farm, Haras du Bois Roussel.

They were Sword Dancer and Dark Star (conqueror of Native Dancer), who were accompanied by Tapalque. In Germany at Gestut Erlenhof, Countess Batthyany stood three stallions – Orsini, Midnight Sun and Waidwerk. Orsini was a big, imposing horse by Ticino out of Oranien by Nuvolari and won 14 of 26 starts, six of them as a juvenile. He captured the Oppenheim Rennen, Zukunfts-Rennen, German 2,000 Guineas, German Derby, Grande International d'Ostende, Oslo Cup, Stockholm Cup, etc. and was runner-up in the Union Rennen, Prix du Moulin de Longchamp (won by Lilya with Blockhaus third). He finished fifth to Australian champion Sailor's Guide in North America's Washington D.C. International Stakes.

Inbred 3 x 4 to the great stallion Athanasius, Orsini was Horse of the Year in Germany, leading sire five times and twice headed the Broodmare Sires' List.

Caro's son Nebos was Germany's Horse of the Year in 1980. Please note Nebos was the 10th foal of his dam, Nostrana. From 18 starts he won 12 including the Zukunfts-Rennen and progressed to win the Union Rennen (defeating Konigsstuhl by a short head), Grosser Preis von Berlin twice, Preis von Europa, Grosser Preis von Dusseldorf, Grosser Preis von Baden-Baden etc. and was runner-up to Konigsstuhl in the German Derby and Aral-Pokal.

Nebos was a highly-strung horse at two and three and sometimes passed this trait on to his superior progeny. This is not surprising since he descends from Nasrullah's line via Grey Sovereign. He has an interesting pedigree pattern. Nebos is linebred to Nogara via her sons Nearco and Niccolo dell'Arca, and via Nogara's daughter Nervesa. In direct female line he traces to Catnip.

I believe descendants of Nebos (especially his granddaughters) will feature in the pedigrees of future European Group winners and I shall wait patiently for predictable success. Not only is Catnip duplicated four times in Nebos' pedigree but also Sainfoin and his sister Sierra form part of his fascinating genotype.

Nebos (1976)	Caro	Fortino II	Grey Sovereign	Nasrullah by Nearco (ex **Nogara**)
				Kong
			Ranavalo II	Relic (to **Sainfoin**)
				Navarra (g'dam **Nogara**)
		Chambord	Chamossaire	Precipitation by Hurry On (to **Sainfoin**)
				Snowberry
			Life Hill	Solario (dam by Sundridge, to **Sierra**)
				Lady of the Snows
	Nostrana	Botticelli	Blue Peter	**Fairway** by Phalaris (to **Sainfoin**)
				Fancy Free
			Buonamica	Niccolo del'Arca (ex **Nogara**)
				Bernina by **Pharos** (to **Sainfoin**)
		Naxos	Ticino	Athanasius
				Terra by Aditi
			Nixe	Arjaman
				Nanon ex Nella da Gubbio ex **Catnip**

Whether the male line of Blandford's son Bahram will continue to flourish in Germany is the big question. Northern Dancer's line has already penetrated Germany.

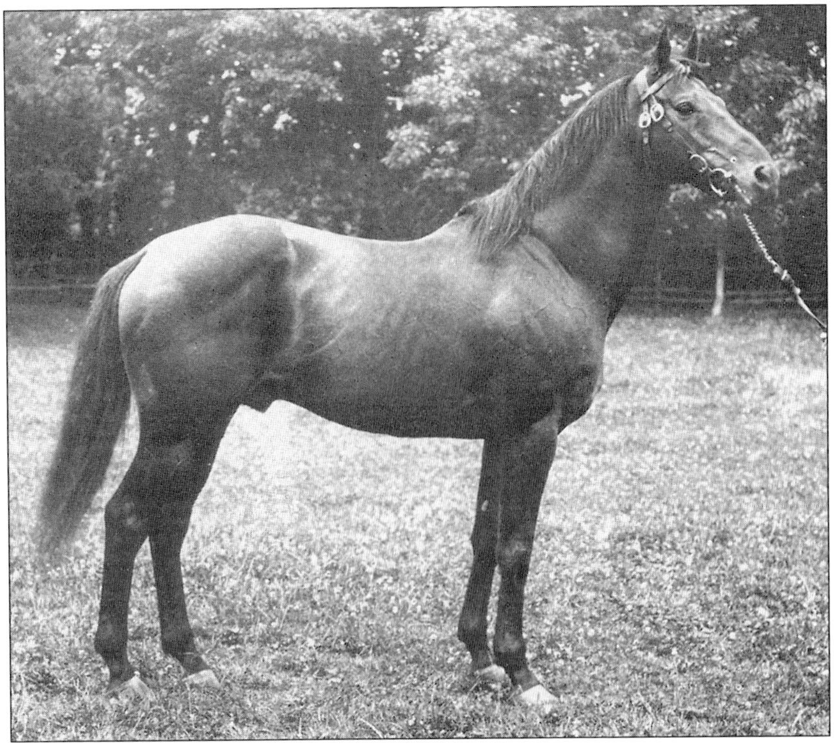

ARD PATRICK, winner of the English Derby in 1902.
He was imported to Germany by Count Lehndorf.

KONIGSSTUHL, Champion 3YO colt and Horse of the Year in Germany.

Northern Dancer's strain is already successful in Germany. Should it dominate in that country during the next decade, I fear Dark Ronald, Alchimist, Konigsstuhl and Neckar lines could be overlooked by local breeders. Even though German-bred mares will carry their influence; it would be a crying shame if breeders fail to support their successful homebred sire material.

Monsun has a chance to become an international sire of sires and revive Blandford's male line. To do this he requires the support of high-class mares from strong families to beget a son to extend the line. Monsun suits mares with the strains of Bayardo, Gainsborough, Hyperion and Teddy. Why?

Maternal strength could be enhanced by linebreeding to the elite mare Black Duchess via her son Bay Ronald (sire of Bayardo). Blandford carries a "daughter" of Black Duchess, while Bay Ronald can reinforce Black Duchess via a "son."

Teddy	Ajax	Flying Fox (inbred to St. Simon and his sister Angelica)
		Amie
	Rondeau	Bay Ronald (son of **Black Duchess**)
		Doremi

Bayardo	Bay Ronald (son of Black **Duchess**)	
	Rosedrop	St. Frusquin by St. Simon
		Rosaline

Blandford	Swynford	St. Simon
		Canterbury Pilgrim
	Blanche (daughter of **Black Duchess**)	

Perhaps Monsun might suit daughters of Selkirk (Sharpen Up-Annie Edge by Nebbiolo) since his genotype features Hyperion's son Rockefella plus Birkhahn.

Nebos is of course the sire of Lebos, winner of the German Derby and linebred 4 x 4 to Ticino via a son and a daughter. In the same year Lebos won his Derby, the Puma Europa Preis was won by Kamiros, a son of Prix de l'Arc de Triomphe winner Star Appeal who is by Appiani (Herbager-Angela Ruccelai by Rockefella) from Sterna (Neckar-Stammesart by Alchimist).

Germany's contribution to the international Thoroughbred gene pool is quite important and should never be overlooked by universal breeders.

German broodmares offer stamina that can be so easily blended with many early-maturing speed strains found in Europe, Australia and the Americas.

Prix de l'Arc de Triomphe winner Urban Sea, English Derby winner Galileo and English 2,000 Guineas winner King's Best confirm the soundness of one of Germany's best female lines. Surely there will be other German lines to succeed on an international basis.

Galileo and King's Best are among the most exciting young sires in Europe at the present time.

NECKAR (Ticino - Nixe by Arjaman), tracing to Catnip's daughter Nera di Bicci. Neckar won the German 2,000 Guineas and Derby.

Countess M. Batthyany's champion NEBOS (by Caro), Horse of the Year in Germany as a four-year-old.

JAPAN, AUSTRALIA, SOUTH AMERICA – NEW MARKETS FOR SIRE PROSPECTS

"Much of the attraction of racing is that to achieve success in any branch is not easy. It requires a great deal of luck, and above all, dedication. In fact, all that anything really worth doing demands." - *John Hislop*

Prize money in England is not keeping pace with the rest of the world and it will be a shame if more British owners race in other countries where purses are so much more lucrative. Japan leads the world with by far the biggest purse structure, even though it still maintains protective restrictions in premier Group races. North America and Australia follow, being more generous regions to attract racehorse owners. Certainly traditional English classics and Pattern races (i.e. Group and Listed stakes races) retain their prestige and are targets for the rich and famous, but surely all owners deserve a chance to redeem training costs.

The horse world awaits the appearance of a dynamic, manipulative, clever, perhaps upstart English person to lead the troops in the right direction and play catch-up with Japan, the United States of America, and Australia. Old school mentality is no longer acceptable in the new century and egos must play second fiddle or else English racing will continue to suffer and gradually decline. The main problem in Britain is the unfortunate lack of unity, foresight and common sense at industry levels. Industry members seem to be frustrated and unwilling to make positive executive decisions. Negative vibes drown innovative thoughts even though measures can be taken to overcome drawbacks. To successfully lobby government officials, Britain needs a true statesman, a leader without any personal agenda, a person to represent a united racing industry – a person with patience, intelligence and charisma to get the job done.

At the present time in Europe there is fierce but healthy competition between John Magnier and partners (Coolmore Stud), Prince Khalid Abdullah (Juddmonte Farms), the Niarchos family, the four Maktoum brothers, the Thompson family (Cheveley Park Stud), the Wildenstein family and the Wertheimer family – hardly much room for the small owner-breeder, one might say!

Yet, on occasions, thank goodness, the small owner-breeder raises a high-class colt or filly to keep European competition interesting, as happened in 2004 when the 19th Earl of Derby raced champion filly Ouija Board. Sadly, there is a trend by small owner-breeders in England and Ireland to bypass flat racing altogether and invest solely in National Hunt runners. Prize money for races in England has not kept pace with other nations and flat racing is in real trouble.

With so many Northern Dancer-line stallions standing at stud in Europe, commercial stallion operators will need to look elsewhere in the world for prospective sire material. Normally these operators would seek outcross or different lines from North America, but more recently operators are seeking sire prospects from South America, Japan and Australasia.

Japanese breeders are about to launch an attack on European and North American racetracks. The signs are evident. Sure, there were a few Japanese-bred horses competing in American Graded stakes and European Group races in the past 10 years, but a much larger raid by Japanese horses is imminent. The people of Japan love to gamble and there are more pedigree enthusiasts in Japan than anywhere else in the world, with the possible exception of Australia.

Japanese breeders are renowned for spending mega-hours researching the ancestries of Thoroughbreds all over the world. They take pride in their homework, remember special inbreeding and linebreeding patterns in the pedigrees of high-class performers and identify members of the strongest stakes-producing families. Before Japan's economy sank, Japanese buyers were active at all major yearling and two-year-old in training sales and big spenders at Tattersalls' and Keeneland's breeding stock sales. They bought into high-class families taking a long-term approach and although buyers were relatively quiet during the past decade, now that the country's economy is on the mend, they will once again seek the best internationally-bred fillies and colts. Oh how history repeats itself!

Recall the years when Eddy Taylor, "Bull" Hancock, William Woodward and others raided Newmarket's sale yards in search of precious fillies and mares to take back to the bluegrass fields of Kentucky or the grasslands of Canada – not to mention the high-class stallion material also purchased from Europe. Japanese buyers are doing exactly the same.

In fact, the leading sire in the world during the past decade was Sunday Silence, based at Shadai Farm in Japan. Sunday Silence led the Sires' List for 10 years. His progeny earnings far outstripped those of Sadler's Wells, Storm Cat, A. P. Indy and Cozzene and he was an extremely prepotent sire. The almost black son of Halo was a phenomenon at stud and his success proves Kentucky's opinion makers can make costly mistakes. You see, there were very few breeders who wanted to help Arthur and Staci Hancock retain Sunday Silence. Arthur is a good salesman – that wasn't the problem. It was Sunday Silence's pedigree. His dam and broodmare sire were called unfashionable, despite the horses' great race record. Arthur couldn't get the horse syndicated and Teruyo Yoshida's family prospered from Kentucky's mistake. Stakes-winning sons and grandsons of Sunday Silence, especially those free of Northern Dancer's strain, are currently on the hitlist of stallion operators around the world. With so many broodmares having Northern Dancer once, twice, three times in their pedigrees, stallions free of Northern Dancer in their make-up will be in demand.

Other lines such as those of Tony Bin (by Kampala) and Brian's Time (by Roberto), both consistent sires of stakes winners in Japan, offer interesting bloodlines. During the next decade, I foresee Japan becoming a target for buyers of non-Northern Dancer stallion prospects. Two other sources will be Australia and South America.

Sunday Silence broke all previous sire records in Japan, eclipsing the statistics of the great Northern Dancer stallion Northern Taste. Sunday Silence and Saint Ballado carry on the excellent work of Halo whose dam, Cosmah (Cosmic Bomb-Almahmoud by Mahmoud), is half-sister to Natalma, dam of Northern Dancer. As anticipated, Almahmoud is destined to play an ever-increasing role in shaping international pedigrees. Sunday Silence was voted North America's Horse of the Year and Champion 3YO colt. He won nine of 14 starts and earned $4,968,554 in a generation of high-class American three-year-olds and possessed the gift of being able to accelerate more than once during a race.

Among Sunday Silence's major triumphs were the Kentucky Derby, Preakness Stakes, Santa Anita Derby, Breeders' Cup Classic, Super Derby and San Felipe Stakes. He missed out becoming a Triple

Crown winner when he was runner-up in the Belmont Stakes. On retirement from racing he went home to Stone Farm. Months later, after failing to syndicate the horse in Kentucky, Arthur and Staci Hancock sold the champion to the Yoshida family who made an offer that was hard to refuse. The son of Halo was then syndicated to stand on the island of Hokkaido.

At stud, Sunday Silence proved his ancestry was world class. He sired more champions in Japan than any sire before him and is proving to be a sire of sires. No doubt he is destined to make an influential broodmare sire because he has covered the best mares Japan has to offer. His granddam Mountain Flower is linebred to Hyperion and to Hyperion's granddam Serenissima (Minoru-Gondolette), she being the dam of Bosworth.

To show how maternal strength has been building up, here is the pedigree of Sunday Silence's granddam who traces to a sister to Beau Pere (Son-in-Law - Cinna), the female line of Brown Bess. Gulf Stream, grandsire of Mountain Flower, was bred by Lord Derby and is inbred to English Oaks winner Canterbury Pilgrim, dam of Chaucer and Swynford. Hillary is inbred to Lord Derby's famous mare Serenissima.

				Gainsborough
			Hyperion	Selene ex **Serenissima**
		Gulf Stream		Fairway by **Phalaris**
			Tide-Way	Drift by Swynford
	Montparnesse (Arg)			Foxhunter by Foxlaw
			Fox Cub	Dorina by La Farina
		Mignon		Barranquero by Verdun
			Mi Pondesa	Pethy
Mountain Flower				**Hyperion** ex Selene ex **Serenissima**
(1964)			Khaled	Éclair
		Hillary		Boswell by Bosworth ex **Serenissima**
			Snow Bunny	La Rose
	Edelweiss			Man o' War (dam by Rock Sand)
			Free France	La France by Sir Gallahad III
		Dowager		Figaro by Colorado by **Phalaris**
			Marcellina	Belle Mere (sister to Beau Pere)

In the pedigree shown above, two ancestors, Fairway and Colorado, are bred on the Phalaris/Chaucer nick. Phalaris brings in Sainfoin. Interestingly, Marcellina, the third dam of Mountain Flower, is linebred to the family of Brown Bess via Polymelus and Belle Mere's dam, Cinna.

When Mountain Flower was matched with the American-bred stallion Understanding it produced Wishing Well, a stakes winner with a triple cross of champion Man o' War, thereby adding more impact from Sainfoin.

Understanding (USA) was by Promised Land (the broodmare sire of champion Spectacular Bid) out of Pretty Ways, a daughter of champion Stymie who is inbred 3 x 3 to champion Man o' War. This union was nothing but sensational!

Stymie (1941)	Equestrian	Equipoise by Pennant Frilette by **Man o' War**
	Sky Watch	On Watch by Colin Sunset Gun by **Man o' War**

Valuable genetic influence was handed down from Domino via Pennant and Colin. Since Understanding is by Promised Land, an extra source of Domino comes via Promised Land's granddam Forever Yours, by Toro, son of The Porter.

Promised Land was by Palestinian by Sun Teddy (Teddy-Sunmelia by Sundridge), thus providing a source of Sainfoin's sister Sierra. Promised Land's dam, Mahmoudess (by Mahmoud), provides another source of Sierra's son Sundridge, an important link with sons of Phalaris.

Mahmoud is out of Mah Mahal by Gainsborough out of Mumtaz Mahal by The Tetrarch out of Lady Josephine by Sundridge. Therefore, Mahmoud supplies a "daughter" of Hyperion's sire, Gainsborough, as well as Sundridge, son of Sierra. When male ancestors are duplicated via both sexes, i.e. son and daughter, it maximizes the chance for similar genes (similar biochemistry) to be deployed on both sides of a foal's chromosomes – thus exploiting superior genes affecting racing class.

In Sunday Silence's pedigree there is an obvious connection between Royal Charger's granddam Mumtaz Begum (Blenheim-Mumtaz Mahal) and her three-parts brother Mahmoud – i.e. Mumtaz Mahal and Blenheim. Supporting Mumtaz Mahal's maternal strength is Selene (dam of Hyperion and Pharamond II) and her dam, Serenissima, as well as the Sainfoin/Sierra mix and duplication of The Tetrarch via a son and a daughter. Promised Land won 21 races $541,707 including the San Juan Capistrano Handicap, Massachusetts Handicap, Roamer Handicap, Pimlico Special and is by Palestinian, winner of 14 races $296,525 including the Brooklyn Handicap, Empire City Handicap, Jersey Stakes and runner-up in the Preakness Stakes.

Sunday Silence	Halo	Hail To Reason	Turn-To by Royal Charger (to Mumtaz Begum) Nothirdchance by Blue Swords
		Cosmah	Cosmic Bomb by Pharamond II (ex **Selene**) Almahmoud by **Mahmoud**
	Wishing Well	Understanding	Promised Land (dam by **Mahmoud**) Pretty Ways by Stymie (inbred to **Man o' War**)
		Mountain Flower	Montparnesse by Gulf Stream by **Hyperion** Edelweiss by Hillary by Khaled by **Hyperion**

Palestinian (1946)	Sun Again	Sun Teddy	Teddy by **Ajax** Sunmelia by Sun Briar by Sundridge
		Hug Again	Stimulus by Ultimus (inbred to Domino) Affection
	Dolly Whisk	Whiskaway	Whisk Broom II by Broomstick Inaugural by Voter
		Dolly Seth	Seth by **Adam** Royal Dolly

Palestinian is linebred to the high-class brothers Ajax and Adam and possesses Sundridge via Sun Briar. Ajax was unbeaten in France. He won the Prix du Jockey Club (French Derby) and Grand Prix de Paris, and was a son of Flying Fox, an English Triple Crown winner. Ajax and his brother Adam each possess eight sources of the elite mare Pocahontas, dam of Stockwell, Rataplan, King Tom and Araucaria. Thus, the genotype of Sunday Silence carries strong maternal influence.

In Australia, despite the growing number of shuttle stallions from Northern Dancer's line and the many stakes-winning sons of Danehill currently at stud, there are high-class Group winners free of Northern Dancer's strain that should appeal to commercial stallion operators in North America and Europe. Already Sunday Silence is making his presence felt in Australia. His granddaughter Hollow Bullet (Tayasu Tsuyoshi-Beat the Bullet by Bite The Bullet) won the VRC Victoria Oaks Gr-1, Wakeful Stakes Gr-2, Tranquil Star Stakes Gr-3 etc., and was runner-up in the 1,000 Guineas Gr-1. She is destined to win more Group races in 2005.

Here is her pedigree showing clever duplication of Promised Land and Buckpasser. Tayasu Tsuyoshi, son of Sunday Silence, is closely related to America's influential stallion Unbridled.

				Hail To Reason by Turn-To
			Halo	Cosmah (ex **Almahmoud**)
		Sunday Silence		Understanding by **Promised Land**
			Wishing Well	Mountain Flower
	Tayasu Tsuyoshi			Fortino II by Grey Sovereign
			Caro	Chambord
		Magaro		**Buckpasser**
			Magic	Aspidistra by Better Self
Hollow Bullet				Bold Bidder by **Bold Ruler**
(2001)			Spectacular Bid	Spectacular by **Promised Land**
		Bite the Bullet		Alydar by Raise a Native
			Lassie's Lady	Lassie Dear by **Buckpasser**
	Beat The Bullet			Rheingold
			Gildoran	Durtal by Lyphard by Northern Dancer
		Gantimpala		Bold Lad (GB) by **Bold Ruler**
			Kampeon	Dolphin Safari by Huntercombe

Australia has a variety of sire lines. The male line of Tourbillon via his champion son Djebel is active through Century's son Rubiton, Australia's Horse of the Year, 10 wins $1,360,330, W.S. Cox Plate, Futurity Stakes, L.K.S. MacKinnon Stakes, Underwood Stakes, Manikato Stakes (all Group 1 events) and sire of more than 310 winners of $28 million to date. Rubiton (Century-Ruby by Seventh Hussar) is the sire of the high-class performers Fields of Omagh, Adam (Aust), Flavour, Rubitano, Monopolize, Rubidium and Millrich.

Rubiton does especially well with mares carrying Nasrullah's strain. His sire, Century (Champion 3YO Sprinter), has an interesting pedigree and was a brilliant racehorse in Australia, winning 11 of 29 starts including the most important Group 1 sprint, the VRC Newmarket Handicap, in new track record time.

Rubiton also won the VRC Sires' Produce Stakes and Lightning Stakes and to date has sired 36 stakes winners. His sire, Century, is linebred to Solario (Gainsborough-Sun Worship by Sundridge), Pharos (Phalaris-Scapa Flow by Chaucer) and classic sire Blandford (Swynford-Blanche by White Eagle). Thus, he carries not only the Sainfoin/Sierra mix but also duplication of Canterbury Pilgrim.

Rubiton (1983)	Century	Better Boy	My Babu	Djebel by Tourbillon
				Perfume II by Badruddin (ex **Mumtaz Mahal**)
			Better So	Mieuxce by Massine
				Soga by **Solario**
		Royal Suite	Rego	Nasrullah (ex daughter of **Mumtaz Mahal**)
				Missy Suntan by son of **Solario**
			Baraganda	Baroda by Bulandshar
				Propaganda by Talking
	Ruby	Seventh Hussar	Queen's Hussar	March Past by Petition by Fair Trial
				Jojo by Vilmorin
			Ann Boleyn	Tudor Minstrel by son of **Hyperion**
				Game of Chance by Big Game by Bahram
		Briar's Toddy	Todman	Star Kingdom by Stardust by **Hyperion**
				Oceana by Columbo
			St. Auriga	Landau (ex Sun Chariot by **Hyperion**)
				Joeletta by St. Magnus (ex **Fair Isle**)

Rubiton comes from a stakes-producing female line, tracing back to Joeletta, a sister to St. Joel (15 wins, MVRC William Reid Stakes). Joeletta produced nine winners including Selvetta, dam of King of the Stars (VRC Carnival Handicap, 2nd The Galaxy Stakes). Readers should note the presence of Fair Isle (Phalaris-Scapa Flow by Chaucer) in the above pedigree. Fair Isle won the English 1,000 Guineas and is the dam of St. Magnus, the sire of Joeletta.

Fair Isle is sister to Pharos and Fairway who both feature in Rubiton's ancestry. In fact, Rubiton possesses many ancestors bred by the 17th Earl of Derby at his famous Woodlands Stud, Newmarket.

Rubiton's son Adam (Aust) has nice sloping shoulders and a strong hip. Standing 16 hands high, Adam (Aust) raced soundly from two to six years, won 12 races and earned $2,033,974. He captured the Stradbroke Handicap Gr-1, George Main Stakes Gr-1 and Theo Marks Quality Stakes Gr-2, was runner-up in the valuable Doomben Ten Thousand Handicap Gr-1 and placed in the Hong Kong Mile Gr-1 at Sha Tin. He stands at High Lane Farm in Victoria. His dam produced 10 winners. Adam is linebred to Hyperion, Lady Juror, Solario, Mumtaz Begum, and Mumtaz Mahal and should suit mares from Northern Dancer's line.

Reenact (Marscay-Role by Gulch-Class Play by Stage Door Johnny) is a young stallion from Star Kingdom's male line standing at Gerry Harvey's Baramul Stud in the Widden Valley. Reenact earned $609,975 and won the QTC Sires' Produce Stakes and Grand Prix Stakes etc.

Here is a successful example of matching Star Kingdom's line with American bloodlines – that of Mr. Prospector, sire of champion Gulch.

SUNDAY SILENCE overpowers Easy Goer in the Preakness Stakes Gr-1.

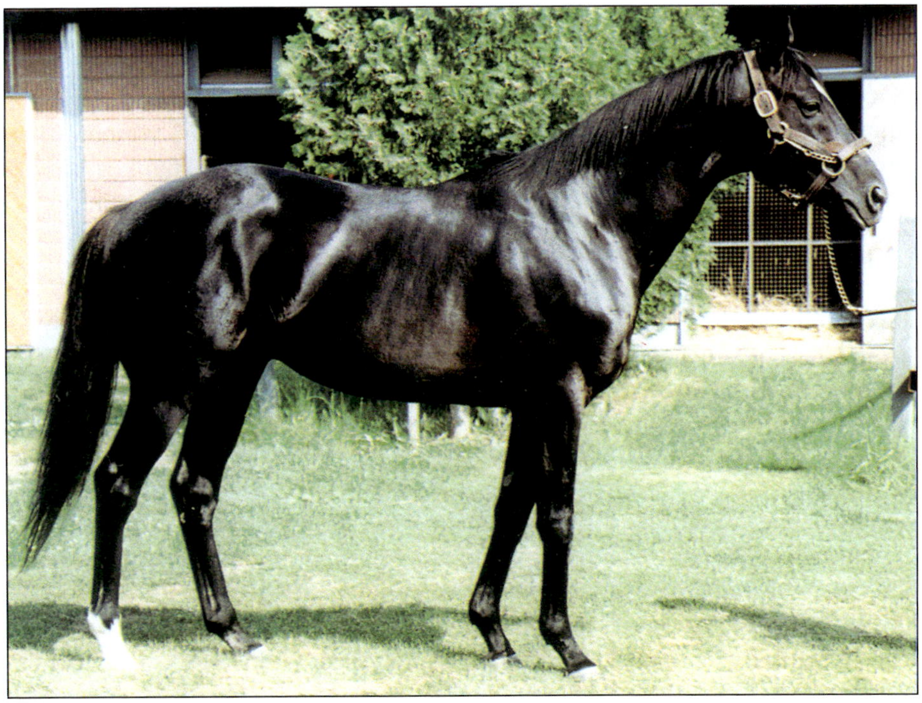

SUNDAY SILENCE, Japan's leading sire and winner of the Breeders' Cup Classic Gr-1 and Kentucky Derby Gr-1.

Reenact is by Marscay (Biscay-Heart of Market by To Market), eight wins including the Golden Slipper Stakes. Marscay sired 66 stakes winners in Australia and is a grandson of Star Kingdom.

Influential sire Zeditave (The Judge-Summoned by Crowned Prince) has been among the leading sires during the past 10 years "down under" and stands at Newhaven Park Stud. This muscular stallion with substance is 16 hands high and descends in male line from the outstanding English juvenile Showdown. Zeditave is free of Northern Dancer's strain. His dam produced 11 winners, five of them Group winners including the brilliant sprinter Alannon, sire of Falvelon.

Zeditave won 14 of 17 starts for $1,313,400 including the Futurity Stakes, Lightning Stakes, Blue Diamond Stakes, and William Reid Stakes (all Group 1 races) and was voted Champion 3YO colt in Australasia. He is the sire of Assertive Lad, Strategic, Sports, Assertive Lass, Zedrich and Magic Albert.

In the past two decades Australian breeders have had access to decent European stallions on a shuttle basis, but to be truthful, only a handful of them really upgraded the progeny of Australian mares. If you take away the very successful shuttle stallions Danehill and Red Ransom, all the others faired well but hardly fulfilled expectations. However, things are changing. Coolmore, Darley and Arrowfield studs are shuttling the very best from Europe, the U.S. and Japan.

Australian breeders now have access to Elusive Quality, Fantastic Light, Hussonet, Falbrav, Galileo, King's Best, Noverre, Giant's Causeway, Orientate, Fusaichi Pegasus, Genuine, Hawk Wing, High Chaparral, Peintre Celebre, Rock of Gibraltar and Johannesburg. Furthermore, New Zealand has Montjeu, a stallion I particularly like who might be destined for fame. Sons of Danehill are extremely popular in Australasia. Arrowfield Stud's young sire Redoute's Choice is "on fire." His son Undoubtedly won the valuable Blue Diamond Stakes Gr-1 for two-year-olds in sensational style, Stratum (whose dam is by Luskin Star) won the $3 million Golden Slipper Stakes Gr-1, and a daughter, Fashions Afield, won the AJC Sires' Produce Stakes Gr-1.

Danzero, a Golden Slipper Stakes winner, is the sire of Australia's Champion 2YO colt Dance Hero, earner of more than Aust$3.2 million and of Danni Martine, a recent Group 1 winner. Encosta de Lago is the sire of Champion 2YO filly Alinghi, winner of the VRC Newmarket Handicap and Blue Diamond Stakes as well as Titanic Jack, earner of $1,207,700. Encosta de Lago stands at Coolmore Stud (Australia).

Australia can boast some of the best performers in the world today.

Many decades ago the leading sire in Japan was Hindostan (Bois Roussel-Sonibai by Solario-Udaipur by Blandford), from Chaucer's male line of St. Simon. Hindostan's granddam was a sister to the successful sire Umidwar, tracing back to Brown Bess, ancestors of Polymelus, Beau Pere and John O' Gaunt. Japanese stallion operators were keen to import English, French or Irish Derby winners as they believe (as did Federico Tesio) these classic winners inherited speed plus stamina.

In South America, one of the most prepotent sires last century was Congreve, a stallion bred in Argentina as long ago as 1924. He was a true champion, winning 12 career victories and crowned Horse of the Year. Among his wins in Argentina were the Gran Premio Carlos Pellegrini, Derby Argentino, 2,000 Guineas, Premio Montevideo etc. Congreve was leading sire in Argentina seven times. His father, Copyright (Tracery-Rectify by William The Third), won the Ascot Gold Vase and descends from the male line of Sainfoin (sire of Rock Sand).

Congreve (Arg) (1924)	Copyright	Tracery	Rock Sand	**Sainfoin** by **Springfield**
				Roquebrune by **St. Simon** by **Galopin**
			Topiary	Orme ex **Angelica** by **Galopin**
				Plaisanterie by Wellingtonia
		Rectify	William The Third	**St. Simon** by **Galopin**
				Gravity by Wisdom
			Simplify	Arklow (Bend Or/Macaroni nick)
				Criosphinx by Rosicrucian
	Per Noi	Perrier	Persimmon	**St. Simon** by **Galopin**
				Perdita by **Hampton**
			Amphora	Amphion
				Sierra by **Springfield**
		My Queen	Batt (GB)	Sheen by **Hampton**
				Vampire by **Galopin**
			Princesa	Esperanza
				Condesa by Earl Clifden

Notes: Linebred 4 x 4 to Sainfoin and his sister Sierra
Linebred to St. Simon and his sister Angelica
Linebred to Galopin via sons and a daughter
Linebred to Hampton via a daughter and a son
Batt is half-brother to English Triple Crown winner Flying Fox.
Ormonde, sire of Orme, is bred on same Bend Or/Macaroni nick as Arklow's dam Lily Agnes.
Perrier's dam, Amphora, is a sister to Sundridge.

This is a remarkable pedigree pattern! No wonder Congreve led the Sires' List for such a long period in Argentina. As expected, he became an influential broodmare sire and a sire of sires. Not surprisingly, he did well with mares carrying Amphora's brother Sundridge. Among stallions standing at stud in South America, I would like to highlight some to indicate the variety of genotypes that survive in that region of the world – including a few male lines already lost in the northern hemisphere.

Egg Toss (Buckpasser-Eggy by Delta Judge-Egg Hunt by Blue Prince)
Good Manners (Nashua-Fun House by The Doge-Recess by Count Fleet)
Cipayo (Alycidon-Tsarina by Tamerlane-Secret Marriage by Owen Tudor), from the male line of Blandford via Blenheim
Tough Critic (Grey Dawn II-In Devotion by Boldnesian-Infatuation by Rosemont)
Salt Marsh (Tom Rolfe-Saline by Sailor-Queen Carloine by Shut Out)
Practicante (Pronto-Extraneza by Penny Post-Epatante by British Empire), from Tourbillon's male line
Pepenador (Lucky Debonair-Ninon II by Never Say Die-My Poppet by My Babu)
Mountdrago (Sheet Anchor-Albara by Tobago-Eritea by Avestruz by Congreve), from Tourbillon's male line
Mat Boy (Matun-Boyera by Pastiche-Braulia by Bonicate), from Teddy's male line
El Serrano (Excell II-Dashing Rock by Dan Kano-Shamrock by Scratch), from Hyperion's male line of Aureole
Babor (Dancing Moss-Bardilla by In The Gloaming-Banderilla by Gulf Stream)

Felicio (Shantung-Fighting Edie by Guersant-Edie Kelly by Bois Roussel)
Waldmeister (Wild Risk-Santa Isabel by Dante-Shamsheeri by Tehran)
Laramie Trail (Swaps-Wildwook by Sir Gaylord-Blue Canoe by Jet Pilot)
Petronisi (Petingo-White Bonnie by Exbury-Snow White by Ballymoss)

Argentina, Brazil and Chile have had access to some of the best bloodlines in the world and so it is not surprising North Americans buy their best stakes performers to race in California where conditions are similar to the home countries.

Cipayo has been a very successful sire in Argentina. A dark brown horse born in 1974, he is by Lacydon from Tsarina by Tamerlane and traces in female line to Alveole, ancestress of Flamingo (English 2,000 Guineas), Honeyway (Champion Stakes), Endless Honey, Messmate, Lord Gayle and the successful German sires Aditi, Arjaman and Alchimist. It is also the female line of Urban Sea, Galileo and King's Best. The third dam of Cipayo is a sister to Honeyway.

Cipayo (Arg) (1974)	Lacydon	Alycidon	Donatello II	Blenheim by **Blandford** by **Swynford**
				Delleana
			Aurora	**Hyperion** by **Gainsborough**
				Rose Red by **Swynford**
		Lackaday	Bobsleigh	**Gainsborough**
				Toboggan
			Lackadaisy	Felstead by Spion Kop by **Spearmint**
				Complacent
	Tsarina	Tamerlane	Persian Gulf	Bahram by **Blandford** by **Swynford**
				Double Life
			Eastern Empress	Nearco by **Pharos**
				Cheveley Lady
		Secret Marriage	Owen Tudor	**Hyperion** by **Gainsborough**
				Mary Tudor by **Pharos**
			Winning Ways	**Fairway**
				Honey Buzzard by Papyrus

Fairway and Pharos are brothers out of Scapa Flow by Chaucer. Hyperion is also out of a daughter of Chaucer. Swynford, sire of Blandford, is half-brother to Chaucer, so there is a fair amount of genetic influence from Canterbury Pilgrim. Other dominant mares duplicated in Cipayo's pedigree are Black Duchess and Serenissima, the latter being dam of Composure, who produced Complacent.

Serenissima (Minoru-Gondolette by Loved One) frequently appears in the pedigrees of Group winners. She is the dam of Selene, Tranquil (English 1,000 Guineas and St. Leger), Bosworth (Ascot Gold Cup), Meditation, Schiavoni, Composure and Siren. Serenissima's dam, Gondolette, produced Great Sport, English Derby winner Sansovino, Piazetta (third dam of English 2,000 Guineas winner Thunderhead II), Ferry (English 1,000 Guineas), Let Fly and Dolabella (dam of Myrobella and Cinderella, granddam of successful New Zealand sire Fair's Fair).

Myrobella, a very smart juvenile, produced Big Game (English 2,000 Guineas) and Snowberry, dam of Chamossaire, winner of the English St. Leger.

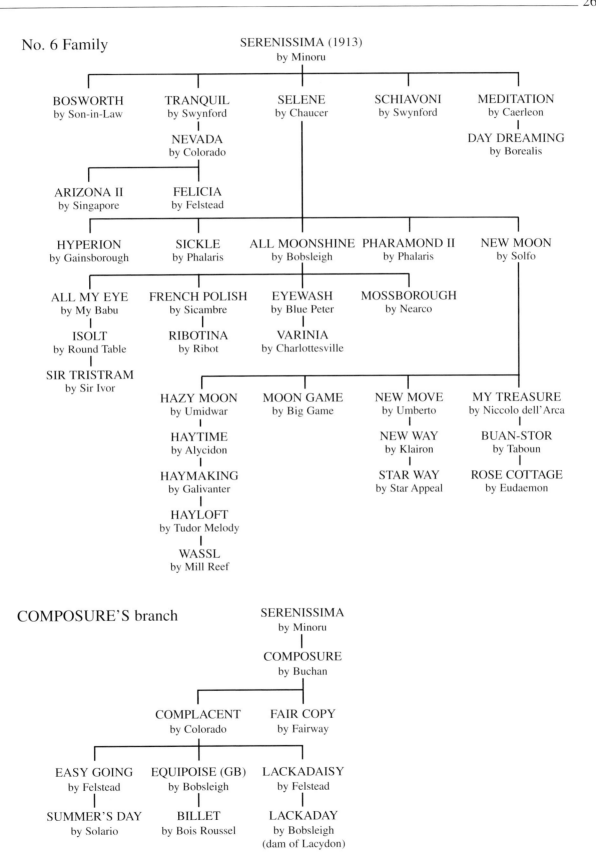

No. 6 Family

- SERENISSIMA (1913) by Minoru
  - BOSWORTH by Son-in-Law
  - TRANQUIL by Swynford
    - NEVADA by Colorado
      - ARIZONA II by Singapore
      - FELICIA by Felstead
  - SELENE by Chaucer
    - HYPERION by Gainsborough
    - SICKLE by Phalaris
    - ALL MOONSHINE by Bobsleigh
      - ALL MY EYE by My Babu
        - ISOLT by Round Table
          - SIR TRISTRAM by Sir Ivor
      - FRENCH POLISH by Sicambre
        - RIBOTINA by Ribot
      - EYEWASH by Blue Peter
        - VARINIA by Charlottesville
      - MOSSBOROUGH by Nearco
    - PHARAMOND II by Phalaris
    - NEW MOON by Solfo
      - HAZY MOON by Umidwar
        - HAYTIME by Alycidon
          - HAYMAKING by Galivanter
            - HAYLOFT by Tudor Melody
              - WASSL by Mill Reef
      - MOON GAME by Big Game
      - NEW MOVE by Umberto
        - NEW WAY by Klairon
          - STAR WAY by Star Appeal
      - MY TREASURE by Niccolo dell'Arca
        - BUAN-STOR by Taboun
          - ROSE COTTAGE by Eudaemon
  - SCHIAVONI by Swynford
  - MEDITATION by Caerleon
    - DAY DREAMING by Borealis

COMPOSURE'S branch

- SERENISSIMA by Minoru
  - COMPOSURE by Buchan
    - COMPLACENT by Colorado
      - EASY GOING by Felstead
        - SUMMER'S DAY by Solario
      - EQUIPOISE (GB) by Bobsleigh
        - BILLET by Bois Roussel
      - LACKADAISY by Felstead
        - LACKADAY by Bobsleigh (dam of Lacydon)
    - FAIR COPY by Fairway

Myrobella is also the third dam of English Derby winner Snow Knight. Myrobella's half-sister Princess Charming (by Phalaris) produced Phalconia, the third dam of successful German sires Pantheon (by Borealis) and Priamos (by Birkhahn).

All Moonshine, three-parts sister to Hyperion, is the dam of Perthenhope (by Nearco) and the third dam of New Zealand's premier sire Sir Tristram, whose son Zabeel is currently among the leading sires in Australasia.

Zabeel (NZ) (1986)	Sir Tristram	Sir Ivor	Sir Gaylord (dam by **Princequillo**)
			Attica by Mr. Trouble by Mahmoud
		Isolt	Round Table by **Princequillo**
			All My Eye by My Babu
	Lady Giselle	Nureyev	Northern Dancer by Nearctic
			Special by Forli
		Valderna	Val de Loir by Vieux Manoir
			Derna by Sunny Boy III

Sir Tristram is inbred to Princequillo and linebred to Lord Derby's famous mare Lavendula II (Pharos-Sweet Lavender by Swynford) via two daughters, viz. Source Sucree (dam of Turn-To) and Perfume II (dam of My Babu). Sir Tristram is also linebred to Selene (dam of Pharamond II and All Moonshine), Mumtaz Mahal and Blandford. Sir Ivor's second dam Athenia is an impeccably bred mare by Pharamond II from Salaminia by Man o' War from champion racemare Alcibiades. It's worth remembering Athenia is three-parts sister to Menow, America's champion racehorse and sire of Tom Fool. South America's influential sire Egg Toss is an excellent broodmare sire. A light-framed brown horse, Egg Toss is one of the few sons of champion Buckpasser to maintain this male line. He stood at Haras La Biznaga and sired many Group winners including Man Toss (1,000 Guineas), Battle Toss (Gran Premio Maipu Gr-1), and Happy Toss as well as Graded stakes winners in California. His dam is linebred to Tracery.

Egg Toss (1977)	Buckpasser	Tom Fool	Menow	Pharamond II (ex **Selene**)
				Alcibiades
			Gaga	Bull Dog by **Teddy**
				Alpoise by Equipoise
		Busanda	War Admiral	Man o' War (dam by Rock Sand)
				Brushup by Sweep
			Businesslike	Blue Larkspur
				La Troienne by **Teddy**
	Eggy	Delta Judge	Traffic Judge	Alibhai by Hyperion (ex **Selene**)
				Traffic Court (to Tracery)
			Beautillion	Noor by Nasrullah by Nearco
				Delta Queen
		Egg Hunt	Blue Prince	Princequillo (dam by Papyrus)
				Blue Denim
			Easterling	Easton (dam by Phalaris)
				French Flower

Babor, a bay stallion born in 1976, was an influential sire in South America who stood at Haras La Quebrada. His victories include the Gran Premio Internacional Carlos Pellegrini Gr-1, one of the most competitive races in the world. Babor also won the Gran Premio Copo de Oro, Gran Premio de Honor (both Group 1 races), Clasico Otono and Clasico Jose P. Ramirez (both Group 2 races).

He is the sire of Larabee (Gran Premio Internacional Carlos Pellegrini, Gran Premio Copa d'Oro, Gran Premio 9 de Julio, Gran Premio Republica Argentina), Octante (Gran Premio J. P. Ramirez), classic winner Offshore, and Foque.

Babor comes from the male line of Ballymoss that no longer exists in Europe. Dancing Moss, the sire of Babor, has as his second dam America's champion racemare Gallorette.

Babor (Arg) (1976)	Dancing Moss	Ballymoss	Mossborough	Nearco by **Pharos**
				All Moonshine (ex **Selene**)
			Indian Call	Singapore
				Flittemere
		Corbette	Native Dancer	Polynesian
				Geisha by Discovery
			Gallorette	Challenger II by **Swynford**
				Gallete by Sir Gallahad III
	Bardilla	In The Gloaming	Crepello	Donatello II by Blenheim
				Crepuscule by Mieuxce
			Sun Cap	Sunny Boy III
				Cappellina
		Banderilla	Gulf Stream	Hyperion (ex **Selene**)
				Tide-Way by **Fairway**
			Banshee	Badruddin (ex Mumtaz Mahal)
				Sissy

Babor is linebred to Selene, Gainsborough, Canterbury Pilgrim (via her sons Swynford and Chaucer) and to two sets of siblings, namely Pharos and Fairway, and Sainfoin and his sister Sierra. Babor's dam has Blandford duplicated via his sons Blenheim and Badruddin.

Challenger II is an interesting horse. He is by Swynford from Sword Play by Great Sport (White Eagle-Gondolette) and Great Sport happens to be a half-brother to Serenissima, dam of Selene who produced Hyperion, Pharamond II and Sickle. White Eagle is of course the broodmare sire of Blandford.

Kaljerry, a grey horse resembling Tourbillon, interests me because his dam, Kaltana, is bred along lines inspired by famous French breeder Marcel Boussac. Kaljerry was a high-class performer in South America and if memory serves me right, was voted Champion Sprinter of his generation. His father, Jerry Honor, sired early maturing stakes winners such as Pretty Boy, Neurologico, Juan Puebloe and Maniatado. Among Kaljerry's best progeny are Kalroll, Kalidoscopio (Gran Premio S. Luro Gr-1), Kalmud (Clasico Club Hipico de Tandril), Kalerre (Clasico R. Aristegui, Clasico Benavides, 2nd Derby Argentino), Kaltrue (Gran Premio Saturnino Unzue Gr-1, Clasico Casares Gr-2), and Kaltia (Clasico Hipodromo de la Plata Gr-2).

Kaljerry	Jerry Honor	Court Martial	Fair Trial	**Fairway** by Phalaris (dam by **Sainfoin**)
				Lady Juror (to Sundridge, ex **Sierra**)
			Instantaneous	Hurry On (dam by **Sainfoin**)
				Picture by **Gainsborough**
		Optimism	Bright News	Stardust by Hyperion by **Gainsborough**
				Inkling
			Emma	Mahmoud by **Blenheim** (and to **Sierra**)
				Pip Emma
	Kaltana	Auriban	Pharis II	**Pharos** by Phalaris (dam by **Sainfoin**)
				Carissima
			Arriba	**Tourbillon**
				Orlanda
		Koulouba	Djebel	**Tourbillon**
				Loika
			Bouillabaisse	**Blenheim** by Blandford
				Becti by Salmon-Trout

Kaljerry belongs to Fair Trial's male line and traces on his female side to Becti, a half-sister to Sind, Seed and Stafaralla (dam of English Derby and St. Leger winner Tehran and of Nebroda, the third dam of multiple stakes winner Majesty's Prince). This is the same family that produced Foolish Pleasure and Eclipse Stakes winner Argur. Jerry Honor is also the sire of Good Time II whose line is still active through his grandson Mogambo (Brz) and via Maniatao.

Another outstanding line is that of Mountdrago (Sheet Anchor-Atbara), winner of the Gran Premio del Jockey Club, Polla de Potrillos and Gran Criterium (all Group 1 events). I believe he still stands stud duty at Haras La Biznaga.

Pretencioso defeated Mountdrago in the Gran Premio Nacional. They were both high-class performers. Pretencioso is by Utopico from Parinas by Great Host. Utopico is by Pronto, a grandson of Tourbillon.

In South America, Bull Dog's male line is trying to survive through Solazo, whereas Hyperion's line continues to do well via Aristophanes and his many sons.

Brazil's Triple Crown winner of 1987 and undefeated Champion 3YO colt is the remarkable horse Itajara (Felicio-Apple Honey by Falkland), winner of the Grande Premio Estado Rio de Janeiro Gr-1 (2,000 Guineas) in race record time, plus the Grande Premio Cruzeiro do Sol (Brazilian Derby) and Grande Premio Jockey Club Brasileiro (St. Leger). Itajara is a masculine bay horse with short cannons. He has a very short rein for such a brilliant performer.

His sire, Felicio, is bred on staying lines, being by Shantung from Fighting Edie by Guersant and traces in female line to Caerlissa, by Phalaris' son Caerleon out of Sister Sarah (the family of Nearctic). Shantung is by French champion juvenile Sicambre by Prince Bio, a male line that has somewhat diminished in France.

Itajara's dam is Brazilian Oaks winner Apple Honey by Falkland, a son of French stayer Right Royal V by Owen Tudor. Itajara's sire, Felicio, showed a glimpse of being high-class when he won the Grand Prix de St. Cloud and Grand Prix Jean Chaudenay carrying the silks of Daniel Wildenstein. In England he was runner-up in the King George VI & Queen Elizabeth Stakes at Ascot. Felicio stood at Haras Sao Jose & Expedictus, as does Itajara, still considered the fastest miler exposed in Brazil.

Blenheim's male line continues through Executioner II, a son of The Axe II (Mahmoud-Blackball, a granddaughter of La Troienne). It will be fascinating and rewarding if any of the surviving male lines of Mahmoud, Tourbillon, Prince Bio, Buckpasser, Gulf Stream, Wild Risk or Court Martial, currently evolving in South America, can resurface in Europe or North America. There is no doubt in my mind high-class stayers are bred in Argentina and Brazil.

Itajara (Brz) (1983)	Felicio	Shantung	Sicambre	Prince Bio by Prince Rose
				Sif by Rialto
			Barley Corn	**Hyperion**
				Schiaparelli by Schiavoni
		Fighting Edie	Guersant	Bubbles by La Farina
				Montagnana by **Brantome**
			Edie Kelly	Bois Roussel by Vatout
				Caerlissa by Caerleon by Phalaris
	Apple Honey	Falkland	Right Royal V	Owen Tudor (**Hyperion/Pharos**)
				Bastia
			Argentina	Nearco by **Pharos** by Phalaris
				Silvery Moon by Solario
		Irish Song	Maki	Formasterus by Asterus
				Canicula by Copyright
			Udaipur (Brz)	Dragon Blanc by **Brantome**
				La Fleche (Brz) by Santarem

In Chile, the leading sire between 2000 and 2004 is Hussonet (Mr. Prospector-Sacahuista by Raja Baba), a stallion with a very high strike rate of stakes winners to starters. John Messara purchased Hussonet for Arrowfield Stud.

I inspected Hussonet shortly after the stallion arrived in Australia and liked him. This dark chestnut stallion seems to be the right type of horse to sire early maturing progeny suitable for Australian conditions. Quite a few years ago I inspected his dam, Sacahuista, in Wayne Lukas' barn at Hollywood Park and admired her physique. She has pronounced forearms and strong hindquarters. Wayne Lukas held a high opinion of the filly and developed her into something special.

Sacahuista was voted U.S. Champion 3YO filly. Her six victories include the Breeders' Cup Distaff, Oak Leaf Stakes, Spinster Stakes (all Grade 1's) as well as the Adirondack Stakes and Schuylerville Stakes. I thought Hussonet resembled Sacahuista's phenotype and inherited her short cannons.

Hussonet is the sire of many champions and Group winners in Chile. Among his progeny are Wild Spirit (Ruffian Handicap Gr-1, Shuvee Handicap Gr-2 in the U.S., Champion 3YO filly in Chile), Penamacor (Horse of the Year in Chile), Host (Horse of the Year in Chile), Printemps (Champion 3YO filly in Chile and Grade 2 winner in the U.S.), Mar De Kara (Champion 2YO and 3YO filly in Chile), Perssonet (Champion 3YO colt in Chile) and National Park (Champion 2YO colt of Chile).

He is half-brother to Ekraar (by Red Ransom), winner of the Gran Premio del Jockey Club, Champagne Stakes, Rose of Lancaster Stakes and runner-up in the Hong Kong Vase and Dubai Sheema Classic.

PEDIGREES OF RECENT GROUP 1 & GRADE 1 WINNERS

"Sweet Catomine's dam is kept at Mill Ridge Farm in Lexington and though her name comes partially from Sweet Life, it could also come from the fact she was foaled on Valentine's Day." - Dan Liebman

When Marty and Pam Wygod's two-year-old filly Sweet Catomine won the 2004 Breeders' Cup Juvenile Stakes so impressively at Lone Star Park, Texas, there were many folk who felt they had seen a truly great juvenile in action. Sweet Catomine is a big, mature filly by Storm Cat out of stakes winner Sweet Life by Kris S., and the first foal of her dam. "Breeding a horse like Sweet Catomine has always been our dream," said Pam Wygod. "Everything we race is a homebred."

Sweet Catomine was Eclipse Award-winning juvenile champion filly in North America. From four lifetime starts she won three and was runner-up in the other. Apart from her stylish Juvenile Stakes victory she captured the Del Mar Debutante Stakes and Oak Leaf Stakes to take her year-end earnings to $799,800.

The thrill of breeding and owning a Grade 1 winner that progresses to be champion of its generation is exciting and rewarding for people who breed to race. Moments like Sweet Catomine's victory are the culmination of years of planning, lots of research before buying foundation breeding stock, and successfully raising equine athletes. Gradually the heartbreaks along the way are overshadowed by success on the racetrack.

The task of breeding a Group or Graded stakes winner is never easy. Even if all the research in the world suggests a certain mating might supply a stakes performer, you still need luck. What appears to be a great match might end in failure because weaker genes suppress those desirable genes you seek. Often repeat matings are required (two or maybe three times) to produce the high-class racehorse indicated from any special pedigree pattern.

In this chapter I highlight pedigrees of some very interesting matings. The pedigrees of champions Ghostzapper and Sweet Catomine are given in an earlier chapter. One of the best two-year-old colts in North America in 2002 was Sky Mesa (Pulpit-Caress by Storm Cat), a bay horse 16.1 hands high who never achieved his potential at three. Undefeated as a juvenile with wins in the Hopeful Stakes and Breeders' Futurity, he was scratched on the morning of the Breeders' Cup Juvenile Stakes won by Vindication. Weighted at 122 on the Experimental Free Handicap, he went on to finish second to Peace Rules in the Haskell Invitational Handicap (with Funny Cide behind) and was placed in the Dwyer Stakes despite twisting a plate halfway through the race.

Sky Mesa has an extraordinary pedigree pattern and is destined to succeed at stud because on both sides of his pedigree he has superior ancestors duplicated. He is inbred (4 x 4) to two daughters of champion Secretariat, with reinforcement of Native Dancer, Raise A Native, Bold Ruler, Princequillo, Round Table and Round Table's sister Monarchy. Sky Mesa traces to Busanda, dam of Buckpasser.

SKY MESA, who stands at Three Chimneys Farm.

CANNY LAD, Champion 2YO colt in Australia from Star Kingdom's male line.

He is out of stakes winner Caress, 13 wins three to five, $666,076, winner of the Poker Stakes, Beaugay Handicap, Athenia Handicap and My Charmer Handicap. Caress is sister to stakes winners Country Cat and Bernstein. The third dam of Sky Mesa is the "elite" mare La Mesa, bred on the successful Princequillo/Nasrullah nick.

La Mesa is by Round Table from Finance by Nasrullah from Busanda by War Admiral and traces directly in female line to La Troienne. Sky Mesa's sire, Pulpit, is linebred to Round Table and his sister Monarchy and stands at Claiborne Farm. Pulpit won four of six starts $728,200 including the Blue Grass Stakes, Fountain of Youth Stakes and finished second in the Florida Derby.

Sky Mesa (2000)	Pulpit	A.P. Indy	Seattle Slew	Bold Reasoning	Boldnesian (dam by **Polynesian**) Reason to Earn
				My Charmer	Poker by **Round Table** by **Princequillo** Fair Charmer
			Weekend Surprise	**Secretariat**	**Bold Ruler** by **Nasrullah** **Somethingroyal** by **Princequillo**
				Lassie Dear	**Raise A Native** by **Native Dancer** Gay Missile by Sir Gaylord
		Preach	Mr. Prospector	**Raise A Native**	**Native Dancer** by **Polynesian** Raise You by Case Ace
				Gold Digger	Nashua by **Nasrullah** Sequence by Count Fleet (to Sundridge)
			Narrate	Honest Pleasure	What A Pleasure by **Bold Ruler** Tularia by Tulyar
				State	Nijinsky II by **Northern Dancer** **Monarchy** by **Princequillo**
	Caress	Storm Cat	Storm Bird	**Northern Dancer**	Nearctic by **Nearco** Natalma by **Native Dancer**
				South Ocean	New Providence by **Bull Page** Shining Sun
			Terlingua	**Secretariat**	**Bold Ruler** by **Nasrullah** **Somethingroyal** by **Princequillo**
				Crimson Saint	Crimson Satan (to Tracery) Bolero Rose by Bolero
		La Affirmed	Affirmed	Exclusive Native	**Raise A Native** by **Native Dancer** Exclusive
				Won't Tell You	Crafty Admiral Scarlet Ribbon (dam by Mahmoud)
			La Mesa	**Round Table**	**Princequillo** **Knight's Daughter**
				Finance	**Nasrullah** (ex Mumtaz Begum) Busanda by War Admiral

Notes: Round Table is a brother to Monarchy.
Poker, Secretariat, La Mesa are bred on the Nasrullah/Princequillo mix.
Nijinsky II and Storm Bird act like genetic cousins.

Sky Mesa's ancestry shows linebreeding to Sainfoin and Sierra, to St. Simon and his sister Angelica, and Nasrullah's "daughter" Glamour helps balance the sons of Nasrullah (i.e. the triple of Bold Ruler plus Nashua). There is a chance Sky Mesa might be prepotent and stamp most of his progeny with his own phenotype. Poker is by Round Table out of Glamour by Nasrullah. (This means Poker is bred the reverse way to Secretariat.) Seattle Slew's dam possesses the sisters Striking and Busher, by War Admiral from Baby League, a daughter of La Troienne and Busanda is, of course, a three-parts sister to Striking and Busher.

Speightstown, winner of the Breeders' Cup Sprint in 2004, has an interesting speed-oriented pedigree. Up to the end of 2004 he had earned $1,258,256.

Once again we see duplication of champion Secretariat via two daughters, but this time the Nasrullah/Princequillo support comes via Chieftain.

Speightstown (1998)	Gone West	Mr. Prospector	Raise A Native	**Native Dancer** by Polynesian
				Raise You
			Gold Digger	Nashua by **Nasrullah**
				Sequence by Count Fleet
		Secrettame	**Secretariat**	**Bold Ruler** by **Nasrullah**
				Somethingroyal by **Princequillo**
			Tamerett	Tim Tam by **Tom Fool**
				Mixed Marriage by Tudor Minstrel
	Silken Cat	Storm Cat	Storm Bird	Northern Dancer (dam by **Native Dancer**)
				South Ocean
			Terlingua	**Secretariat** by **Bold Ruler**
				Crimson Saint
		Silken Doll	Chieftain	**Bold Ruler** by **Nasrullah**
				Pocahontas (dam by **Princequillo**)
			Insilca	Buckpasser by **Tom Fool**
				Copper Canyon

Aaron U. Jones and Marie Jones are the breeders of Speightstown, a chestnut sprinter that also won the Dwyer Stakes, Gotham Stakes, Withers Stakes and was runner-up in the Wood Memorial, Peter Pan and Hutcheson Stakes.

The 2004 Breeders' Cup Filly and Mare Turf Stakes was won by Europe's Champion 3YO filly Ouija Board, owned and bred by the 19th Earl of Derby. Ouija Board was born when her dam, Selection Board, was 19 years old and is the mare's first stakes winner. Here is an instance where persistence was rewarded.

Selection Board went barren in 1990 and 2000, slipped in 1993 and 1994, and before her champion daughter was born produced six winners, two being stakes-placed. Her owner's faith is admirable because Selection Board was a non-winner. However, she is well bred being half-sister to the smart horse Teleprompter, English and Irish Champion Older Male and winner of the Arlington Million, Queen Elizabeth II Stakes and Pacemaker International Stakes etc.

Ouija Board hails from the first crop of the Darley-owned stallion Cape Cross (Green Desert-Park Appeal by Ahonoora), Champion Older Male in England whose wins include the Lockinge Stakes, Celebration Mile and Queen Anne Stakes.

				Northern Dancer by Nearctic
			Danzig	Pas de Nom by Admiral's Voyage
		Green Desert		Sir Ivor by Sir Gaylord by Turn-To
			Foreign Courier	Courtly Dee by Never Bend
	Cape Cross			Lorenzaccio (dam by **The Phoenix**)
			Ahonoora	Helen Nicholls by Martial
		Park Appeal		Balidar (dam by **The Phoenix**)
			Balidaress	Innocence by Sea Hawk II by Herbager
Ouija Board (2001)				Tudor Minstrel (to Lady Juror)
			Tudor Melody	Matelda by Dante
		Welsh Pageant		Court Martial (to Lady Juror)
			Picture Light	Queen of Light (dam by **Donatello II**)
	Selection Board			Tom Fool by Menow
			Silly Season	Double Deal II by son of Solario
		Ouija		Alycidon by **Donatello II**
			Samanda	Gradisca

				Nearco by Pharos
			Nearctic	Lady Angela by **Hyperion**
		Northern Dancer		**Native Dancer** by Polynesian
			Natalma	Almahmoud by Mahmoud
	Sadler's Wells			Hail To Reason by Turn-To
			Bold Reason	**Lalun** by Djeddah (to **Tourbillon**)
		Fairy Bridge		Forli by Aristophanes by **Hyperion**
			Special	Thong by Nantallah by **Nasrullah**
High Chaparral (1999)				Mill Reef by Never Bend (ex **Lalun**)
			Shirley Heights	Hardiemma
		Darshaan		Abdos
			Delsy	Kelty (to Tourzima by **Tourbillon**)
	Kasora			Sharpen Up by Atan by **Native Dancer**
			Kris	Doubly Sure by Reliance II
		Kozana		Hugh Lupus (to **Tourbillon**)
			Koblenza	Kalimara by Norseman

High Chaparral, bred in Ireland by Mr. S. Coughlan, was purchased by the partnership of Sue Magnier and Michael Tabor. High Chaparral is a true stayer that won 10 of 13 starts for the equivalent of $5.3 million including the English Derby, Irish Derby, 2002 Breeders' Cup Turf, and dead-heated again with Johren in the same event in 2003. High Chaparral also won the Racing Post Trophy, Irish Champion Stakes, Royal Whip etc. His pedigree shows linebreeding to the elite mare Lalun (Djeddah-Be Faithful by Bimelech), winner of the Kentucky Oaks, and to Native Dancer, Djebel, Nearco, Nasrullah and Tourbillon.

High Chaparral's second dam Kozana was Co-Champion 3YO filly in France, winner of the Prix de Malleret, runner-up in the Prix de Moulin de Longchamp, and third in the Prix de l'Arc de Triomphe. The third dam Koblenza won the French 1,000 Guineas for the Aga Khan.

				Nearctic ex Lady Angela (Hyperion/Tracery)
			Northern Dancer	Natalma ex Almahmoud
		Danzig		Admiral's Voyage (to War Admiral)
			Pas de Nom	Petitioner by son of Fair Trial (Lady Juror)
	Danehill			Ribot (to Papyrus by Tracery)
			His Majesty	Flower Bowl by Alibhai (Hyperion/Tracery)
		Razyana		Buckpasser (dam by War Admiral)
			Spring Adieu	Natalma ex Almahmoud
Rock of Gibraltar (1999)				Nearctic ex Lady Angela (Hyperion/Tracery)
			Northern Dancer	Natalma ex Almahmoud
		Be My Guest		Tudor Minstrel (ex Sansonet ex Lady Juror)
			What A Treat	Rare Treat by Stymie (x 2 Man o' War)
	Offshore Boom			Bold Ruler by Nasrullah (ex Mumtaz Begum)
			Bold Lad (GB)	Barn Pride by Democratic
		Push A Button		Prince John by Princequillo (dam by Papyrus)
			River Lady	Nile Lily by Roman (dam by Buchan)

Europe's Horse of the Year in 2002 was Rock of Gibraltar, winner of 10 of 13 starts with earnings in excess of 1 million pounds. If one simply looked at the first three generations of his pedigree you'd come to the conclusion that inbreeding to two sons of Northern Dancer was the reason for his success. However, in phenotype, Rock of Gibraltar doesn't resemble Northern Dancer. He is a different type, and I see His Majesty's input coming through. Like many of the successful Danehill tribe he appears to be slightly back at the knee on his nearside, a common trait inherited from Natalma.

Rock of Gibraltar's pedigree, when extended, reveals a complex pattern with many superior ancestors forming his ancestry. His pedigree shows a triple of Natalma and her dam, Almahmoud (by Mahmoud, a three-quarters brother to Nasrullah's dam), duplication of Man o' War (dam by Rock Sand), duplication of Papyrus and his father, Tracery (son of Rock Sand), and duplication of Sundridge via Lady Josephine (dam of Lady Juror and Mumtaz Mahal). Boosting additional speed is Sundridge's English Derby-winning son Sunstar, sire of Buchan (twice winner of the Eclipse Stakes). The female line of Rock of Gibraltar goes back to River Lady, dam of Riverman, a high-class miler and successful sire. Danehill has been successful with mares from Northern Dancer's line, perhaps because it causes a triple of Almahmoud.

Machiavellian is out of the elite mare Coup de Folie, a stakes winner inbred to Almahmoud. Champion 2YO colt in France, Machiavellian was among the leading sires in Europe. His son Street Cry won the valuable Dubai World Cup by more than four lengths. Bred by Sheikh Mohammed bin Rashid al-Maktoum, Street Cry is out of Irish Oaks winner Helen Street by England's Horse of the Year Troy (who is making his mark as a broodmare sire).

Helen Street produced Helsinki, a stakes-placed winning daughter of Machiavellian that produced Europe's Champion 2YO colt Shamardal, winner of the Dewhurst Stakes. Street Cry's pedigree reveals linebreeding to Nasrullah and his three-quarter brother Royal Charger, supported by Mahmoud, thus adding fast fiber muscle from Mumtaz Mahal, plus Fair Trial whose dam, Lady Juror, supplies more Sundridge to the pattern. Obviously the concentration of Sainfoin and Sierra hyped up speed!

Street Cry (1998)	Machiavellian	Mr. Prospector	Raise A Native	**Native Dancer** by Polynesian
				Raise You
			Gold Digger	Nashua by **Nasrullah**
				Sequence by Count Fleet (to Sundridge)
		Coup de Folie	Halo	Hail To Reason by son of **Royal Charger**
				Cosmah ex **Almahmoud**
			Raise The Standard	Hoist the Flag by Tom Rolfe (to **Princequillo**)
				Natalma (**Native Dancer** - **Almahmoud**)
	Helen Street	Troy	Petingo	Petition by **Fair Trial** (dam Lady Juror)
				Alcazar by Alycidon
			La Milo	Hornbeam (dam by **Nasrullah**)
				Pin Prick
		Waterway	Riverman	Never Bend by **Nasrullah**
				River Lady by Prince John by **Princequillo**
			Boulevard	Pall Mall by Palestine by **Fair Trial** (Lady Juror)
				Costa Solar by Worden II by Wild Risk

Australia's Champion 3YO colt at a middle distance in 2002 was Helenus, winner of the Victoria Derby, Rosehill Guineas, Caulfield Guineas (all Group 1 races), Moonee Valley Vase and Bill Stutt Stakes. He is a son of Helissio, Champion 3YO colt in Europe, eight wins including the Prix de l'Arc de Triomphe. The dam of Helenus is by Java Gold, winner of the Travers Stakes and now at stud in Germany. This is the family of classic winner Carrozza. Helenus earned $2,114,680 and recently retired to Heytesbury Stud in Western Australia. He was a sound performer linebred four times to Princequillo and twice to Northern Dancer. Prince Tenderfoot is bred on the same Princequillo/Nasrullah nick as Poker, the broodmare sire of Seattle Slew. Graustark's broodmare sire, Alibhai, is bred on the same Hyperion/Tracery mix as Nearctic's dam, Lady Angela.

Helenus (Aust) (1999)	Helissio	Fairy King	**Northern Dancer**	Nearctic
				Natalma by Native Dancer
			Fairy Bridge	Bold Reason (ex Lalun)
				Special by Forli
		Helice	Slewpy	Seattle Slew (dam by Poker, g'son **Princequillo**)
				Rare Bouquet by Prince John by **Princequillo**
			Hirondelle	Val de l'Orne by Val de Loir
				Hermanville by Cutlass
	Worldwise Elsie	Java Gold	Key to the Mint	Graustark by Ribot
				Key Bridge by **Princequillo**
			Javamine	Nijinsky II by **Northern Dancer**
				Dusky Evening by Tim Tam
		Tender Camilla	Prince Tenderfoot	Blue Prince by **Princequillo**
				La Tendresse by Grey Sovereign
			Camilla Edge	Alcide by Alycidon
				Carrozza by Dante

Here are some high-class performers with interesting pedigree patterns. The first is Islington, six wins $1,553,043 and Champion 3YO filly of England in 2002, winner of the Breeders' Cup Filly & Mare Turf Stakes, Yorkshire Oaks (twice), Nassau Stakes and Musidora Stakes. Alinghi is Australia's Champion Sprinter whose wins include the Newmarket Handicap, 1,000 Guineas and Blue Diamond Stakes (all Group 1's). Declan's Moon was voted U.S. Champion 2YO colt. Good Reward won the Hollywood Derby and has Storm Bird linked with his genetic cousin Nijinsky II.

Islington (1999)	Sadler's Wells	Northern Dancer	Nearctic
			Natalma
		Fairy Bridge	Bold Reason (ex **Lalun**)
			Special
	Hellenic	Darshaan	Shirley Heights (to **Lalun**)
			Delsy by Abdos
		Grecian Sea	Homeric by Ragusa
			Sea Venture by Diatome

Alinghi (Aust) (2001)	Encosta de Lago(Aust)	Fairy King	Northern Dancer
			Fairy Bridge by Bold Reason
		Shoal Creek	Star Way by Star Appeal
			Rolls by Mr. Prospector
	Oceanfast	Monde Bleu	Last Tycoon (dam by **Mill Reef**)
			Make Plans by Go Marching
		Affluent	Shirley Heights by **Mill Reef**
			Marcela by Reform

Declan's Moon (2002)	Malibu Moon	A.P. Indy	Seattle Slew
			Weekend Surprise (x 2 **Somethingroyal**)
		Macoumba	**Mr. Prospector**
			Maximova
	Vee Vee Star	Norquestor	Conquistador Cielo by **Mr. Prospector**
			Linda North
		Fabulous Vee	Somethingfabulous ex **Somethingroyal**
			Ms Vee Vee

Good Reward	Storm Cat	**Storm Bird**	**Northern Dancer**
			South Ocean
		Terlingua	Secretariat
			Crimson Saint
	Heavenly Prize	Seeking The Gold	Mr. Prospector
			Con Game by Buckpasser
		Oh What A Dance	**Nijinsky II** by **Northern Dancer**
			Blitey

Rock Hard Ten (2001)	Kris S.	Roberto	**Hail To Reason** by Turn-To
			Bramalea by **Nashua**
		Sharp Queen	Princequillo
			Bridgework
	Tersa	Mr. Prospector	Raise A Native
			Gold Digger by **Nashua**
		Peacefully	Jacinto
			Morning Calm by **Hail To Reason**

Motivator	Montjeu	Sadler's Wells	Northern Dancer dam by **Native Dancer**
			Fairy Bridge by Bold Reason
		Floripedes	Top Ville by High Top
			Toute Cry
	Out West	Gone West	Mr. Prospector by son of **Native Dancer**
			Secrettame by Secretariat
		Chellingoua	Sharpen Up by Atan by **Native Dancer**
			Uncommitted by Buckpasser

Rock Hard Ten won the Malibu Stakes and Santa Anita Handicap. Motivator won the Racing Post Trophy and has the pedigree of a potential classic runner with his triple of Native Dancer. Motivator was bred by Deerfield Farm in England and is owned by the Royal Ascot Racing Club. Zenno Rob Roy won the valuable Japan Cup and The Tenno Sho etc and was bred by Shiraoi Farm in Japan, also the breeder of Time Paradox who won the Japan Cup Dirt and The Breeders' Gold Cup. Time Paradox comes from the same family as Sakura Laurel.

Zenno Rob Roy (Jpn) (2000)	Sunday Silence	Halo	Hail To Reason by Turn-To
			Cosmah (ex Almahmoud)
		Wishing Well	Understanding by Promised Land
			Mountain Flower
	Roamin Rachel	Mining	Mr. Prospector
			I Pass by Buckpasser
		One Smart Lady	Clever Trick
			Pia's Lady by Pia Star

Time Paradox (Jpn)	Brian's Time	Roberto	Hail To Reason by **Turn-To**
			Bramalea by Nashua
		Kelley's Day	Graustark by Ribot
			Golden Trail by Hasty Road
	Jolie Zaza	Alzao	Lyphard by Northern Dancer
			Lady Rebecca by Sir Ivor (to **Turn-To**)
		Bold Lady	Bold Lad (ex Misty Morn by Princequillo)
			Tredam by High Treason

The champion mare in Australasia is Makybe Diva (Desert King-Tugela by Riverman) who was conceived in Ireland. One of the greatest staying mares ever seen in Australia, with an incredible burst of acceleration at the finish of her races, Makybe Diva won the VRC Melbourne Cup twice, Australian Cup, Sydney Cup, VRC Queen Elizabeth Stakes, The BMW Stakes etc., and may travel overseas either to France for the Prix de l'Arc de Triomphe at Longchamp or race in Japan. She is linebred three times to Northern Dancer (via two sons and a daughter) and her dam, Tugela (USA), is linebred to Nasrullah and Royal Charger. In fact, there is strong concentration of Mumtaz Mahal and Lady Juror in the pedigree pattern.

Bred and owned by Mr. Tony Santic and trained by Lee Freedman, Makybe Diva set a new track record when she won the Australian Cup. The mare's earnings approach Aust$10 million.

Makybe Diva is out of a mare that started twice but did not win. The female lines trace to Noble Fancy (Vaguely Noble-Amerigo's Fancy). At the 2005 Sydney Easter Yearling Sales a half-brother to Makybe Diva brought a record price of $2.5 million and was bought by Bob Ingham, the owner of Woodlands Stud.

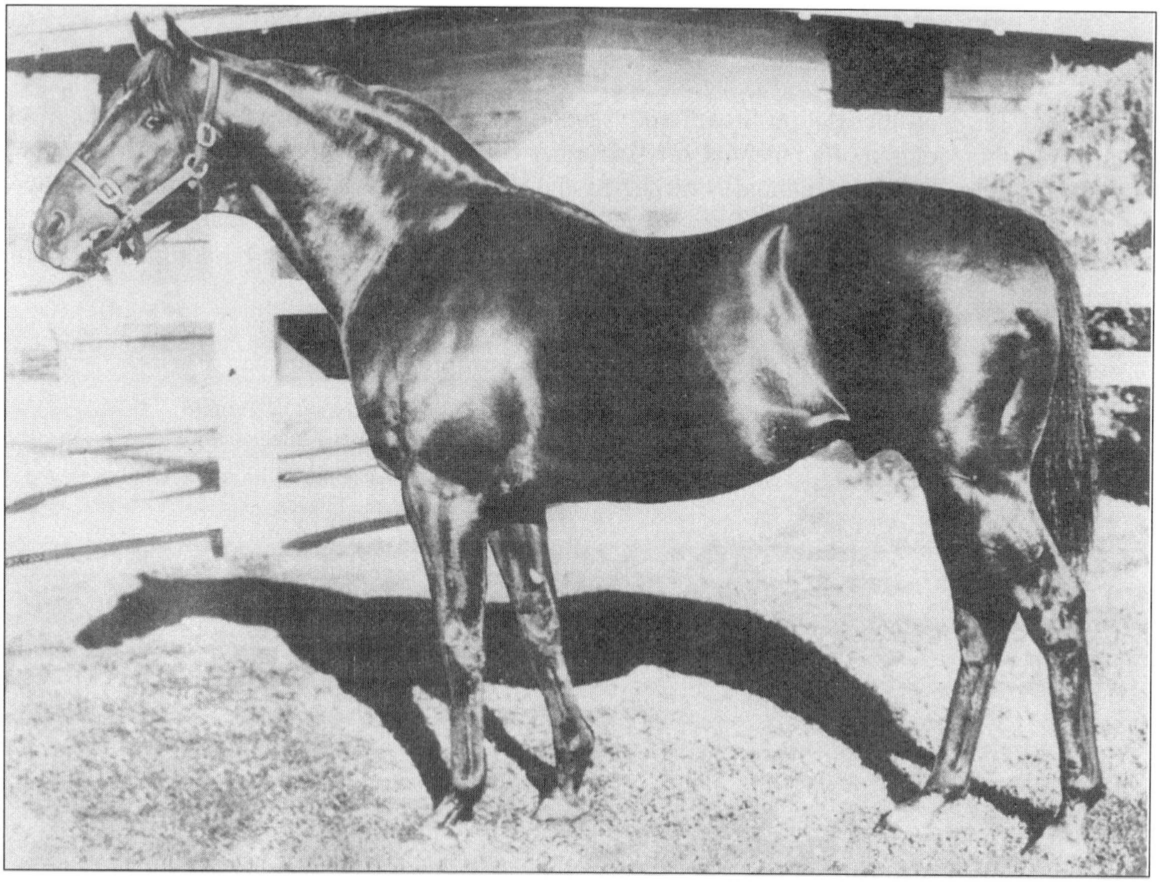

STAR KINGDOM (Stardust - Impromptu by Concerto), who was a phenomenal sire in Australia. He is inbred to Sunstar, son of Sundridge. Star Kingdom is a grandson of Hyperion and traces in direct female line to Canterbury Pilgrim.

Magical Romance (2002)	Barathea	Sadler's Wells	Northern Dancer Fairy Bridge by Bold Reason (ex **Lalun**)
		Brocade	Habitat by Sir Gaylord Canton Silk by Runnymede
	Shouk	Shirley Heights	Mill Reef by Never Bend (ex **Lalun**) Hardiemma by Hardicanute
		Souk	Ahonoora by Lorenzaccio Soumana (ex Faziebad)

Divine Proportions (2002)	Kingmambo	Mr. Prospector	Raise A Native by **Native Dancer** Gold Digger
		Miesque	Nureyev (**Northern Dancer** - **Special**) Pasadoble by Prove Out
	Myth To Reality	Sadler's Wells	**Northern Dancer** Fairy Bridge (**Lalun** & **Special**)
		Millieme	Mill Reef by Never Bend (**Lalun**) Hardiemma

Magical Romance won the Cheveley Park Stakes. She is linebred to Lalun, as is the dam of champion Divine Proportions, winner of the Prix Marcel Boussac, Prix Morny and Prix Robert Papin. Bago, Champion 2YO of Europe, at three won the Prix de l'Arc de Triomphe. Bago and Divine Proportions were both bred by the Niarchos family. Bago's second dam is a sister to Machiavellian. Oratorio won the Prix Jean Luc Legardere and was runner-up to Shamardal in the Dewhurst Stakes. Oratorio is linebred to champion Native Dancer and Nearco, both via daughter and son.

Bago (1999)	Nashwan	Blushing Groom	Red God by Nasrullah Runaway Bride by Wild Risk
		Height of Fashion	Bustino by Busted by Crepello Highclere by Queen's Hussar
	Moonlight's Box	Nureyev	Northern Dancer (to **Almahmoud**) Special by Forli (linebred to Lady Juror)
		Coup de Genie	Mr. Prospector Coup de Folie (x 2 to **Almahmoud**)

Oratorio (2002)	Danehill	Danzig	Northern Dancer (ex **Natalma**) Pas de Nom
		Razyana	His Majesty by Ribot Spring Adieu (ex **Natalma**)
	Mahrah	Vaguely Noble	Vienna by Aureole by Hyperion Noble Lassie by **Nearco**
		Montage	Alydar by Raise A Native Katonka by Minnesota Mac

			Literat by Birkhahn
		Surumu	Surama by Reliance II
	Acatenango		Aggressor II by Combat (to Lady Juror)
		Aggravate	Raven Locks by Mr. Jinks
Sabiango (Ger) (1998)			Golden Eagle by Right Royal V
		Beau's Eagle	Beaufield by Maribeau
	Spirit of Eagles		Big Spruce by Herbager
		Big Spirit	Beautiful Spirit by Bold Bidder

Sabiango won the Charles Whittingham Memorial Handicap, Kentucky Cup Turf Handicap, Oppenheim Union-Rennen etc., and is half-brother to German Champion Older Male Silvano. Fire Wall won the valuable Premio Carlos Pellegrini in Argentina. The game mare Salt Champ won the Santa Monica Handicap, Polla de Potrancas, etc. She was Champion 3YO filly in Argentina. Grand Armee has earned $4 million in Australia with wins in the Doncaster Handicap, Ranvet Stakes, Queen Elizabeth Stakes etc. He is another product of the Storm Bird/Nijinsky II mix.

			Stop The Music by Hail To Reason
		Cure the Blues	Quick Cure by Dr. Fager
	Incurable Optimist		Seattle Slew
		Miss Turlington	Class Play by Stage Door Johnny
Fire Wall (Arg) (2001)			Nureyev (to Lady Juror)
		Rudy's Fantasy	Rainbow's Edge by Crème dela Creme
	Fat Timer		Saint Sever by Lyphard (to Lady Juror)
		Flaminia	Nocera by Good Manners by Nashua

			Vice Regent by Northern Dancer
		Deputy Minister	Mint Copy
	Salt Lake		Queen City Lad by Olden Times
		Take Lady Anne	Lovita H. by Take Away
Salt Champ (Arg) (2000)			Cipayo by Lacydon
		Fotzcarraldo	Stall Only
	Wandel		Cipot by El Centauro
		La Brujula	North Star by Cambremont

			Storm Bird
		Storm Cat	Terlingua by Secretariat
	Hennessy		Hawaii by Utrillo
		Island Kitty	T. C. Kitten by Tom Cat
Grand Armee (Aust) (1998)			Sir Tristram
		Marauding	Biscalowe by Biscay
	Tambour		Whiskey Road by **Nijinsky II**
		Voltage	Electric Belle

Lohnro (Aust) (1998)	Octagonal	Zabeel	Sir Tristram (inbred to Princequillo) Lady Giselle by Nureyev (dam by **Forli**)
		Eight Carat	Pieces of Eight by Relic Klairessa (to Tessa Gillian)
	Shadea	Straight Strike	Mr. Prospector Bend Not by Never Bend by Nasrullah
		Concia	First Consul by **Forli** My Tricia by Hermes

Elvstroem (Aust) (2000)	Danehill	Danzig	Northern Dancer (ex **Natalma**) Pas de Nom by Admiral's Voyage
		Razyana	His Majesty by Ribot Spring Adieu (ex **Natalma**)
	Olympic Aim	Marscay	Biscay by Star Kingdom Heart of Market by To Market
		Gold Vink	Gold Sovereign by Grey Sovereign Goudvink by Dogger Bank

Lohnro (linebred to Forli) was Australia's Horse of the Year in 2003-2004 with 26 wins and $5,790,510. Elvstroem is an outstanding racehorse. His wins include the Caulfield Cup, Victoria Derby and Autumn Classic. Elvstroem has earned more than $5 million and ranks as one of the best weight-for-age horses in Australia. He showed his talent by winning the valuable Dubai Duty Free Stakes. Tarlow won the Santa Margarita Invitational Handicap and La Canada Stakes. Wild Iris has earned $574,460 and is the winner of the Australian Oaks and Adrian Knox Stakes.

Tarlow (2001)	Stormin Fever	Storm Cat	Storm Bird by Northern Dancer Terlingua by Secretariat
		Penant Fever	Seattle Slew Letty's Pennant
	Madame Bear	Dreadnought	Lt. Stevens (ex Rough Shod II) Misty Memory by Court Martial
		Sister Bear	For The Moment by What A Pleasure Roses of Love by Dancer's Image

Wild Iris (Aust) (2000)	Spectrum	Rainbow Quest	Blushing Groom by son of **Nasrullah** I Will Follow by Herbager
		River Dancer	Irish River by Riverman Dancing Shadow by Dancer's Image
	Wild Violet	Archregent	Vice Regent Respond by Canadian Champ
		Fiancee	Baguette by Rego by **Nasrullah** Attentive by Wilkes by Court Martial

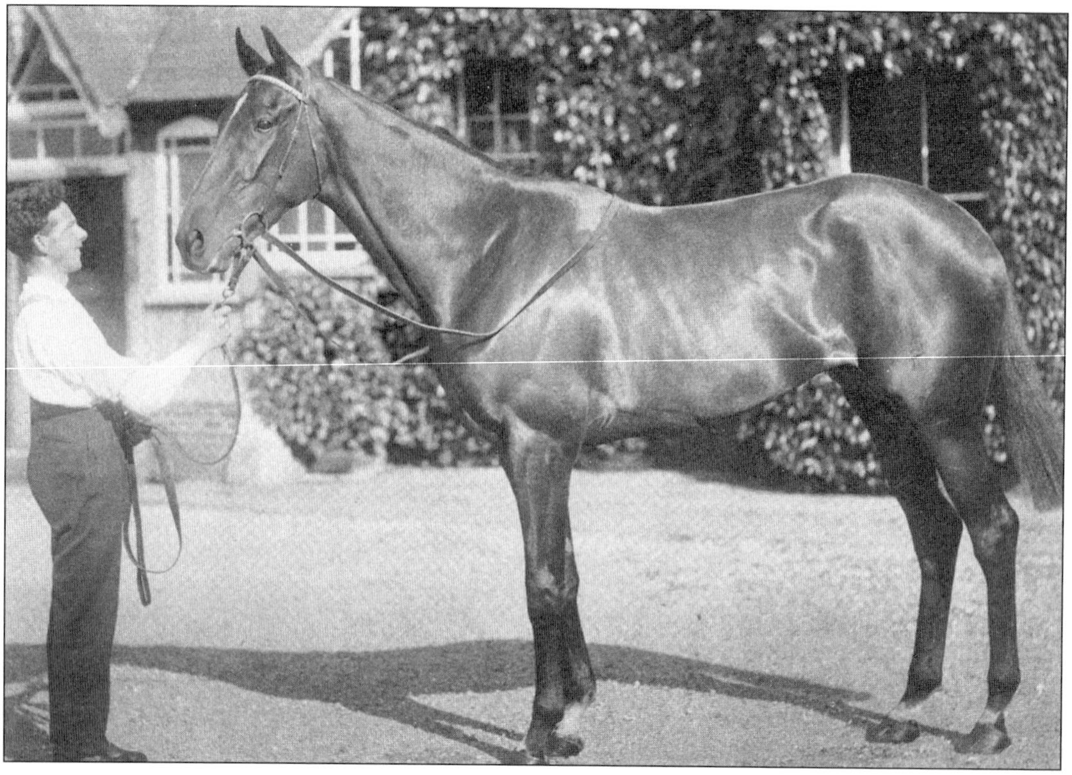

LADY JOSEPHINE, by Sundridge, dam of Lady Juror and Mumtaz Mahal.

TUDOR MINSTREL, Champion 2YO colt in England, winner of the English 2,000 Guineas. He is by Owen Tudor out of Sansonnet by Sansovino out of Lady Juror.

Admire Groove (2000)	Sunday Silence	Halo	Hail To Reason by Turn-To
			Cosmah (ex **Almahmoud**)
		Wishing Well	Understanding by Promised Land
			Mountain Flower
	Air Groove	Tony Bin	Kampala by Kalamoun
			Severn Bridge by Hornbeam
		Dyna Carle	Northern Taste by Northern Dancer (**A**)
			Shadai Feather by Guersant

Wilko (2002)	Awesome Again	Deputy Minister	Vice Regent
			Mint Copy
		Primal Force	Blushing Groom
			Prime Prospect by Mr. Prospector
	Native Roots	Indian Ridge	Ahonoora by Lorenzaccio
			Hillbrow by Swing Easy
		Phazania	Tap On Wood by Sallust
			Contrail by Roan Rocket

Admire Groove won the Queen Elizabeth II Commemorative Cup in Japan. He is linebred to the elite mare Almahmoud. Wilko won the Breeders' Cup Juvenile Stakes. He was co-highweight with Declan's Moon on North America's Experimental Free Handicap. Singletary won the Breeders' Cup Mile, defeating Antonius Pius and Six Perfections. Pleasantly Perfect won the Breeders' Cup Classic, Dubai World Cup, Pacific Classic Stakes and has earned more than $7.5 million. He was bred by Clovelly Farms and trained by Richard Mandella for Diamond A Racing Corporation.

Singletary (2000)	Sultry Song	Cox's Ridge	Best Turn by Turn-To by **Royal Charger**
			Our Martha
		Sultry Sun	Buckfinder by Buckpasser
			Sunny Dame by Damascus
	Joiski's Star	Star de Naskra	Naskra by Nasram by **Nasrullah**
			Candle Star
		Joi'Ski	Key to the Mint by Graustark
			Tatalah (dam by **Nasrullah**)

Pleasantly Perfect (1998)	Pleasant Colony	His Majesty	Ribot by Tenerani
			Flower Bowl by Alibhai
		Sun Colony	Sunrise Flight (ex Misty Morn)
			Colonia by Cockrullah
	Regal State	Affirmed	Exclusive Native by Raise A Native
			Won't Tell You by Crafty Admiral
		La Trinite	Lyphard by Northern Dancer
			Promessa by Darius II

Sharp Lisa (2002)	Dixieland Band	Northern Dancer	Nearctic by Nearco
			Natalma by Native Dancer
		Mississippi Mud	Delta Judge by Traffic Judge by **Alibhai**
			Sand Buggy by Warfare (gs of **Alibhai**)
	Winter's Gone	Dynaformer	Roberto by Hail To Reason
			Andover Way by **His Majesty** (**Alibhai**)
		Stark Winter	**Graustark** (dam by **Alibhai**)
			Winter Wren by Princequillo

Mr. Light (Arg) & Miss Loren (Arg)	Numerous	Mr. Prospector	Raise A Native by Native Dancer
			Gold Digger by **Nashua**
		Number	Nijinsky II by Northern Dancer
			Special by **Forli** by **Aristophanes**
	Luminare	Forlitano	Good Manners by **Nashua**
			Forlita (ex **Trevisana** by **Aristophanes**)
		Luminaria	Pepenador by Lucky Debonair
			Luna Araucaria by Seleno

Sharp Lisa (linebred six times to Tracery, four times to Alibhai) won the Las Virgenes Stakes. Her dam is inbred to the brothers His Majesty and Graustark. Champion Mare in Argentina, Miss Loren is a sister to Mr. Light who set a new world record for a mile in 1:31.41. They are inbred (4 x 4) to brother and sister Forli and Trevisana. The brilliant colt Undoubtedly won the valuable Blue Diamond Stakes in Australia. For Gainsborough Stud, the author designed the pedigree of Zafeen, winner of the St. James' Palace Stakes, Mill Reef Stakes, and 2nd English 2,000 Guineas.

Undoubtedly (2002)	Redoute's Choice	Danehill	Danzig by Northern Dancer (to **A**)
			Razyana (to **Almahmoud**)
		Samantha's Choice	Canny Lad by Bletchingly
			Dancing Show by Nijinsky II (to **A**)
	Kiss A Halo	Don't Say Halo	Halo (g'dam **Almahmoud**)
			Never Babble by Never Bend
		Matihi Bay	Manihi by Matrice
			Grey Hostess by Coeur Volant

Zafeen (2000)	Zafonic	Gone West	Mr. Prospector
			Secrettame by Secretariat
		Zaizafon	The Minstrel by Northern Dancer
			Mofida by Right Tack
	Shy Lady	Kaldoun	Caro by Fortino II
			Katana by Le Haar
		Shy Danseuse	Groom Dancer by Blushing Groom
			Shy Princess by Irish River

Haafhd	Alhaarth	Unfuwain	Northern Dancer by Nearctic
			Height of Fashion by Bustino
		Irish Valley	Irish River by Riverman by Never Bend
			Green Valley by Val de Loir
	Al Bahathri	Blushing Groom	Red God by Nasrullah
			Runaway Bride by Wild Risk
		Chain Store	Noholme II by Star Kingdom
			General Store by To Market

Smarty Jones (2001)	Elusive Quality	Gone West	Mr. Prospector
			Secrettame by Secretariat
		Touch of Greatness	Hero's Honor (dam by Graustark)
			Ivory Wand by Sir Ivor
	I'll Get Along	Smile	In Reality by Intentionally
			Sunny Smile by Boldnesian
		Don't Worry Bout Me	Foolish Pleasure by What A Pleasure
			Stolen Base by Herbager

Silent Witness (1999)	El Moxie	Conquistador Cielo	Mr. Prospector (g'son **Native Dancer**)
			K D Princess
		Raise the Standard	Hoist the Flag
			Natalma by **Native Dancer**
	Jade Tiara	Bureaucracy	Lord Ballina by Bletchingly
			Tulla Doll by Oncidium
		Jade Amanda	Grosvenor by Sir Tristram by Sir Ivor
			Comptroller

Haafhd, bred by Sheikh Hamdan bin Rashid al-Maktoum won the English 2,000 Guineas and Champion Stakes. He is an example of the successful cross of Northern Dancer with Blushing Groom and Star Kingdom (duplicating Hyperion, Tracery, Sainfoin and Sierra).

Smarty Jones, who stands at Three Chimneys Farm, was North America's Champion 3YO colt in 2004. He won the Kentucky Derby, Preakness Stakes etc., and is linebred to Polynesian and Bold Ruler. He traces to La Troienne. Silent Witness is Hong Kong's unbeaten Champion Sprinter – perhaps the fastest short-course sprinter in the world. He is by El Moxie, a useful son of Natalma's daughter Raise The Standard, and therefore related to Machiavellian, Danehill and Northern Dancer.

Choisir (Danehill Dancer-Great Selection by Lunchtime), winner of the Newmarket Handicap Group 1 in Australia, was sent to England where he defeated the best English sprinters at Royal Ascot. British racing journalists were surprised at Choisir's two sprint victories in the same week (Golden Jubilee Stakes Group 1 and King's Stand Stakes Group 2) but had they studied Choisir's times in Australia, they should have been pre-warned. Choisir won seven of 23 starts for almost $2 million in earnings and shuttles for Coolmore Stud.

Australia is now a major source of high-class sprinter-milers in the world.

Queen's Logic (1999)	Grand Lodge	Chief's Crown	Danzig by Northern Dancer
			Six Crowns by Secretariat (**Somethingroyal**)
		La Papagena	Habitat by Sir Gaylord (ex **Somethingroyal**)
			Magic Flute by Tudor Melody
	Lagrion	Diesis	Sharpen Up by Atan by Native Dancer
			Doubly Sure by Reliance II
		Wrap It Up	Mount Hagen by Bold Bidder
			Doc Nan by Francis S.

Monarchos (1998)	Maria's Mon	Wavering Monarch	Majestic Light (dam by **Ribot**)
			Uncommitted by Buckpasser
		Carlotta Maria	Caro by Fortino II
			Water Mallone by Naskra
	Regal Band	Dixieland Band	Northern Dancer
			Mississippi Mud by Delta Judge
		Royal Roberta	Roberto by Hail To Reason
			Regal Road by Graustark by **Ribot**

Boreal (Ger) (1998)	Java Gold	Key To The Mint	Graustark by Ribot
			Key Bridge by Princequillo
		Javamine	Nijinsky II by Northern Dancer
			Dusky Evening by Tim Tam
	Britannia	Tarim	Tudor Melody by son of **Owen Tudor**
			Tamerelle by Tamerlane
		Bonna	Salvo by Right Royal V by **Owen Tudor**
			Birgit by Altrek

Queen's Logic was Champion 2YO filly in Europe for Mr. Jaber Abdullah. She was unbeaten at two. Her victories include the Cheveley Park Stakes, Lowther Stakes and Queen Mary Stakes.

Monarchos won the Kentucky Derby and Florida Derby and stands at Claiborne Farm. He is linebred to champion Ribot, Alibhai, the gray mare Boudoir II (by Mahmoud) and possesses concentrations of Tracery.

Coronation Cup and German Derby winner Boreal (by Java Gold) is out of a mare inbred to English Derby winner Owen Tudor (Hyperion-Mary Tudor by Pharos). Boreal (Ger.) is linebred to Pharos, Nearco, Hyperion and Selene. His dam, Britannia, won the German St. Leger, Deutscher Stutenpreis and was runner-up in the German Oaks. She produced another German Derby winner, Borgia (by Acatenango). Java Gold won the Travers Stakes and his champion father is linebred to Tracery.

Two high-class racehorses linebred to Wild Risk are Noverre (Rahy out of Danseur Fabuleux by Northern Dancer out of Fabuleux Jane by Le Fabuleux, son of Wild Risk) who won the Sussex Stakes, Champagne Stakes etc., and earned 974,350 pounds for Sheikh Mohammed bin Rashid al-Maktoum; and Pin Oak Stud's homebred stallion Broken Vow (Unbridled-Wedding Vow by Nijinsky II-Wedding Picture by Blushing Groom).

CONCLUSION – REINFORCE GREAT ANCESTORS

"The basic problem in Europe was that the level of prize money was too low, and rising too slowly to encourage wider ownership of Thoroughbreds. The only surefire way to make money out of a yearling colt was to have him develop into a high-class racehorse who could be sold for stud duty, and realistically, the odds against that were remote."

- Tony Morris (Thoroughbred Stallions)

Can pedigree research benefit the horse breeder if soundness and temperament are considered when designing racehorse matings? I believe it can, otherwise I would not have spent a lifetime trying to follow genetic traits from generation to generation.

Pedigrees supply detailed information. An individual's pedigree is a reflection of its ancestry, providing information about performance, racing class, courage and even indicates a distance range. Each ancestor possesses individual characteristics and different degrees of racing class. Whereas some ancestors are dominant and breed reasonably true to their specific phenotype, most Thoroughbred ancestors inherit and express recessive genes (hidden characteristics) hitherto unknown in their families.

When I began to write *Designing Speed in the Racehorse*, my aim was to make young people more aware of the genetic background of today's major stakes winners – important ancestors who transmitted speed, especially Sainfoin and his sister Sierra and the famous mare Pocahontas.

Stakes performers need to be bred from high-class bloodlines, be raised properly, educated with patience and skill, and well trained to reach their potential. Last but not least, they require to be ridden by experienced jockeys. Stakes performers require a suitable temperament for competitive racing and conserve energy wisely. Quite often we read about accidents and injuries serious enough to jeopardize or terminate a potentially smart horse's racing career. There are young stallions standing at stud that showed amazing speed before their career was cut short by accident rather than unsoundness. Danzig is a typical example.

I have tried to be impartial with research. While subjective opinion weaves its way through the text, I make no apology because we are all entitled to form opinions. I simply wanted to share information and knowledge collected over time. Unfortunately, there are no golden rules that can be applied in the Thoroughbred breeding business.

Breeding the racehorse remains an inexact science.

There are no experts who can predict the future athletic ability of a young foal or unbroken yearling. On occasion an outstanding weanling might indicate it will be something special on the racetrack, and although an assessment is based on gut feeling and intuition, it still remains a calculated guess. Even in-depth analysis of a yearling's DNA does not enable anyone to make accurate predictions about its potential racetrack ability; and in any case, if this were really possible, it would rob the breeding and racing industry of mystery, magic, hope and wishful thinking.

Can DNA analysis of a yearling accurately tell whether it inherits motivation (the will-to-win), suitable temperament, high-class speed and sufficient energy to develop into a stakes performer? Can DNA analysis of any of our young children accurately assess whether one of them might be capable of developing into a top athlete, superior enough to compete at the Olympic Games? I don't believe anyone can tell us at the present time. So what can we do to maximize the chance to breed a stakes winner? The first requirement is to own broodmares from successful female lines – stakes-producing families. Mares from below-average female lines or with poor fertility should be culled and replaced with above average fillies.

Ideally, racetrack performance is the ultimate guide. Superior racehorses win Group or Graded stakes races. However, young mares that showed a lack of ability on the racetrack who are half-siblings or very closely related to Group or Graded stakes winners should always be given an opportunity to produce runners. In all probability they carry many valuable genes to pass on to the next generation, even if they showed below-average ability themselves. One has to rely on the strength of successful families. You see, of the broodmare population in any Thoroughbred breeding country, less than six percent of the gene pool is responsible for producing Group or Graded stakes performers. With overproduction a serious economic factor, breeders should focus attention on major stakes-producing female lines. Only if you are sentimental and unconcerned about costs (or if you live in Ireland where hope springs eternal) should you keep mares that belong in the bottom half of the gene pool. If you breed to race, you have the opportunity to buy some of the best bloodlines in the world, even those deemed less fashionable by commercial sales people – bloodlines that continue to produce the very best stakes winners. If you breed to race you may select less expensive stallions and not be concerned about temporary fashion. "Sheep follow sheep" as the saying goes in Australia. Instead, your aim will be to breed for the racetrack with absolute freedom to make choices and they will be sensible choices because your intention is to race your homebreds. Even if you are a committed commercial breeder I recommend you consider having a separate program whereby you design a few matings with the aim to retain some foals to race.

Conclusion: There are a number of "phases" involved in the evolution of equine speed. Perhaps it began in Europe with English Derby winner Sainfoin (Springfield-Sanda) and his sister Sierra (dam of English champion sprinter Sundridge) or perhaps earlier via famous mare Pocahontas (by Glencoe) and the great stallion St. Simon. In North America it likely began with the importation of Glencoe followed later by descendants of Domino. The biochemistry of each of these ancestors must have been uniquely different to all other ancestors. To my mind, either they possessed valuable mutated genes, some perhaps altering the mitochondria of cells, or else fast fiber muscle naturally evolved from a mixture of specific strains. (Mutated genes could have been located on X sex chromosomes.) Even without scientific proof, I am convinced sex-linked genes exist in the Thoroughbred breed and these genes are located solely on the X sex chromosome and transmitted via a zigzag path.

During my life I observed identifiable traits (characteristics handed down from generation to generation) clearly traceable to specific ancestors. I am amazed at how many outstanding colts resemble their maternal grandsire – their broodmare sire. Secretariat looked more like Princequillo than his father, Bold Ruler. War Admiral looked more like Sweep than his sire, Man o' War. Mr. Prospector resembled Nashua, not Raise A Native. Maria's Mon resembles his broodmare sire, Caro.

The first phase of early-maturing speed involved the following players:

SAINFOIN (1887)	Springfield	St. Albans	**Stockwell** (ex **Pocahontas** by Glencoe)
			Bribery
		Viridis	Marsyas by Orlando
			Maid of Palmyra
	Sanda	Wenlock	Lord Clifden by Newminster
			Mineral by **Rataplan** (ex **Pocahontas** by Glencoe)
		Sandal	**Stockwell** (ex **Pocahontas** by Glencoe)
			Lady Evelyn by Don John

SUNDRIDGE (1898)	Amphion	Rosebery	Speculum by Vedette
			Ladylike by **Newminster**
		Suicide	Hermit by **Newminster**
			The Ratcatcher's Daughter by **Rataplan** (**P**)
	Sierra	Springfield	St. Albans by **Stockwell** (ex **Pocahontas**)
			Viridis by Marsyas
		Sanda	Wenlock dam by **Rataplan** (ex **Pocahontas**)
			Sandal by **Stockwell** (ex **Pocahontas**)

Sierra's dam, Sanda, is incestuously inbred to the brothers Rataplan and Stockwell, sons of the famous mare Pocahontas. Stockwell was a phenomenal sire in England and is often referred to as the "Emperor of Stallions." He is a brother to Rataplan and half-brother to King Tom, sire of the dam of St. Simon. The brothers Stockwell and Rataplan were inbred to three full siblings, all of the very highest class, namely Whalebone, Whisker and their sister Web. They were by Waxy from the outstanding mare Penelope.

STOCKWELL (1849) and his brother RATAPLAN (1850)	The Baron	Birdcatcher	Sir Hercules by **Whalebone**
			Guiccioli by Bob Booty
		Echidna	Economist by **Whisker**
			Miss Pratt, dam by **Orville**
	Pocahontas	Glencoe	Sultan by Selim
			Trampoline ex **Web**
		Marpessa	Muley by **Orville**
			Clare by Marmion

Pocahontas was by Glencoe, who only had light duties in England before his export to North America where he became leading sire. Glencoe was a rich chestnut horse (bred by the fifth Lord Jersey), winner of the English 2,000 Guineas, Ascot Gold Cup, Goodwood Cup etc. Glencoe established the male line of Vandal-Virgil-Hindoo-Hanover-Hamburg.

Pocahontas produced 15 foals and is, in my opinion, the greatest mare in the history of Thoroughbred breeding. She was an extremely dominant individual.

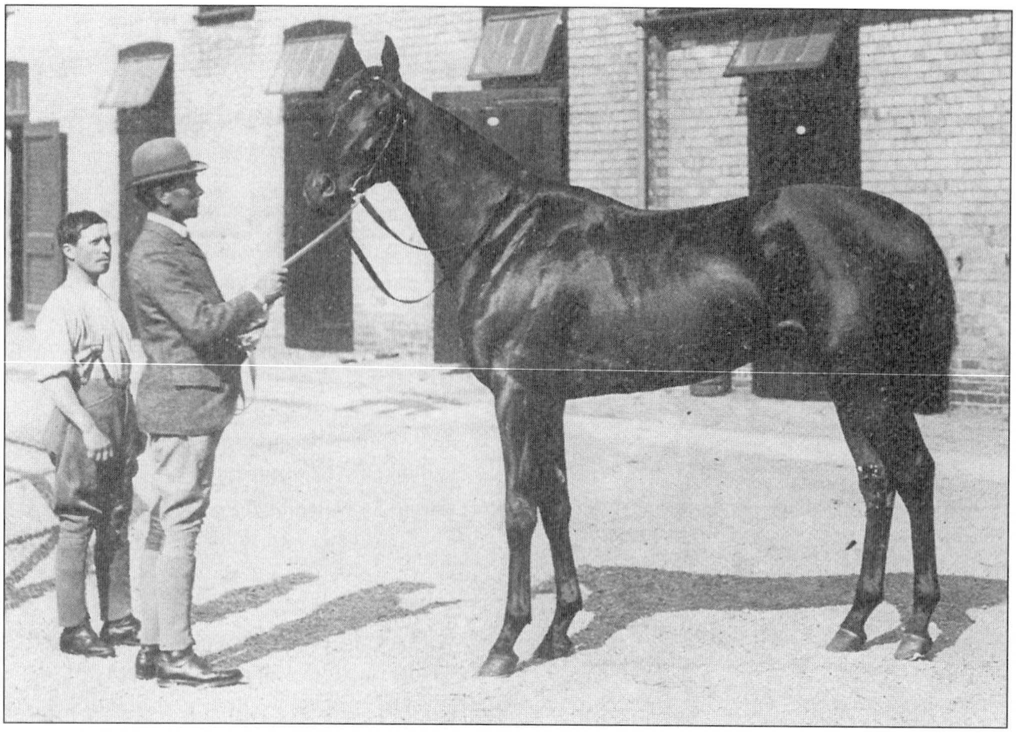

English Triple Crown winner ROCK SAND, son of Sainfoin. He is the sire of Tracery.

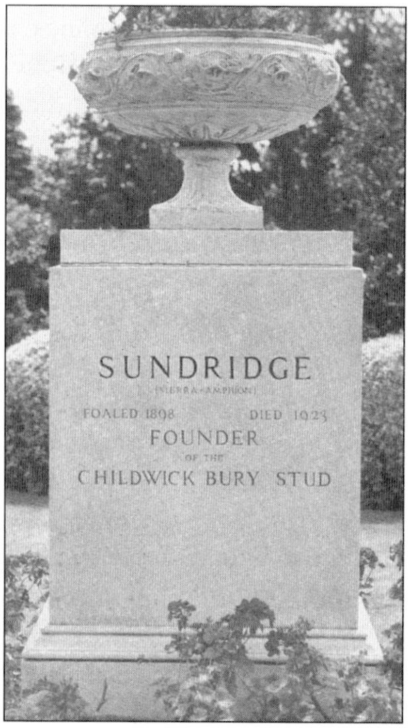

The headstone of champion sprinter SUNDRIDGE.

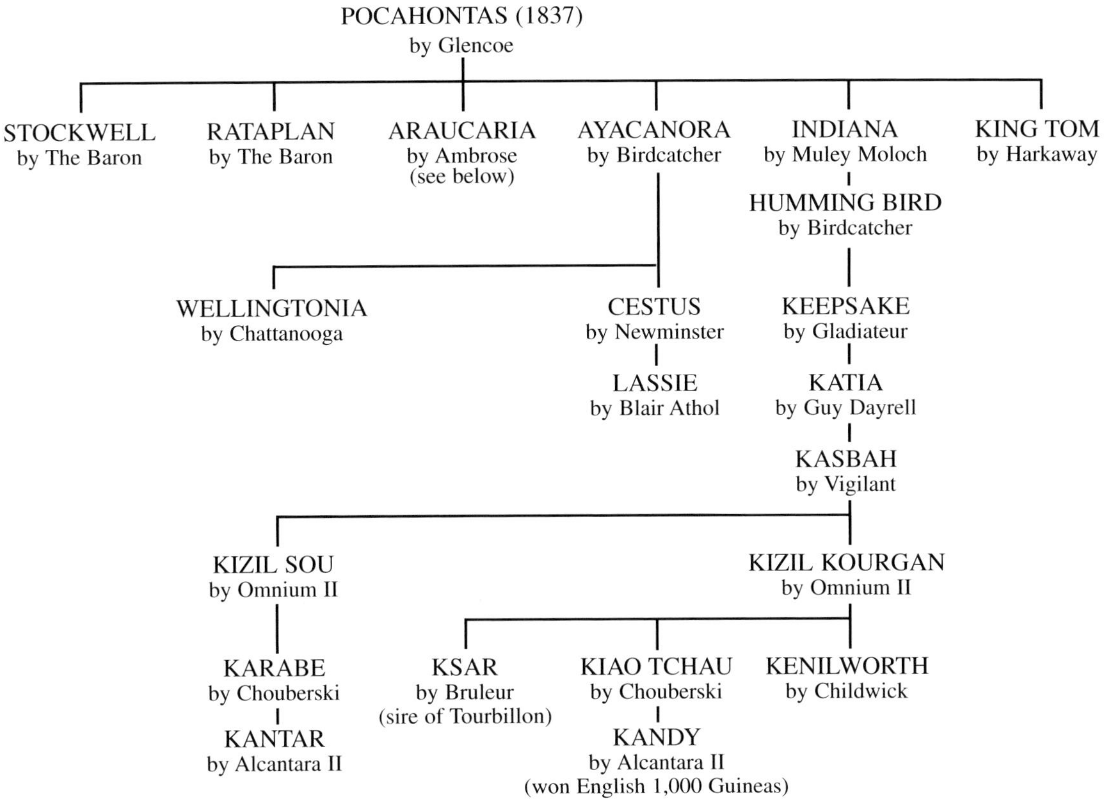
POCAHONTAS (1837)
by Glencoe
STOCKWELL
by The Baron
RATAPLAN
by The Baron
ARAUCARIA
by Ambrose
(see below)
AYACANORA
by Birdcatcher
INDIANA
by Muley Moloch
KING TOM
by Harkaway
HUMMING BIRD
by Birdcatcher
WELLINGTONIA
by Chattanooga
CESTUS
by Newminster
KEEPSAKE
by Gladiateur
LASSIE
by Blair Athol
KATIA
by Guy Dayrell
KASBAH
by Vigilant
KIZIL SOU
by Omnium II
KIZIL KOURGAN
by Omnium II
KARABE
by Chouberski
KSAR
by Bruleur
(sire of Tourbillon)
KIAO TCHAU
by Chouberski
KENILWORTH
by Childwick
KANTAR
by Alcantara II
KANDY
by Alcantara II
(won English 1,000 Guineas)

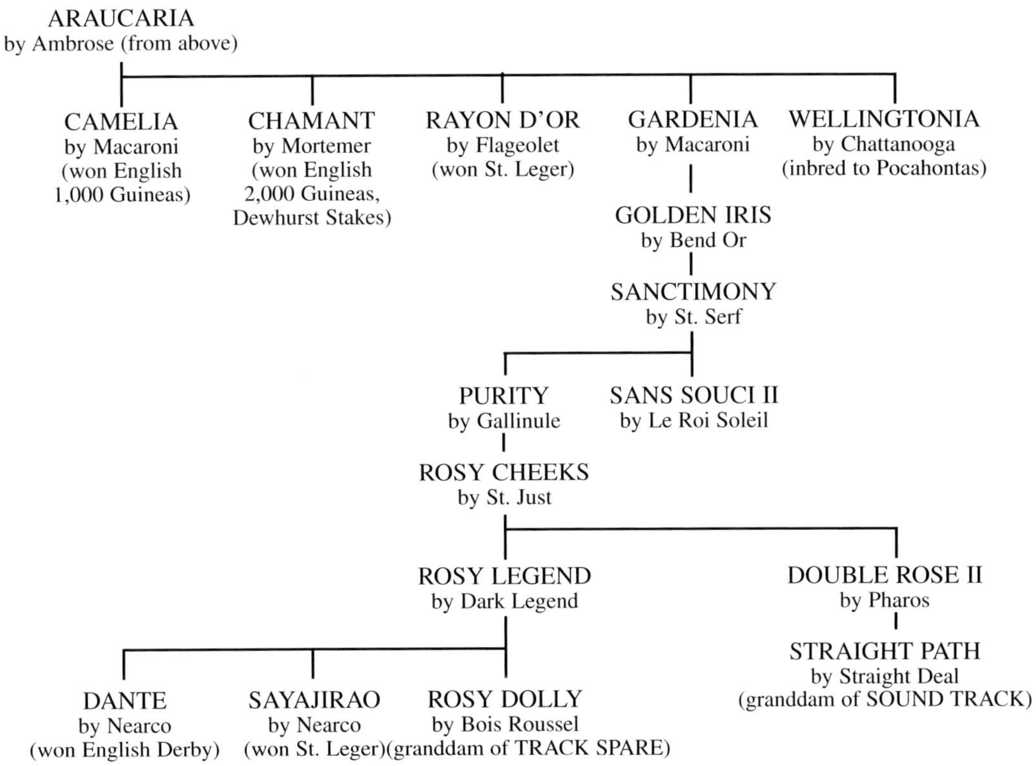
ARAUCARIA
by Ambrose (from above)
CAMELIA
by Macaroni
(won English
1,000 Guineas)
CHAMANT
by Mortemer
(won English
2,000 Guineas,
Dewhurst Stakes)
RAYON D'OR
by Flageolet
(won St. Leger)
GARDENIA
by Macaroni
WELLINGTONIA
by Chattanooga
(inbred to Pocahontas)
GOLDEN IRIS
by Bend Or
SANCTIMONY
by St. Serf
PURITY
by Gallinule
SANS SOUCI II
by Le Roi Soleil
ROSY CHEEKS
by St. Just
ROSY LEGEND
by Dark Legend
DOUBLE ROSE II
by Pharos
STRAIGHT PATH
by Straight Deal
(granddam of SOUND TRACK)
DANTE
by Nearco
(won English Derby)
SAYAJIRAO
by Nearco
(won St. Leger)
ROSY DOLLY
by Bois Roussel
(granddam of TRACK SPARE)

The connection between Stockwell, Rataplan and King Tom (the three best sons of Pocahontas) with Tracery is evident once we extend Tracery's pedigree. Rock Sand, a Triple Crown winner, has five sources of Pocahontas. Tracery has nine!

Tracery (1909)	Rock Sand	Sainfoin	Springfield by a son of **Stockwell**
			Sanda (to **Rataplan** & **Stockwell**)
		Roquebrune	**St. Simon** (dam by **King Tom**)
			St. Marguerite (dam by **Stockwell**)
	Topiary	Orme	Ormonde (grandson of **Stockwell**)
			Angelica (dam by **King Tom**)
		Plaisanterie	Wellingtonia (two **daughters of Pocahontas**)
			Poetess by Trocadero

Wellingtonia was incestuously inbred 3 x 2 to Pocahontas via two daughters. There are very few ancestors in modern pedigrees that can offer "daughters" of Pocahontas. Whenever Wellingtonia appears in a pedigree, take notice of him because when his descendants meet up with descendants of Pocahontas's three sons, it causes electricity! Somewhere I read famous French breeder Edmond Blanc duplicated Pocahontas via her best daughters, on purpose, to produce Wellingtonia.

Wellingtonia (1869)	Chattanooga	Orlando	**Touchstone**
			Vulture
		Ayacanora	Birdcatcher
			Pocahontas by Glencoe
	Araucaria	Ambrose	**Touchstone**
			Annette by Priam
		Pocahontas	Glencoe
			Marpessa by Muley

Did such close inbreeding to Pocahontas cause a favorable, spontaneous mutation, perhaps altering a tiny cluster of genes in Wellingtonia's genotype? If so, might any alteration affect Wellingtonia's DNA?

Other ancestors with linebreeding to Pocahontas exclusively via her sons were successful, but in hindsight, not as successful as descendants with the addition of either the Sainfoin/Sierra mix or the Tracery/Sundridge mix, or both. Even if we discard for a moment valuable genetic input from Pocahontas' dam, Marpessa, Wellingtonia is inbred to Glencoe and Touchstone, superior stallions of the highest order. However, there is another interesting ancestor to consider, Marpessa's sire, Muley, who provides classic speed. He is hardly ever mentioned in the annals of turf history, yet he was impeccably bred, being by dominant stallion Orville from the classic-winning mare Eleanor by Whiskey. Eleanor won the English Derby and Oaks and is a sister to Julia, dam of English Derby winner Phantom, and to Cressida, dam of English Derby winner Priam. Marpessa's family is one of the very best in the General Stud Book and represents tremendous staying power.

Sainfoin never received credit in Europe for his significant contribution to the establishment of speed in the breed. Maybe I understand how this came about. Sainfoin was a product of Her Majesty Queen Victoria's Hampton Court Stud and yearlings raised were never pumped up with feed – the infrastructure was quite basic.

Quoting from Roger Mortimer's book *The History of the Derby Stakes*, he states: "In the last century it was the custom to sneer at the yearlings bred at the Royal Stud at Hampton Court and to call them the Hampton Court Rats. However, the fact remains that Sainfoin, winner of the Derby in 1890, and Memoir, winner of the Oaks and the St. Leger that year, were both bred at Hampton Court."

"Sainfoin was a beautifully made little chestnut colt by Springfield out of Sanda by Wenlock. John Porter and Sir Robert Jardine both took a fancy to Sainfoin at the Hampton Court Sale and bought him in partnership for 500 guineas."

Sainfoin won the Ashley Stakes at his only start at two years and made progress through winter growing to 15.2 hands high. In April he won the Sandown Esher Stakes easily and caught the attention of Sir James Miller who offered to buy the colt. Sir Robert and his trainer agreed to sell Sainfoin for 6,000 pounds plus half the Derby stake as a contingency. John Porter believed the 2,000 Guineas winner Surefoot would surely win the Derby and thought Sainfoin might not be able to defeat him. However, after Sainfoin won the Dee Stakes at Chester for his new owner, bookmakers slashed the colt's price for the Epsom classic.

Although Surefoot started odds-on for the Derby, he sweated up badly at the start on a track that was soaked with rain. Orwell took the lead followed by Sainfoin, Rathbeal and Surefoot. Into the home stretch, Sainfoin passed the leader. He ran on valiantly to win by three-parts of a length from French invader Le Nord, with Orwell third, ahead of Surefoot. At his next start, Sainfoin was runner-up to the smart horse Amphion in the Hardwicke Stakes, then finished fourth to Memoir in the St. Leger, weakening badly over the last two furlongs.

At four, he suffered with sore feet and finished third in the Imperial Plate and unplaced in a race at Newmarket. At five, Sir James wanted Sainfoin to win the City and Suburban Handicap but the colt was shuffled and interfered with, and finished unplaced. Sainfoin should have been retired after his unplaced St. Leger effort. His race record was spoiled and clearly this affected his stud career because initially he was not patronized by leading breeders and had to struggle up the ladder of success. Nor did it help when Sainfoin's owner, Sir James Miller, became ill and passed away in 1906, but not before Sainfoin had sired a champion son in Rock Sand. Eventually Sainfoin was sold to Lord Carnarvon and completed his stud career in Ireland up until 1911, the year he died. Sainfoin never led the Sires' List, but was a decent sire of winners, a very successful broodmare sire, and above all else, a sire of sires.

The second phase in the evolution of speed began in England with Lord Derby's sprinter Phalaris (Polymelus-Bromus by Sainfoin) and Jack Joel's champion sprinter Sundridge. Phalaris sired classic winners, especially from daughters of St. Simon's son Chaucer, a match supplying additional impact from Pocahontas. Unbeaten Hurry On (Marcovil-Tout Suite by Sainfoin) became a leading sire in England and lifted Sainfoin's image.

Lady Josephine (Sundridge-Americus Girl by Americus) produced three talented progeny, namely Champion 2YO filly Mumtaz Mahal (by The Tetrarch), Lady Juror (by Son-in-Law) and her brother Samphire. Lady Juror produced Fair Trial (colt by Fairway, son of Phalaris), as well as Riot (filly by Colorado, son of Phalaris), The Recorder (colt by Captain Cuttle), Jurisdiction (filly by Abbot's Trace), The Black Abbot (colt by Abbot's Trace) and Sansonnet (filly by Sansovino). Sansonnet produced champion Tudor Minstrel. Jurisdiction is the third dam of brilliant miler and successful sire Kashmir II, winner of the English 2,000 Guineas.

Riot produced English Oaks winner Commotion, the dam of Faux Tirage, Combat and Aristophanes (sire of Forli, Argentina's Horse of the Year).

Mumtaz Mahal created a dynasty. Her sons Mirza II and Badruddin were successful sires imparting brilliance while her most famous daughters were Mumtaz Begum (dam of Nasrullah, Rivaz, Malindi and Sun Princess, dam of Royal Charger), Mah Mahal (dam of champion Mahmoud, Pherozshah and Mah Iran, dam of Migoli) and Rustom Mahal (dam of champion Abernant).

Rock Sand and his son Tracery also hyped up classic speed on an international basis, especially via Northern Dancer's sire Nearctic, Alibhai and the influential stallion Princequillo. America's champion Man o' War (out of a daughter of Rock Sand) became an influential sire and broodmare sire.

Fast fiber muscle along with highly tuned nervous systems flowed from these ancestors and while this was happening, Domino's early maturing speed was quickly establishing itself in North America. When Domino's strain linked up with descendants of Pocahontas (especially via her three sons) it reinforced English 2,000 Guineas winner Glencoe and the results were explosive!

Dominant strains will linger for many generations – strains like Northern Dancer, Nasrullah, Mahmoud, Princequillo, Tracery, Domino, Phalaris, Sainfoin and Sundridge.

Charles Morton, private trainer for Jack Joel, commented about the high regard he held for the owner of Childwick Bury Stud and for his champion sprinter Sundridge. He wrote, "I remained with Mr. Joel for 25 years because he not only understands the breeding of horses and training of Thoroughbred horses, but also knows human nature. He loves his horses. He bought Sundridge for 1,450 guineas from Sir Samuel Scott, and Sundridge proved to be one of the greatest bargains of all time. Morny Cannon, who usually rode him, never understood why Sir Samuel sold the horse."

Sundridge retired to Childwick Bury Stud and stood at a fee of nine guineas. As the years passed by his fee increased to 300 guineas and commercial breeders were happy to pay it, but neither owner nor trainer realized they possessed in Sundridge the horse who would be largely responsible for the foundation of the Childwick Bury Stud. For Jack Joel, Sundridge sired a Derby winner, an Oaks and 1,000 Guineas winner and among his many other offspring Sundridge sired Sun Worship, the dam of Solario. Jack Joel always said Jest (Sundridge-Absurdity) was the best filly he ever bred and Sunstar (Sundridge-Doris) the best colt. Sunstar won the English 2,000 Guineas and Derby. His dam, Doris, was a small mare by Loved One, given to him by his brother "Solly" as a present. Sunstar might have been a great racehorse had it not been for a strained suspensory ligament that happened in between his classic victories. In the circumstances, the son of Sundridge must have been a courageous horse to win at Epsom. At stud, Sunstar was exceptionally fertile and sired 269 winners including Sunny Jane (English Oaks), Craig An Eran (English 2,000 Guineas) and Buchan (Eclipse Stakes twice), leading sire in England in 1927.

The third phase of the evolution of speed comprises descendants of the aforementioned horses – the era of Nasrullah, Royal Charger, Mahmoud, War Admiral, Court Martial, Petition, Tudor Minstrel etc., and the whole Domino tribe. Linebreeding to Nasrullah and his three-parts brother Royal Charger is extremely successful, as is the Nasrullah link with Fair Trial. These strains eventually crossed successfully with Princequillo, who carries Tracery via Papyrus.

ARTHUR B. HANCOCK III, co-breeder of three Kentucky Derby winners – Gato del Sol, Sunday Silence and Fusaichi Pegasus.

SWEET CATOMINE (by Storm Cat) winning the Santa Ysabel Stakes.

Tracery, a champion racehorse at three in England, has **nine lines of Pocahontas by Glencoe!**

Tracery (Rock Sand-Topiary by Orme) was always admired by the Italian genius Federico Tesio, who used Tracery and Papyrus in his breeding program. Consider for a moment a scenario whereby there would be no Northern Dancer in the world today had Sister Sarah not been born. Sister Sarah is by Tracery's son Abbot's Trace from Sarita.

Sister Sarah produced Lady Angela, the dam of Canadian champion Nearctic, sire of Northern Dancer.

There would be no Danehill either if Tesio had not used Tracery's son Papyrus to breed the mare Barbara Burrini, granddam of champion Ribot who sired His Majesty, a horse linebred to a "son" and "daughter" of Tracery. His Majesty is, of course, the broodmare sire of Danehill (and Danehill inherits even more powerful influence from Tracery via Northern Dancer's sire, Nearctic).

So you see, pedigree research can teach us to identify superior, athletic lines and sometimes explains why lines succeed when others fail. The genetic affinity that exists between Nasrullah and Princequillo (whose dam is by Papyrus, son of Tracery) resulted in many champions being born and naturally it is exceedingly effective when reinforced. In Australia, the cross of Nasrullah with Star Kingdom's strain was nearly always successful, resulting in high-class sprinter-milers at Group level. This match duplicated Sainfoin and Sierra several times. As mentioned earlier, Star Kingdom was inbred to Sunstar, son of Sundridge.

Linebreeding to champion Native Dancer via a "son" and a "daughter" is a successful method used to produce stakes runners and the most frequently used example of this link is the combination of Northern Dancer with Mr. Prospector. Northern Dancer is out of a "daughter" of Native Dancer whereas Mr. Prospector is by a "son," Raise A Native. Kentucky Derby winner Fusaichi Pegasus is bred on this cross.

In conclusion, great racehorses such as Secretariat and Seattle Slew in North America, and Mill Reef and Sadler's Wells in Europe, owe their racing class to superior ancestors. Although there were many outstanding three-year-olds to perform in the past two decades, we still await the appearance of another Triple Crown winner.

Up until now, Sainfoin and his sister Sierra (dam of English champion sprinter Sundridge) were forgotten heroes. Perhaps in the future they will be remembered with respect.

Today, competition is of such a high standard for the classics and Group or Graded stakes races that it is exceedingly difficult to win any of these major events.

As for the cynics who doubt a few genes can travel many generations, consider this fact. Every Thoroughbred racehorse with the gray coat color traces back without a single break to one of only a few gray horses that established the Thoroughbred breed, and almost all of today's gray horses trace back without a single break to the Alcock's Arabian, a gray stallion born in 1704.

Alcock's Arabian went by various names. He is the same stallion known as Akaster Turk, Sutton's Turk, Honeywood's Arabian and Turner's White Turk.

No gray colt or filly can inherit the gray coat color unless at least one of its parents carries the genes that cause pigment deficiency.

75 Years - The Aga Khan's Racing and Breeding Studs by Georg Lange, published in 1998, Dortmund, Germany.

A Quarter-Century of American Racing by various authors including Joe Estes and Joe H. Palmer, published by The Blood-Horse Publications in 1941, in Lexington, Kentucky.

American Race Horses various year books, by various authors, published by The Countryman Press, Woodstock, Vermont, USA.

Dormello-Olgiata two volumes, 1961-61 and 1966-67, published in 1962 and 1967 in Milan, Italy. (Various authors).

From Here To The Bugle by Frank Jennings, published in 1949 in Kentucky, USA.

Life Itself, Its Origin and Nature by Dr. Francis Crick, published in 1981 by MacDonald & Co., London, England.

Molecular & Cellular Biology by Wolfe, published in 1993 in the USA.

Pacemaker magazine, various issues, published in England on a monthly basis.

Pedigrees of Leading Winners two volumes, published in 1981 and 1995 by J. A. Allen & Co, London, England.

Private pedigree charts compiled by the author.

Racing and breeding manuscripts, penned by various authors, in the possession of Messrs. R.E. and G. B. Way, Burrough Green, Newmarket, England.

Register of Thoroughbred Stallions various year books, published between 1900 and 1974 in London, England.

The Blood Horse Stallion Register published annually in Lexington, Kentucky.

The Breed of the Racehorse by Friedrich Becker, published in 1936 by The British Bloodstock Agency, London, England.

The Chemistry of Life by Dr. Steven Rose, published in 1991 by Penguin Books.

The Classic Pedigree (1770-1989) by Michael Church, published in 1990 by The Racing Post, in London, England.

The Double Helix by Dr. James D. Watson, published in 1980 by W. W. Norton & Company, in New York and London.

The Energy of Life by Dr. Guy Brown, Ph D., published in 1999 in London, England.

The European Racehorse various issues 1950 to 1965, published in England.

The Great Breeders and Their Methods by Abram S. Hewitt, published in 1982 by the Thoroughbred Record, Lexington, Kentucky.

The Great Stallion Book by Richard Ulbrich, published in 1986, Hobart, Australia.

The History of the Derby Stakes by Roger Mortimer, published in England 1973.

The History of Thoroughbred Racing in America by William H. P. Robertson, published in 1970 in New York, New York, U.S.A.

The Stallion Book a Weatherby Publication - various years, printed in England.

The Thoroughbred Record Sire Book published annually in Lexington, Kentucky.

Thoroughbred Pedigree Charts by H. E. Keylock published in 1935 by The British Bloodstock Agency, London, England.

Thoroughbred Stallions by Tony Morris, published in 1990 by The Crowood Press, Swindon, Wilshire, England.

Various issues of *The Blood Horse* magazine, published in Lexington, Kentucky.

Various scientific articles and papers published by authors at Cambridge and Oxford Universities, England, and New York and California, USA.